Botanic Garden and The Domain
Pages 104–117

Kings Cross and Darlinghurst
Pages 118–123

Paddington
Pages 124–129

ANIC GARDEN
THE DOMAIN

KINGS CROSS
AND
DARLINGHURST

PADDINGTON

EYEWITNESS TRAVEL

SYDNEY

EYEWITNESS TRAVEL

SYDNEY

Main Contributor **Ken Brass & Kirsty McKenzie**

LONDON, NEW YORK,
MELBOURNE, MUNICH AND DELHI
www.dk.com

Produced by The Watermark Press, Sydney, Australia

Project Editor Siobhán O'Connor

Art Editor Claire Edwards

Editors Robert Coupe, Leith Hillard, Jane Sheard

Designers Katie Peacock, Claire Ricketts, Noel Wendtman

Dorling Kindersley Limited

Senior Editor Fay Franklin

Senior Art Editor Jane Ewart

Senior Revisions Editor Esther Labi

Contributors

Anna Bruechert, John Dengate, Carrie Hutchinson, Graham Jahn,
Kim Saville, Susan Skelly, Deborah Soden

Photographers

Max Alexander, Simon Blackall, Michael Nicholson, Rob Reichenfeld, Alan Williams

Illustrators

Richard Draper, Stephen Gyapay, Alex Lavroff Associates, The Overall Picture, Robbie Polley

Printed and bound in China

First published in Great Britain in 1996
by Dorling Kindersley Limited
80 Strand, London, WC2R 0RL

15 16 17 18 10 9 8 7 6 5 4 3 2 1

**Reprinted with revisions 1997, 1999, 2000, 2001,
2002 (twice), 2003, 2005, 2006, 2008, 2010, 2012, 2015**

Copyright 1997, 2015 © Dorling Kindersley Limited, London

A Penguin Random House Company

A CIP catalogue record is available from the British Library

ISBN 978-0-2410-0702-0

MIX
Paper from
responsible sources
FSC™ C018179
www.fsc.org

Front cover main image: Sydney Opera House at dusk

◄ Sydney Opera House, photographed from the east, shortly after sunrise

Contents

How to Use this Guide **6**

Introducing Sydney

Four Great Days
in Sydney **10**

Façade of the Art Gallery of New South
Wales, built between 1896 and 1909

Putting Sydney on the
Map **14**

The History of Sydney **20**

Sydney at a Glance **34**

Sydney Through the Year
50

Sun-worshippers bask on Tamarama Beach

Sporting Sydney **54**

The City Shoreline **58**

Sydney Area by Area

The Rocks and Circular Quay **64**

City Centre **80**

Darling Harbour and Surry Hills **92**

Botanic Garden and The Domain **104**

Kings Cross and Darlinghurst **118**

Paddington **124**

Further Afield **130**

Four Guided Walks **142**

Detail of a mural that can be seen inside Sydney Opera House

Beyond Sydney

Exploring Beyond Sydney **154**

Pittwater and Ku-ring-gai Chase **156**

Hawkesbury Tour **158**

Hunter Valley **160**

Blue Mountains **162**

Southern Highlands Tour **164**

Royal National Park **166**

Dramatic rock cleft known as Jacob's Ladder, near The Gap

Travellers' Needs

Where to Stay **170**

Where to Eat and Drink **180**

Shops and Markets **198**

Entertainment in Sydney **208**

Survival Guide

Practical Information **218**

Travel Information **228**

Sydney Street Finder **238**

General Index **250**

Acknowledgments **263**

Transport Map
Inside Back Cover

Sydney Tower – the city's tallest structure

HOW TO USE THIS GUIDE

This guide helps you to get the most from your visit to Sydney. It provides both expert recommendations and detailed practical information. *Introducing Sydney* locates the city geographically, sets modern Sydney in its historical and cultural context and describes events through the entire year. *Sydney at a Glance* is an overview of the city's main attractions, including a feature on the city shoreline and Sydney's best beaches. *Sydney Area by Area* is the main sightseeing section, covering all the sights, with photographs, maps and drawings. *Further Afield* looks at sights just outside the city centre while *Beyond Sydney* explores other places close to Sydney. Carefully researched tips on hotels, restaurants, pubs and entertainment venues are found in *Travellers' Needs*. The *Survival Guide* contains useful practical advice on everything from the Australian telephone system to public transport.

Finding your way around the sightseeing section

The centre of Sydney has been divided into six sightseeing areas. Each area has its own chapter and is colour-coded for easy reference. Every chapter opens with a list of the sights described. All sights are numbered and plotted on an *Area Map*. Detailed information for each sight is presented in numerical order, making it easy to locate within the chapter.

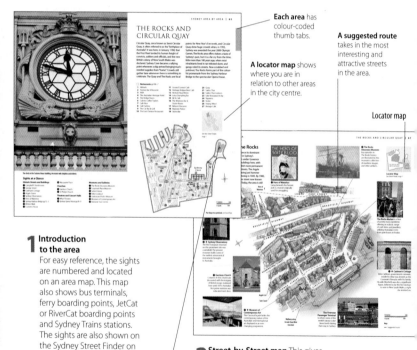

Each area has colour-coded thumb tabs.

A locator map shows where you are in relation to other areas in the city centre.

A suggested route takes in the most interesting and attractive streets in the area.

Locator map

1 Introduction to the area
For easy reference, the sights are numbered and located on an area map. This map also shows bus terminals, ferry boarding points, JetCat or RiverCat boarding points and Sydney Trains stations. The sights are also shown on the Sydney Street Finder on pages 240–45.

2 Street-by-Street map This gives a bird's eye view of the most important parts of each sightseeing area. The numbering of the sights ties in with the area map and the fuller descriptions on the pages that follow.

The area shaded pink is shown in greater detail on the Street-by-Street map on the following pages.

Sydney Area Map

The coloured areas shown on this map (see pp18–19) are the six main sightseeing areas – each covered by a full chapter in *Sydney Area by Area* (pp62–151). The six areas are highlighted on other maps throughout the book. In *Sydney at a Glance* (pp34–49), for example, they help locate the top sights, including art galleries and museums and parks and reserves. They are also used to show some of the best hotels (pp174–9), the top restaurants, cafés and pubs (pp186–97) and great shopping areas (pp200–1).

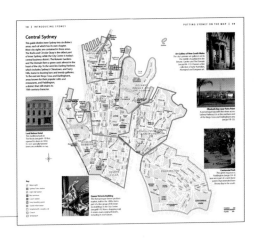

Façades of important buildings are often shown to help you recognize them quickly.

Numbers refer to each sight's position on the area map and its place in the chapter.

Practical information lists all the information you need to visit every sight, including a map reference to the Street Finder (pp240–45).

The visitors' checklist provides all the practical information needed to plan your visit.

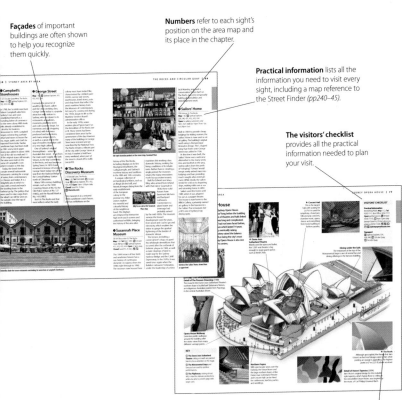

3 Detailed information on each sight
All the important sights in Sydney are described individually. They are listed in order, following the numbering on the area map. Addresses and practical information are provided. The key to the symbols used is on the back flap.

Stars indicate the features no visitor should miss.

4 Sydney's top sights Museums and galleries have colour-coded floorplans to help you locate the most interesting exhibits; historic buildings are dissected to reveal their interiors.

INTRODUCING
SYDNEY

Great Days in Sydney   10–13

Putting Sydney on the Map   14–19

The History of Sydney   20–33

Sydney at a Glance   34–49

Sydney Through the Year   50–53

Sporting Sydney   54–57

The City Shoreline   58–61

GREAT DAYS IN SYDNEY

Planning a one-day itinerary to take in the best that Sydney has to offer need not be a challenge. The magnificent harbour or beaches, as well as cultural and architectural highlights, would ideally be included. These four itineraries offer a mix of activities in different parts of Sydney, all accessible by public transport. They are designed to be flexible – you might choose to leave out some stops or include other attractions that are nearby. Prices show the cost for two adults or for a family of two adults and two children, including food and drinks.

Sydney Opera House and Harbour Bridge by night

Around the Harbour

Two adults allow at least A$125

- **The view from Sydney Harbour Bridge**
- **A tour of The Rocks**
- **Ferry ride to Manly**
- **Sunset over the harbour**

Morning

Start early at an Australian icon, the **Sydney Harbour Bridge** (see pp72–3), built in 1932. Cross on the pedestrian walkway or, from $198 per person, let BridgeClimb guide you to the top of the steel arch bridge (bookings are essential). Climbs depart every ten minutes, and take 3½ hours including orientation. The view at the top is well worth it. Recharge with a pit stop at one of the cafés or restaurants in the vicinity (see pp186–7); there's everything from pastries to Chinese food.

Explore the historic Rocks area where you'll find the convict-carved Argyle Cut and the military **Garrison Church** (see pp70–71). Cobblestoned alleys lead to the original docks of Old Sydney Town at **Campbell's Store-houses** (see p68) and **Cadman's Cottage** (see p70), Sydney's oldest surviving dwelling. Finish your stroll at Circular Quay.

Afternoon

Enjoy a classic ferry trip to **Manly** (see p135). Once there, stroll down the Corso to the ocean beach or walk around the headland (see pp148–9). Buy fish and chips and eat them on the beach, or try some parasailing, boating or kayaking, activities that are on offer at the jetty. Treat yourself to a beer at the Manly Wharf Hotel (see p197) where you can find a window seat and watch the sunset over the harbour. End the day with the return ferry back to Circular Quay. Take in the lights of the city by the harbour as night falls.

Art and Opera

Two adults allow at least A$175

- **Colonial buildings on Macquarie Street**
- **Aboriginal art at the Yiribana Gallery**
- **The Royal Botanic Garden**
- **Sydney Opera House**

Morning

Stroll down **Macquarie Street** (see pp114–17), named after Governor Lachlan Macquarie. You can still see several of the buildings he commissioned here. Other architectural gems include the **Hyde Park Barracks** (see pp116–17) and **St James' Church** (see p117), both designed by convict James Greenway. The old Rum Hospital now houses the **Sydney Mint** (see p116) and **Parliament House** (see pp114–15), where free tours run every half hour. At the **State Library of NSW** (see p114), you can tread on a mosaic replica of the Tasman Map, illustrating 17th-century voyages to Australia.

Henry Moore sculpture outside the Art Gallery of New South Wales

◀ Australian Aboriginal mural, by Danny and Jamie Eastwood

Afternoon
Across **The Domain** *(see p109)*, the **Art Gallery of New South Wales** *(see pp110–13)* houses both traditional and modern Aboriginal art in the Yiribana Gallery, the largest space in the world devoted to the art of Indigenous Australians. Rest weary legs and enjoy lunch in the gallery's café *(see p191)*, then stroll along to the scenic **Mrs Macquaries Chair** *(see p108)* for a fine view across the harbour before taking the Fleet Steps down the hill into the **Royal Botanic Garden** *(see pp106–7)*. On the other side of Farm Cove is **Sydney Opera House** *(see pp76–9)*. Stop in at the Opera Bar *(see pp186–7)*, then take a tour of the world-famous building (booking is recommended). If you want to make an evening of it, last-minute tickets are sometimes available for an opera, play or concert.

Giraffe at Taronga Zoo, on the foreshore of Sydney Harbour

do laps. Then stretch your legs with the Bondi-to-Bronte section of the famous cliff walk *(see pp146–7)*. When you reach Bronte, find somewhere for a refreshing drink, then head to Oxford Street, Paddington, to begin browsing the glamorous boutiques. The renowned **Paddington Markets** *(see p128)* are open every Saturday.

Afternoon
Take lunch in the leafy surrounds of beautiful Queen Street at Crème Café *(see p194)*, then, if you wish, visit the store of prominent designer Akira Isofawa *(see p205)*. Stop by the London Tavern *(see p126)*, the area's oldest pub, before exploring the streets of terraced houses near Five Ways. Admire the art at Olsen Irwin Gallery (No. 63 Jersey Road), Australian Galleries (No. 15 Roylston Street) and Martin Browne Contemporary (No. 15 Hampden Street). Later, have a drink at the Tilbury Hotel *(see p194)* in Woolloomooloo and cap off the day with a pie from Harry's Café de Wheels *(see p193)* on the Finger Wharf.

Beaches and Browsing

Two adults allow at least A$140

- **Breakfast at Bondi Beach**
- **A cliff-top walk**
- **Fashion, terraces and galleries in Paddington**
- **Cocktails on the Finger Wharf**

Morning
Have breakfast at **Bondi Beach**'s Icebergs Bistro *(see p197)*, at the legendary Bondi Icebergs (on weekends) or at the Crabbe Hole *(see p196)*. Admire the view and watch the die-hard swimmers

Bathers enjoying the golden sand and surf at Bronte Beach

Family Fun

Family of 4 allow at least A$325

- **A spin through the city's main streets**
- **Ferry and Sky Safari**
- **Koalas, kangaroos and platypuses at Taronga Zoo**
- **Up high in Sydney Tower**

Morning
Start with a lap of the city's main streets on the free 555 shuttle bus, hopping off at Circular Quay. Buy a ZooPass from Circular Quay then take a ferry to **Taronga Zoo** *(see pp136–7)*. Your ZooPass includes a return ferry trip and zoo entrance. Take the included Sky Safari cable car ride to the main entrance. Here you'll find information on koala viewing and the daily seal and bird shows. Spend the morning exploring the zoo, making sure you stop by all of the native Australian animals, including monotremes, platypuses and echidnas. Buy ice creams to eat as you walk.

Afternoon
Have lunch at one of the many kiosks in the zoo, before heading back to the wharf for the return ferry. Finish off the day at **Sydney Tower** *(see p85)*. Ride the lift to the Sydney Tower Eye Observation Deck and take in a tour of Sydney in the 4-D cinema. Use a telescope to spot the zoo and other landmarks as far away as the Blue Mountains on a clear day, or enjoy the sunset.

2 Days in Sydney

- Take centre stage on an Opera House tour
- See one of the world's biggest collections of Aboriginal art
- Journey across the harbour to Manly Beach

Day 1

Morning Start your day with a behind-the-scenes tour at the **Sydney Opera House** (pp76–9). Stand on the Concert Hall stage and admire the stunning interior of this landmark before having breakfast in the "green room". Afterwards, take the harbour foreshore walk to the **Royal Botanic Garden** (pp106–7), established as Australia's first farm, and join a guided tour of the exotic plants and historic monuments. Buy a snack from the kiosk, and picnic in the park.

Afternoon Exit the gardens near the **Art Gallery of New South Wales** (pp110–13), and visit its famous Yiribana Gallery, which features one of the world's largest collections of Aboriginal and Torres Strait Islander art. Stroll along Macquarie Street to **The Mint** (p116), a former coining factory and the oldest public building in the city centre. Then head to Darling Harbour to watch the dugongs and sharks at **Sea Life Sydney Aquarium** (p98).

Day 2

Morning Catch a ferry from Circular Quay to **Manly** (p135). Stroll the shop-lined Corso to the surf beach, and walk the track to Shelly Beach marine preserve. Have lunch overlooking the water before your return ferry trip.

Afternoon Walk to the **Museum of Contemporary Art** (p75), home to more than 4,000 modern artworks. Meander through The Rocks' historic streets to the BridgeClimb head-quarters for a three-and-a-half hour adventure to the top of the **Harbour Bridge** (pp72–3).

The stunning interior of the beautifully restored Queen Victoria Building

3 Days in Sydney

- Step aboard a replica of the *Endeavour* at Darling Harbour
- Admire the splendour of the Queen Victoria Building
- Follow in convicts' footsteps at Hyde Park Barracks

Day 1

Morning Starting at Darling Harbour, walk across the **Pyrmont Bridge** (p100) to the **Australian National Maritime Museum** (pp96–7). Roam the wharves and explore historic vessels, including a replica of Captain Cook's *Endeavour*, then meet native Australian animals at **Wild Life Sydney** (p99).

Afternoon Catch a ferry to Circular Quay. Visit **The Rocks Discovery Museum** (pp68–9) to learn about the area's history. Walk through The Rocks to the pedestrian deck of the Harbour

Bridge. Go up the sandstone **Pylon Lookout** (p70) for an overview of the bridge's creation and great views.

Day 2

Morning Combine shopping, history and architecture at the immaculately restored **Queen Victoria Building** (p84), with its stained-glass windows and clocks. Head to Circular Quay, enjoying entertainment from waterfront street buskers.

Afternoon Take a ferry ride to Manly, passing small harbour island Fort Denison and **North Head** (p135), where the harbour starts. Wander along Manly Cove to dive with sharks at **Manly Sea Life Sanctuary** (p135). Have a sunset drink on Manly Wharf before returning.

Day 3

Morning Stroll through Hyde Park (pp88–9). Walk along tree-lined pathways and past the Archibald Fountain's grand sculptures. Sink into a convict hammock at **Hyde Park Barracks** (pp116–17), formerly home to 50,000 convicts. Later, peek inside the stately reading room in the Mitchell Wing of the **State Library of NSW** (p114).

Afternoon Walk through **The Domain** (p109) to the Art Gallery of New South Wales, and take a free tour of the gallery highlights. Wind through the Royal Botanic Garden to the Sydney Opera House. Admire the beauty of its famous white sails with evening drinks by the water's edge.

Manly Cove, as viewed from Sydney Harbour National Park

5 Days in Sydney

- Watch the sun set from the top of the Harbour Bridge
- Feel the sand between your toes at iconic Bondi Beach
- Take in the rugged beauty of the Blue Mountains

Day 1

Morning Start your day watching harbour life at Circular Quay, or get the adrenaline flowing with a spin in a jet boat. Walk to the Museum of Contemporary Art and admire the stunning works on display there. Enjoy lunch at one of the area's historic pubs.

Afternoon Step back in time with a stroll through The Rocks and the dramatic **Argyle Cut** *(p66)*, a passage cut through sandstone by convicts. Then join BridgeClimb for a twilight ascent of the Harbour Bridge, and watch the sun set over the city.

The lake at the peaceful Chinese Garden of Friendship, in Darling Harbour

Day 2

Morning Head to Hyde Park for a game of chess on the giant outdoor board near St James Station, stroll to the grand **Archibald Fountain** *(p88)*, featuring Apollo, then visit the **Anzac Memorial** reflection pool *(p88)* and museum commemorating those who served in war.

A bench decorated with a mosaic of lifeguards at Bondi Beach

Afternoon Take advantage of the park's proximity to Oxford Street and travel to **Paddington** *(pp126–7)*. Stroll down beautiful Queen Street with its antiques stores, galleries and cafés, and continue on to **Bondi Beach** *(p139)*. Take the stunning Bondi-to-Bronte coastal walk and return for a drink overlooking the ocean at one of the seaside cafés.

Day 3

Morning Shop till you drop in the world's most expensive retail floor space, **Pitt St Mall** *(pp204–5)*. Window shop in the Victorian-style **Strand Arcade** *(p86)*, which was completely rebuilt after a fire in 1997. Afterwards, take in some culture with a tour of the majestic **State Theatre** *(p84)*, with its exquisite architectural features, important artworks and the world's second-biggest chandelier.

Afternoon Escape the hustle and bustle of the city, entering the Royal Botanic Garden from Macquarie Street to admire the **Conservatorium of Music** *(p108)*, a striking Neo-Gothic building housing one of the nation's most prestigious music colleges. Afterwards, head to stately **Government House** *(p108)*, the former residence of the governor of New South Wales. En route, look out for noisy flying foxes (large bats) and cockatoos. Exit near the Art Gallery of New South Wales, and enjoy free entry to its impressive collections. Make your way to the Opera House for an evening show.

Day 4

Morning Take a ferry to Sydney's zoo with a view, **Taronga Zoo** *(pp136–7)*. Get the cable car to the top of the hill, and visit some of the many fascinating animal enclosures on your way back down. The absence of bars and fences allows you to get up close to many of the animals, including wombats, koalas and elephants. Don't miss the QBE Free Flight Bird Show *(see p137)*.

Afternoon Catch the ferry to Darling Harbour. Enjoy the quiet solitude of the **Chinese Garden of Friendship** *(pp100–1)*. Children will enjoy the Darling Quarter playground, with water games, rope climbing nets and slides. Head back to bustling **Chinatown** *(p101)* for a great-value dinner and some souvenir shopping.

Day 5

Morning to afternoon Venture from the city with a day trip to Katoomba, in the Greater **Blue Mountains** World Heritage Area *(pp162–3)*. Hire a car, take a train or join a bus tour to experience the rugged beauty of the vast Australian bush. Visit Echo Point lookout for spectacular views of the iconic **Three Sisters** rock formation *(p162)* and learn its Aboriginal dreamtime legend. Take the Giant Stairway down to the valley floor, and glide between clifftops on the glass-floored Scenic Skyway cablecar (www.scenicworld.com.au) before returning to Sydney.

Putting Sydney on the Map

Situated on Australia's eastern coastline within the state of New South Wales, Sydney spreads with the rare luxury of space – 3,700 sq km (1,430 sq miles) in all – around what is often described as one of the finest harbours in the world. Greater Sydney is home to more than 4 million people and, while it is not the nation's capital, it is Australia's oldest and largest city, as well as its media and financial centre. Sydney is also the main gateway to Australia and it enjoys good air, road and rail links to other major centres.

Southeast Asia and the Pacific Rim

Key

-  International airport
- Domestic airport
- Passenger ship terminal
- Freeway or motorway
- Highway
- Railway
- State boundary

Greater Sydney and Environs

Palm
Beach

Mona
Vale

Hornsby

Penrith

Blacktown

Glenbrook

Parramatta

Chatswood

Manly

See next page

Burwood

Bondi

Bankstown

Sydney
Airport

Maroubra

Campbelltown

Sutherland

Cronulla

afura Sea

Torres Strait
Cape York

*Gulf of
Carpentaria*

*Groote
Eylandt*

*Mornington
Island*

Cooktown

Cairns

ERN

ORY

Mount Isa

Townsville

Proserpine

Great Barrier Reef

Mackay

QUEENSLAND

Longreach

Rockhampton

Blackall

Hervey Bay

*Fraser
Island*

Diamantina

Charleville

Maroochydore

Toowoomba

Brisbane

Coolangatta

Moree

*Lake
Eyre*

STRALIA

Bourke

Coffs Harbour

*Lake
Torrens*

Broken
Hill

Darling

N E W

S O U T H

W A L E S

Dubbo

Whyalla

Murray

Maitland

Newcastle

Sydney

Mildura

Wagga Wagga

Wollongong

Adelaide

Canberra

*ngaroo
Island*

VICTORIA

**STRALIAN
CAPITAL
TERRITORY**

Melbourne

Geelong

Tasman Sea

*King
Island*

Bass Strait

*Flinders
Island*

Devonport

Launceston

T A S M A

Hobart

Pacific Ocean

0 kilometres   500

0 miles   250

Central Sydney and Suburbs

Sydney has gradually expanded to fill both sides of the harbour.
Parramatta to the west was once a separate settlement, but is
now very much a part of the city. To the east are the beaches
and seaside suburbs that have come to typify Sydney living.
The area as a whole is served by CityRail lines and roads.

↗ Newcastle

PYMBLE

*LANE COVE
NATIONAL
PARK*

Lane Cove

EPPING

NORTH ROCKS ROAD

CARLINGFORD ROAD

MARSDEN ROAD

PENNANT HILLS ROAD

← Windsor

55

40

RUTLEDGE ST

KISSING POINT ROAD

EPPING ROAD

BLAXLAND ROAD

LANE COVE ROAD

RYDE ROAD

PITTWATER ROAD

LADY

Lane Co

● Parramatta

PARRAMATTA

VICTORIA ROAD

VICTORIA ROAD

Rydalmere

Meadowbank

Sydney
Olympic Park

Silverwater
Bridge

RYDE

Ryde
Bridge

RYDE

RYDE ROAD

40

← Penrith

4

WESTERN MOTORWAY

PARRAMATTA ROAD

SILVERWATER ROAD

Parramatta River

D

Gladesville

AUBURN

45

HOMEBUSH BAY DRIVE

CONCORD ROAD

Abbotsford

Chiswick

ROAD

CONCORD

LYONS

44

4

GREAT WESTERN HIGHWAY

21

27

BURWOOD

RAMSAY ST

JOSEPH STREET

CENTENARY DRIVE

HOMEBUSH ROAD

STRATHFIELD

BURWOOD ROAD

FREDERICK ST

5

3

LIVERPOOL ROAD

ASHFIELD

OLD CANTERBURY ROAD

NEW

M

ROBERTS ROAD

27

GEORGES RIVER ROAD

Cooks

5

PUNCHBOWL ROAD

BEXLEY ROAD

ROAD

KINGSGROVE ROAD

WILLIAM STREET

54

CANTERBURY ROAD

MOOREFIELDS ROAD

KING GEORGES ROAD

FOREST ROAD

55

Princ

5

3

STONEY CREEK ROAD

HURSTVILLE

↓ Wollongong

Key

▢	Central Sydney
▢	Parks and reserves
▢	Sydney Olympic Park
✈	Airport
🚉	Central Railway Station
⛴	Ferry boarding point
⛴	RiverCat boarding point
③	Metroad route
═	Freeway or motorway
▬	Major road
┈	Minor road
—	Railway
═ ═	Tunnel

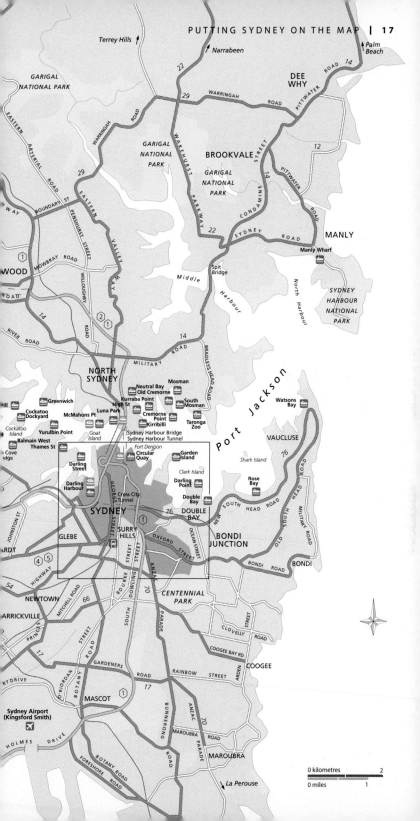

Central Sydney

This guide divides inner Sydney into six distinct areas, each of which has its own chapter. Most city sights are contained in these areas. The Rocks and Circular Quay is the oldest part of inner Sydney, while the City Centre is today's central business district. The Botanic Gardens and The Domain form a green oasis almost in the heart of the city. To the west lies Darling Harbour, which includes Sydney's Chinatown, and Surry Hills, home to buzzing bars and trendy galleries. To the east are Kings Cross and Darlinghurst, areas known for their popular cafés and restaurants, and Paddington, a district that still retains its 19th-century character.

Lord Nelson Hotel
This traditional pub in The Rocks (see pp64–79) first opened its doors in 1834. Its own specially brewed beers are available on tap.

Key

▨	Major sight
🚆	Sydney Trains station
🚋	Light Rail station
🚌	Bus terminus
🚌	Coach station
⛴	Ferry boarding point
ℹ	Tourist information
✚	Hospital with casualty unit
✝	Church
✡	Synagogue

Queen Victoria Building
This Romanesque former produce market, built in the 1890s, forms part of a fine group of Victorian-era buildings in the City Centre (see pp80–91). Now a shopping mall, it retains many original features, including its roof statues.

Art Gallery of New South Wales
The city's premier art gallery is set in the middle of parkland in the Botanic Garden and The Domain *(see pp104–17)*. It houses a fine collection of early Australian, Aboriginal and European art.

Elizabeth Bay near Potts Point
A picturesque bay with fine views across Sydney Harbour, it is at the northern end of the Kings Cross and Darlinghurst area *(see pp118–23)*.

Centennial Park
This green expanse in Paddington *(see pp124–9)* was once part of a sand dune system that extended from Botany Bay in the south.

Fort Denison

Farm Cove

AL NIC EN

OTANIC DEN AND DOMAIN

rt Gallery of ew South ales

MRS MACQUARIES ROAD

COWPER WHARF ROADWAY

CHALLIS AVE

NICHOLSON ST

BROUGHAM STREET

VICTORIA STREET

MACLEAY STREET

HUGHES ST

GREENKNOWE AVE

ELIZABETH BAY RD

FORBES STREET

BOURKE ST

Kings Cross

WILLIAM STREET

DARLINGHURST ROAD

WARD AVENUE

ELIZABETH BAY

KINGS CROSS ROAD

CRAIGEND STREET

KINGS CROSS AND DARLINGHURST

LIVERPOOL STREET

URTON ST

DARLINGHURST ROAD

VICTORIA STREET

WOMERAH AVENUE

LOR ARE

BOUNDARY STREET

GLENMORE ROAD

BROWN STREET

ORMOND STREET

STAFFORD STREET

PADDINGTON

OXFORD STREET

UNDERWOOD STREET

PADDINGTON STREET

SELWYN STREET

GREENS ROAD

MOORE PARK ROAD

RENNY STREET

LEINSTER STREET

GORDON STREET

MOORE STREET

GLENMORE ROAD

QUEEN STREET

JAMES STREET

OXFORD STREET

MOORE PARK

DRIVER

ALLIANZ STADIUM

Kippax Lake

GREGORY AVENUE

SYDNEY CRICKET GROUND

THE ENTERTAINMENT QUARTER

CENTENNIAL LANE

LANG ROAD

CENTENNIAL PARK

0 metres 250
0 yards 250

THE HISTORY OF SYDNEY

The first inhabitants of Australia were the Aboriginal peoples. Their history began in a time called the Dreaming when the Ancestor Spirits emerged from the earth and gave form to the landscape. Anthropologists believe the Aboriginal peoples arrived from Asia more than 50,000 years ago. Clans lived in the area now known as Sydney, until the arrival of Europeans caused violent disruption to this world.

In 1768, Captain James Cook began a search for the fabled "great south land". Travelling in the wake of other European explorers, he was the first to set foot on the east coast of the land the Dutch had named New Holland, and claimed it for King and country. He landed at Botany Bay in 1770, naming the coast New South Wales.

At the suggestion of Sir Joseph Banks, Cook's botanist on HMS *Endeavour*, a penal colony was established here to relieve Britain's overflowing prisons. The First Fleet of 11 ships reached Botany Bay in 1788, commanded by Captain Arthur Phillip. He felt the land there was too swampy and the bay windswept. Just to the north, however, he found "one of the finest harbours in the world," naming it Sydney Cove, after the Home Department's Secretary of State. Here, 1,485 convicts,

guards, officers, officials, wives and children landed on 26 January, now commemorated as Australia Day. This marked the beginning of the rapid devastation of the Aboriginal peoples, as they fell to introduced diseases and battled an undeclared war against the settlers. Full citizenship rights were finally granted to the Aboriginal peoples in 1973, and their traditions are now accorded respect.

The city of Sydney soon flourished, with the construction of impressive public buildings befitting an emerging maritime power. In 1901, amid a burgeoning nationalism, the Federation drew the country's six colonies together and New South Wales became a state of Australia.

In its two centuries of European settlement, Sydney has experienced alternating periods of growth and decline. It has weathered the effects of gold rush and trade booms, depressions and world wars, to establish a distinctive city marked by a vibrant eclecticism. The underlying British culture, married with Aboriginal influences and successive waves of Asian and European migration, has produced today's modern cosmopolitan city.

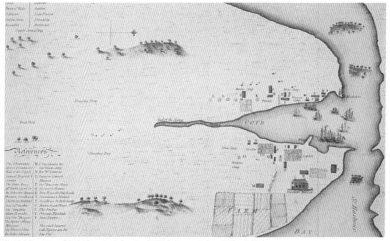

Sketch & Description of the Settlement at Sydney Cove (1788), by transported convict Francis Fowkes

◀ *Desmond, a New South Wales Chief* (about 1825), by Augustus Earle

Sydney's Original Inhabitants

Anthropologists believe that Aboriginal peoples reached Sydney Harbour at least 50,000 years ago. One of the clans of coastal Sydney was the Eora people. Their campsites were usually close to the shore, particularly in the summer when fish were plentiful. Plant and animal foods supplemented their seafood diet. Artistic expression was a way of life, with their shields decorated with ochre, designs carved on their implements, and their bodies adorned with scars, animal teeth and feathers. Sacred and social ceremonies are still vital today. Oral traditions recount stories of the Dreaming *(see p21)* and describe the Eora's strong attachment to the land.

Aborigines Fishing (1819) Sixty-seven Eora canoes were counted in the harbour on a single day. Spears were used as tools and weapons.

Bero
Wa

Glenbrook Crossing
The Red Hand Caves near Glenbrook in the lower Blue Mountains contain stencils where ochre was blown over outstretched hands.

The name Parramatta means "place where eels lie down or sleep", or "the head of the river".

Glenbrook •

Parramatta •

Cabramatta •

Cabramatta means "land where the cobra grub is found".

Red Ochre and Shell Paint Holder
Ochre was a commonly used material in rock painting. Finely ground, then mixed with water and a binding agent, it would be applied by brush or hand.

Aboriginal Rock Art

There are approximately 5,500 known rock art sites in the Sydney basin alone. Early colonists such as Watkin Tench said that paintings and engravings were on every kind of surface. The history of colonization was also recorded in rock engravings, with depictions of the arrival of ships and fighting.

43,000–38,000BC Tools found in a gravel pit beside Nepean River are among the oldest firmly dated signs of human occupation in Australia

Diprotodon

20,000 Humans lived in the Blue Mountains despite extreme conditions. Remains found of the largest mammal, *Diprotodon*, date back to this period

11,000 Bur
excava
Victoria of
than 40 indiv
of this

50,000 BC

20,000 BC

28,000 Funerary rites at Lake Mungo, NSW. Complete skeleton has been found of man buried at this time

18,000 People now inhabit the entire continent, from the deserts to the mountains

23,000 One of the world's earliest known cremations carried out in Western NSW

13,000 Final stages of Ice Age, with small glaciers in the Snowy Mountains

u-ring-gai
named after
ans who lived
this coastal
strict. It is rich in
ck engravings.

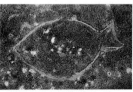

Hunting and Fishing Implements
Multi-pronged Eora spears were used for fishing, while canoes were shaped from a single piece of bark. Boomerangs are still used today for hunting and music making.

Where to See Aboriginal Rock Art and Artifacts

The soft sandstone of Sydney was a natural canvas. Much of the rock art of the original inhabitants remains and can be found on walking trails in Ku-ring-gai Chase National Park *(see pp156–7)* and in the Royal National Park *(p167)*. The National Parks & Wildlife shop at Cadman's Cottage *(p70)* has a range of pamphlets about Aboriginal sites.

Fish Carving at West Head
This area in Ku-ring-gai Chase has 51 figures and is acknowledged as one of the richest sites in the greater Sydney region.

Gumbooya Reserve in suburban Allambie Heights has a collection of 68 rock carvings. This human figure appears to be inside or on top of a whale.

The name Bondi comes from the word *boondi*, meaning "the sound of water crashing".

Allambie Heights

Bondi

Coogee

Maroubra

Coogee means "bad smell of rotten seaweed washed ashore".

Maroubra comes either from the *merooberah* tribe, or means "place where shells are found".

Bundeena

Shell Fish-Hooks
Introduced from the Torres Strait, these hooks were ground-down mollusc shells.

This python skeleton is on view at the Australian Museum *(see pp90–91)*, along with a large collection of Aboriginal artifacts.

Water Carrier
These bags were usually made of kangaroo skin. The skin was removed in one piece and either turned inside out or tanned with the sap from a gum tree.

8,000 BC The oldest returning boomerangs are in use in South Australia

5,000 BC Dingo reaches Australia, thought to have been brought by seafarers

Captain James Cook

AD 1606 Dutch ship, *Duyfken*, records first European sighting of the continent. Lands on the eastern coast of Gulf of Carpentaria

),000 BC

AD 1

,000–8,500 BC
smania is separated
om mainland Australia
rising seas

Copperplate print of a dingo

AD 1700 Macassans search for trepang or sea slugs off Australia's north coast

AD 1770 James Cook lands at Botany Bay

The Early Colony

The colony's beginnings were rugged and hungry, imbued with a spirit that would give Sydney its unique character. Convicts were put to work establishing roads and constructing buildings out of mud, reeds, unseasoned wood and mortar made from a crushed shell mixture. From these simple beginnings, a town grew. Officers of the New South Wales Corps became farmers, encouraged to work their land alongside convict labour. Because the soldiers paid for work and goods in rum, they soon became known as the Rum Corps, in 1808 overthrowing Governor Bligh (of *Bounty* fame) when he threatened their privileges. By the early 1800s farms were producing crops, with supplies arriving more regularly – as were convicts and settlers with more appropriate skills and trades.

Growth of the City
☐ Today ▨ 1810

Boat building at the Government dockyard

Pitts Row

First Fleet Ship (c.1787)
This painting by Francis Holman shows three angles of the *Borrowdale*, one of the fleet's three commercial storeships.

Government House

Scrimshaw
Engraving bone or shell was a skilful way to pass time during long months spent at sea.

A View of Sydney Cove
This idyllic image, drawn by Edward Dayes and engraved by F Jukes in 1804, shows the Aboriginal peoples living peacefully within the infant colony alongside the flourishing maritime and agricultural industries. In fact, they had been entirely ostracized from the life and prosperity of the town by this time.

1787 The First Fleet leaves Portsmouth, bound for Botany Bay

1788 The First Fleet arrives, the first white child is born in the colony, and the first man is hanged

Barrington, the convict and thespian star of The Revenge

1796 *The Revenge* opens Sydney's first, but short-lived, playhouse, simply named The Theatre

1785

1790

1795

Bennelong pictured in European finery

1789 The Aboriginal Bennelong is held captive and ordered to act as an intermediary between the whites and blacks

1790 First detachment of the New South Wales Corps arrives in the colony. Fears of starvation are lessened with the arrival of the supply ship *Lady Juliana*

1793 Arrival of the first free settlers

1797 Merino sheep a from Cape of Good H

The Arrest of Bligh
This shameful, and invented, scene shows the hated Governor William Bligh, in full regalia, hiding under a servant's bed to avoid arrest by the NSW Rum Corps in 1808.

Where to See Early Colonial Sydney

The Rocks was the hub of early Sydney. Wharves, warehouses, hotels, rough houses and even rougher characters gave it its colour. Dramatic cuts were made in the rocky point to provide building materials and filling for the construction of Circular Quay, and allow for streets. The houses are gone, except for Cadman's Cottage (see p70), but the irregular, labyrinthine lanes still give the flavour of convict history.

The buildings may look impressive, but most were poorly built with inferior materials.

Male and female convicts housed separately

Waratah (1803)
John Lewin, naturalist and engraver, drew delicate and faithful representations of the local flora and fauna.

Barracks housing NSW Rum Corps

Elizabeth Farm (pp140–41) at Parramatta is the oldest surviving building in Australia. It was built by convicts using lime mortar from the penal colony of Norfolk Island.

Experiment Farm Cottage, an early dwelling (see p141), displays marked convict-made bricks. Masons also marked each brick, as they were paid according to the number laid.

Kangaroo (1813)
Naturalists were amazed at Sydney's vast array of strange plant and animal species. The first pictures sent back to England caused a sensation.

1799 Explorers Bass and Flinders complete their circumnavigation of Van Diemen's Land (now Tasmania), before returning to Port Jackson

1803 The first issue of the weekly Sydney Gazette, Australia's first newspaper, is published

1808 Rum Rebellion brings social upheaval. Estimated population of New South Wales stands at 9,100

1800

1805

1810

1801 Ticket-of-leave system introduced, enabling the convicts to work for wages and to choose their own master

1804 Irish convict uprising at Castle Hill

1802 Aboriginal leader Pemulwy is shot and killed following the killing of four white men by Aboriginal men

Love token

1810 New convict arrivals craft such items as love tokens

The Georgian Era

Sydney's early decades were times of turbulence and growth. Lachlan Macquarie, governor from 1810 to 1821, was one of the most significant figures. He took over a town-cum-jail and left behind a fully fledged city with a sense of civic pride. Noted for his sympathetic attitude to convicts and freed women and men, he commissioned many fine buildings, including work by convict Francis Greenway *(see p116)*. When Macquarie left in 1822, Sydney boasted main roads, regular streets and an organized police system. By the 1830s, trade had expanded, and labour and land were plentiful. In 1840, transportation of convicts was abolished. A decade of lively debate followed: on immigration, religion and education.

Growth of the City
☐ Today   ▨ 1825

The domed saloon is elliptical, and has a cantilevered staircase.

Bedroom

The breakfast room was used for informal dining.

View from the Summit
Blaxland, Lawson and Wentworth were the first Europeans to cross the Blue Mountains in 1813. Augustus Earle's painting shows convicts working on a road into this fertile area.

The kitchen was originally in a separate block to avoid the danger of fire.

The Macquaries
Governor Macquarie and his wife Elizabeth arrived in the city with a brief to "improve the morals of the Colonists".

Elizabeth Bay House

This extravagant Regency villa was built from 1835–9 for Colonial Secretary Alexander Macleay (see p122). After only six years' occupancy, lavish building and household expenses forced him into bankruptcy.

1814 Holey dollar eases coin shortage

Holey dollar and dump, made from Spanish coins

1820 Macquarie Chair crafted of she-oak and wallaby skin

Macquarie Chair

1830 Sir Thomas Mitchell discovers megafauna fossils in New South Wales

1810	1815	1820	1825	

1816 Convict architect Francis Greenway designs his first building, Macquarie Lighthouse

1817 The Bank of NSW opens. Macquarie recommends adoption of the name Australia for the continent, as suggested by explorer Matthew Flinders

1831 First Austra novel, *Quintus Servin* is printed and publish

1824 Hume and Hovell are the first Europeans to see the Snowy Mountains

Lyrebird (1813)
As the colony continued to expand, more exotic birds and animals were found. The male of this species has an impressive tail that spreads into the shape of a lyre.

Where to See Georgian Sydney

Governor Macquarie designated the street now bearing his name *(see pp114–17)* as the ceremonial centre of the city. It has an elegant collection of buildings: the Hyde Park Barracks, St James' Church, the Sydney Mint, Parliament House and Sydney Hospital. Other fine examples are the Victoria Barracks *(p129)*, Vaucluse House *(p138)* and Macquarie Lighthouse *(p139)*.

Old Government House, the oldest surviving public building in Australia *(see p141)*, was erected in 1799. Additions ordered by Governor Macquarie were completed in 1816.

Servants' quarters

Aboriginal Explorer
Bungaree took part in the first circumnavigation of the continent, sailing with Matthew Flinders.

Drawing room

The Classical design was to be complemented by a colonnade, but money ran out.

High Fashion, 1838
Stylish ladies would promenade through Hyde Park *(see pp88–9)* in the very latest London fashions, which were available from the David Jones department store.

The dining room was furnished in a florid style out of keeping with the Neo-Classical architecture.

Naturalist and author, Charles Darwin

1842 Sydney town becomes a city

1838 Myall Creek massacre of Aboriginal peoples

1844 Edward Geoghegan's Australian musical comedy, *The Currency Lass*, first performed

1850 Work begins on NSW's first railway line, from Sydney to Parramatta

1835 | **1840** | **1845** | **1850**

1836 Charles Darwin visits Sydney on HMS *Beagle*

1837 Victoria is crowned Queen of England

1841 Female Immigrants' Home established in Sydney by Caroline Chisholm. Gas lights illuminate Sydney

1840 Transportation of convicts to NSW is abolished

1848 Parramatta's Female Factory, a notorious women's prison, closes down

Caroline Chisholm, philanthropist

Victorian Sydney

In the 1850s, gold was discovered in New South Wales and Sydney came alive with gold seekers, big spenders and a new wave of settlers. It was the start of a peaceful period of solid growth. Education became compulsory, an art gallery was opened and the Australian Academy of Arts held its first exhibition. The city skyline became more complex, with spires and "tall" buildings. Terrace houses proliferated. Victorian decorum and social behaviour borrowed from the mother country flourished, with much social visiting and sporting enthusiasm. It was an age of pleasure gardens and regattas, but also a time of unruliness and political agitation. In the 1890s, fervent nationalism and an Australian identity began to take shape as the country moved towards Federation.

Growth of the City
☐ Today ▨ 1881

The structure was built of hollow pine.

The dome was 30 m (98 ft) in diameter.

Mrs Macquaries Chair (1855)
This prime harbour viewing spot *(see p108)*, with the seat carved from rock for the governor's wife, was "the daily resort of all the fashionable people in Sydney".

Boer War
The 1st Australian Horse division was praised for its bushcraft, horsemanship and accurate shooting.

The Garden Palace

Built in the Botanic Garden especially for the occasion, in 1879–80, the Garden Palace hosted the first international exhibition held in the southern hemisphere. Twenty nations took part. Sadly, the building and most of its contents were destroyed by fire in 1882.

Henry Parkes

1851 The discovery of gold near Bathurst, west of the Blue Mountains, sparks a gold rush

1868 The Duke of Edinburgh visits and survives an assassination attempt. The Prince Alfred Hospital is later named in his honour

1872 He Parkes elected N Premier

1850

1860

1870

1857 *Dunbar* wrecked at The Gap with the loss of 121 lives and only one survivor

Henry Lawson, notable poet and author of short stories

1867 Henry Lawson born

1869 Trend in the colony towards the segregation of Aboriginal peoples on reserves and settlements

1870 The last British troops withdraw from the colony

The Waverly
This clipper brig, with its extra sails and tall masts, enabled the fast transport of wool exports and fortune seekers hastening to newly discovered colonial gold fields.

Where to See Victorian Sydney

Sydney's buildings reflect the spirit of the age. The Queen Victoria Building (*see p84*), Sydney Town Hall (*p89*) and Martin Place (*p86*) mark grand civic spaces. In stark contrast, the Argyle Terraces and Susannah Place (*p69*) in The Rocks give some idea of the cramped living conditions endured by the working class.

The "Strasburg" Clock
In 1887, Sydney clockmaker Richard Smith began work on this astronomical model now in the Powerhouse Museum (*see pp102–3*).

Some of the exhibits held in the Powerhouse Museum (*see pp102–3*) were rescued from this burning building.

The exhibition attracted over one million people.

St Mary's Cathedral (*see p88*), built in Gothic Revival style, is thought to be the largest Christian church in the former "Empire", outside Britain.

Arthur Streeton
In 1891, Streeton and Tom Roberts, both Australian Impressionist painters, set up an artists' camp overlooking Sydney Harbour in Mosman.

Victorian terrace houses, decorated with iron lace, began to fill the streets of Paddington (*see pp124–9*) and Glebe (*p133*) from the 1870s onwards.

---

7 Caroline Chisholm, a philanthropist who helped immigrant women, dies

1880 The *Bulletin* magazine is launched. Captain Moonlight, a notorious bushranger, is hanged

1890 First electric trams run between Bondi Junction and Waverley

Tivoli Theatre programme

1896 Moving pictures come to the Tivoli Theatre

1880

1890

1879 Steam tramway travels from the city to Redfern

Steam tram

1891 Labor Party enters the political arena

1888 Louisa Lawson's journal *Dawn* published

1900 Queen Victoria consents to the formation of the Commonwealth of Australia. Bubonic plague breaks out

Sydney Between the Wars

Federation took place on 1 January 1901 and New South Wales became a state of the Australian nation. In Sydney, new wharves were built, roads widened and slums cleared. The 1920s were colourful and optimistic in "the city of pleasure". The skyline bristled with cranes as modern structures replaced their ornate predecessors. The country was hit hard by the Great Depression in 1931, but economic salvation came in the form of rising wool prices and growth in manufacturing. The opening of the Sydney Harbour Bridge in 1932 was a consolidation of all the changes brought by Federation and urbanization.

Growth of the City
☐ Today ▨ 1945

The poster depicts the youthful vigour of the nation.

Home in the Suburbs
The Federation bungalow became a unique architectural style *(see p41)*. Verandas, gables and chimneys featured amid much red brick.

Surf lifesaver

"Making Do"
This chair, made in 1910, used packing case timber, cotton reels, fencing wire and the mouldings of picture frames.

Bronzed Lifesavers
No surf beach was complete without these supervisors forever looking to sea.

Sydney Harbour Bridge
After nine years of construction, the largest crowd ever seen in Sydney greeted the bridge's opening. Considered a wonder of engineering at the time, it linked the harbour's north and south shores.

Miles Franklin

1901 Miles Franklin's *My Brilliant Career* is published

1912 High-rise era begins in Sydney with the erection of the 14-storey Culwulla Chambers in Macquarie Street. First surfboard arrives in Sydney from Hawaii

1920 Prince Edward, the Prince of Wales, visits

1918 Sydneysiders greet the Armistice riotously

1900

1910

19

1902 Women win the right to vote in New South Wales

1907 Trunk line between Melbourne and Sydney opens

Poster for telephone trunk line

1919 The Archibald Prize for portraiture is first awarded. Influenza epidemic hits Sydney

1901 Proclamation of the Commonwealth of Australia. Edmund Barton elected as first prime minister

1915 Anzacs land at Gallipoli

Luna Park

This harbourside amusement park opened in 1935 *(see p134)*. A maniacally grinning face looms at the entranceway. Millions of Australians recall the terrifying thrill of running the gauntlet through the gaping mouth as children.

Where to See Early 20th-Century Sydney

The years after Federation yielded stylish and sensible buildings like Central Railway Station, the Commonwealth Bank in Martin Place *(see pp42–3)* and the State Library of New South Wales. The suburbs of Haberfield and Strathfield best exemplify the Federation style of gentrified residential housing.

One million people crossed the bridge on its opening day.

Donald Bradman

The 1932 English team used "dirty" tactics to outsmart this brilliant cricketer, almost causing a diplomatic rift with Great Britain.

The Anzac Memorial (1934) is in Hyde Park *(see pp88–9)*. The Art Deco memorial, with its reflecting pool, commemorates all Australians killed in wars.

The wireless became a popular fixture in most sitting rooms in the 1930s. This 1935 AWA Radiolette is held at the Powerhouse Museum *(see pp102–03)*.

Australian Women's Weekly
This magazine, first published in 1933, becomes a family institution full of homespun wisdom, recipes, stories and handy hints.

1924 Sydney swimmer Andrew "Boy" Charlton wins a gold medal at the Paris Olympics

Painted glass pub sign

1937 Heyday of painted glass pub art depicting local heroes

1938 Sydney celebrates her 150th anniversary

1942 Japanese midget submarines enter Sydney Harbour

1930

1940

1928 Kingsford Smith and Ulm make first flight across Pacific in the *Southern Cross*

Kingsford Smith, Ulm

1935 Luna Park opens

1932 Sydney Harbour Bridge opens

1939 Australia declares war on Germany

1941 Australia declares war on Japan

1945 Street celebrations mark the end of World War II

Postwar Sydney

The postwar baby boom was accompanied by mass immigration and the suburban sprawl. The hippie movement gave youth an extrovert voice that imbued the 1960s with an air of flamboyance. Australian involvement in the Vietnam War led to political unrest in the early 1970s, relieved for one seminal moment by the 1973 opening of the Sydney Opera House *(see pp76–9)*. In the 1980s, vast sums were spent on skyscrapers and glossy redevelopments like Darling Harbour, and on bicentennial celebrations. The city's potential was recognized in 1993 with the announcement that Sydney would host the year 2000 Olympics.

Growth of the City
☐ Today   ▨ 1966

Drag queens pose in their Hollywood-style sequined finery or lampoon public figures of the day.

Sydney to Hobart Yacht Race
Australia's most prestigious and treacherous yacht race runs over 1,167 km (725 miles). Each Boxing Day since 1945, spectators have watched yachts jostle at the starting line.

Elaborate floats and costumes can take a year to make, with prizes given to the best.

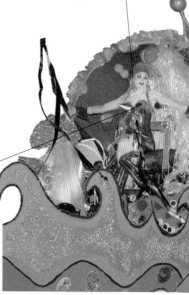

Bicentenary
The re-enactment of the First Fleet's journey ended in Sydney Harbour on Australia Day, 1988. A chaotic flotilla greeted the "tall ships".

Mardi Gras Festival
What began as a protest march involving 1,000 peo in 1978 is now a multi-million-dollar boost for Australian tourism. While the parade lasts for one ru and riotous night only (see p51), the surrounding international festival offers a month of art, sporting and community events.

1950		1960		1970		1980
1950 Petrol, butter and tea rationing ends	**1958** Qantas Airlines embarks on its first round-the-world flights	*Johnny O'Keefe*	**1965** Conscription re-introduced; first regular army battalion sent to Vietnam	**1973** Official opening of the Sydney Opera House		**1979** Sydney's Eastern Suburb Railway opens
1954 Elizabeth II is the first reigning monarch to visit Australia	**1959** Population of Australia reaches 10 million	**1964** Rocker Johnny O'Keefe, "The Wild One", continues to top the music charts		**1973** Patrick White wins the Nobel Prize for Literature		**1978** Brett Whitel wins Archibald Pri Wynne Prize and Sulman Prize for th works of art

Patrick White

Green Bans

In the 1970s, the militant building union placed work bans on developments in the inner city considered destructive to the environment or cultural heritage.

Mr Eternity

Arthur Stace (1885–1967), a reformed alcoholic, was inspired by an evangelist who said that he wanted to "shout eternity through the streets of Sydney". "I felt a powerful call from the Lord to write 'Eternity.'" At least 50 times a day, for over 30 years, he chalked this word in perfect copperplate on the footpaths and walls of the city. A plaque in Sydney Square pays tribute to Mr Eternity's endeavours.

The parade of ornate floats and showy dance troupes stretches for over 2 km (1¼ miles).

Arthur Stace and "Eternity", 1963

Ned Kelly

This 1946 portrait of legendary hero Ned Kelly is by Sir Sidney Nolan (1917–92), an important postwar painter.

Floats are marshalled in Elizabeth Street, before travelling along Oxford and Flinders Streets.

Oz Magazine, 1963–73

This satirical magazine, which had a major international influence, was the mouthpiece of an irreverent generation. It was declared obscene in 1964.

Aboriginal Land Rights

In 1975, the first handover of land was made to Vincent Lingiari, representative of the Gurindji people, by Prime Minister Gough Whitlam.

1990 Population of Australia reaches 17 million

1997 INXS singer Michael Hutchence commits suicide in a Sydney hotel

2003 Memorial unveiled to the 202 people killed in Bali bombing (2002)

2006 Sydney stages first Live Earth concert replicated simultaneously worldwide

2010 Population of Australia reaches 22 million

2014 Dame Marie Bashir, the first female Governor of NSW, retires after 13 years in the role

1990　　　**2000**　　　**2010**　　　**2020**

1992 Sydney Harbour Tunnel opens

1989 Earthquake strikes Newcastle causing extensive damage

2008 Sydney hosts World Youth Day

2000 Sydney plays host to the first Olympic Games of the new millennium

2010 Julia Gillard named as country's first female Prime Minister

2013 Bushfires rage through the Blue Mountains area, devastating several small communities

SYDNEY AT A GLANCE

There are more than 100 places of interest described in the *Area by Area* section of this book. A broad range of sights is covered: from the colonial simplicity of Hyde Park Barracks *(see pp116–17)* to the ornate Victorian terraces of Paddington; from the tranquillity of Centennial Park *(see p129)* to the bustle of the cafés and shops of Oxford Street. To help you make the most of your stay, the following 14 pages are a time-saving guide to the best Sydney has to offer. Museums and galleries, architecture and parks and reserves all have sections of their own. There is also a guide to the diverse cultures that have helped to shape the city into what it is today. Below is a selection of attractions that no visitor should miss.

Sydney's Top Ten Attractions

The Rocks
See pp64–79

Sydney Opera House
See pp76–9

Royal Botanic Garden
See pp106–7

Art Gallery of New South Wales
See pp110–13

Sydney Tower
See p85

Oxford Street and Paddington
See pp118–29

Darling Harbour and Chinatown
See pp92–103

Taronga Zoo
See pp136–7

Harbour ferries
See pp234–5

Sydney's beaches
See pp56–7

◀ Sydney Harbour Bridge *(see pp72–3)* and city skyline, from Lavender Bay

Sydney's Best: Museums and Galleries

Sydney is well endowed with museums and galleries, and, in line with the growing interest in social history, much emphasis is placed on the lifestyles of past and present Sydneysiders. Small museums are also a feature of the Sydney scene, with a number of historic houses recalling the colonial days. These are covered in greater depth on pages 38–9. Most of the major collections are housed in architecturally significant buildings – the Classical façade of the Art Gallery of NSW makes it a city landmark, while the Museum of Contemporary Art has given new life to a 1950s Art Deco-style building at Circular Quay.

Museum of Sydney
The *Edge of the Trees* is an interactive installation by the entrance.

THE ROCKS AND CIRCULAR QUAY

Museum of Contemporary Art
This waterfront space is Australia's only museum dedicated to exhibiting national and international contemporary art.

CITY CENTRE

The National Maritime Museum
The museum is the home port for HMS *Endeavour*, a replica of the vessel that charted Australia's east coast in 1770, with Captain Cook in command.

DARLING HARBOUR AND SURRY HILLS

0 metres   500
0 yards   500

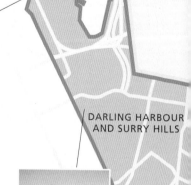

Powerhouse Museum
This museum, set in a former power station, uses both traditional and interactive displays to explore Australian innovations in science and technology.

Art Gallery of New South Wales
The Australian collection includes colonial watercolours which, to avoid deterioration, are only shown for a few weeks each year. Charles Meere's *Australian Beach Pattern* (1940) is among more recent works.

Elizabeth Bay House
The dining room is elegantly furnished to the 1840s period, when the Colonial Secretary Alexander Macleay briefly lived in the house that ultimately caused his bankruptcy.

BOTANIC GARDEN AND THE DOMAIN

KINGS CROSS AND DARLINGHURST

Hyde Park Barracks Museum
Originally built by convicts for their own incarceration, these barracks were later home to poor female immigrants. Exhibits recall the daily life of these occupants.

PADDINGTON

Australian Museum
Discover the Earth's age, find out about meteorites, volcanic activity and dinosaurs at Australia's largest natural history museum.

Sydney Jewish Museum
The history of the city's Jewish community is documented here. Included is a reconstruction of George Street in 1848, a major location for Jewish businesses.

Exploring Sydney's Museums and Galleries

Sydney boasts a rich variety of museums and galleries that reflect the cultural, artistic and historical heritage of this, the country's oldest city – and of Australia as a whole. The growth of such institutions parallels a corresponding growth in public interest in all things cultural, a phenomenon that seems at odds with Sydney's predominantly hedonistic image. In fact, Sydney has a long-standing cultural tradition, one that has not always been widely recognized. It may even surprise some people that museums and galleries attract more people than high-profile football matches.

Detail from Window of Dreams at the National Maritime Museum

Collage on one of the internal doors of the Brett Whiteley Studio

Visual Arts

The **Art Gallery of NSW** has one of the finest existing collections of modern Australian and Aboriginal art. It also boasts an outstanding collection of late 19th- and early 20th-century English and Australian works as well as a gallery devoted to Asian art and a collection of contemporary and photographic works. Thematic temporary exhibitions are also a regular feature here.

The far newer **Museum of Contemporary Art** (MCA) is best known for its impressive blockbuster exhibitions. Many of these take advantage of its prime harbour site to create a fine sense of spectacle. It also has a considerable permanent collection, and hosts literary readings and talks.

The **Brett Whiteley Studio**, housed in the studio of the late artist, commemorates the life and works of perhaps the most celebrated and controversial Sydney painter of the late 20th century.

The substantial collection of Australian painting and sculpture held by the **S H Ervin Gallery** is supplemented by frequent thematic and other specialized exhibitions.

Technology and Natural History

The undisputed leader in this area is the **Powerhouse**, with traditional and interactive displays covering fields as diverse as space travel, silent films and solar energy.

The **Australian National Maritime Museum** has the world's fastest boat, *Spirit of Australia*, as part of its indoor/outdoor display. Also part of their fleet are the destroyer HMAS *Vampire*, the *Onslow* (a submarine), and the *James Craig* (1874), a three-masted barque.

The **Australian Museum**, in contrast, emphasizes natural history with its displays of the exotic and extinct: from birds, insects and rock samples to giant Australian megafauna.

Aboriginal Culture

With more than 200 works, both traditional and contemporary, on display, the **Art Gallery of NSW**'s Yiribana Gallery has the best and most comprehensive

Jabarrgwa Wurrabadalumba's *Dugong Hunt* (1948), Art Gallery of NSW

collection of Aboriginal art in the country. The **Australian Museum** has displays ranging from rocks and minerals, birds and insects to the permanent indigenous exhibition. In its community access space, it also presents performances that celebrate Aboriginal culture.

The First Australians exhibit at the **Australian National Maritime Museum** includes audio and video material, with traditional tools made by Aboriginal communities.

The **Museum of Sydney** uses images, artifacts and oral histories to evoke the life of the Eora, the indigenous people of the Sydney region, up to the years of first contact with the European colonists.

Colonial History

Elizabeth Bay House's superb interior is furnished to show early colonial life at its most elegant, but while at first the house may appear to celebrate a success story, the enormous cost of its construction brought bankruptcy to its owner. Also built in grand style, **Vaucluse House** celebrates the life and times of W C Wentworth, explorer and politician.

Experiment Farm Cottage, **Hambledon Cottage** and **Elizabeth Farm** in and around Parramatta are testament

Water dip at Experiment Farm Cottage

to the crucial role of agriculture in the survival of a colony that was brought to the brink of starvation. The former has been restored as a gentleman's cottage of the mid-19th century, while the latter two have been furnished to the period of 1820–50. Parramatta's **Old Government House** was once the vice-regal "inland" residence. The colonial furniture on display predates 1855.

The **Museum of Sydney** is built on the site of the first Government House, close to Sydney Cove. On display are unearthed relics from that building, some of which are

The Georgian-style front bedroom in the cottage at Elizabeth Farm

visible under windows at the entrance to the museum.

Susannah Place Museum looks at working-class life in the 19th century. **Cadman's Cottage**, also in The Rocks, is a simple stone dwelling dating from 1816 and the city's oldest extant building. Adjacent is the **Sailors' Home**, built in 1864 as lodgings for visiting sailors. It now houses the Billich Art Gallery, as well as a restaurant and the Sailors Thai Canteen noodle bar *(see p187)*. The important role of gold in the history of Australia and how it determined patterns of migration and expansion are shown at the **Powerhouse Museum**. **Hyde Park Barracks Museum** evokes the often brutal lives and times of the convicts who were housed there in the early 19th century, while not neglecting its other place in history as an immigration depot.

Side view of the veranda at Elizabeth Farm, near Parramatta

Specialist Museums

Author May Gibbs' home on the harbour, **Nutcote**, has been refurbished in the style of the 1930s. The **Justice and Police Museum** examines a far less comfortable history, investigating Australian crime and punishment, while the Caroline Simpson Library & Research Collection at **The Mint** covers the history of Australian homes and gardens. Experiences of Jewish migrants to Australia and the story of the Holocaust are examined at the **Sydney Jewish Museum**.

Finding the Museums and Galleries

Art Gallery of NSW   pp110–13
Australian Museum   pp90–91
Australian National Maritime
    Museum   pp96–7
Brett Whiteley Studio   p132
Cadman's Cottage   p70
Elizabeth Bay House   p122
Elizabeth Farm   pp140–41
Experiment Farm Cottage   p141
Hambledon Cottage   p141
Hyde Park Barracks
    Museum   pp116–17
Justice and Police Museum   p74
The Mint   p116
Museum of Contemporary
    Art   p75
Museum of Sydney   p87
Nutcote   pp134–5
Old Government House   p141
Powerhouse Museum   pp102–3
S H Ervin Gallery, National
    Trust Centre   p75
Susannah Place Museum   p69
Sydney Jewish Museum   p123
Vaucluse House   p138

Sydney's Best: Architecture

For such a young city, Sydney possesses a remarkable diversity of architectural styles. They range from the simplicity of Francis Greenway's Georgian buildings *(see p116)* to Jørn Utzon's Expressionist Sydney Opera House *(see pp76–9)*. Practical Colonial structures gave way to elaborate Victorian edifices such as Sydney Town Hall, and the same passion for detail is seen on a smaller scale in Paddington's terraces. Later, Federation warehouses and bungalows brought in a uniquely Australian style.

Colonial Convict
The first structures were very simple yet formal English-style cottages with shingled roofs and no verandas. Cadman's Cottage is a fine representative of this style.

Contemporary
Governor Phillip Tower is a modern commercial building incorporating a historical site *(see p87)*.

THE ROCKS AND CIRCULAR QUAY

Colonial Georgian
Francis Greenway's courthouse design was ordered to be adapted to suit the purposes of a church. St James' Church is the result.

CITY CENTRE

American Revivalism
Shopping arcades connecting streets, such as the Queen Victoria Building, were 1890s vogue.

DARLING HARBOUR AND SURRY HILLS

Contemporary Expressionism
Innovations in sports stadiums and museum architecture, such as the National Maritime Museum, emphasize roof design and the silhouette.

Victorian
The Town Hall interior includes Australia's first pressed metal ceiling, installed for fear that the organ would vibrate a plaster one loose.

| 0 metres | 500 |
| 0 yards | 500 |

Interwar Architecture
Bruce Dellit's Anzac Memorial in Hyde Park, with sculptures by Raynor Hoff, encapsulates the spirit, form and detail of Art Deco.

Modern Expressionism
One of the world's greatest examples of 20th-century architecture, Jørn Utzon's Sydney Opera House beat 234 entries in a design competition. Work commenced in 1959 and, despite the architect's resignation in 1966, it was opened in 1973.

Early Colonial
The first buildings of character and quality, such as Hyde Park Barracks, were for the government.

Australian Regency
During the 1830s, the best designed villas were the work of John Verge. Elizabeth Bay House was his masterpiece.

BOTANIC GARDEN AND THE DOMAIN

Colonial Grecian
Greek Revival was the major style for public buildings, such as the Darlinghurst Court House, designed by the Colonial Architect in the 1820–50 period.

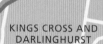

KINGS CROSS AND DARLINGHURST

Victorian Iron Lace
Festooned with a filigree of cast-iron lace in a wide range of prefabricated patterns, Paddington verandas demonstrate 1880s workmanship.

PADDINGTON

Colonial Military
Victoria Barracks, designed by engineers, is an impressive example of a well-preserved Georgian military compound.

Exploring Sydney's Architecture

While European settlement in Sydney has a relatively short history, architectural styles have rapidly evolved from provincial British buildings and the simplicity of convict structures. From the mid-19th century until the present day, architectural innovations have borrowed from a range of international trends to create vernacular styles more suited to local materials and conditions. The signs of affluence and austerity, from gold rush to depression, are also manifested in bricks and mortar.

Façade of the Colonial Susannah Place, with corner shop window

Colonial Architecture

Little remains of the Colonial buildings from 1790–1830. The few structures still standing have a simple robustness and unassuming dignity. They rely more on form, proportion and mass than on detail.

The Rocks area has one of the best collections of early Colonial buildings: **Cadman's Cottage** (1816), the **Argyle Stores** (1826) and **Susannah Place Museum** (1844). The Georgian **Hyde Park Barracks** (1819) and **St James' Church** (1820), by Francis Greenway *(see p116)*, as well as the Greek Revival **Darlinghurst Court House** (1835) and **Victoria Barracks** (1841–8) are excellent examples of this period.

Australian Regency

Just as the Colonial style was reaching its zenith, the city's increasingly moneyed society abandoned it as undignified and unfashionable. London's residential architecture, exemplified by John Soane under the Prince Regent's patronage, was in favour from the 1830s to the 1850s. Fine examples of this shift towards Regency are John Verge's stylish town houses at **39–41 Lower Fort Street** (1834–6), The Rocks, and the adjoining **Bligh House** built for a wealthy merchant in 1833 in High Colonial style complete with Greek Classical Doric veranda columns.

Regency-style homes often had Grecian, French and Italian details. **Elizabeth Bay House** (1835–8), internally the finest of all John Verge's works, is particularly noted for its cantilevered staircase rising to the arcaded gallery. The cast-iron Ionic-columned **Tusculum Villa** (1831) by the same architect at Potts Point *(see p120)* is unusual in that it is encircled by a double-storeyed veranda, now partially enclosed.

Entrance detail from the Victorian St Patrick's Seminary in Manly

Victorian

This prosperous era featured confident business people and merchants who designed their own premises. Tracts of the city west of York Street and south of Bathurst Street are testimony to these self-assured projects. The cast-iron and glass **Strand Arcade** (1891) by J B Spencer originally included a gas and electricity system, and hydraulic lifts.

Government architect James Barnet's best work includes the "Venetian Renaissance" style **General Post Office**, Martin Place (1864–87), and the extravagant **Lands Department Building** (1877–90) with its four iron staircases and, originally, patent lifts operated by water power. The **Great Synagogue** (1878), **St Mary's Cathedral** (1882), **St Patrick's Seminary** (1885), **Sydney Town Hall** and **Paddington Street** are also of this period.

American Revivalism

After federation in 1901, architects looked to styles such as Edwardian, American Romanesque and Beaux Arts from overseas for commercial buildings. The former **National Mutual Building** (1892) by Edward Raht set the change of direction, followed by warehouse buildings in Sussex and Kent Streets. The Romanesque **Queen Victoria Building**

The Australian Regency-style Bligh House in Dawes Point

(1893–98) was a grand council project by George McRae. The Beaux Arts **Commonwealth Savings Bank** (1928) features an elaborate chamber in Neo-Classical style.

Interwar Architecture

Architecture between World Wars I and II produced skyscrapers such as the **City Mutual Life Assurance Building** (1936), by Emil Sodersten. This building exhibits German Expressionist influences such as pleated or zigzag windows.

Two important structures are the **ANZAC Memorial** (1929–34) in Hyde Park and **Delfin House** (1938–40), by the Art Deco architect Bruce Dellit. The latter, a skyscraper, features a vaulted ceiling and a granite arch decorated with an allegory of modern life.

The 67-storey MLC Centre in Martin Place, by architect Harry Seidler

Modern Architecture

From the mid-1950s, modern architecture was introduced to the city through glass-clad curtain-walled office blocks, proportioned like matchboxes on their ends. The contrasting expressed frame approach of **Australia Square** (1961–7) gives structural stability to one of the world's tallest lightweight concrete office towers. This city block was formed by amalgamating 30 properties. Harry Seidler's **MLC Centre** (1975–8) is a 67-storey

Federation Architecture

This distinctly urban style of architecture developed to meet the demands of the prosperous, newly emerging middle classes at the time of Federation in 1901. Particular features are high-pitched roofs, which form a picturesque composition or architectural tableau, incorporating intricate gables, wide verandas and chimneys. The decorative timber fretwork the verandas and archways and the leadlight windows reveal the influence of the Art Nouveau period, as do the vibrant red roof tiles. Patriotic references are seen throughout, and Australian flora and fauna are recurring decorative motifs.

"Verona" in The Appian Way, Burwood

office tower comprising a reinforced concrete tube structure with column-free floors.

Jørn Utzon's **Sydney Opera House** (1959–73) is widely regarded as one of the architectural wonders of the world.

Contemporary Architecture

The elliptical **Allianz Stadium** (1985–8) and the **Australian National Maritime Museum** (1986–9), both by Philip Cox, make use of advanced steel engineering systems. Detailed masonry has made a return to commercial buildings such as the highly regarded **Governor Phillip Tower** (1989–94). The dictates of office design do not detract from the historical Museum of Sydney, ingeniously sited on the lower floors.

The **ABN-AMRO Tower** at Aurora Place (2000) was designed by Renzo Piano and was awarded the Sulman Prize for Architecture in 2004.

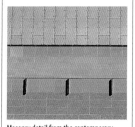

Masonry detail from the contemporary Governor Phillip Tower

Where to Find the Buildings

ABN-AMRO Tower, Cnr Phillip & Bent St. **Map** 1 C4.
Allianz Stadium. **Map** 5 C4.
Anzac Memorial *p88*
Argyle Stores *p70*
Australia Square, Cnr George & Bond Sts. **Map** 1 B3.
Australian National Maritime Museum *pp96–7*
Bligh House, 43 Lower Fort St, Dawes Point. **Map** 1 B2.
Cadman's Cottage *p70*
City Mutual Life Assurance Building, Cnr Hunter & Bligh Sts. **Map** 1 B4.
Commonwealth Savings Bank of Australia, Martin Pl. *p86*
Darlinghurst Court House *p123*
Delfin House, 16–18 O'Connell St. **Map** 1 B4.
Elizabeth Bay House *p122*
General Post Office, Martin Pl *p86*
Governor Phillip Tower *p87*
Great Synagogue *p88*
Hyde Park Barracks *pp116–17*
Lands Department Building *p86*
39–41 Lower Fort Street, Dawes Point. **Map** 1 A2.
MLC Centre, Martin Place *p86*
National Mutual Building, 350 George St. **Map** 1 B4.
Paddington Street *p128*
Queen Victoria Building *p84*
St James' Church *p117*
St Mary's Cathedral *p88*
St Patrick's Seminary *p149*
Strand Arcade *p86*
Susannah Place Museum *p69*
Sydney Opera House *pp76–9*
Sydney Town Hall *p89*
Tusculum Villa *p120*
Victoria Barracks *p129*

Sydney's Many Cultures

Sydney has one of the world's most cosmopolitan societies, reflected in the extraordinary variety of restaurants, religions, community centres and cultural activities to be found throughout the city and its environs. Over 235 birthplaces outside Australia were named in the last census. Indeed, the Sydney telephone directory lists interpreting services for 22 languages, including Greek, Italian, Spanish, Chinese, Vietnamese, Turkish, Korean and Arabic, and many of these groups have their own newspapers. While immigrants have settled all over the city, there are still pockets of Sydney that retain a distinctive ethnic flavour.

Thai Community
Thai culinary traditions have caused a revolution in Sydney eating houses. The Loy Krathong Festival in Parramatta celebrates the transplanted Thai culture.

Auburn Mosque
This lavish mosque rises above the thriving Turkish businesses nearby.

Thailand

Turkey

Cambodian
Cabramatta is the hub of the Cambodian community. Songkran, the three-day new year celebration is held at Bonnyrigg.

Cambodia

Vietnam

Philippines

Lebanon

Filipinos
Over 60 per cent of this rapidly expanding migrant group arrive as the brides of Australian men.

Vietnamese
This sculpture of a cow stands in Cabramatta's Freedom Plaza, an area offering all the sights, smells and street life of Southeast Asia.

Lakemba
A living monument to Islam, the fastest growing religion in Australia, this centre is a meeting place for local Lebanese people.

0 kilometres   4

0 miles   2

Little Italy
Long home to the Italian community, Leichhardt evokes the flavour of Europe with its bars, cafés, restaurants and a sprawling annual street fair.

Irish Parade
Sydney's first settlers, many of them Irish, made their home in The Rocks. With its proliferation of pubs, it is the focal point for jubilant St Patrick's Day celebrations on 17 March each year.

Jewish Delicatessen
The sizeable Jewish community in the city's eastern suburbs, about half of whom were born in Australia, is well served by kosher supermarkets and butchers' shops.

Ireland

Italy

China

Israel

Greece

Indigenous Australia

Aboriginal Peoples
Redfern Park hosts a Survival concert every 26 January, the culmination of a week of cultural exchange.

St Nicholas Church
Marrickville's Greek Orthodox church is the home of worship for the community, mostly based in the southern suburbs.

Chinese New Year
Each year, revellers pack Dixon Street, at the heart of Chinatown, to celebrate with fireworks and Chinese dragons.

Sydney's Best: Parks and Reserves

Sydney is almost completely surrounded by national parks and intact bushland. There are also a number of national parks and reserves within Greater Sydney itself. Here, the visitor can gain some idea of how the landscape looked before the arrival of European settlers. The city parks, too, are filled with plant and animal life. The more formal plantings of both native and exotic species are countered by the indigenous birds and animals that have adapted and made the urban environment their home. One of the highlights of a trip to Sydney is the huge variety of birds to be seen, from large birds of prey such as sea eagles and kites, to the shyer species such as wrens and tiny finches.

Garigal National Park
Rainforest and moist gullies provide shelter for superb lyrebirds and sugar gliders.

Lane Cove National Park
The open eucalypt forest is dotted with grass trees, as well as fine stands of red and blue gums. The rosella, a type of parrot, is common.

North Arm Walk
In spring, grevilleas and flannel flowers bloom profusely on this foreshore walk.

Bicentennial Park
Situated at Homebush Bay on the Parramatta River, the park features a mangrove habitat. It attracts many water birds, including pelicans.

Hyde Park
Situated on the edge of the city centre, the park provides a peaceful respite from the hectic streets. The native iris is just one of the plants found in the lush gardens. The sacred ibis, a water bird, is often seen.

Middle Head and Obelisk Bay
Gun emplacements, tunnels and bunkers built in the 1870s to protect Sydney from invasion by sea dot the area. The superb fairy wren lives here and water dragons can at times be seen basking on rocks.

North Head
Coastal heathland, with banksias, tea trees and casuarinas, dominates the cliff tops. On the leeward side, moist forest surrounds tiny harbour beaches.

Grotto Point
Bottlebrushes, grevilleas and flannel flowers line paths winding through the bush to the lighthouse.

South Head
Unique plant species such as the sundew cover this heathland.

Bradleys Head
The headland is a nesting place for the ringtail possum. Noisy flocks of rainbow lorikeets are also often in residence.

```
0 kilometres        4
0 miles        2
```

Nielsen Park
The kookaburra is easily identified by its call, which sounds like laughter.

The Domain
Palms and Moreton Bay figs are a feature of this former common. The Australian magpie, with its black and white plumage, is a frequent visitor.

Centennial Park
Open expanses and groves of paperbark and eucalypt trees bring sulphur-crested cockatoos en masse. The brushtail possum is a shy creature that comes out at night.

Moore Park
Huge Moreton Bay figs provide an urban habitat for the flying fox.

Exploring the Parks and Reserves

Despite 200 years of European settlement, Sydney's parks and reserves contain a surprising variety of native wildlife. Approximately 2,000 species of native plants, 1,000 cultivated and weed species and 300 bird species have managed to adapt favourably to the changes.

Several quite distinct vegetation types are protected in the bushland around Sydney, and these in turn provide shelter for a wide range of birds and animals. Even the more formal parks such as Hyde Park and the Royal Botanic Garden are home to many indigenous species, allowing the visitor a glimpse of the city's diverse wildlife.

Colourful and noisy rainbow lorikeets at Manly's Collins Beach

Coastal Hinterland

One reason Sydney has so many heathland parks, such as those found at South Head and North Head, is that the soil along the city's coastline is deficient in almost every known nutrient. What these areas lack in fertility, they make up for in species diversity.

Heathland contains literally hundreds of species of plants, including some unique flora that have adapted to the poor soil. The most surprising ones are the carnivorous plants, which rely on passing insects for their food. The tiny sundew (*Drosera spatulata*), so called because of its sparkling foliage, is the commonest of the carnivorous species. This low-growing plant snares insects on its sticky, reddish leaves, which lie flat on the ground. You will often stumble across them where walking tracks pass through swampy ground, waiting patiently for a

Red bottlebrush (*Callistemon sp.*)

victim. Two other distinctive plants are casuarinas (*Allocasuarina* species*) and banksias (*Banksia* species), both of which attract smaller birds such as honeyeaters and blue wrens.

Rainforest and Moist Forest

Rainforest remnants do exist in a few parts of Sydney, especially in the Royal National Park to the south of the city (*see pp166–7*). Small pockets can also be found in Garigal National Park, Ku-ring-gai Chase (*see pp156–7*) and some gullies running down to Middle Harbour. The superb lyrebird (*Menura novaehollandiae*) is a feature of these forest areas. The sugar glider (*Petaurus breviceps*), a small species of possum, can sometimes be heard calling to its mate during the night.

The deadliest spider in the world, the Sydney funnel-web (*Atrax robustus, see p91*), also lives here, but you are unlikely to see

one unless you poke under rocks and logs. A common plant in this habitat is the cabbage tree palm (*Livistona australis*). Its heart was used as a vegetable by the early European settlers.

The soft tree fern (*Dicksonia antarctica*) decorates the gullies and creeks of moist forest. You may see a ringtail possum (*Pseudocheirus peregrinus*) nest at the top of one of these ferns at Bradleys Head. The nest looks rather like a hairy football and is found in hollow trees or ferns and shrubs.

Rainbow lorikeets (*Trichoglossus haematodus*) also inhabit Bradleys Head, as well as Clifton Gardens and Collins Beach. Early in the morning, they shoot through the forest canopy like iridescent bullets.

Open Eucalypt Forest

Some of Sydney's finest smooth-barked apple gums (*Angophora costata*) are in the Lane Cove National Park. These ancient trees, with their gnarled pinkish trunks, lend an almost "lost world" feeling.

Tall and straight blue gums (*Eucalyptus saligna*) stand in the lower reaches of the park, where the soil is better, while the smaller grey-white scribbly gum (*Eucalyptus rossii*), with its distinctive gum veins, lives on higher slopes. If you examine the markings on a scribbly gum closely, you will see they start out thin, gradually become thicker, then take a U-turn and stop. This is the track made by an *ogmograptis* caterpillar the

Coastal heathland lining the cliff tops at Manly's North Head

previous year. The grubs that made the track become small, brownish-grey moths and are commonly seen in eucalypt or gum forests.

Grass trees (*Xanthorrhoea* species*)*, also common in open eucalypt forest, are an ancient plant species with a tall spike that bears white flowers in spring. Lyrebirds, echidnas, currawongs and black snakes are predominant wildlife. The snakes, although beautiful, should be treated with caution.

A smooth-barked apple gum in Lane Cove National Park

Wetlands

More than 60 per cent of New South Wales' coastal wetlands have been lost. This makes the remaining areas of wetland especially important. Most of Sydney's wetlands are mangrove swamps, with some of the best preserved examples at Bicentennial Park and the North Arm Walking Track.

A grey mangrove swamp near the Lane Cove National Park

Mangrove swamps are one of the most hostile places for a plant or animal to live. There is no fresh water and, unlike soil, the mud has no oxygen whatsoever below the very surface level. Mangroves have developed some fascinating ways around these problems.

First, excess salt is excreted from their leaves. Secondly, they get oxygen to the roots by pushing special peg-like roots, called pneumatophores, into the air. At low tide, these can be clearly seen around the base of most mangroves. They allow air to diffuse down into the roots so that they can survive the stifling conditions under the mud. The Sydney rock oyster (*Saccostrea commercialis*), a popular local delicacy, is found in mangrove areas, particularly around the Hawkesbury and Botany Bay.

City Parks

An amazing number of birds and animals make the city parks their home. Silver gulls (*Larus novae-hollandiae*) and sulphur-crested cockatoos (*Cacatua galerita*) are frequent daytime visitors to Hyde Park, Centennial Park, The Domain and the Botanic Garden.

After dark, brush-tailed possums (*Trichosurus vulpecula*) go in search of food and may be seen scavenging in rubbish bins. Also a night creature, the fruit-eating grey-headed flying fox (*Pteropus poliocephalus*) can be

The nocturnal grey-headed flying fox, at rest during the daytime

seen swooping through the trees. There is sometimes a temporary colony of these mammals in the Botanic Garden, where they hang upside down from trees in the park. Most of Sydney's flying foxes come from a large colony in Gordon, in the city's north.

Moore Park and The Domain are good places to spot flying foxes and they also have wonderful specimens of Moreton Bay and other fig species.

While paperbarks (*Melaleuca* species) are a feature of Centennial Park, a range of palms can be seen in the Botanic Garden. The exquisite superb fairy-wren (*Malurus cyaneus*) can also be seen here, flitting between shrubs, while overhead honeyeaters dart after each other in the tree canopy.

Strangler Figs

The majestic figs in the city parks hide a dark secret. While most of the Moreton Bay figs (*Ficus macrophylla*) you see have been grown by gardeners long past, in the wild these trees have a different origin. They start as a tiny seedling, sprouted from a seed dropped by a bird in the fork of a tree. Over decades, the pencil-thin roots grow downwards. Once they reach the ground, new roots are sent down, forming a lacy network around the trunk of the host tree. They eventually become an iron-hard cage around the host tree's trunk so that it dies and rots away, leaving the fig with a hollow trunk.

The Moreton Bay fig, with its massive spreading canopy

SYDNEY THROUGH THE YEAR

Sydney's temperate climate allows for the enjoyment of outdoor activities throughout the year. Seasons in Sydney are the opposite of those in the northern hemisphere. September ushers in the three months of spring; summer stretches from December to February; March, April and May are the autumn months; while the shorter days and falling temperatures of June announce the onset of winter. In reality, however, Sydney seasons often merge into one another with little to mark their changeover. Balmy nights, the sweet, pervasive scent of jasmine blossom and the colourful blooming of shrubs and flowers are typical of spring. Summer caters for sun- and surf-lovers as well as being Sydney's festival season. Autumn, with warm days and cooler nights, is often perfect for bushwalks and picnics. And the crisp days of winter are ideal for historic walks and exploring art galleries and museums.

Spring

With the warmer weather, the profusion of spring flowers brings the city's parks and gardens excitingly to life. Food, art and music festivals abound. Footballers finish their seasons with action-packed grand finals, professional and backyard cricketers warm up for their summer competitions and the horse-racing fraternity gets ready to place its bets.

Spring display of tulip beds at the Leura Garden Festival

September
David Jones Spring Flower Show *(first two weeks)*, Elizabeth Street department store. Breathtaking floral artwork fills the ground floor.
Primavera *(Sep–mid-Nov)*. Highly regarded talent-spotting show at the Museum of Contemporary Art *(see p75)*.
Tulip Time Bowral *(late Sep–early Oct)*, Bowral *(see p164)*. A two-week festival of open gardens, talks, specialist shows and 100,000 tulips in bloom.
Spring Racing Carnival *(Sep–Oct)*. The horse-racing action is shared between Rosehill racecourse and the Royal Randwick racecourse.

Kite-flying on Bondi Beach at the Festival of the Winds

Festival of the Winds *(dates vary)*, Bondi Beach *(see p139)*. Multicultural kite-flying festival.
New South Wales Rugby Union Grand Final *(see p54)*, Sydney Football Stadium.

October
Australian Rugby League Grand Final *(first Sun)*, ANZ Stadium, Homebush.
Manly International Jazz Festival *(Labour Day weekend)*. World-class jazz at a variety of venues *(see p135)*.
Fiesta *(Labour Day weekend)*, Darling Harbour *(see pp94–5)*. Fiestas, parades and festivals from all nations, including music, arts, dance, puppets and fireworks.
Leura Garden Festival *(early Oct)*, Blue Mountains *(see pp162–3)*. A village fair launches the festival, when magnificent private gardens featuring flower displays of a particularly high standard may be viewed.
Bathurst 1000 *(second Sun)*, Mount Panorama Circuit, Bathurst. The premier endurance event on Australia's motor-sport calendar.
Sculpture by the Sea *(late Oct–early Nov)*, Bondi Beach. Hugely popular outdoor exhibition of fantastic sculptures on the path between Bondi and Tamarama beaches.

November
Melbourne Cup Day *(first Tue)*. The city almost grinds to a halt mid-afternoon to tune in to Australia's most popular horse race. Restaurants and hotels offer special luncheons on the day.
Sydney to the Gong Bicycle Ride *(first Sun)*. From Moore Park to Wollongong. Over 10,000 cyclists of all standards do this 92-km (57-mile) ride.

Average Daily Hours of Sunshine

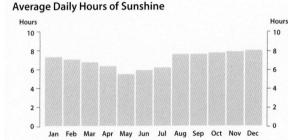

Hours

Jan Feb Mar Apr May Jun Jul Aug Sep Oct Nov Dec

Sunshine Hours
A sunny climate is one of Sydney's main attractions. There are very few days with no sunshine at all, even in the middle of winter. An up-to-date weather forecast is available by telephoning 1196. Coastal weather conditions can be obtained by dialling 11541.

Summer

Sydney turns festive in the summer months. Christmas pageants and open-air carol singing in The Domain mark the start of the season. Then there is the Sydney Festival, three weeks of cultural events and other popular entertainment, culminating in Australia Day celebrations on 26 January. Summer, too, brings a feast for sport lovers, with surfing and life-saving events, yacht races and both local and international cricket matches.

"Santa Claus" at the surf: Christmas Day celebrations on Bondi Beach

December

Carols in The Domain (*second Sat before Christmas*). Carols by candlelight in the parkland of the city's favourite outdoor gathering spot (*see p109*).
Tropfest (*first Sun*), Centennial Park. Outdoor screenings of the competition finalists in this popular short-film festival.
Sydney to Hobart Yacht Race (*26 Dec*). The harbour teems with small craft as they escort racing yachts out to sea for the start of their journey.
New Year's Eve (*31 Dec*). Street parties in The Rocks and Circular Quay and fireworks displays in Sydney Harbour.

January

Opera in The Domain (*one Sat*), The Domain (*see p109*). A free performance of highlights from productions staged by Opera Australia.
Symphony in The Domain (*one Sat*), The Domain (*see p109*). Free concert by the Sydney Symphony Orchestra.
Cricket Test matches and one-day internationals at Sydney Cricket Ground (*see p54*).
Flickerfest (*early–mid-Jan*), Bondi Pavilion (*see pp146–7*). Festival of Australian and international short films and animation.
Festival of Sydney (*three weeks*). Fantastic music, theatre and art events are staged.
Apia Sydney International (*mid-Jan*), Olympic Park Tennis Centre. Week-long tennis tournament attracting some of the top players in the world.
Ferrython (*26 Jan*), Sydney Harbour. Ferries compete for

line honours, as do rigged competitors in the Tall Ships Race held on the same day.
Australia Day Concert (*26 Jan*). Music concerts take place all over the city to celebrate this national holiday.
Chinese New Year (*late Jan or early Feb*). Lion dancing, fire-crackers and other New Year festivities held in Chinatown (*see p101*), Darling Harbour and Cabramatta (*p44*).

Chinese New Year lion

February

Mardi Gras Festival, various inner-city venues (*see pp32–3*). A month of events culminating in a street parade, mainly on Oxford Street, usually running from late Feb or early March.
North Bondi Classic Ocean Swim (*one Sun in early Feb*), North Bondi (*see p139*). A popular 2-km (1½-mile) race that any swimmer is eligible to enter.
Coogee Surf Carnival (*first weekend*), Coogee (*see p57*).

Australia Day Tall Ships race in Sydney Harbour

Average Monthly Rainfall

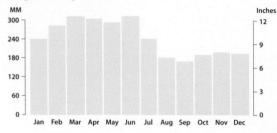

Rainfall Chart
Autumn is Sydney's rainiest season, with March being the wettest month, while spring is the driest time of year. Rainfall, however, can often be unpredictable. Long stretches of sunny weather are common, but so, too, are periods of unrelenting rain.

Autumn

After the humidity of the summer, autumn brings fresh mornings and cooler days that are tailor-made for outdoor pursuits. There are many sporting and cultural events – some of them colourful and eccentric – to tempt the visitor. For many, the Royal Easter Show is the highlight of the season. Anzac Day (25 April) is a national holiday on which Australians commemorate their war dead.

March

Dragon Boat Races Festival *(late Feb–early Mar)*, Darling Harbour *(see pp94–5)*. Brilliantly decorated Chinese dragon boats race across Cockle Bay.
ArtExpress *(all month)*, Art Gallery of NSW *(pp110–13)*. Exhibition of major artworks by the pick of the state's best graduating students.

St Patrick's Day beer

Seniors Week *(mid-Mar)*, statewide. Activities and events, many of them free, including talks, exhibitions and concerts for the state's older citizens.
St Patrick's Day Parade *(17 Mar, or closest Sun)*. Hyde Park *(see pp88–9)* to The Domain. Pubs serve green beer on the day.
Sydney Regatta *(early Mar)*. One of the largest competitive keelboat regattas in Australia.
Autumn Racing Carnival *(six weeks during Mar and Apr)*. Sydney's premier horseracing event, held at Randwick racecourse, with millions of dollars in prize money up for grabs.

Easter

Sydney Royal Easter Show *(opens for two weeks over Easter period)*, Olympic Park, Homebush. Country meets city for around 14 days of ring events, livestock and produce judging, wood-

Entrant in a woodchopping competition at the Easter Show

chopping competitions, sheep-dog trials, craft displays and sideshow alley attractions.

April

National Trust Heritage Festival *(dates vary)*. Celebration of the natural and cultural heritage of Sydney (see www.nsw.nationaltrust.org.au).
Anzac Day *(25 Apr)*. Dawn remembrance service held at the Cenotaph, Martin Place *(see p86)*, with a parade by war veterans along George Street.

May

Sydney Writers' Festival *(dates vary, one week mid-May)*, Pier 4/5 Hickson Road, Walsh Bay. Australia's finest literary celebration, with more than 300 events featuring Australian and international writers and publishers.
Sydney Half Marathon *(Sun in May)*, from Pier One, The Rocks. A 21-km (13-mile) run open to all standards.
Vivid Festival *(late May–early Jun)*. Sydney is transformed into a canvas of lights, music and creative forums.

Traditional decorative dragon boats on Darling Harbour's Cockle Bay

Average Monthly Temperature

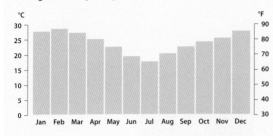

Temperature Chart
This chart gives the average minimum and maximum temperatures for Sydney. Spring and autumn are generally free of extremes, but be prepared for sudden cold snaps in winter and occasional bursts of oppressive humid heat in summer.

Winter

Winter in Sydney can be cold enough to require warm jackets; temperatures at night may drop dramatically away from the coast. The days are often clear and sometimes surprisingly mild. Arts are a major feature of winter. There are lots of exhibitions and the Sydney Film Festival, which no film buff will want to miss.

June

Manly Food and Wine Festival *(first weekend)*, Manly Beach *(see p135)*. Annual food and wine festival plus train rides, bouncy castles and more for children.

Queen's Birthday Weekend *(early Jun)*, Darling Harbour *(see pp94–5)*. This long weekend of celebrations also marks the official opening of the Australian ski season.

Sydney Film Festival *(two weeks mid-Jun)*, State Theatre *(see p84)*. The latest short and feature films, as well as retrospectives and showcases.

Winter Magic Festival *(weekend closest to winter solstice)*, Katoomba. Celebrate the winter solstice with elves and fairies in a street parade.

July

Biennale of Sydney *(two months, mid-year)*, various venues. International festival, held in even-numbered years, encompassing and showcasing many forms of visual art, from painting and

The familiar logo of the Film Festival

Australian soldiers or "Diggers" at an Anzac Day ceremony

installations to photography and performance art.

Yulefest *(throughout winter)*, Blue Mountains *(see pp162–3)*. Hotels, guesthouses and some restaurants celebrate a midwinter "Christmas" with log fires and all the Yuletide trimmings.

NAIDOC (National Aboriginal and Torres Strait Islander) Week *(dates vary)*. Week-long celebrations to build awareness and understanding of Aboriginal culture and history.

The Rocks Aroma Festival *(late Jul)*, The Rocks *(see pp66–7)*. A festival celebrating ground coffee, spices and teas.

Splendour in the Grass *(late Jul)*, Byron Bay. A weekend of alternative music and arts.

Archibald, Wynne and Sulman exhibitions *(Jul–Sep)*, Art Gallery of NSW *(pp110–13)*. Annual exhibition of competition entries for prestigious prizes in portrait, landscape and genre painting.

Public Holidays

New Year's Day (1 Jan)

Australia Day (26 Jan)

Good Friday (variable)

Easter Monday (variable)

Anzac Day (25 Apr)

Queen's Birthday (second Mon in Jun)

Bank Holiday (first Mon in Aug: only banks and some financial institutions are closed)

Labour Day (first Mon in Oct)

Christmas Day (25 Dec)

Boxing Day (26 Dec)

August

Sydney International Boat Show *(early Aug)*, Convention and Exhibition Centre and Cockle Bay Marina, Darling Harbour *(see p95)*.

City to Surf Race *(second Sun)*. From the city to Bondi Beach *(see p139)*. A 14-km (9-mile) community event that attracts all types, from amateurs to leading marathon runners.

Runners in the City to Surf Race, surging down William Street

SPORTING SYDNEY

Throughout Australia sport is a way of life and Sydney is no exception. On any day you'll see locals on golf courses at dawn, running around the streets keeping fit, or having a quick set of tennis after work. At weekends, during summer and winter, there is no end to the variety of sports you can watch. Thousands gather at Allianz Stadium and Sydney Cricket Ground every weekend while, for those who cannot make it, sport reigns supreme on weekend television.

Cricket

During the summer months Test cricket and one-day internationals are played at the Sydney Cricket Ground (SCG). Tickets for weekday sessions of the Tests can often be bought at the gate, although it is advisable to book well in advance (through **Ticketek**) for weekend sessions of Test matches and for all the one-day international matches.

Rugby League and Rugby Union

The popularity of rugby league knows no bounds here. This is what people are referring to when they talk about "the footy". There are three major competition levels: national, State of Origin – which matches Queensland against New South Wales – and Tests. The National Rugby League (NRL) competition fields teams from all over Sydney as well as Newcastle, Canberra, Melbourne, Brisbane, the Gold Coast, Far North Queensland and Auckland, New Zealand.

Many of these matches are held in different areas of Sydney, although the ANZ Stadium at

Australia's Wallabies playing the All Blacks in a Rugby Test

Sydney Olympic Park is by far the biggest venue. Tickets for State of Origin and Test matches often sell out instantly.

Rugby union is the second most popular game. Again, matches at Test level sell out very quickly. For some premium trans-Tasman rivalry, catch a Test match between Australia's "Wallabies" and the New Zealand "All Blacks".

Golf and Tennis

Golf enthusiasts need not do without their round of golf. There are many courses throughout Sydney where visitors are welcome at all times.

These include **Moore Park**, **St Michael's** and **Warringah** golf courses. It is sensible to phone beforehand for a booking, especially at weekends.

Tennis is another favoured sport. Courts available for hire can be found all over Sydney. Many centres also have flood-lit courts available for night time. Try **Cooper Park** or **Parkland Sports** Centre.

Playing golf at Moore Park, one of Sydney's public courses

Australian Rules Football

Although not as popular as in Melbourne, "Aussie Rules" has a strong following in Sydney. The original local team, the Sydney Swans, plays its home games at the Sydney Cricket Ground. A second Sydney-based team, the Greater Western Sydney Giants, plays at Homebush. Check a local paper for details.

Rivalry between the Sydney supporters and their Melbourne counterparts is always strong. Tickets can usually be bought at the ground on match day.

Basketball

Basketball is a popular spectator and recreational sport in the city. Sydney has male and female teams competing in the National Basketball League. The men's games, held at the Sydney Entertainment Centre, Haymarket (until the end of 2016, when they move

Aerial view showing both Allianz Stadium and Sydney Cricket Ground

Aerial view of the Allianz Stadium at Moore Park

to the Olympic Park), have much of the pizzazz, colour and excitement of American basketball. Tickets can be purchased from Ticketek, on the phone or on the Internet.

Cycling and Inline Skating

Sydney has excellent, safe locations for the whole family to go cycling. One of the most frequented is Centennial Park *(see p129)*. You can hire bicycles and safety helmets from **Centennial Park Cycles**.

Another popular pastime in summer is inline skating, and skaters can often be seen on the paths of the city's parks as well as on the streets.

Rollerblading.com.au runs tours starting at Milsons Point to all parts of Sydney. If you're unsteady, they also do group and private lessons.

For those who like to keep both feet firmly on the ground, you can watch skateboarders and inline skaters practising their moves at the ramps at Bondi Beach *(see p139)*.

Inline skaters enjoying a summer evening on the city's streets

Horse Riding

For a leisurely ride, head to Centennial Park or contact the **Centennial Parklands Equestrian Centre**. They will give details of the five riding schools that operate in the park. **Shelby Equestrian Centre** conducts trail rides through Ku-ring-gai Chase National Park *(see pp156–7)*.

Further afield, you can enjoy the scenery of the Blue Mountains *(see pp162–3)* on horseback. The **Megalong Australian Heritage Centre** has rides lasting from one hour to overnight. All levels of experience are catered for.

Horse riding in one of the parks surrounding the city centre

Adventure Sports

You can participate in guided bushwalking, mountain biking, canyoning, rock climbing and abseiling expeditions in the nearby Blue Mountains National Park. The **Blue Mountains Adventure Company** runs one-day or multi-day courses and trips for all standards of adventurer.

In the city, **BridgeClimb** offers 2½- and 3½-hour guided climbs to the summit of Sydney Harbour Bridge.

DIRECTORY

Blue Mountains Adventure Company
84a Bathurst Rd, Katoomba.
Tel 4782 1271. W **bmac.com.au**

BridgeClimb
3 Cumberland St, The Rocks, Sydney. **Tel** 8274 7777.
W **bridgeclimb.com.**

Centennial Park Cycles
50 Clovelly Rd, Randwick.
Tel 9398 5027.
W **cyclehire.com.au**

Centennial Parklands Equestrian Centre
Cnr Lang & Cook Rds, Moore Park.
Map 6 D5. **Tel** 9332 2809.
W **cpequestrian.com.au**

Cooper Park Tennis Courts
Off Suttie Rd, Double Bay.
Tel 9389 3100.
W **cptennis.com.au**

Megalong Australian Heritage Centre
Megalong Valley Rd, Megalong Valley. **Tel** 4787 8188.
W **megalongcc.com.au**

Moore Park Golf Club
Cnr Cleveland St & Anzac Parade, Moore Park. **Map** 5 B5.
Tel 9663 1064.
W **mooreparkgolf.com.au**

Parkland Sports
Cnr Anzac Parade & Lang Rd, Moore Park. **Tel** 9662 7033.

Rollerblading.com.au
Tel 0411 872 022.

St Michael's Golf Club
Jennifer St, Little Bay.
Tel 9311 0688.
W **stmichaelsgolf.com.au**

Shelby Equestrian Centre
90 Booralie Rd, Terrey Hills.
Tel 9450 1745.
W **shelbyec.com.au**

Ticketek
Tel 132849. W **ticketek.com.au**

Warringah Golf Club
397 Condamine St, North Manly.
Tel 9905 4028.

Sydney's Beaches

As Sydney is a city built around the water, it is no wonder that many of its recreational activities involve the sand, sea and sun. There are many harbour and surf beaches in Sydney, most of them accessible by bus *(see p231)*. Even if you're not a swimmer, the beaches offer a chance to get away from it all for a day or weekend and enjoy the fresh air and relaxed way of life.

A group of scuba divers preparing to enter the water at Gordons Bay

Swimming

Harbour beaches such as Camp Cove, Shark Bay and Balmoral Beach are generally smaller and more sheltered than the ocean beaches. The latter have surf lifesavers in distinctive red and yellow caps. Surf lifesaving carnivals are held throughout summer. Call **Surf Life Saving NSW** for a calendar of events. District councils also provide their own lifeguards, who wear blue uniforms. Rules about swimming are rigorously enforced, so try to familiarize yourself with beach signage.

The beaches can sometimes become polluted. Find up-to-date details at **Beach Watch and Harbour Watch Information**.

Surfing

Surfing is more a way of life than a leisure activity for some Sydneysiders. If you're a beginner, try Bondi, Bronte, Palm Beach or Collaroy.

Two of the best surf beaches are Maroubra and Narrabeen. Bear in mind that local surfers know one another well and do not take kindly to "intruders" who drop in on their waves or

leave litter on their beaches. To hire a surfboard, try Bondi Surf Co on Campbell Parade, Bondi Beach, or Aloha Surf on Pittwater Road, Manly. If you would like to learn, there are two surf schools: **Manly Surf School** and **Lets Go Surfing** at Bondi Beach. They also hire out boards and wetsuits.

Windsurfing and Sailing

There are locations around Sydney suitable for every level of windsurfer. Boards can be hired from **Balmoral Sailing School** at Balmoral Beach. Good spots include Palm Beach, Narrabeen Lakes, La Perouse, Brighton-Le-Sands and Kurnell Point (for beginner and intermediate boarders) and Long Reef Beach, Palm Beach and Collaroy (for the more experienced windsurfer).

One of the best ways to see the harbour is while sailing. A sailing boat, including a skipper, can be hired for the afternoon from the **East Sail** sailing club. If you'd like to learn how to sail, the sailing club has two-day courses and also hires out sailing boats and motor cruisers to experienced sailors.

Scuba Diving

There are some excellent dive spots around Sydney, especially in winter when the water is clear, if a little cold. More favoured spots are Gordons Bay, Shelly Beach, and Camp Cove.

Pro Dive Coogee offers a complete range of courses, escorted dives, introductory dives for beginners, and hire equipment. **Dive Centre Manly** also runs courses and introductory dives, hires equipment and conducts boat dives seven days a week.

DIRECTORY

Balmoral Sailing School
Balmoral Park, The Esplanade, Mosman. **Tel** 9960 5344.
W sailingschool.com.au

Beach Watch and Harbour Watch Information
W environment.nsw.gov.au/beach

Dive Centre Manly
10 Belgrave St, Manly.
Tel 9977 4355.
W divesydney.com.au

East Sail
d'Albora Marinas, New Beach Rd, Rushcutters Bay. **Tel** 9327 1166.
W eastsail.com.au

Lets Go Surfing
128 Ramsgate Ave North Bondi.
Tel 9365 1800.
W letsgosurfing.com.au

Manly Surf School
North Steyne Rd, Manly.
Tel 9977 6977.
W manlysurfschool.com.au

Pro Dive Coogee
27 Alfreda St, Coogee. **Tel** 9665 6333. W prodivesydney.com

Surf Life Saving NSW
Tel 9471 8000.
W surflifesaving.com.au

Rock baths and surf lifesaving club at Coogee Beach

Top 30 beaches

These beaches have been selected for their safe swimming, water sports, facilities available or their picturesque setting.

	Swimming Pool	Surfing	Windsurfing	Fishing	Scuba Diving	Picnic/Barbecue	Restaurant/Café
Avalon	●	●	●			●	
Balmoral	●		●	●		●	●
The Basin	●					●	
Bilgola							
Bondi Beach	●	●		●	●	●	●
Bronte	●	●		●	●	●	●
Camp Cove					●		
Clifton Gardens	●		●	●	●		
Clovelly	●				●		●
Coogee	●		●	●		●	●
Curl Curl	●	●		●			
Dee Why	●	●			●		●
Fairy Bower					●		
Fishermans Beach		●	●	●			
Freshwater	●	●					●
Gordons Bay				●	●		
Long Reef		●	●		●		
Manly Beach	●				●	●	●
Maroubra		●	●	●		●	
Narrabeen	●	●		●		●	
Newport Beach	●	●	●	●		●	
Obelisk Bay							
Palm Beach	●	●	●	●	●	●	
Parsley Bay	●						
Seven Shillings Beach	●					●	
Shark Bay	●					●	●
Shelly Beach					●	●	●
Tamarama		●			●	●	●
Watsons Bay	●		●	●	●		●
Whale Beach	●	●	●	●		●	●

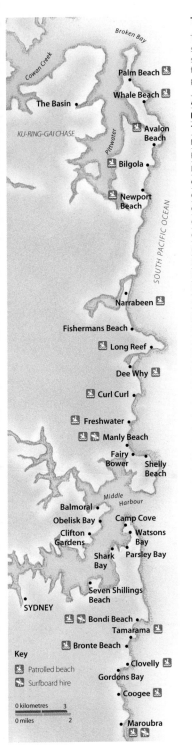

Broken Bay
Cowan Creek
Palm Beach
Whale Beach
The Basin
KU-RING-GAI CHASE
Pittwater
Avalon Beach
Bilgola
Newport Beach
SOUTH PACIFIC OCEAN
Narrabeen
Fishermans Beach
Long Reef
Dee Why
Curl Curl
Freshwater
Manly Beach
Fairy Bower
Shelly Beach
Middle Harbour
Balmoral
Obelisk Bay
Camp Cove
Clifton Gardens
Watsons Bay
Shark Bay
Parsley Bay
Seven Shillings Beach
SYDNEY
Bondi Beach
Tamarama
Bronte Beach
Clovelly
Gordons Bay
Coogee
Maroubra

Key

🏖 Patrolled beach
🏄 Surfboard hire

0 kilometres   3
0 miles   2

The Types of Waves

Cresting waves can be identified by the foam that is created as they break from the top. These waves are ideal for board riding and body surfing.

Plunging waves curl into a tube before breaking close to the shore. Fondly known as "dumpers", these waves should only be tackled by experienced surfers.

Surging waves are those that don't appear to break. They often travel way into the beach before breaking and can easily sweep a young child off its feet.

Garden Island to Farm Cove

Sydney's vast harbour, also named Port Jackson after a Secretary in the British Admiralty (who promptly changed his name), is a drowned river valley which was transformed over millions of years. Its intricate coastal geography of headlands and secluded bays can sometimes confound even lifelong residents. This waterway was the lifeblood of the early colony, with the maritime industry a vital source of wealth and supply. The legacies of alternate recessions and booms can be viewed along the shoreline: a representative story in a nation where an estimated 70 per cent of the population cling to the coastal cities, especially along the eastern seaboard.

The city skyline is a result of random development. The 1960s indiscriminate destruction of architectural history was halted, and towers now stand amid Victorian buildings.

Two harbour beacons, known as "wedding cakes" because of their three tiers, are solar powered and equipped with a fail-safe back-up. There are around 350 buoys and beacons now in operation.

KEY

① **Garden Island** marks a 1940s construction project with 12 ha (30 acres) reclaimed from the harbour.

② **The barracks** for the naval garrison date from 1888.

③ **Woolloomooloo Finger Wharf** has been developed as a dynamic dining and residential complex.

0 metres		250
0 yards		250

Sailing on the harbour is a pastime not exclusively reserved for the rich and elite. Of the several hundred thousand pleasure boats registered, some are available for hire while others take out groups of inexperienced sailors.

Mrs Macquaries Chair is a carved rock seat (*see p106*) by Mrs Macquaries Road. In the early days of the colony this was the site of a fruit and vegetable garden, which was farmed until 1805.

The Andrew (Boy) Charlton Pool is a favourite bathing spot for inner-city residents, and is named after the Sydneysider who, at the age of 16, won an Olympic gold medal in 1924. It was erected in 1963 on the Domain Baths' site, which had a grandstand for 1,700 spectators.

Locator Map
See Street Finder, map 2

Harry's Café de Wheels, a snack van, is a Sydney culinary institution, and has been operating continuously since 1945. Photographs of celebrity customers are pinned to the van.

The Royal Botanic Garden displays both flowering and non-flowering plants. Here the first trees were planted by the new European colonists; some of these trees survive today.

Farm Cove has long been a mooring place for visiting naval vessels. The land opposite, now the Botanic Garden, has been continuously cultivated for over 200 years.

Sydney Cove to Walsh Bay

It is estimated that over 70 km (43 miles) of harbour foreshore have been lost as a result of the massive land reclamation projects carried out since the 1840s. That the 13 islands existing when the First Fleet arrived in 1788 have now been reduced to just eight is a startling indication of rapid and profound geographical transformation. Redevelopments around the Circular Muay and Walsh Bay area from the 1980s have opened up the waterfront for public use and enjoyment, acknowledging it as the city's greatest natural asset. Sydney's environmental and architectural aspirations recognize the need to integrate city and harbour.

Conservatorium of Music

1857 Man O'War Steps

The Sydney Opera House was designed to take advantage of its spectacular setting. The roofs shine during the day and seem to glow at night. The building can appear as a visionary landscape to the pedestrian onlooker.

Government House, a Gothic Revival building, was home to the state's governors until 1996

Harbour cruises regularly depart from Circular Quay, taking visitors out and about both during the day and in the evening. They are an incomparable way to see the city and its waterways.

| 0 metres | 250 |
| 0 yards | 250 |

The Sydney Harbour Bridge was also known as the "Iron Lung" at the time of its construction. During the Great Depression it provided on-site work for approximately 1,400, while many more were employed in the specialist workshops.

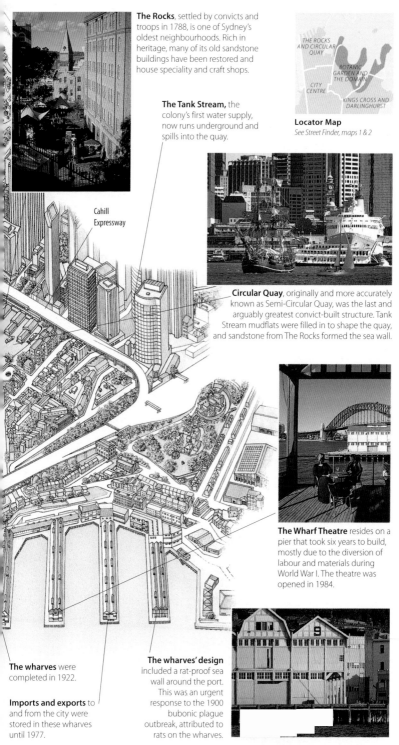

The Rocks, settled by convicts and troops in 1788, is one of Sydney's oldest neighbourhoods. Rich in heritage, many of its old sandstone buildings have been restored and house speciality and craft shops.

The Tank Stream, the colony's first water supply, now runs underground and spills into the quay.

Locator Map
See Street Finder, maps 1 & 2

Cahill Expressway

Circular Quay, originally and more accurately known as Semi-Circular Quay, was the last and arguably greatest convict-built structure. Tank Stream mudflats were filled in to shape the quay, and sandstone from The Rocks formed the sea wall.

The Wharf Theatre resides on a pier that took six years to build, mostly due to the diversion of labour and materials during World War I. The theatre was opened in 1984.

The wharves were completed in 1922.

Imports and exports to and from the city were stored in these wharves until 1977.

The wharves' design included a rat-proof sea wall around the port. This was an urgent response to the 1900 bubonic plague outbreak, attributed to rats on the wharves.

View across Sydney Cove to Circular Quay ▶

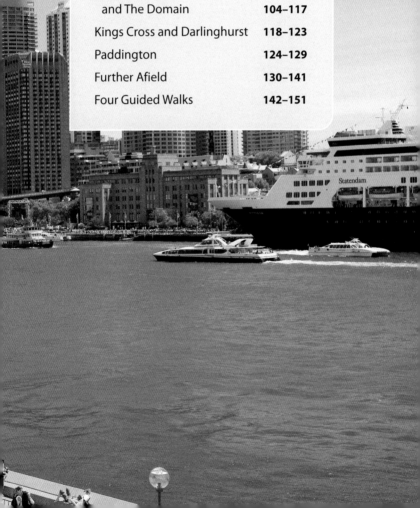

SYDNEY AREA BY AREA

The Rocks and Circular Quay   **64–79**

City Centre   **80–91**

Darling Harbour and Surry Hills   **92–103**

Botanic Garden
  and The Domain   **104–117**

Kings Cross and Darlinghurst   **118–123**

Paddington   **124–129**

Further Afield   **130–141**

Four Guided Walks   **142–151**

The clock on the Customs House building, decorated with dolphins and tridents

Sights at a Glance

Historic Streets and Buildings

1 Campbell's Storehouses
2 George Street
6 Cadman's Cottage
8 Argyle Stores
10 Sydney Observatory
11 Hero of Waterloo
13 Sydney Harbour Bridge pp72–3
15 Writers' Walk
17 Customs House

18 Macquarie Place

Churches

9 Garrison Church
21 St Philip's Church

Theatres and Concert Halls

12 Wharf Theatre
14 Sydney Opera House pp76–9

Museums and Galleries

3 The Rocks Discovery Museum
4 Susannah Place Museum
5 Sailors' Home
7 Pylon Lookout
16 Justice and Police Museum
19 Museum of Contemporary Art
20 National Trust Centre

THE ROCKS AND CIRCULAR QUAY

Circular Quay, once known as Semi-Circular Quay, is often referred to as the "birthplace of Australia". It was here, in January 1788, that the First Fleet landed its human freight of convicts, soldiers and officials, and the new British colony of New South Wales was declared. Sydney Cove became a rallying point whenever a ship arrived bringing much-needed supplies from "home". Crowds still gather here whenever there is something to celebrate. The Quay and The Rocks are focal points for New Year's Eve revels, and Circular Quay drew huge crowds when, in 1993, Sydney was awarded the year 2000 Olympic Games. The Rocks area offers visitors a taste of Sydney's past, but it is a far cry from the time, little more than 100 years ago, when most inhabitants lived in rat-infested slums and gangs ruled its streets. Now scrubbed and polished, The Rocks forms part of the colourful promenade from the Sydney Harbour Bridge to the spectacular Opera House.

☐ **Restaurants** *pp186–7*

1 Altitude
2 Ananas Bar & Brasserie
3 ARIA
4 The Australian Heritage Hotel
5 The Bridge Room
6 Cabrito Coffee Traders
7 Café Nice
8 Café Sydney
9 The Cut Bar & Grill
10 The East Chinese Restaurant

11 Ground Control Café
12 Heritage Belgian Beer Café
13 Hickson Road Bistro
14 Lotus Dumpling Bar
15 MCA Café
16 The Morrison Bar & Oyster Room
17 Nelson's Brasserie
18 Neptune Palace
19 Opera Bar

20 Quay
21 Sailors Thai
22 Sailors Thai Canteen
23 Saké Restaurant & Bar
24 Tapavino
25 Yoshii
26 Young Alfred
27 Vintage Café

See also Street Finder, map 1

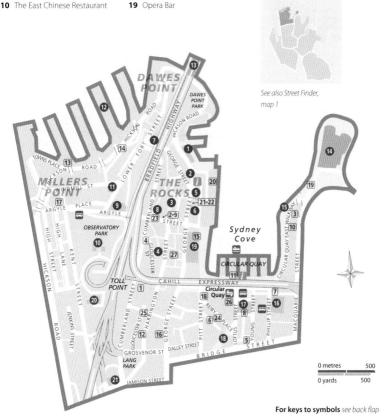

0 metres 500
0 yards 500

For keys to symbols *see back flap*

Street-by-Street: The Rocks

Named for the rugged cliffs that were once its dominant feature, this area has played a vital role in Sydney's development. In 1788, the First Fleeters under Governor Phillip's command erected makeshift buildings here, with the convicts' hard labour used to establish more permanent structures in the form of rough-hewn streets. The Argyle Cut, a road carved through solid rock using just hammer and chisel, took 18 years to build, beginning in 1843. By 1900, The Rocks was overrun with disease; the street now known as Suez Canal was once Sewer's Canal. Today, the area is still rich in colonial history and colour.

⓫ Hero of Waterloo
Lying beneath this historic pub is a tunnel originally used for smuggling.

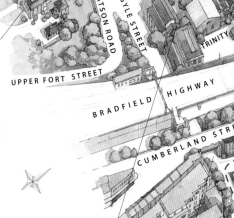

⓾ ★ Sydney Observatory
The first European structure on this prominent site was a windmill. The present museum holds some of the earliest astronomical instruments brought to Australia.

❾ Garrison Church
Columns in this church are decorated with the insignia of British troops stationed here until 1870. Australia's first prime minister was educated next door.

Argyle Cut

Suez Canal

⓳ ★ Museum of Contemporary Art
The Classical façade belies the contemporary nature of the Australian and international art displayed in an ever-changing programme.

Walkway along Circular Quay West foreshore

❸ The Rocks Discovery Museum
Key episodes in The Rocks' history are illustrated by this museum's collection of maritime images and other artifacts.

Locator Map
See Street Finder, map 1

The Rocks Market is a hive of activity every weekend, offering an eclectic range of craft items and jewellery utilizing Australian icons from gum leaves to koalas.

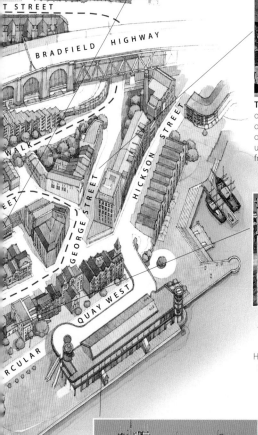

T STREET

BRADFIELD HIGHWAY

WALK

HICKSON STREET

GEORGE STREET

EET

QUAY WEST

RCULAR

❻ ★ Cadman's Cottage
John Cadman, government coxswain, resided in what was known as the Coxswain's Barracks with his family. His wife Elizabeth was also a significant figure, believed to be the first woman to vote in New South Wales, a right she insisted on.

The Overseas Passenger Terminal is where some of the world's luxury cruise liners berth during their stay in Sydney.

0 metres	100
0 yards	100

Key

— Suggested route

❶ Campbell's Storehouses

7–27 Circular Quay West; The Rocks.
Map 1 B2. 🚌 Sydney Explorer, 431, 432, 433, 434. ♿

In 1798, the Scottish merchant Robert Campbell sailed into Sydney Cove and soon established himself as a founding father of commerce for the new colony. With trade links already established in Calcutta, his business blossomed. In 1839, Campbell began constructing a private wharf and stores to house the tea, sugar, spirits and cloth he imported from India. Twelve sandstone bays had been built by 1861 and a brick upper storey was added in about 1890. Part of the old sea wall and 11 of the original stores still remain. The area soon took on the name of Campbell's Cove, which it retains to this day.

Today, the bond stores contain several harbourside restaurants catering for a range of tastes, from contemporary to Chinese and Italian. It is a delightful area in which to relax with a meal and watch the bustling boats in the harbour go by. The pulleys that were used to raise cargo from the wharf can still be seen on the outside, near the top of the building.

❷ George Street

Map 1 B2. 🚌 Sydney Explorer, 431, 432, 433, 434.

Formerly the preserve of wealthy merchants, sailors and the city's working class, George Street today is a popular attraction with visitors to Sydney, who are drawn to its restaurants, art galleries, museums, jewellery stores and craft souvenir shops. For memento and gift shopping it is ideal, with few mass-produced and tacky items, and many unique pieces, as well as a great deal in the way of modern Australian craft of a very high calibre.

One of Sydney's original thoroughfares – some say Australia's first street – it ran from the main water supply, the Tank Stream, to the tiny community in the Rocks, and was known as Spring Street. In 1810 it was renamed in honour of George III. George Street today runs all the way from the Harbour Bridge to the Central Railway Station north of Chinatown.

Many 19th-century buildings remain, such as the 1844 Counting House at No. 43, the Old Police station at No. 127 (1882), and the Russell Hotel at No. 143 (1887).

But it is The Rocks end that most reflects what the early colony must have looked like, characterized by cobbled pavements, narrow side streets, warehouses, bond stores, pubs and shop fronts that reflect the area's maritime history. Even the Museum of Contemporary Art *(see p75)*, constructed during the 1950s, began its life as the Maritime Services Board's administration offices.

In the early 1970s, union workers placed "green bans" on the demolition of The Rocks *(see p33)*. These streets had been considered slum areas by the government of the day. However many of the buildings in George Street were restored and are now listed by the National Trust. The Rocks remains a vibrant part of the city, with George Street at its hub. A market is held here every weekend, when part of the street is closed off to traffic *(see p203)*.

❸ The Rocks Discovery Museum

2–6 Kendall Lane, The Rocks.
Map 1 B2. **Tel** 9240 8680. 🚢 Circular Quay. 🚌 Sydney Explorer, 431, 432, 433, 434. **Open** 10am–5:30pm daily. **Closed** Good Fri, 25 Dec.
🆆 therocks.com

This museum is in a restored 1850s sandstone coach house, and has exhibitions on the

Umbrellas shade the terrace restaurants overlooking the waterfront at Campbell's Storehouses

Old-style Australian products at the corner shop, Susannah Place

history of the The Rocks, including displays on its first Aboriginal inhabitants, the Cadigal people, and Sydney's maritime history and traditions in the 18th and 19th centuries.

A unique collection of archaeological artifacts, such as an illegal alcohol still, and historical images dating from the early establishment of the European colony to the postwar era, helps visitors explore the eventful and colourful history of this neighbourhood. The displays are enhanced by interactive high-tech touch screens and audiovisual exhibits, bringing the history of the area alive.

❹ Susannah Place Museum

58–64 Gloucester St, The Rocks. **Map** 1 B2. **Tel** 9241 1893. 🚋 Circular Quay, Wynyard. 🚌 Sydney Explorer, 431, 432, 433, 434. **Open** 2–5pm daily. **Closed** Good Fri, 25 Dec. 🐾 🅿

This 1844 terrace of four brick and sandstone houses has a rare history of continuous domestic occupancy from the 1840s right through to 1990. The museum now housed here

examines this working-class domestic history, evoking the living conditions of its inhabitants. Rather than re-creating a single period, the museum retains the many renovations made by successive tenants.

Built for Edward and Mary Riley, who arrived from Ireland with their niece Susannah in 1838, these solid houses have basement kitchens and backyard outhouses. Connections to piped water and sewerage had probably arrived by the mid-1850s. The museum surveys the houses' development over the years, from wood and coal to gas and electricity, which enables the visitor to gauge the gradual lightening of the burden of domestic labour.

The terrace, including a corner grocer's shop, escaped the wholesale demolitions that occurred after the outbreak of bubonic plague in 1900, as well as later clearings of land to make way for the Sydney Harbour Bridge and the Cahill Expressway. In the 1970s, it was saved once again when the Builders Labourers' Federation, under the leadership of activist

THE FAMOUS **Billy Tea** 250 g NET

Billy Tea on sale at the Susannah Place shop

Jack Mundey, imposed a conservation "green ban" on The Rocks (see p33), temporarily halting all demolition and redevelopment work.

❺ Sailors' Home

106 George St, The Rocks. **Map** 1 B2. 🚌 Sydney Explorer, 339, 340, 431, 432, 433, 434. **Open** to gallery customers only: 9am–7pm daily (to 10pm Thurs–Sat; to 8.30pm Sun)

Built in 1864 to provide cheap lodgings for visiting seamen, the Sailors' Home is now used as an art gallery. The building's original north wing is Romanesque Revival in design. The L-shaped wing that fronts onto George Street was added in 1926.

At the time it was built, the Sailors' Home was a welcome alternative to the many seedy inns and brothels in the area, saving sailors from the perils of "crimping". "Crimps" would tempt newly arrived men into lodgings and bars providing much-sought-after entertainment. While drunk, the sailors would be sold on to departing ships, waking miles out at sea and returning home in debt.

Sailors used the home until 1980, when it was adapted for use as a puppet theatre. The house is now home to the Billich Gallery, a privately owned art gallery. In the basement is the Sailors Thai restaurant (see p187), one of Sydney's top dining spots.

Interior of the Sailors' Home, viewed from an upper level

Façade of Cadman's Cottage, the oldest extant building in the city

❻ Cadman's Cottage

110 George St, The Rocks.
Map 1 B2. **Tel** 9247 5033. 431, 432, 433 434. **Closed** to the public.

Dwarfed by the adjacent Sailors' Home, of which it was once part, this small historic site is no longer open to the public, though it is possible to walk around the outside of it. Built in 1816 to house the crews of the governor's boats, it is Sydney's oldest surviving dwelling.

The cottage is named after John Cadman, a convict who was transported in 1798 for stealing horses. By 1813, he was coxswain of a timber boat and the following year received an unconditional pardon. In 1821, he was granted a full pardon. Six years later, he was made boat superintendent of government craft and took up residence in the four-room cottage that now bears his name.

Cadman married Elizabeth Mortimer in 1830. She had also arrived in Sydney as a convict, sentenced to seven years transportation for the theft of one hairbrush. The couple, along with Elizabeth's two daughters, lived in the cottage until 1846.

When Cadman's Cottage was built it stood on the foreshore of Sydney Harbour. At high tide, the water used to lap just 2.5 m (8 ft) from the door.

Now, as a result of successive land reclamations such as the filling in of Circular Quay in the 1870s, it is set well back from the waterfront.

❼ Pylon Lookout

South-east pylon, Sydney Harbour Bridge. **Map** 1 B1. **Tel** 9240 1100. Sydney Explorer, 431, 432, 433, 434. **Open** 10am–5pm daily. **Closed** 25 Dec.
W pylonlookout.com.au

This site not only offers visitors one of the best views of Sydney from the top, but it also houses a series of exhibitions about the building and history of the Sydney Harbour Bridge. Take the time to absorb the stories and gaze upon the artifacts and stained-glass memorial feature windows as you walk the 200 steps from the bridge's pedestrian deck to the upper reaches of the sandstone pylon.

❽ Argyle Stores

12–20 Argyle St, The Rocks. **Map** 1 B2. Sydney Explorer, 431, 432, 433, 434. **Open** 10am–6pm daily. **Closed** Good Fri, 25 Dec.

The Argyle Stores consists of a number of warehouses set around a cobbled courtyard. They have been converted into a retail complex of mostly accessories and fashion shops that retains its period character.

Built between 1826 and the early 1880s, the stores held imported goods such as spirits. All goods forfeited for the non-payment of duties were auctioned in the courtyard. The oldest store was built for Captain John Piper, but it was confiscated and sold after his arrest for embezzlement.

The Argyle Centre, as seen from the cobbled courtyard

❾ Garrison Church

Cnr Argyle and Lower Fort Sts, Millers Point. **Map** 1 A2. **Tel** 9247 1071. 431, 433. **Open** 9am–6pm daily. **W** thegarrisonchurch.org.au

The Holy Trinity Church is known as the Garrison Church because it was the colony's first military church. Officers and men from various British regiments, stationed at Dawes Point fort, came for morning prayers until 1870.

Historic exhibits are located inside the sandstone pylon

Henry Ginn designed the church and, in 1840, the foundation stone was laid. In 1855, the architect Edmund Blacket was engaged to enlarge the church to accommodate up to 600 people. These extensions, minus the spire that Blacket proposed, were completed in 1878. Regimental plaques hung along interior walls recall the church's military associations.

Other features to look out for are the brilliantly coloured east window and the carved red cedar pulpit. The window was donated by a devout parishioner, Dr James Mitchell, scion of a leading Sydney family. The church also houses a museum displaying early Australian military and historical items.

East window, Garrison Church

⑩ Sydney Observatory

Watson Rd, Observatory Hill, The Rocks. **Map** 1 A2. **Tel** 9921 3485. 🚌 Sydney Explorer, 343, 431, 432. **Open** 10am–5pm daily. Night viewings Mon–Sat: phone to book. **Closed** Good Fri, 25 & 26 Dec. 🅿 ♿ 🎦 ⓦ sydneyobservatory.com.au

In 1982, this domed building, which had been a centre for astronomical observation and research for almost 125 years, became the city's astronomy museum. It has interactive equipment and games, along with night sky viewings; it is essential to book for these.

The building began life in the 1850s as a time-ball tower. At 1pm daily, the ball on top of the tower dropped to signal the correct time. A cannon was fired simultaneously at Fort Denison. This custom continues today (see p109).

In the 1880s, some of the first astronomical photographs of the southern sky were taken here. From 1890–1962, the observatory mapped 750,000 stars as part of an international project that produced an atlas of the entire night sky.

⑪ Hero of Waterloo

81 Lower Fort St, The Rocks. **Map** 1 A2. **Tel** 9252 4553. 🚌 431, 432, 433, 434. **Open** 10am–11pm Mon & Tue, 10am–11:30pm Wed–Sat, 10am–10pm Sun. **Closed** Good Fri, 25 Dec. ♿ ground floor only.

This picturesque old inn is welcoming in the winter, when its log fires and cosy ambience offer respite from the chill outside. Built in 1844 from sandstone excavated from the Argyle Cut, this was a favourite drinking place for the nearby garrison's soldiers. Unscrupulous sea captains were said to use the hotel to recruit. Patrons who drank themselves into a stupor were pushed into the cellars through a trapdoor. From here they were carried along underground tunnels to the wharves nearby and onto waiting ships.

⑫ Wharf Theatre

Pier 4, Hickson Rd, Walsh Bay. **Map** 1 A1. **Tel** 9250 1700. 🚌 430, 431, 432, 433, 434. Box office: **Tel** 9250 1777. **Open** 9am–7pm Mon, 9am–8:30pm Tue–Fri, 11am–8:30pm Sat. ♿ phone in advance. ⓦ sydneytheatre.com.au
See Entertainment, p210.

In 1984, the then recently formed Sydney Theatre Company took possession of this early 20th-century finger wharf at Walsh Bay. Pier 4/5 is

The corner façade of the Hero of Waterloo hotel in Millers Point

one of four finger wharves at Walsh Bay, reminders of the time when this was a busy part of the city's maritime industry.

The site fulfilled the Sydney Theatre Company's need for a base large enough to hold theatres, rehearsal rooms and administration offices. The ingenious conversion of the once-derelict heritage building into a modern theatre complex is recognized as an outstanding architectural achievement.

Since then, the main theatre has been a venue for many of the company's productions. It has seen premieres of plays from leading Australian playwrights such as Michael Gow and David Williamson, as well as performances of new works from overseas.

At the tip of the wharf, the bright and breezy bar area commands superb harbour views across to the Harbour Bridge (see pp72–3).

The Wharf Theatre, a former finger wharf, jutting on to Walsh Bay

⓭ Sydney Harbour Bridge

Completed in 1932, the construction of the Sydney Harbour Bridge was an economic feat, given the depressed times, as well as an engineering triumph. Prior to this, the only links between the city centre on the south side of the harbour and the residential north side were by ferry or via a circuitous 20-km (12½-mile) road route with five bridge crossings. Known as the "Coathanger", the single-span arch bridge was manufactured in sections and took eight years to build, including the railway line. Loans for the total cost of approximately 6.25 million Australian pounds were paid off in 1988. Intrepid visitors can make the vertiginous climb to its summit, with spectacular views as reward.

The 1932 Opening
The ceremony was disrupted when zealous royalist Francis de Groot rode forward and cut the ribbon in honour, he claimed, of King and Empire.

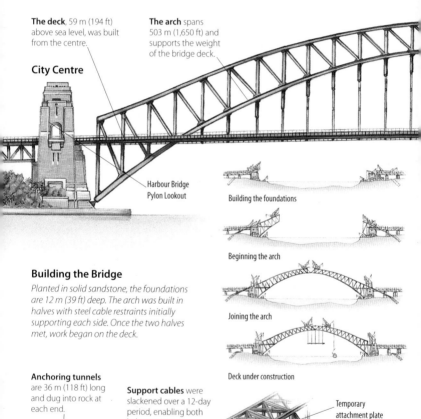

The deck, 59 m (194 ft) above sea level, was built from the centre.

The arch spans 503 m (1,650 ft) and supports the weight of the bridge deck.

City Centre

Harbour Bridge Pylon Lookout

Building the foundations

Beginning the arch

Joining the arch

Deck under construction

Building the Bridge

Planted in solid sandstone, the foundations are 12 m (39 ft) deep. The arch was built in halves with steel cable restraints initially supporting each side. Once the two halves met, work began on the deck.

Anchoring tunnels are 36 m (118 ft) long and dug into rock at each end.

Support cables were slackened over a 12-day period, enabling both halves to join.

Temporary attachment plate

The Bridge Design
The steel arch of the bridge supports the deck, with hinges at either end bearing the bridge's full weight and spreading the load to the foundations. The hinges allow the structure to move as the steel expands and contracts in response to wind and extreme temperatures.

BridgeClimb
Thousands of people have enjoyed the spectacular bridge-top views after a 2.5- or 3.5-hour guided tour up ladders, cat-walks and finally the upper arch of the bridge (see p55).

Over 150,000 vehicles cross the bridge each day, about 15 times as many as in 1932.

Bridge Workers
The bridge was built by 1,400 workers, 16 of whom were killed in accidents during construction.

North Shore

Maintenance
Painting the bridge has become a metaphor for an endless task. Approximately 30,000 litres (6,593 gal) of paint are required for each coat, enough to cover an area equivalent to 60 soccer pitches.

The vertical hangers support the slanting crossbeams which, in turn, carry the deck.

Father of the Bridge
Chief engineer Dr John Bradfield shakes the hand of the driver of the first train to cross the bridge. Over a 20-year period, Bradfield supervised all aspects of the bridge's design and construction. At the opening ceremony, the highway linking the harbour's south side and northern suburbs was named in his honour.

Maintenance
Painting the bridge has become a metaphor for an endless task. Approximately 30,000 litres (6,593 gal) of paint are required for each coat, enough to cover an area equivalent to 60 soccer pitches.

Strolling along a section of the Writers' Walk at Circular Quay

⑭ Sydney Opera House

See pp76–9.

⑮ Writers' Walk

Circular Quay. **Map** 1 C2. Circular Quay routes.

This series of plaques is set in the pavement at regular intervals between East and West Circular Quay. It gives the visitor the chance to ponder the observations of famous Australian writers, both past and present, as well as the musings of some noted literary visitors.

Each plaque is dedicated to a particular writer, with a quotation and a brief biographical note. Australian writers include novelists Miles Franklin and Peter Carey, poets Oodgeroo Noonuccal and Judith Wright, humorists Barry Humphries and Clive James, and the influential feminist writer Germaine Greer. Among visiting writers are Charles Darwin, Joseph Conrad and Mark Twain.

⑯ Justice and Police Museum

Cnr Albert & Phillip sts. **Map** 1 C3. **Tel** 9252 1144. Circular Quay routes. **Open** 10am–5pm Sat & Sun (daily Jan & NSW school hols). **Closed** Good Fri, 25 Dec. restricted.

The museum's buildings were originally the Water Police Court, designed by Edmund Blacket in 1856; Water Police

Station, designed by Alexander Dawson in 1858; and Police Court designed by James Barnet in 1885. Here the rough-and-tumble underworld of quayside crime, from the petty to the violent, was dealt swift and, at times, harsh justice. The museum exhibits bear vivid testimony to that turbulent period, as they document and re-create legal and criminal history. Late Victorian legal proceedings can be easily imagined in the fully restored courtroom.

Menacing implements from knuckledusters to bludgeons are displayed as the macabre relics of violent and notorious crimes. Other aspects of policing and justice are highlighted in regularly changing exhibitions. The bushranger exhibit, prison artifacts, and forensic display powerfully evoke the realities of the justice system in Australia.

Montage of criminal "mug shots", Justice and Police Museum

⑰ Customs House

31 Alfred St, Circular Quay. **Map** 1 B3. **Tel** 9242 8551. Circular Quay routes. **Open** 8am–midnight Mon–Sat (from 10am Sat), 11am–5pm Sun & pub hols. **Closed** Good Fri, 25 Dec.

Colonial architect James Barnet designed this 1885 sandstone Classical Revival building on the site of an earlier Customs House. It recalls the days when trading ships loaded and unloaded their goods at the quay. Features include columns in polished granite, a sculpted coat of arms and a clock face, added in 1897, bearing a pair of tridents and dolphins. Customs House reopened in 2005 after major refurbishment. Facilities include a City Library with a reading room and exhibition space, and an open lounge area with an international newspaper and magazine salon, Internet access and bar. On the roof, Café Sydney offers great views.

Detail from Customs House

⑱ Macquarie Place

Map 1 B3. Circular Quay routes.

In 1810, governor Lachlan Macquarie created this park on what was once part of the vegetable garden of the first Government House. The sandstone obelisk, designed by convict architect Francis Greenway (*see p116*), was erected in 1818 to mark the starting point for all roads in the colony. The gas lamps recall the fact that this was also the site of Sydney's first street lamp, installed in 1826.

Also in this little triangle of history are the remains of the bow anchor and cannon from HMS *Sirius*, flagship of the First Fleet. There is also a statue of Thomas Mort, a 19th-century industrialist whose vast business interests embraced gold, coal and copper mining, dairy and cotton farming, wool auctioning and ship repair. These days his statue is a marshalling place for the city's somewhat kamikaze bicycle couriers.

Façade of the Museum of Contemporary Art

⑲ Museum of Contemporary Art

Circular Quay West, The Rocks.
Map 1 B2. **Tel** 9245 2400. 🚌 Sydney Explorer, 431, 432, 433, 434. **Open** 10am–5pm daily. **Closed** 25 Dec.
♿ 📷 🌐 mca.com.au

Sydney's substantial collection of contemporary art has grown steadily, but largely out of public view, since 1943. This was the year John Power died, leaving his art collection and a financial bequest to the University of Sydney.

In 1991 the permanent collection, including works by Hockney, Warhol, Lichtenstein and Christo, was transferred to this 1950s Art Deco-style former Maritime Services Board Building. The museum also hosts temporary exhibitions of works by both Australian and International artists.

The grassed area at the front of the building is an ideal location for a harbour-front picnic. The MCA Store sells distinctive gifts by Australian designers, as well as books on contemporary art and design.

⑳ National Trust Centre

Observatory Hill, Watson Rd, The Rocks. **Map** 1 A3. **Tel** 9258 0123.
🚌 Sydney Explorer, 343, 431, 432, 433, 434. **Open** 9am–5pm Mon–Fri. Gallery: **Open** 11am–5pm Tue–Sun.
Closed public hols. ♿ 📷 🛍

The buildings that form the headquarters of the conservation organization, the National Trust of Australia (NSW), date from 1815, when Macquarie chose the site on Observatory Hill for a military hospital.

Today they house a café and the S H Ervin Gallery, with changing exhibitions throughout the year, designed to explore the richness and diversity of Australian Art.

㉑ St Philip's Church

3 York St (enter from Jamison St).
Map 1 A3. **Tel** 9247 1071.
🚌 George St routes. **Open** 9am–5pm Mon–Fri. **Closed** 26 Jan. 📷 🛕 8:30am, 10:15am, 6pm Sun.
🌐 yorkstreetanglican.com

Despite its elevated site, this Victorian Gothic church seems overshadowed in its modern setting. Yet, when it was first built, the tall square tower with its decorative pinnacles was a local landmark.

Begun in 1848, St Philip's is by Edmund Blacket, dubbed "the Christopher Wren of Australia" for the 58 churches he designed. In 1851, work was disrupted when its stone-masons left for the gold fields, but was completed by 1856.

A peal of bells was donated in 1858, with another added in 1888 to mark Sydney's centenary. These bells are still in use.

The interior and pipe organ of St Philip's Anglican church

The Founding of Australia, by Algernon Talmage, which hangs in Parliament House (see pp114–15)

A Flagpole on the Mudflats

It is easy to miss the modest flagpole in Loftus Street near Customs House. It flies a flag, the Union Jack, on the spot where Australia's first ceremonial flag-raising took place. On 26 January 1788, Captain Arthur Phillip came ashore to hoist the flag and declare the foundation of the colony. A toast to the King was drunk and a musket volley fired. On the same day, the rest of the First Fleet arrived from Botany Bay to join Phillip and his men. (On this date each year, the country marks Australia Day with a national holiday.) In 1788, the flagpole was on the edge of mudflats on Sydney Cove. Today, because of the large amount of land reclaimed to build Circular Quay, it is some distance from the water's edge.

⓮ Sydney Opera House

No building on earth looks like the Sydney Opera House. Popularly known as the "Opera House" long before the building was complete, it is, in fact, a complex of theatres and halls linked beneath its famous shells. Its birth was long and complicated. Many of the construction problems had not been faced before, resulting in an architectural adventure which lasted 14 years *(see p79)*. An appeal fund was set up, eventually raising $900,000, while the Opera House Lottery raised the balance of the $102 million final cost. As well as being the city's most popular tourist attraction, the Sydney Opera House is also one of the world's busiest performing arts centres.

★ **Dame Joan Sutherland Theatre**
Mainly used for opera and ballet, this 1,507-seat theatre is big enough to stage grand operas such as Verdi's *Aida*.

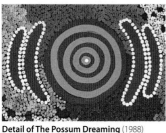

Detail of The Possum Dreaming (1988)
The mural in the Dame Joan Sutherland Theatre's northern foyer is by Michael Tjakamarra Nelson, an indigenous Australian painter from Papunga, in the central Australian desert.

Opera House Walkway
Extensive public walkways around the building offer the visitor views from many different vantage points.

KEY

① **The Dame Joan Sutherland Theatre** ceiling and walls are painted black to focus attention on the stage.

② **The Monumental Steps** and forecourt are used for outdoor performances.

③ **The Playhouse**, seating almost 400, is ideal for intimate productions while also able to present plays with larger casts.

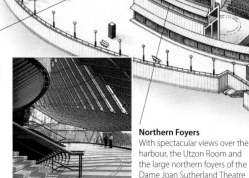

Northern Foyers
With spectacular views over the harbour, the Utzon Room and the large northern foyers of the Dame Joan Sutherland Theatre and Concert Hall can be hired for conferences, lunches, parties and weddings.

★ Concert Hall
This is the largest hall, with seating for 2,679. It is used for symphony, choral, jazz, folk and pop concerts, chamber music, opera, dance and everything from body building to fashion parades.

Dining under the Sails
The restaurant at the top of the Monumental Steps is one of several bar and dining offerings in the famous building.

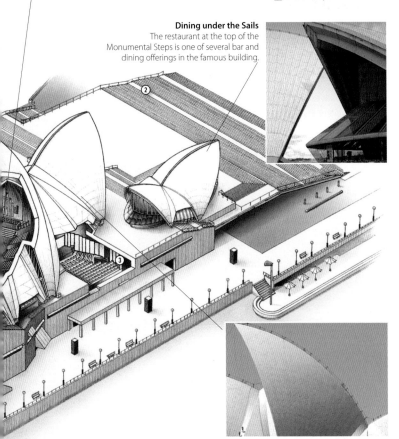

★ The Roofs
Although apocryphal, the theory that Jørn Utzon's arched roof design came to him while peeling an orange is appealing. The highest point is 67 m (221 ft) above sea level.

Detail of Utzon's Tapestry (2004)
Jørn Utzon's original design for this Gobelin-style tapestry, which hangs floor to ceiling in the remodelled Utzon Room, was inspired by the music of Carl Philipp Emanuel Bach.

Exploring Sydney Opera House

The Sydney Opera House covers almost 2 ha (4.5 acres), and is the fourth building to stand on this prominent site. Underneath the ten spectacular roofs of varying planes and textures lies a complex maze of more than 1,000 rooms of all shapes and sizes. One of the world's busiest performing arts centres, the Opera House hosts more than 3,000 events every year.

Sydney Dance Company poster advertising a production of *Poppy*

A scene from *Coppelia*, being performed in the Dame Joan Sutherland Theatre

extends back 25 m (82 ft), while the orchestra pit accommodates up to 70–80 musicians. It is rumoured that Box C plays host to a resident ghost.

Concert Hall

The rich concert acoustics under the vaulted ceiling of this venue are much admired. Sumptuous Australian wood panelling and the 18 acoustic rings above the stage clearly reflect back the sound. The 10,500 pipe Grand Organ was designed and built by Ronald Sharp from 1969–79.

Drama Theatre, Studio and Playhouse

The Drama Theatre was not in the original building plan, so jackhammers were brought in to hack it out of the concrete.

Dame Joan Sutherland Theatre

The relatively compact size of this venue makes for an intimate experience, and stage designers show off the theatre's great versatility for both opera and dance. The proscenium opening is 12 m (39 ft) wide, and the stage

Refrigerated aluminium panels in the ceiling control the temperature.

The Playhouse is used for small-cast plays and is also a fully equipped cinema. The Sydney Theatre Company *(see p71)* puts on at least one performance here every year.

The Studio hosts innovative, contemporary music and performances in an intimate space that seats just 350 people.

Backstage

Artists performing at the Opera House have the use of five rehearsal studios, 60 dressing rooms and suites and a green room complete with restaurant, bar and lounge.

The scene-changing machinery works on very well-oiled wheels; most crucial in the Dame Joan Sutherland Theatre where there is regularly a nightly change of performance, with an average of 14 operas being performed in repertoire each year.

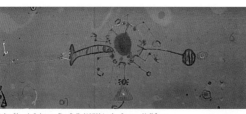

John Olsen's *Salute to Five Bells* (1973) in the Concert Hall foyer

1955 International design competition announced

Old tram shed at Bennelong Point

1957 Utzon's design wins and a lottery is established to finance the building

1963 Building of roof shells begins

Roof in mid-construction

1973 Opera House officially opened by Queen Elizabeth II

2003 Prote sprays "No slogan in re paint on th famous she

1945	1950	1955	1960	1965	1970	2003

1959 Construction begins

1948 Sir Eugene Goossens lobbies government and Bennelong Point is chosen as opera house site

1963 Utzon opens Sydney office

1966 Utzon resigns. Australian architects appointed to complete interior design

1967 Concrete roof shells completed

1973 Prokofiev's opera *War and Peace* is the first public performance in Opera House

The Design of the Opera House

In 1957, Jørn Utzon won the international competition to design the Sydney Opera House. He envisaged a living sculpture that could be viewed from any angle – land, air or sea – with the roofs as a "fifth façade". It was boldly conceived, posing architectural and engineering problems that Utzon's initial compendium of sketches did not begin to solve. When construction began in 1959, the intricate design proved impossible to execute and had to be greatly modified. The project remained so controversial that Utzon resigned in 1966 and an Australian design team completed the building's interior. In 1999 Utzon agreed to be involved in guiding future changes to the building. Since Utzon's death in 2008, his son Jan has taken on this role.

The Red Book, as submitted for the 1957 design competition, contains Utzon's original concept sketches for the Sydney Opera House.

Segmented globe

Segments separated

Roof comes into view

Several pieces cut out of a globe were used in an ingenious manner by architect Jørn Utzon to make up the now familiar shell roof structure.

Utzon's Opera House Model

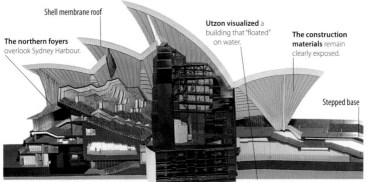

Shell membrane roof

The northern foyers overlook Sydney Harbour.

Utzon visualized a building that "floated" on water.

The construction materials remain clearly exposed.

Stepped base

Utzon's original interiors and many of his design features now exist only in model form. The architect donated his models and plans to the State Library of NSW (see p114).

The pre-cast roof has its inspiration in nature. The basic idea for the formwork of the roof was taken from the fanlike ribs of a palm. Realizing this deceptively simple idea took Utzon six years of design work.

The roof tiles were not fixed in place individually, but installed in panels to create the smooth and continuous roof surface.

The mythological figure of Apollo atop the Archibald Fountain, Hyde Park

Sights at a Glance

Historic Streets and Buildings

① Marble Bar
② Queen Victoria Building
⑤ Strand Arcade
⑥ Martin Place
⑦ Lands Department Building
⑫ Sydney Town Hall

Museums and Galleries

⑧ Museum of Sydney
⑭ Australian Museum *pp90–91*

Landmarks

④ Sydney Tower *p85*

Cathedrals and Synagogues

⑨ St Mary's Cathedral
⑪ Great Synagogue
⑬ St Andrew's Cathedral

Parks and Gardens

⑩ Hyde Park

Theatres

③ State Theatre

0 metres 500
0 yards 500

CITY CENTRE

Australia's first thoroughfare, George Street, was originally lined with clusters of mud and wattle huts. The gold rushes brought bustling prosperity, and by the 1880s shops and the architecturally majestic edifices of banks dominated the area. The city's first skyscraper – Culwulla Chambers in Castlereagh Street – was completed in 1913, but the city council then imposed a 46-m (150-ft) height restriction which remained in place until 1956. Hyde Park, on the edge of the city centre, was first used as a racecourse,

attracting illegal betting and gambling taverns to Elizabeth Street. The park later hosted other amusements: wrestling matches, circuses, public hangings and, from 1804 onwards, cricket matches between the army and the town. Today it provides a peaceful oasis, while the city's commercial centre is an area of glamorous boutiques, department stores, arcades and malls. Various exercise needs are also catered for: the Cook & Phillip Park Centre in College Street is a great pool and gym complex.

Restaurants *pp187–9*

1 Baker Bros. Espresso Bar	**7** Chophouse	**13** Glass Brasserie
2 Bambini Trust	**8** Danjee	**14** GPO Pizza by Wood
3 Barrafina	**9** Diethnes	**15** Indochine Café
4 Bistrode CBD	**10** est.	**16** Machiavelli
5 Bodhi in the Park	**11** Felix	**17** Madame Nhu
6 Bridge Street Garage	**12** Gowings Bar & Grill	**18** Mother Chu's Vegetarian Kitchen
		19 Mr Wong
		20 Pablo and Rusty's
		21 Rockpool
		22 Rockpool Bar & Grill
		23 Spice Temple
		24 Sushi e
		25 Sushi Hotara
		26 Tetsuya's
		27 Workshop Expresso
		28 York Lane

See also Street Finder, maps 1, 4 & 5

For keys to symbols *see back flap*

Street-by-Street: City Centre

Although closely rivalled by Melbourne, this is the business and commercial capital of Australia. Vibrant by day, at night the streets are far less busy when office workers and shoppers have gone home. The comparatively small city centre of this sprawling metropolis seems to be almost jammed into a few city blocks. Because Sydney grew in such a haphazard fashion, with many of today's streets following tracks from the harbour originally made by bullocks, there was no allowance for the expansion of the burgeoning city into what has become a major international centre. A colourful night scene of cafés, restaurants and theatres is emerging, however, as more people return to the city centre to live.

❷ ★ Queen Victoria Building
Taking up an entire city block, this 1898 former produce market has been lovingly restored and is now a shopping mall.

❸ State Theatre
A gem from the era when the movies reigned, this glittering and richly decorated 1929 cinema was once hailed as "the Empire's greatest theatre".

```
0 metres        100
0 yards         100
```

The Queen Victoria Statue was found after a worldwide search in 1983 ended in a small Irish village. It had lain forgotten and neglected since being removed from the front of the Irish Parliament in 1947.

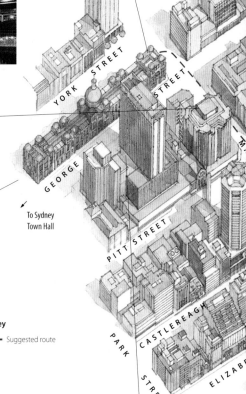

To Sydney
Town Hall

Key
— Suggested route

❶ Marble Bar
Once a landmark bar in the 1893 Tattersalls Hotel, it was dismantled and re-erected in the Sydney Hilton in 1973.

❺ Strand Arcade
A reminder of the late 19th century Victorian era when Sydney was famed as a city of elegant shopping arcades, this faithfully restored example is said to have been the finest of them all.

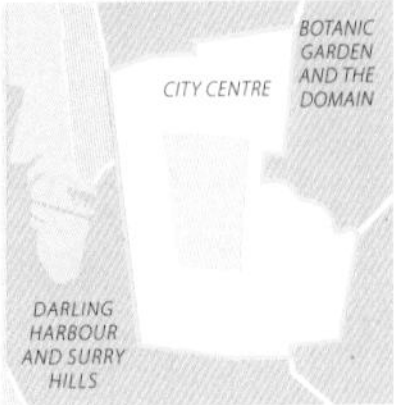

Locator Map
See Street Finder, maps 1 & 4

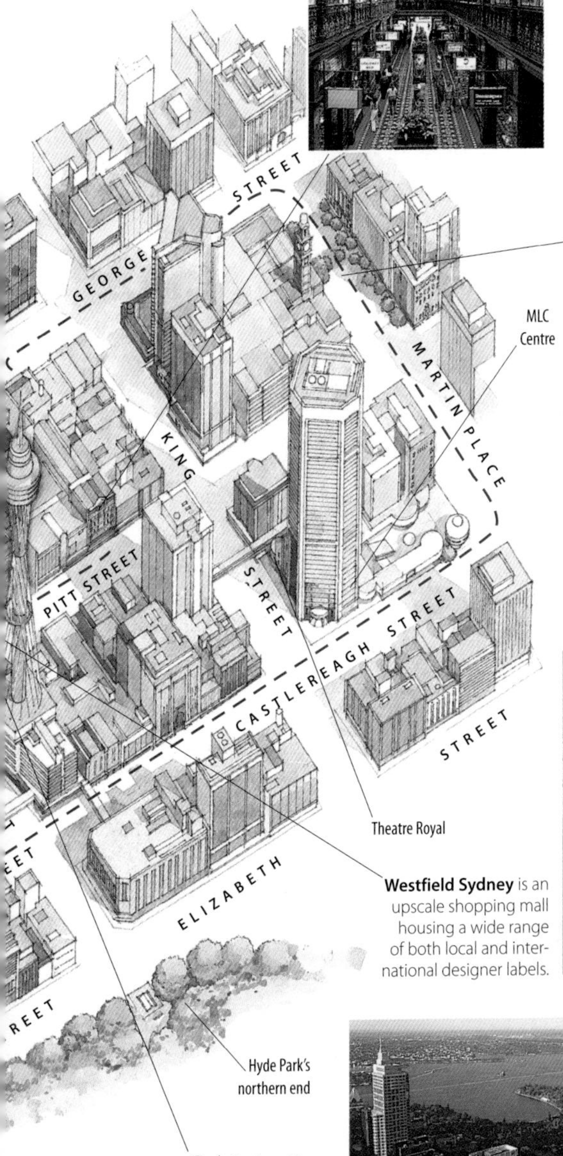

MLC Centre

❻ ★ Martin Place
Martin Place's 1929 Art Deco Cenotaph is the site of annual Anzac Day war remembrance services.

Theatre Royal

Westfield Sydney is an upscale shopping mall housing a wide range of both local and international designer labels.

Hyde Park's northern end

❹ ★ Sydney Tower
The tower tops the city skyline, giving a bird's eye view of the whole of Sydney. It rises 305 m (1,000 ft) above the ground and can be seen from as far away as the Blue Mountains.

Entrance to the Marble Bar, in the basement level of the Hilton Sydney

❶ Marble Bar

488 George St. **Map** 1 B5. **Tel** 9266 2000. 🚍 George St routes. **Open** 4pm to late Mon–Thu, 4pm–2am Fri & Sat, 4–11pm Sun. **Closed** public hols.

The Marble Bar, originally part of George Adams' Tattersalls Hotel built in 1893, is an inspired link with the Sydney of an earlier era. The bar, whose rich and decadent Italian Renaissance style had made it a local institution, was dismantled before the demolition of the hotel in 1969. Its colonnade entrance, fireplaces and counters were re-erected in the Sydney Hilton basement and reopened in 1973.

During the week, the bar attracts a broad range of city workers for after-work drinks. On Fridays and at weekends if a band is playing, the bar bustles with a younger crowd who come to hear mostly jazz and rhythm and blues music.

❷ Queen Victoria Building

455 George St. **Map** 1 B5. **Tel** 9264 9209. 🚍 George St routes. **Open** 9am–6pm Mon–Sat, 11am–5pm Sun. 🚻 🛒 *See Shops and Markets: pp198 and 200.* 🅦 **qvb.com.au**

French Designer Pierre Cardin called the Queen Victoria Building "the most beautiful shopping centre in the world". Yet this spacious, ornate Romanesque building, better known as the QVB, began life as the Sydney produce market. The dust, flies, grime and shouts as horses struggled with heavy loads on the slippery ramps are now difficult to imagine. Completed to the design of City Architect George McRae in 1898, the dominant features are the central dome, sheathed in copper, as are the 20 smaller domes, and the glass barrel-vault roof which lets in a flood of natural light.

Roof detail, Queen Victoria Building

The market closed at the end of World War I and the building fell into disrepair. It had various roles during this time, including that of City Library. By the 1950s, after extensive remodelling and neglect, it was threatened with demolition.

Refurbished at a cost of over A\$75 million, the QVB reopened in 1986 as a grand shopping gallery, with over 190 shops and boutiques on four levels. At the Town Hall end a wishing well incorporates a stone from Blarney Castle, Ireland and a sculpture of Islay, beloved dog of Queen Victoria. In 1983, a worldwide search began for a statue of the queen herself. One was finally found in the village of Daingean, Republic of Ireland, where it had lain forgotten since its removal from the front of the Irish Parliament in 1947.

Fully restored, the Queen Victoria Statue stands near the wishing well. Inside the QVB, suspended from the ceiling, is the Royal Clock. Weighing more than 1 tonne and over 5 m (17 ft) tall, the clock was designed by Neil Glasser in 1982. The upper structure features part of Balmoral Castle above a copy of the four dials of Big Ben. At one minute to every hour, a fanfare is played and there follows a parade depicting six scenes from the lives of various kings and queens of England.

❸ State Theatre

49 Market St. **Map** 1 B5. **Tel** 9373 6655. 🚍 George St routes. Box office: **Open** 9am–5:30pm Mon–Fri. **Closed** Good Fri, 25 Dec. 🚻 📷 10am & 1pm Mon–Wed; bookings essential. 🅦 **statetheatre.com.au.**

When it opened in 1929, this picture palace was hailed as the finest that local craftsmanship could achieve. The State Theatre is one of the best examples in Australia of the architectural fantasies used to entice people to the movies.

Its Cinema Baroque style is evident right from the Gothic foyer, with its vaulted ceiling, mosaic floor, richly decorated marble columns and statues. Inside the brass and bronze doors, the auditorium, which seats over 2,000 people, is lit by a 20,000-piece chandelier. The Wurlitzer organ (currently under repair) rises from below stage just before performances. Now one of Sydney's premier concert and theatre venues, it is also the main base for the Sydney Film Festival, held in June each year *(see p53)*.

The ornately decorated Gothic foyer of the State Theatre

❹ Sydney Tower

The highest observation deck in the southern hemisphere, the Sydney Tower was conceived as part of a 1970s shopping centre, but was not completed until 1981. About one million visitors a year admire the stunning views, often stretching for over 85 km (53 miles). A landmark in itself, it can be seen from almost anywhere in the city, and far beyond. Visitors can also take a 45-minute Skywalk tour on a platform around the turret's exterior.

Sydney Tower Eye Observation Deck
Views stretch to Pittwater in the north, Botany Bay to the south, westwards to the Blue Mountains, and out to the sea.

The 30-m (98-ft) spire completes the total 305 m (1,000 ft) of the tower's height.

The water tank holds 162,000 litres (35,500 gallons) and acts as an enormous stabilizer on very windy days.

Skywalk

Level 4: Observation deck

Level 3: Private event space

Level 2: Buffet restaurant

Level 1: A la carte restaurant

The turret's nine levels include two restaurants, a café and the Observation Level.

The windows comprise three layers. The outer has a gold dust coating. The frame design prevents panes falling outwards.

The 56 cables weigh seven tonnes each. If laid end to end, they would reach from New Zealand to Sydney.

The shaft is designed to withstand wind speeds expected only once in 500 years.

The stairs are two separate, fireproofed emergency escape routes.

Double-decker lifts can carry up to 2,000 people per hour. At full speed, a lift takes only 40 seconds to ascend the 76 floors to the Observation Level.

The 4-D cinema experience takes you on a journey around Sydney.

Construction of Turret
The nine turret levels were erected on the roof of the base building, then hoisted up the shaft using hydraulic jacks.

New Year's Eve
Every year, visitors flock to Sydney's highest observation deck to watch the fireworks over the city and Harbour Bridge.

❺ Strand Arcade

412–414 George St. **Map** 1 B5.
Tel 9232 4199. 🚌 George St routes.
Open 9am–5:30pm Mon–Wed &
Fri, 9am–9pm Thu, 9am–8pm Sat,
11am–4pm Sun. **Closed** some public
hols, 25 & 26 Dec. 🚻 *See Shops and
Markets: pp198–201.*

Victorian Sydney was a city of
grand shopping arcades. The
Strand, joining George and Pitt
Streets and designed by English
architect John Spencer, was the
finest jewel in the city's crown.
The blaze of publicity surrounding
its opening in April 1892 was
equalled only by the natural
light pouring through the glass
roof and the artificial glare from
the chandeliers, each carrying
50 jets of gas as well as 50 lamps.
   The boutiques and shops in
the galleries make window
shopping a delight in this airy
building which, after a fire in
1976, was restored to its original
splendour. Be sure to stop, as
shoppers have done since
opening day, for refreshments
at one of the beautiful coffee
shops in the arcade.

Interior of National Australia Bank, George Street end of Martin Place

The Pitt Street entrance to the majestic
Strand Arcade

❻ Martin Place

Map 1 B4. 🚌 George St & Elizabeth St
routes. 🚉 Martin Place.

Running from George Street
across Pitt, Castlereagh and
Elizabeth Streets to Macquarie
Street, this plaza was opened
in 1891 and made a traffic-free
precinct in 1971. It is busiest at
lunchtime when city workers
enjoy their sandwiches while
watching free entertainment,
sponsored by the Sydney City

Council, in a performance space
near Castlereagh Street.
   Every Anzac Day, a national
day of war remembrance on
25 April, the focus moves to the
Cenotaph at the George Street
end. Thousands of past and
present servicemen and women
attend a dawn service and
wreath-laying ceremony,
followed by a march-past. The
shrine, with bronze statues of a
soldier and a sailor on a granite
base, by Bertram MacKennal,
was unveiled in 1929.
   On the southern side of the
Cenotaph is the symmetrical
façade of the Renaissance-style
General Post Office,
considered to be the finest
building by James Barnet,
Colonial Architect. Con-
struction of the GPO, as
Sydneysiders call it, took
place between 1866 and
1874, with additions in Pitt
Street between 1881 and
1885. Most controversial
were the relief figures
executed by Tomaso
Sani. Although Barnet
declared that the figures
represented Australians
in realistic form, they were
labelled "grotesque".
   The Commonwealth Savings
Bank is further north, just after
the intersection with Pitt Street.
Built in 1928, this distinctive

**Statue of explorer
Gregory Blaxland**

Beaux-Arts building has a pink
granite façade with four huge
Ionic columns.
   The next building along is
the MLC Centre, a famous
skyscraper designed by Harry
Seidler *(see p43).*

❼ Lands Department Building

23 Bridge St. **Map** 1 B3. 🚌 325,
George St routes. **Open** only 2 weeks,
dates vary. 🚻

Designed by the Colonial
Architect James Barnet, this
three-storey Classical Revival
sandstone edifice was built
between 1877 and 1890.
As with the GPO building,
Pyrmont sandstone was
used for the exterior.
Decisions about the sub-
division of much of rural
eastern Australia were made
in offices within. Statues of
explorers and legislators
who "promoted
settlement" fill 23 of the
façade's 48 niches; the
remainder are still
empty. The luminaries
include the explorers Hovell
and Hume, Sir Thomas Mitchell,
Blaxland, Lawson and Wentworth
(see p138), Ludwig Leichhardt,
Bass and Matthew Flinders and
the botanist Sir Joseph Banks.

❽ Museum of Sydney

Cnr Bridge & Phillip Sts. **Map** 1 B3.
Tel 9251 5988. 🚌 Circular Quay
routes. **Open** 9:30am–5pm daily.
Closed Good Fri, 25 Dec. 🅿 🖥 ⬭
📷 ♿ 🅦 **sydneylivingmuseums.
com.au/museum-of-sydney**

Situated at the base of Governor
Phillip Tower, the Museum of
Sydney is on the site of the first
Government House, the home,
office and seat of authority for
the first nine governors of NSW
from 1788 until its demolition
in 1846. The design assimilates
a valuable archaeological site
into a modern office block.
The museum itself traces the
city's turbulent history, from
the 1788 arrival of the British
colonists until the present day.

Indigenous Peoples

The museum sits on Cadigal
land. A gallery explores the
culture, history, continuity and
place of Sydney's original
Aboriginal inhabitants, and the
"turning point" of colonization/
invasion. Collectors' chests
hold items of daily use such
as flint and ochre, each piece
painstakingly catalogued and
evocatively interpreted.

There are two audio-visual
exhibits which explore the
history of indigenous peoples

The Viewing Cube, Level 3, overlooking the
piazza to Circular Quay

from a contemporary perspective. In the square at the front
of the complex, the acclaimed
Edge of the Trees sculpture, a
collection of 29 sandstone, steel
and wooden pillars, symbolizes
the first contact
between the
Aboriginal peoples
and Europeans.
Haunting voices
in the Eora tongue
fill the space.
Inscribed in the
wood are signa-
tures of the First
Fleeters and names
of botanical species
in both the indigenous language
and Latin. Incisions made in the
pillars are filled with organic
materials such as ash, feathers,
bone, shells and human hair.

The Trade Wall display
on Level 2

History of Sydney

Outside the museum, a paving
pattern outlines the site of
the first Government House.
Original foundations, lost under
street level for many years,
can be seen here through a
window. Inside the entrance a
viewing floor reveals more
foundations. A segment of wall
has been reconstructed using
sandstone excavated during
archaeological exploration of
the site.

The Colony display on Level 2
focuses on Sydney during the
critical decade of the 1840s when
convict transportation ended,
the town officially became a
city and suffered an economic
depression. There is also a set of
scale models of the 11 First Fleet
ships. The Museum
presents stories
of the Fleet's
journey, arrival,
first contacts
with indigenous
people and the
survival challenges
faced by those on
board. On Level 3,
20th century
Sydney is explored
with panoramic images of the
developing city providing a
vivid backdrop. The Museum of
Sydney has a regular changing
exhibition programme.

Edge of the Trees sculptural installation, by Janet Laurence and Fiona Foley (1995)

Gothic Revival-style façade of St Mary's Cathedral

❾ St Mary's Cathedral

St. Mary's Rd. **Map** 1 C5. **Tel** 9220 0400. ▦ Elizabeth St routes. **Open** 6:30am–6pm Mon–Fri, 6:30am–7pm Sat & Sun. ⚑ with advance notice. 🎟 by prior arrangement. 🖳 stmaryscathedral.org.au

Although Catholics arrived with the First Fleet, the celebration of Mass was at first prohibited in case the priests provoked civil strife among the colony's large Irish Catholic population. The first priests were appointed in 1820 and services allowed. In 1821, Governor Macquarie laid the foundation stone for

St Mary's Chapel on the site of today's cathedral, the first land granted to the Catholic Church in Australia.

The initial section of the Gothic Revival-style cathedral was opened in 1882. In 1928, the building was completed, but without the twin southern spires proposed by the architect, William Wardell. By the entrance steps are statues of Australia's first cardinal, Moran, and Archbishop Kelly who laid the stone for the final stage in 1913. They were sculpted by Bertram MacKennal,

also responsible for the Martin Place Cenotaph (see p86) and the Shakespeare group outside the State Library (see p114). The crypt houses a historical exhibition of the early Sydney church. The terrazzo mosaic floor here took 15 years to complete.

⓫ Great Synagogue

187 Elizabeth St, entrance on 166 Castlereagh St. **Map** 1 B5. **Tel** 9267 2477. ▦ 333, 380, 394. **Open** for services and tours. **Closed** public & Jewish hols. ⚑ advance notice. 🎟 🖳 greatsynagogue.org.au

The longest established Jewish Orthodox congregation in Australia assembles in this synagogue, consecrated in 1878. Although Jews had arrived with the First Fleet, worship did not begin until the 1820s. With its carved entrance columns and magnificent stained-glass windows, the synagogue is perhaps the finest work of Thomas Rowe, the architect of Sydney Hospital (see p115). The panelled ceiling is decorated with hundreds of tiny gold leaf stars.

Candelabra from the Great Synagogue

❿ Hyde Park

Map 1 B5. ▦ Elizabeth St routes.

Fenced and named after its London equivalent by Governor Macquarie in 1810, Hyde Park marked the outskirts of the township. It was a popular exercise field for garrison troops and later incorporated a racecourse and a cricket pitch.

Tomb of the Unknown Soldier in the Art Deco Anzac Memorial

Though much smaller today than the original park, it still provides a peaceful haven in the middle of the bustling city centre.

Anzac Memorial
The 30-m- (98-ft-) high Art Deco memorial, reflected in the poplar-lined Pool of Remembrance, commemorates those Australians who were killed at war in the service of their country. Opened in 1934, the Anzac Memorial now includes a photographic and military artifact exhibition downstairs.

Sandringham Garden
In spring, the pergola in this sunken garden is a cascade of mauve-flowering wisteria. The garden, a memorial to the English kings George V and George VI, was opened by Queen Elizabeth II in 1954.

Diana, goddess of purity and the chase, Archibald Fountain

Archibald Fountain
This bronze and granite fountain commemorates the French and Australian World War I alliance. It was completed by François Sicard in 1932 and donated by J F Archibald, one of the founders of the *Bulletin*, a popular literary magazine which encouraged the work of Henry Lawson and "Banjo" Paterson, among many others. It was Archibald's bequest that established the Archibald Prize for portraiture (see p53).

The Grand Organ in Sydney Town Hall's Centennial Hall

⑫ Sydney Town Hall

483 George St. **Map** 4 E2. **Tel** 9265 9333. George St routes. **Open** 8:30am–6pm Mon–Fri. **Closed** public hols. **W** sydneytownhall.com.au

The steps of this sandstone building, central to George Street's Victorian architecture, have been a favourite Sydney meeting place since it opened in 1869. Walled burial grounds had originally covered the site.

It is a fine example of high Victorian architecture. The original architect, J H Wilson, died during its construction, as did several of the architects who followed. The vestibule – an elegant salon with intricate plasterwork, lavish stained glass and a crystal chandelier – is the work of Albert Bond. The Bradbridge brothers completed the clock tower in 1884. From 1888–9, other architects were used for the Centennial Hall, with its coffered zinc ceiling and the imposing 19th-century Grand Organ with over 8,500 pipes.

On the façade, you will see numerous carved lion heads. Just to the north of the main entrance, facing George Street, a lion has been carved with one eye shut. This oddity appeared because of the head stone-mason's habit of checking the line of the stonework by closing one eye. The sly joke was not found until work was finished.

Some people have concluded that Sydney Town Hall became the city's most elaborate building by accident, as each architect strove to outdo similar buildings in Manchester and Liverpool. Today, it makes a magnificent event venue.

⑬ St Andrew's Cathedral

Sydney Square, Cnr George & Bathurst Sts. **Map** 4 E3. **Tel** 9265 1661. George St routes. **Open** contact the cathedral for opening hours and tour times. **W** sydneycathedral.com

While the foundation stone for the country's oldest cathedral was laid in 1819, almost 50 years elapsed before the building was consecrated in 1868. The Gothic Revival design is by Edmund Blacket, whose ashes are interred here. Inspired by York Minster in England, the twin towers were completed in 1874. In 1949, the main entrance was moved to the eastern end near George Street.

The Great Bible, St Andrew's Cathedral

Inside are memorials to Sydney pioneers, including Thomas Mort (see p74), as well as a collection of religious memorabilia.

The southern wall incorporates stones from London's St Paul's Cathedral, Westminster Abbey and the House of Lords.

Obelisk

This monument was dubbed "Thornton's Scent Bottle" after the mayor of Sydney who had it erected in 1857. The mock-Egyptian edifice is in fact a ventilator for a sewer.

Emden Gun

Standing at the corner of College and Liverpool Streets, this monument commemorates a World War I naval action. HMAS *Sydney* destroyed the German raider *Emden* off the Cocos Islands on 9 November 1914, and 180 crew members were taken prisoner.

City Circle Railway

The park we see today bears very little resemblance to the Hyde Park of old. In fact, the dictates of city railway tunnels have largely created its present landscape. Tunnels were excavated through an open cut that ran through the park, and after the rail system was opened in 1926 the entire area had to be remodelled and replanted.

Busby's Bore Fountain

This is a reminder of Busby's Bore, the city's first piped water supply opened in 1837. John Busby, a civil engineer, conceived and supervised the construction of the 4.4-km (2¾-mile) tunnel. It carried water from bores on Lachlan Swamp, now within Centennial Park (see p129), to horse-drawn water carriers on the corner of Elizabeth Street and Park Street.

Game in progress on the giant chessboard, near Busby's Bore Fountain

⑭ Australian Museum

The Australian Museum, the nation's leading natural science museum, founded in 1827, was the first museum established and remains the premier showcase of Australian natural history. The main building, an impressive sandstone structure with a marble staircase, faces Hyde Park. Architect Mortimer Lewis was forced to resign his position when building costs began to far exceed the budget. Construction was completed in the 1860s by James Barnet. The collection provides a journey across Australia and the near Pacific, covering biology and both natural and cultural history. Museum visitors can take part in informative behind-the-scenes tours, which are held every Saturday.

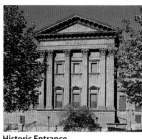

Historic Entrance
The façade features massive Corinthian square pillars or piers.

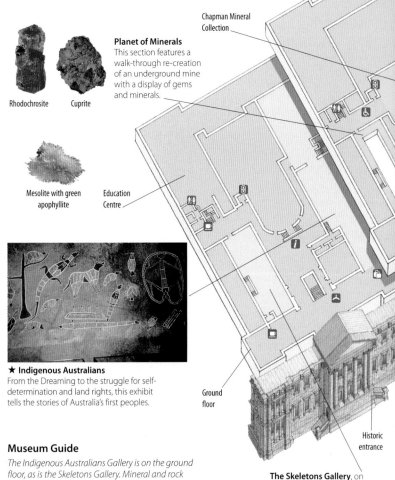

Rhodochrosite   Cuprite

Mesolite with green apophyllite

Planet of Minerals
This section features a walk-through re-creation of an underground mine with a display of gems and minerals.

Chapman Mineral Collection

Education Centre

★ **Indigenous Australians**
From the Dreaming to the struggle for self-determination and land rights, this exhibit tells the stories of Australia's first peoples.

Ground floor

Historic entrance

Museum Guide

The Indigenous Australians Gallery is on the ground floor, as is the Skeletons Gallery. Mineral and rock exhibits are in two galleries on level 1. Birds and Insects are found on level 2, along with Kidspace, Surviving Australia and Dinosaurs.

The Skeletons Gallery, on the ground floor, provides a different perspective on natural history.

★ Search & Discover
Sydneysiders bring bugs, rocks and bones to this hands-on area for identification. The public can also access an online research facility.

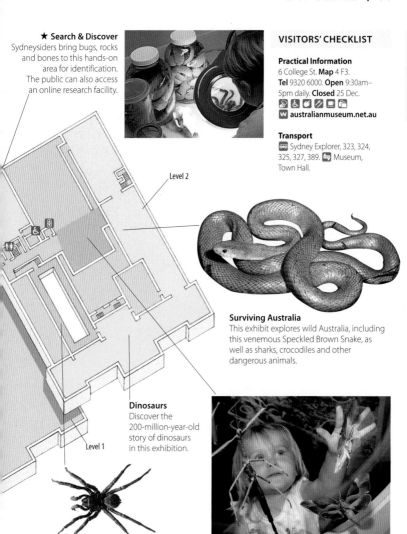

Level 2

Level 1

VISITORS' CHECKLIST

Practical Information
6 College St. **Map** 4 F3.
Tel 9320 6000. **Open** 9:30am–5pm daily. **Closed** 25 Dec.
🖼️🚻🎫🎫🖥️📷
Ⓦ **australianmuseum.net.au**

Transport
🚌 Sydney Explorer, 323, 324, 325, 327, 389. 🚌 Museum, Town Hall.

Surviving Australia
This exhibit explores wild Australia, including this venemous Speckled Brown Snake, as well as sharks, crocodiles and other dangerous animals.

Dinosaurs
Discover the 200-million-year-old story of dinosaurs in this exhibition.

Birds and Insects
Australia's most poisonous spider, the male of the funnel-web species, dwells exclusively in the Greater Sydney region.

★ Kidspace
This mini museum is designed especially for children aged five and under to investigate the natural world.

Key to Floorplan
- 🔲 Dinosaurs
- 🔲 Kidspace
- 🔲 Surviving Australia
- 🔲 Indigenous Australians
- 🔲 Temporary exhibition space
- 🔲 Non-exhibition space
- 🔲 Plants and Minerals
- 🔲 Birds and Insects
- 🔲 Search & Discover
- 🔲 Skeletons Gallery

"Welcome Stranger" Gold Nugget Cast

In 1869, the largest gold nugget ever found in Australia was discovered in Victoria. It weighed 71.06 kg (156 lb). The museum holds a cast of the original in a display examining the impact of the gold rush, when the Australian population doubled in ten years.

← 67.5 cm (26¹/₂ in) wide →

View across Darling Harbour towards the city

Sights at a Glance

Historic Districts and Buildings
④ Pyrmont Bridge
⑤ King Street Wharf
⑧ Chinatown
⑫ Surry Hills

Museums and Galleries
① *Australian National Maritime Museum pp96–7*
⑪ *Powerhouse Museum pp102–3*

Parks and Gardens
⑦ Chinese Garden of Friendship

Entertainment
② *Sea Life Sydney Aquarium p98*
③ *Wild Life Sydney p99*
⑥ Convention and Exhibition Centre

Theatres
⑨ Capitol Theatre

Markets
⑩ Paddy's Markets

0 metres 250
0 yards 250

DARLING HARBOUR AND SURRY HILLS

Darling Harbour is named after the seventh governor of New South Wales, Ralph Darling, and was originally called Cockle Bay because of the molluscs early European settlers collected here. It was an unsavoury place in the late 19th century, known for its thieves' dens and bawdy houses. The docks were an embarkation point for wool and other exports. As Sydney Harbour industry declined, Darling Harbour became rundown, only to be revived as a focal point of the 1988 Bicentenary. Today, Darling Harbour is a popular and lively area of Sydney, with a 2015 redevelopment adding more residential and commercial facilities.

Until the 1940s, Surry Hills was a depressed, inner city slum area, vividly described in Ruth Park's celebrated novel *The Harp in the South*. In the postwar years, it became home to new migrants and the garment and fashion trade. More recently, young professionals have moved in, lured by pretty Victorian terraces and proximity to the city.

☐ Restaurants pp189–191

1 Bar Zini
2 BBQ King
3 Berta
4 Bodega
5 Café del Mer
6 Café Morso
7 Caysorn Thai
8 Chat Thai
9 Devon
10 Din Fai Fung
11 El Loco at Slip Inn
12 Encasa
13 Golden Century
14 Home Café & Thai Restaurant
15 King Street Brewhouse
16 Kobe Jones
17 Longrain
18 Mahjong Room
19 The Malaya
20 Mamak
21 Marigold
22 Marque
23 Mohr Fish
24 Momofuku Seiobo
25 MoVida
26 Nick's Bar & Grill
27 Pasteur
28 Reuben Hills
29 Sepia
30 Steerson's Steakhouse
31 Taste Baguette on Sussex Lane
32 Zaafran

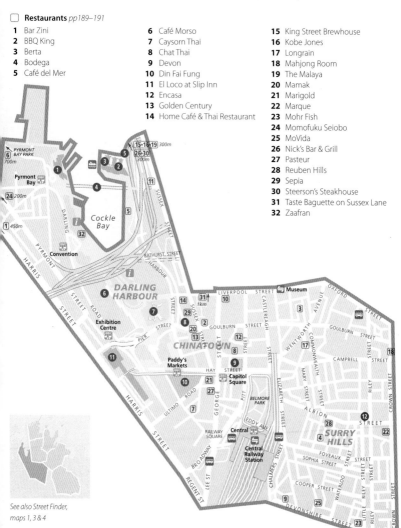

See also Street Finder, maps 1, 3 & 4

Street-by-Street: Darling Harbour

Darling Harbour was New South Wales' bicentennial gift to itself. This imaginative urban redevelopment, in the heart of Sydney, covers a 54-ha (133-acre) site that was once a busy industrial centre and international shipping terminal catering for the local wool, grain, timber and coal trades. In 1984 the Darling Harbour Authority was formed to examine the area's commercial options. The resulting complex opened in 1988, complete with the Australian National Maritime Museum and Sydney Aquarium, two of the city's tourist highlights. Free outdoor entertainment, for children in particular, is a regular feature, and there are many shops, cafés and restaurants, as well as several major hotels overlooking the bay.

Harbourside Complex offers restaurants and cafés with superb views over the water to the city skyline. There is also a wide range of speciality shops, selling unusual gifts and other items.

ICC Sydney, set in the redeveloped Convention and Exhibition Centre, will open in December 2016.

The Tidal Cascades sunken fountain was designed by Robert Woodward, also responsible for the El Alamein Fountain *(see p122)*. The double spiral of water and paths replicates the circular shape of the Convention Centre.

❻ IMAX Darling Harbour features the world's largest screen and shows a range of new-release movies and documentaries.

Chinese Garden of Friendship

The Chinese Garden of Friendship is a haven of peace and tranquillity in the heart of Sydney. Its landscaping, with winding pathways, waterfalls, lakes and pavilions, offers an insight into the rich culture of China.

Key

— Suggested route

❹ Pyrmont Bridge
The swingspan bridge opens for vessels up to 14 m (46 ft) tall.

Locator Map
See Street Finder, maps 3 & 4

A historic fleet of 14 vessels is docked at the museum's wharves, making it one of the world's largest collections held at a museum.

Star City Casino

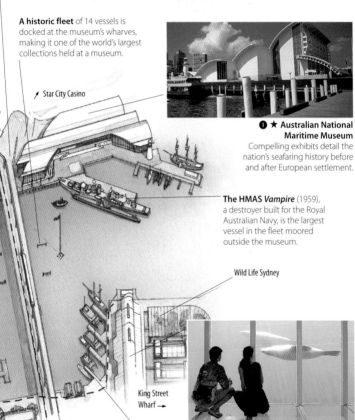

❶ ★ Australian National Maritime Museum
Compelling exhibits detail the nation's seafaring history before and after European settlement.

The HMAS *Vampire* (1959), a destroyer built for the Royal Australian Navy, is the largest vessel in the fleet moored outside the museum.

Wild Life Sydney

King Street Wharf →

Wharf for harbour cruise departures

❷ ★ Sea Life Sydney Aquarium
The aquatic life of Sydney Harbour, the open ocean and the Great Barrier Reef is displayed in massive tanks, which can be seen from underwater walkways.

Cockle Bay Wharf is vibrant and colourful, and an exciting food and entertainment precinct.

0 metres	100
0 yards	100

❶ Australian National Maritime Museum

Bounded as it is by the sea, Australia's history is inextricably linked to maritime traditions. The museum displays material in a broad range of permanent and temporary thematic exhibits, many with interactive elements. As well as artifacts relating to the enduring Aboriginal maritime cultures, the exhibits survey the history of European exploratory voyages in the Pacific, the arrival of convict ships, successive waves of migration, water sports and recreation, and naval life. Historic vessels on show at the wharf include a flimsy Vietnamese refugee boat, sailing, fishing and pearling boats, a navy patrol boat and a World War II commando raider.

Museum Façade
The billowing steel roof design by Philip Cox suggests both the surging sea and the sails of a ship.

Passengers
The model of the *Orcades* reflects the grace of 1950s liners. This display also charts harrowing sea voyages made by migrants and refugees.

Eora Indigenous Gallery – First People traces the seafaring traditions of Aboriginal peoples and Torres Strait Islanders.

The Tasman Light was used in a Tasmanian lighthouse.

★ Navigators
This 1754 engraving of an East Indian sea creature is a European vision of the uncharted, exotic "great south".

The *Sirius* anchor is from a 1790 wreck off Norfolk Island.

Main entrance (sea level)

Key to Floorplan

- ⬜ Navigators and Eora Indigenous Gallery – First People
- ⬜ Passengers
- ⬜ Commerce
- ⬜ Watermarks
- ⬜ Navy
- ⬜ Linked by the Sea: USA Gallery
- ⬜ Temporary exhibitions
- ⬜ Non-exhibition space

The Navy exhibit examines naval life in war and peace, as well as the history of colonial navies.

Linked by the Sea honours enduring links between the US and Australia. American traders stopped off in Australia on their way to China.

Commerce

This 1903 Painters' and Dockers' Union banner was carried by waterfront workers in marches. It shows the *Niagara* entering the dry dock at Cockatoo Island *(see p108)*.

VISITORS' CHECKLIST

Practical Information

2 Murray St, Darling Harbour. **Map** 3 C2. **Tel** 9298 3777. **Open** 9:30am–5pm daily (Jan: 6pm). **Closed** 25 Dec. (special exhibitions, submarine, *Endeavour* & destroyer). anmm.gov.au

Transport

Sydney Explorer, 443, 888. Town Hall. Pyrmont Bay.

Level 1

★ Watermarks

This 1960s poster for Bondi beach is part of the museum's "Watermarks – Adventure, Sport and Play" exhibition. The displays, including fully rigged boats and profiles of world champion scullers and swimmers, celebrate Australia's love affair with the water.

Gallery One

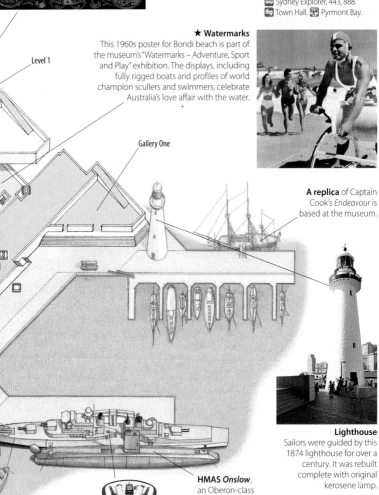

A replica of Captain Cook's *Endeavour* is based at the museum.

Lighthouse

Sailors were guided by this 1874 lighthouse for over a century. It was rebuilt complete with original kerosene lamp.

HMAS *Onslow*, an Oberon-class submarine.

★ HMAS *Vampire*

The museum's largest vessel is the 1959 Royal Australian Navy destroyer, whose insignia is shown. Tours of "The Bat" are accompanied by simulated battle action sounds.

Museum Guide

The Watermarks, Navy and Linked by the Sea: USA Gallery exhibits are located on the main entrance level (sea level). The Eora Indigenous Gallery – First People, Navigators, Passengers and Commerce sections are found on the first level.

❷ Sea Life Sydney Aquarium

Sydney Aquarium contains the largest, most comprehensive collection of Australian aquatic wildlife, with over 12,000 animals from 650 species. Both freshwater and marine exhibits simulate the animals' natural environments. For many visitors, the highlight is a walk "on the ocean floor" through the floating oceanarium with 165 m (480 ft) of acrylic underwater tunnels. These allow close observation of sharks, stingrays and schools of fish. None of the displays is harmful to the creatures, and many of the tanks display practical information about environmental hazards.

VISITORS' CHECKLIST

Practical Information
Aquarium Wharf, Darling Harbour.
Map 4 D2. **Tel** 1800 614 069.
Open 9am–7pm daily (last adm 6pm). 🐾 ♿ 🖥 🖵 📷
W sydneyaquarium.com.au
Transport
🚌 Sydney Explorer, George St. 🚌 Darling Harbour. 🚆 Town Hall. 🚇 Paddy's Markets.

Exploring the Tropical Touch Pool

Exploring Sydney Aquarium
Built on a pier in Darling Harbour, Sydney Aquarium comprises over 4,000 sq m (43,000 sq ft) of exhibition space and is one of the largest aquariums in the world. Exhibits are organised by theme and take the visitor on a journey through the different marine habitats of the Australian continent. On entering, visitors are led through the Northern Rivers and Southern Rivers sections, featuring animals such as platypuses and freshwater fish, before reaching the Southern Oceans and Northern Oceans areas where the oceanariums and touch pool can be found.

It is worth checking the website to coincide a visit with one of the feeding times. There are also "tank talks" when a trained diver can be asked questions while they are feeding sharks in the Great Barrier Reef Oceanarium. Also, for an added cost, visitors can ride out on a glass-bottom boat to watch and feed the sharks first hand or take a 20-minute snorkel in a transparent enclosure.

Attractions
Sydney Aquarium offers a great variety of exhibits and animal encounters.

Platypuses
Endemic to the rivers, streams, billabongs and lakes of the east coast and Tasmania, the platypus is an iconic symbol of Australia. When discovered by Europeans, the animal's strange collection of physical attributes, including a duck-like bill and otter's tail, was once thought to be some kind of elaborate hoax.

Claws
This exhibit features the world's largest crab species – the Japanese Spider Crab. It can grow to a claw-to-claw span of almost 4 m (13 ft).

Mermaid Lagoon
An exciting addition to the aquarium in 2008 were two dugongs (sea cows) – only six are currently held in captivity. These docile, herbivorous mammals can reach up to 3 m (9.8 ft) in length and live for more than 70 years. Named "Pig" and "Wuru" (an Aboriginal word meaning "young child"), the dugongs were originally rescued as orphaned calves.

Touch Pool
There is a touch pool in the aquarium, giving the visitor the rare chance to touch, with care, marine life found along the coastline. It includes sea urchins, tubeworms, crabs and sea stars.

Shark Walk and Shark Valley
Through an underwater tunnel, visitors can encounter huge stingrays, shoals of fish as well as the largest sharks on display in the aquarium – the critically endangered grey nurse shark.

Great Barrier Reef Oceanarium
The world's largest coral reef extends along 2,300 km (1,430 miles) of Australia's coast. Vibrant tangs, angelfish and spiny lionfish are on display as well as tropical sharks and rays. At the end of the oceanarium, the floor-to-ceiling Reef Theatre glass panel offers an unparalleled spectacle of the colourful, exotic creatures.

Sharks and hundreds of other fish on view from the Reef Theatre

❸ Wild Life Sydney

Wild Life Sydney contains over 100 Australian land-dwelling species, including insects, birds, reptiles and mammals. Together with the nearby aquarium, the complex comprises the world's largest collection of native Australian animal species to be housed in one location. In the heart of Darling Harbour, the undulating see-through mesh roof is a sight to behold in itself. Although compact in size, the zoo contains nine different temperature- and humidity-controlled habitats, and the experience is enhanced by soundscapes, graphics and interactive models.

Visitors can get close to kangaroos at Wild Life Sydney

Exploring Wild Life Sydney

There are joint tickets available for Wild Life Sydney and Sydney Aquarium and both sites can be visited in one day; another pass also includes Sydney Tower Eye.

Exhibits are laid out over three floors with one kilometre (0.6 miles) of enclosed walkways. The habitats are climate controlled and visitors largely view the animals through vast viewing panels.

Throughout the day, feeds and talks are given by the keepers, and visitors get the chance to get closer to and sometimes touch the animals, under supervision. Another good option is to book a group or "VIP" guided tour.

Attractions

Wild Life Sydney groups the animals by their natural habitats, housing intriguing, often unique, species that are native to the Australian continent.

Butterfly Tropics

The butterfly tropics zone contains such spectacular species as the Zebra, Blue Triangle and Ulysses butterflies, the latter with its huge 14-cm (5.5-in) wingspan. During guided tours visitors get to gently hold the butterflies.

Frilled-Neck Lizard

Native to the dry landscape of the Kimberley in north Western Australia, this bizarre-looking lizard flares the folds of skin around its neck when feeling threatened or scared. It will also hiss and lunge to ward off predators. It used to feature on the Australian 2c coin.

Nocturnal Animals

The Nightfall exhibit features animals that venture out in the dark, such as possums, bilbies, bats, quolls, geckos, betongs and gliders, including the "false vampire bat" of Australia's north.

Invertebrates

This habitat contains all kinds of creepy crawlies such as the carnivorous praying mantis, the giant rhinoceros cockroach and the world's most dangerous spider – the Sydney funnel-web.

Koalas

A raised walkway under the open-air mesh roof winds through the koala and wallaby habitats and allows visitors to get closer to these cuddly, iconic animals and even have a photo taken with them. The koala's diet of eucalyptus leaves is so low in nutrients it has to conserve energy by moving slowly and sleeping a lot.

Yellow-Footed Rock Wallaby

Bounding about on rocks in the Wallaby Cliff habitat, this stripy-tailed wallaby is perhaps the most attractive of the kangaroo species, so much so it used to be hunted for its beautiful fur. Its huge feet have strong muscles and a brush of stiff hairs to help it get around over rocky terrain.

Koala

Southern Cassowary

This distinctive blue-necked bird, a close relation of the emu, is considered the most dangerous bird in the world. It has powerful talons and one spear-like inner claw which can reach up to 12 cm (4.7 in) in length. This flightless bird is capable of killing dogs and even humans if provoked. Around half of the bird species in Australia are found nowhere else in the world.

❹ Pyrmont Bridge

Darling Harbour. **Map** 1 A5. 🚌 George St. 🚈 Paddy's Markets. ♿ 📷

Pyrmont Bridge opened in 1902. The world's oldest electrically operated swingspan bridge, it was fully functional before Sydney's streets were lit by electricity. It was the second Pyrmont Bridge and provided access to what, at the time, was a busy international shipping terminal with warehouses and wool stores. Electricity for the new bridge came from the Ultimo power station, the building that now houses the city's Powerhouse Museum (see pp102–3).

Percy Allan, the bridge's designer, achieved overseas recognition for his two central steel swingspans and went on to design 583 more bridges in the course of his career. J J Bradfield, the designer of the Sydney Harbour Bridge (see pp72–3), was also involved in construction of this bridge.

The 369-m- (1,200-ft-) long Pyrmont Bridge has 14 spans, with only the two central swingspans being made of steel. The remaining spans are made of ironbark, an Australian hardwood timber. The bridge was permanently closed to road traffic in 1981, but reopened to pedestrians when the Darling Harbour complex opened in 1988. It is also popular with cyclists riding to work.

The view from Pyrmont Bridge looking up towards the city centre

Cockle Bay Wharf and the eight-storey-high IMAX Theatre at Darling Harbour

The central steel swingspans are still driven by their original motor. The bridge is opened regularly to allow boats access to and from Cockle Bay.

❺ King Street Wharf

Lime St, between King St and Erskine St. **Map** 4 D1. 🚌 George St. 🚈 Paddy's Markets. 🍴 🚭 📷 🍷 ♿ 🌐 **kingstreetwharf.com.au**

Journalists from nearby newspaper offices and city workers flock to this harbourside venue, which combines a working wharf with an aggressively modern glass and steel shrine to café society. Passengers arrive and depart in style on ferries, water taxis and rivercats.

The complex is flush with bars that vie for the best views, and restaurants including Thai, Japanese, Italian and Modern Australian. Midway along the wharf is a boutique brewery that caters for those who revere the best kind of cleansing ales. There are residents here as well in low-rise apartments set back from the water on the city side.

❻ IMAX Darling Harbour

Wheat Rd, Darling Harbour. **Map** 4 D3. 🚌 George St. 🚈 Paddy's Markets. **Tel** 9281 3300. **Open** daily. 📷 ♿ 🌐 **imax.com.au**

The IMAX Theatre is hard to miss, with its large yellow-and-black chequered exterior. Once you are inside, the screen is hard to miss, too – it is equal to eight storeys in height. IMAX screens a diverse range of films in both 2-D and 3-D, including the latest releases. It also shows specially made documentaries on topics such as nature and space that are well suited to the particularly large screens.

❼ Chinese Garden of Friendship

Darling Harbour. **Map** 4 D3. **Tel** 9240 8500. 🚌 George St. 🚈 Paddy's Markets. **Open** 9:30am–5pm daily. **Closed** Good Fri, 25 Dec. 📷 📺 ♿ limited. 🌐 **chinese gardens.com.au**

The Chinese Garden of Friendship was built in 1988. It is a tranquil refuge from the city streets. The garden's design was a gift to Sydney from its Chinese sister city of Guangdong. The Dragon Wall is in the lower section beside the lake. It has glazed carvings of two dragons, one representing Guangdong province and the other the state of New South Wales. In the centre of the wall, a carved pearl, symbolizing prosperity, is lifted by the waves. The lake is covered with lotus and water lilies for much of the year and a rock monster guards against evil. On the other side of the lake is the Twin Pavilion. Waratahs (New South Wales's floral symbol) and flowering apricots are carved into its woodwork, and also grow at its base.

A tea house, found at the top of the stairs in the Tea House Courtyard, serves traditional Chinese tea and cakes.

❽ Chinatown

Dixon St Plaza, Sydney. **Map** 4 D4.
🚊 George St. 🚉 Paddy's Markets.

Originally concentrated around Dixon and Hay Streets, Chinatown is expanding to fill Sydney's Haymarket area, stretching west to Harris Street, south to Broadway and east to Castlereagh Street. It is close to the Sydney Entertainment Centre, where some of the world's best-known rock and pop stars perform and indoor sporting events are held.

For years, Chinatown was a run-down district at the edge of the city's produce markets. Today Dixon Street, its main thoroughfare, has been spruced up, with street lanterns and archways, and a new wave of Asian migrants fills the now upmarket restaurants.

Towering over the corner of George Street and Hay Street is a sculpture by artist Lin Li, *Golden Water Mouth* (1999). Made from the trunk of a eucalyptus tree covered in gold-leaf, it is said to bring good fortune to the area.

Chinatown is a distinctive area with greengrocers, traditional herbalists and butchers' shops with wind-dried ducks hanging in their windows. Jewellers, clothing shops and confectioners fill the arcades.

❾ Capitol Theatre

13 Campbell St, Haymarket. **Map** 4 E4.
Tel 9320 5000. 🚊 George St routes.
🚉 Capitol. **Open** performances only.
Box office: **Open** 9am–5pm Mon–Fri &
2 hrs before shows. ♿
🌐 **capitoltheatre.com.au**

In the mid-1800s a cattle and corn market was situated here. It became Paddy's Market Bazaar with sideshows and an outdoor theatre, in turn replaced by a circus with a floodable ring. The present building was erected in the 1920s as a luxurious picture palace. In the mid-1990s, the cinema was restored, in keeping with the original theme of a Florentine Garden.

The Capitol reopened as a lyric theatre with productions staged beneath a Mediterranean-blue ceiling studded with stars reflecting the southern sky.

❿ Paddy's Markets

Cnr Thomas & Hay sts, Haymarket. **Map**
4 D4. **Tel** 1300 361 589. 🚊 George St.
🚉 Paddy's Markets. **Open** 10am–6pm
Wed–Sat & public holiday Mons.
Closed 25 Apr, 25 Dec. ♿
See also Shops and Markets: p203.
🌐 **paddysmarkets.com.au**

Haymarket, in Chinatown, is home to Paddy's Markets, Sydney's oldest market. It has been in this area, on a number of sites, since 1869 (with only one five-year absence). The name's origin is uncertain, but is believed to have come from either the Chinese, who originally supplied much of its produce, or the Irish, their main customers.

Once the shopping centre for the inner-city poor, Paddy's Markets is now an integral part of an ambitious development including residential apartments and the Market City Shopping Centre. However, the familiar clamour and chaotic bargain-hunting atmosphere of the original marketplace remain. Every weekend the market has up to 800 stalls selling everything from fresh produce to chickens, puppies, electrical products and leather goods.

⓫ Powerhouse Museum

See pp102–3.

⓬ Surry Hills

Map 5 A2–5. **Tel** 9699 3444. 🚌 301,
302, 303, 304, 339. *See Shops and
Markets p203.*

A curious mixture of fashion and seediness can be found on the streets of Surry Hills. Newly renovated houses stand alongside dilapidated dwellings, while streets of elegant Victorian terraces abut modern high-rise flats and factory warehouses.

For the visitor, the suburb offers a wide range of ethnic cuisines, often at bargain prices. It is famed for its Lebanese and Turkish restaurants, but you will also find Indian, Chinese, Thai, French and numerous Italian eateries scattered around the suburb, along with smart and casual cafés and stylish pubs.

Once the centre of Sydney's garment and fashion trade, Surry Hills is still home to a number of factory outlets where clothing, haberdashery and lingerie can be bought at below retail prices. A wide range of alternative fashion and retro clothing shops can also be found at the Oxford Street end of Crown Street.

Pavilion in the grounds of the Chinese Garden of Friendship

⓫ Powerhouse Museum

This former power station, completed in 1902 to provide power for Sydney's tramway system, was redesigned to cater for the needs of an interactive, hands-on museum. The revamped Powerhouse opened in 1988. The early collection was housed in the Garden Palace where the 1879 international exhibition of invention and industry from around the world was held. Few exhibits survived the devastating 1882 fire, and today's huge and ever-expanding collection was gathered after this disaster. The building's monumental scale provides an ideal context for the epic sweep of ideas encompassed within: everything from the realm of space and technology to the decorative and domestic arts. The museum emphasizes Australian innovations and achievements, celebrating both the extraordinary and the everyday.

What's It Like to Live in Space?
Find out how astronauts live and work in space, and experience weightlessness in the zero gravity space lab.

Transport
Discover the air, land and sea vehicles that helped shape our way of life.

Level 2

★ **Experimentations**
Explore the principles of temperature, pressure, electricity, magnetism, light, gravity, motion and chemistry in this exciting interactive exhibit.

Level 1

Nuclear Matters
This is a great space in which to explore the complex worlds of nuclear science, medicine and power.

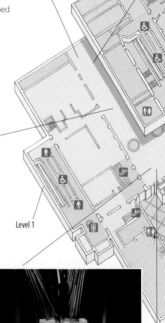

Ecologic shows the science behind global warming and what can be done to prevent it

Museum Guide

The museum is housed in two buildings: the former Powerhouse and the Neville Wran building. There are over 20 exhibitions on four levels, descending from Level 4. The shop, entrance and temporary exhibits are on Level 3. Level 2 has thematic exhibits. Level 1 has experiments and displays on space, transport and computers.

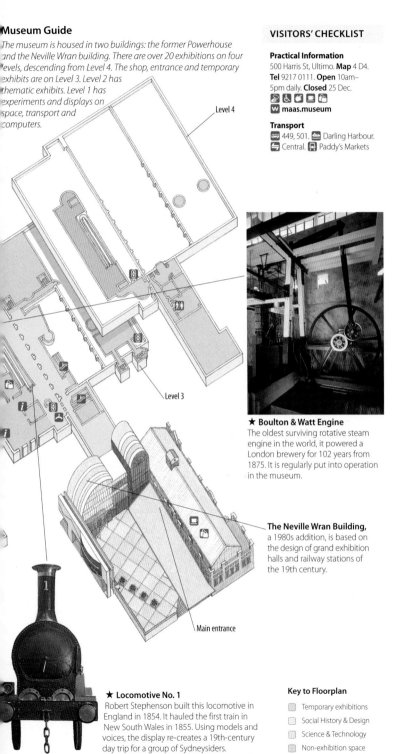

Level 4

Level 3

Main entrance

VISITORS' CHECKLIST

Practical Information
500 Harris St, Ultimo. **Map** 4 D4.
Tel 9217 0111. **Open** 10am–
5pm daily. **Closed** 25 Dec.
♿ 🅿 🚻 📷 ♿
W maas.museum

Transport
🚌 449, 501. 🚢 Darling Harbour.
🚆 Central. 🚆 Paddy's Markets

★ Boulton & Watt Engine
The oldest surviving rotative steam engine in the world, it powered a London brewery for 102 years from 1875. It is regularly put into operation in the museum.

The Neville Wran Building,
a 1980s addition, is based on the design of grand exhibition halls and railway stations of the 19th century.

★ Locomotive No. 1
Robert Stephenson built this locomotive in England in 1854. It hauled the first train in New South Wales in 1855. Using models and voices, the display re-creates a 19th-century day trip for a group of Sydneysiders.

Key to Floorplan

- 🟦 Temporary exhibitions
- ⬜ Social History & Design
- 🟦 Science & Technology
- 🟦 Non-exhibition space

BOTANIC GARDEN AND THE DOMAIN

This tranquil part of Sydney can seem a world away from the bustle of the city centre. It is rich in the remnants of Sydney's convict and colonial past: the site of the first farm, and the boulevard-like Macquarie Street where the barracks, hospital, church and mint – bastions of civic power – are among the oldest surviving public buildings in Australia. This street continues to assert its dominance today as the home of the state government of New South Wales. The Domain, an open,

grassy space, was originally set aside by the colony's first governor for his private use. Today it is a democratic place with joggers and touch footballers sidestepping picnickers. In January, during the Festival of Sydney, it hosts outdoor concerts with thousands of people enjoying fine music. The Botanic Garden, which with The Domain was the site of Australia's first park, is a haven where visitors can stroll around and enjoy the extensive collection of native and exotic flora.

Sights at a Glance

Historic Streets and Buildings

2 Conservatorium of Music
3 Government House
6 Woolloomooloo Finger Wharf
9 State Library of NSW
10 Parliament House
11 Sydney Hospital
12 The Mint
13 Hyde Park Barracks Museum

Museums and Galleries

7 Art Gallery of New South Wales pp110–13

Churches

14 St James' Church

Islands

5 Fort Denison

Monuments

4 Mrs Macquaries Chair

Parks and Gardens

1 Royal Botanic Garden pp106–7
8 The Domain

☐ Restaurants pp191–2

1 Aki's
2 Botanic Garden Café
3 Botanic Garden Restaurant
4 Café at the Gallery
5 Charlie's
6 China Doll
7 Chiswick at the Gallery
8 The Hyde Park Barracks Café
9 Kingsleys Sydney
10 Otto Ristorante

11 The Pavilion Kiosk
12 The Pavilion Restaurant
13 Poolside Café
14 Manta
15 Sienna Marina

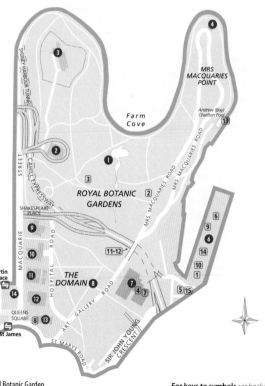

0 metres 250
0 yards 250

See also Street Finder,
maps 1 & 2

◀ The lush surroundings of the Royal Botanic Garden

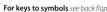

For keys to symbols see back flap

❶ Royal Botanic Garden

The Royal Botanic Garden, an oasis of 30 ha (74 acres) in the heart of the city, occupies a superb position, wrapped around Farm Cove at the harbour's edge. Established in 1816 as a series of pathways through shrubbery, it is the oldest scientific institution in the country and houses an outstanding collection of plants from Australia and overseas. A living museum, the garden is also the site of the first farm in the fledgling colony. Fountains, statues and monuments are today scattered throughout. Plant specimens collected by Joseph Banks on Captain James Cook's epic voyage along the east coast of Australia in 1770 are displayed in the National Herbarium of New South Wales, an important centre for research on Australian plants.

Locator Map
See Street Finder, maps 1 & 2

★ **Palm Grove**
Begun in 1862, this cool summer haven is one of the world's finest outdoor collections of palms. There are about 180 species. Borders planted with kaffir lilies make a colourful display in springtime.

★ **Herb Garden**
Herbs from around the world used for a wide variety of purposes – culinary, medicinal and aromatic – are on display here. A sensory fountain and a sundial modelled on the celestial sphere are also features.

KEY

① **Government House (1897)**

② **Cadi Jam Ora**, a bush tucker display, features native plants that would have grown on the site prior to colonial settlement.

③ **Wollemi Pine**

★ **Sydney Fernery**
Opened in 1993, on the site where earlier ferneries had previously stood, this feature garden is a tribute to some of the most ancient plants on earth.

Macquarie Wall
In 1810, work began on this 290-m- (950-ft-) long wall intended to separate the convict domain from the town's "respectable Class of Inhabitants". Only a small section remains standing today.

Choragic Monument (1870)
This replica of the marble monument of Lysicrates in Athens was sculpted in sandstone by Walter McGill.

★ **Australia's First Farm**
It is claimed that some Middle Garden oblong beds follow the direction of the first furrows ploughed in the colony.

National Herbarium of New South Wales
Over one million dried plant specimens document biological diversity. The charting of new plants provides essential information for conservation decision making.

0 metres   200
0 yards   200

❷ Conservatorium of Music

Macquarie St. **Map** 1 C3. **Tel** 9351 1222.
🚌 Sydney Explorer, Circular Quay
routes. **Open** 9am–5pm Mon–Fri, 9am–
6pm Sat (public areas only). **Closed**
pub hols, Easter Sat, 24 Dec–2 Jan. ♿
📷 Wed, Thu & Sat by appt (call 0404
256 256). Free concerts: 1:10pm Wed
(donation). 🌐 **music.sydney.edu.au**

When it was finished in 821,
this striking castellated Colonial
Gothic building was meant to
be stables and servants' quarters
for Government House, but
construction of the latter was
delayed for almost 25 years. That
stables should be built in so grand
a style, and at such great cost,
brought forth cries of outrage
and led to bitter arguments
between the architect, Francis
Greenway *(see p116)*, and
Governor Macquarie – and a
decree that all future building
plans be submitted to London.

Between 1908 and 1915,
"Greenway's folly" underwent a
dramatic transformation. A concert hall, roofed in grey slate,
was built on the central courtyard
and the entire building was
converted for the use of the new
Sydney Conservatorium of Music.

The Conservatorium's
facilities include a café which
holds lunchtime concerts
during the school term and an
upper level with harbour views.
"The Con" continues to be a
training ground for future
musicians as well as being a
great place to visit.

HMS *Orlando* in dry dock at Cockatoo
Island in the 1890s

❸ Government House

Macquarie St. **Map** 1 C2. **Tel** 9931 5222.
🚌 Sydney Explorer, Circular Quay
routes. House: **Open** 10:30am–3pm
Fri–Sun (guided tour only; ID required).
Closed Good Fri, 25 Dec. Garden:
Open 10am–4pm daily. ♿ 📷 every
30 mins. 🌐 **hht.net.au/museums**

What used to be the official
residence of the governor of
New South Wales overlooks
the harbour from within the
Royal Botanic Garden, but
the grandiose, somewhat
sombre, turreted Gothic
Revival edifice seems curiously
out of place in its beautiful
park setting.

It was built of local sandstone
and cedar between 1837 and
1845. A fine collection of
19th- and early 20th-century
furnishings is housed within.

The History of Cockatoo Island

Now deserted, the largest of the 12
Sydney Harbour islands was used
to store grain from the 1830s. It was
a penal establishment from the
1840s to 1908, with prisoners being
put to work constructing dock
facilities. The infamous bushranger
"Captain Thunderbolt" made his
escape from Cockatoo in 1863 by
swimming across to the mainland.
From the 1870s to the 1960s,
Cockatoo Island was a thriving
naval dockyard and shipyard,
the hub of Australian industry.

Resting on the carved stone seat of
Mrs Macquaries Chair

❹ Mrs Macquaries Chair

Mrs Macquaries Rd. **Map** 2 E2.
🚌 Sydney Explorer, 441, 442. ♿

The scenic Mrs Macquaries
Road winds alongside much
of what is now the city's
Royal Botanic Garden, from
Farm Cove to Woolloomooloo
Bay and back again. The road
was built in 1816 at the
instigation of Elizabeth
Macquarie, wife of the
Governor. In the same year,
a stone bench, inscribed with
details of the new road, was
carved into the rock at the point
where Mrs Macquarie would
stop to admire the view on her
daily constitutional.

Although today the outlook
from this famous landmark is
much changed, it is just as
arresting, taking in the broad
sweep of the harbour and foreshore with all its landmarks.

The Conservatorium of Music, at the edge of the Royal Botanic Garden

Historic Woolloomooloo Finger Wharf redevelopment, including apartments, restaurants and a hotel

❺ Fort Denison

Sydney Harbour. **Map** 2 E1. **Tel** 9361 5208. 🚢 from Circular Quay. **Closed** 25 Dec. 📷 🔲 📷 phone to book. 🆆 fortdenison.com.au

First named Rock Island, this prominent, rocky outcrop in Sydney Harbour was very quickly dubbed "Pinchgut". This was probably because of the meagre rations given to convicts who were confined there as punishment. It had a grim history of incarceration in the early years of the colony.

In 1796, con-victed murderer Francis Morgan was hanged on the island in chains. His body was left to rot on the gallows for three years as a grisly warning to the other convicts.

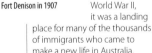

Fort Denison in 1907

Between 1855 and 1857, the Martello tower (the only one in Australia), gun battery and barracks that now occupy the island were built as part of Sydney's defences and the site was renamed after the governor of the time. The gun, still fired at 1pm each day, was an important aid for navigation, allowing mariners to set their ships' chronometers.

Today the island is a popular tourist spot, commanding spectacular views of Sydney Harbour, the Opera House and Kirribilli. To explore Fort Denison, book a boat tour from Cadman Cottage.

❻ Woolloomooloo Finger Wharf

Cowper Wharf Roadway, Woolloomooloo. **Map** 2 E4. 🚌 Sydney Explorer, 311.

This is the largest of several finger wharves that jut out into the harbour. The wharf, completed in 1914, was one of the points of embarkation for soldiers bound for both world wars. Following World War II, it was a landing place for many of the thousands of immigrants who came to make a new life in Australia.

The wharf was the subject of public controversy in the late 1980s and early 1990s, when demolition plans were thwarted by conservation groups. Since then, this National Trust-listed maritime site has been redeveloped to include a hotel, lively restaurants and bars, and apartments.

❼ Art Gallery of New South Wales

See pp110–13.

❾ The Domain

Art Gallery Rd. **Map** 1 C4. 🚌 Sydney Explorer, 111, 411. ♿

People who swarm to the January concerts and other Festival of Sydney events in The Domain *(see p51)* are part of a long-standing tradition.

This extensive public space has long been a rallying point for crowds of Sydneysiders whenever emotive issues of public importance have arisen, such as the attempt in 1916 to introduce military conscription or the dismissal of the elected federal government by the then governor-general in 1975.

From the 1890s, part of The Domain was also used as the Sydney version of "Speakers' Corner". Today, you are more likely to see joggers or office workers playing touch football in their lunch hours, or simply enjoying the shade.

A dramatic view of Sydney Opera House from Mrs Macquaries Chair

❼ Art Gallery of New South Wales

Established in 1871, the art gallery has occupied its present imposing building since 1897. Designed by the Colonial Architect WL Vernon, the gallery doubled in size following 1988 building extensions. Two equestrian bronzes – *The Offerings of Peace* and *The Offerings of War* – greet the visitor on entry. The gallery itself houses some of the finest works of art in Australia, with permanent collections of Australian, Aboriginal, European, Asian and contemporary art. The Yiribana Gallery is one of the largest in the world to exclusively exhibit Aboriginal and Torres Strait Islander art and culture. Free guided tours take place daily, covering Aboriginal art, highlights of the collection or major exhibitions.

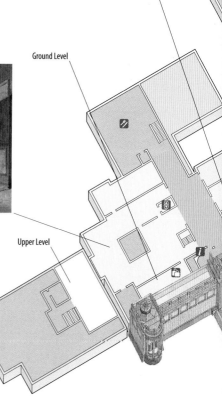

Lower Level 3

Ground Level

Upper Level

Mars and the Vestal Virgin (1638)
This oil on canvas by Parisian painter Jacques Blanchard (1600–38) depicts Mars's encounter with a Vestal Virgin, who subsequently gave birth to Romulus and Remus, founders of Rome.

Sofala (1947) Russell Drysdale's visions of Australia show "ghost" towns laid waste by devastating natural forces such as drought.

Gallery Guide

There are five levels. The Upper Level, Ground Level and Lower Level 1 host temporary exhibitions. The Ground Level also showcases European and Australian works. The Contemporary Galleries on Lower Level 2 have the most comprehensive collection of contemporary art in the country. On Lower Level 3 is the Yiribana Aboriginal Gallery.

★ Pukumani Grave Posts (1958)
Carved by Tiwi artists of Melville Island (north of Australia), these magnificent funerary posts were specially commissioned for the art gallery.

Lower Level 2

Padmapani
This extremely large, softly glowing, resplendent Nepalese work is made of copper and is remarkable for being cast in one piece.

Lower Level

Natives on the Ouse River, Van Diemen's Land (1838)
English-Australian artist John Glover was dubbed the father of Australian landscape painting for his bright depictions of the Van Diemen's Land bush (now Tasmania).

★ The Golden Fleece (1894)
Also known as Shearing at Newstead, this work by Tom Roberts marks the coming of age of Australian Impressionist art.

The sandstone entrance was added in 1909.

Key to Floorplan
- ☐ Australian Art
- ☐ European Art
- ▦ Asian Art
- ☐ Modern Gallery (20th-Century European Art)
- ▨ Contemporary Art
- ▦ Domain Theatre
- ☐ Yiribana Aboriginal Gallery
- ▨ Temporary exhibition space
- ▨ Photography Gallery

Exploring the Art Gallery's Collection

Although local works had been collected since 1875 the gallery did not seriously begin seeking Australian and non-British art until the 1920s, and not until the 1940s did it begin acquiring Aboriginal and Torres Strait Islander paintings. These contrasting collections are now its great strength. Major temporary exhibitions are also regularly staged, with the annual Archibald, Wynne and Sulman prizes being most controversial and highly entertaining.

Grace Cossington Smith's *The Curve of the Bridge* (1928–9)

Australian Art

Among the most important colonial works is John Glover's *Natives on the Ouse River, Van Diemen's Land* (1838), an image of doomed Tasmanian Aborigines.

The old wing holds paintings from the Heidelberg School of Australian Impressionism. Charles Conder's *Departure of the Orient – Circular Quay* (1888) and Tom Robert's *The Golden Fleece – Shearing at Newstead* (1894) hang alongside fine works by Frederick McCubbin and Arthur Streeton. Rupert Bunny's sensuous

Summer Time (c.1907) and *A Summer Morning* (c.1908), and George Lambert's heroic *Across the Black Soil Plains* (1899), impress with their huge size and complex compositions.

Australia was slow to take up Modernism. *Implement Blue* (1927) and *Western Australian Gum Blossom* (1928), both by Margaret Preston, are her most assertive works of the 1920s. The Gallery's paintings by Sidney Nolan exploit myths of early Australian history, and range from *Boy in Township* (1943) to *Burke* (c.1962). There are fine holdings of William Dobell and Russell Drysdale, as well as important collections of Arthur Boyd, Fred Williams, Grace Cossington Smith and Brett Whiteley (*see p132*).

European Art

The scope of the scattered European collection ranges from Medieval to modern art. British art from the late 19th to the early 20th centuries forms an outstanding component.

Among the Old Masters are some significant Italian works that reflect Caravaggio's influence. There are also several

Three Bathers, an Ernst Ludwig Kirchner painting from 1913

notable works from the Renaissance in Sienese and Florentine styles. Hogarth, Turner and Joshua Reynolds are represented, as are Neo-Classical works. *The Visit of the Queen of Sheba to King Solomon* (1884–90) by Edward Poynter has been on display since 1892. Ford Madox Brown's *Chaucer at the Court of Edward III* (1845–51) is the most commanding work in the Pre-Raphaelite collection.

The Impressionists and Post-Impressionists, represented by late 1880s Pissarro and Monet, are housed in the newest gallery wing. Bonnard, Kandinsky, Braque and many other well-known European artists are also here. *Old Woman in Ermine* (1946) by Max Beckmann and *Three Bathers* (1913) by Ernst Ludwig Kirchner are strong examples of German Expressionism. The gallery's first Picasso, *Nude in a Rocking Chair* (1956), was purchased in 1981. Among the distinguished sculptures on show is Henry Moore's *Reclining Figure: Angles* (1980), which is displayed by the side of the entrance.

Photography

Australian photography from 1975 to today, represented in all its various forms, is a major part of the collection. In recent years, however, the emphasis has been on building up a body of 19th-century Australian work in a range of early mediums. Nearly 3,000 prints constitute this collection with pieces by

Brett Whiteley's vivid *The balcony 2* from 1975

Charles Kerry, Charles Bayliss and Harold Cazneaux, the latter a major figure of early 20th-century Pictorialism. Such international photographers as Muybridge, Robert Mapplethorpe and Man Ray are also represented here.

Asian Art

This collection is one of the finest in Australia. Chinese art is represented by a chronological presentation of works from the pre-Shang dynasty (c.1600–1027 BC) to the 20th century. The Ming porcelains, earthenware funerary pieces *(mingqi)* and the sculptures deserve close attention.

The Japanese painting collection contains fine examples by major artists of the Edo period (1615–1867). The Indian and Southeast Asian holdings consist of lacquer, ceramics and sculptures, with painting displays changing regularly.

Prints and Drawings

As so many of the works in this collection are fragile, the exhibitions are changed frequently. The collection represents the European tradition from the High Renaissance to the 19th and 20th centuries, with work by Rembrandt, Constable, William Blake and Edvard Munch. A strong bias towards Sydney artists from the past 100 years has resulted in a fine gathering of work by Thea Proctor, Norman and Lionel Lindsay, and Lloyd Rees.

Egon Schiele's *Poster for the Vienna Secession* (1918)

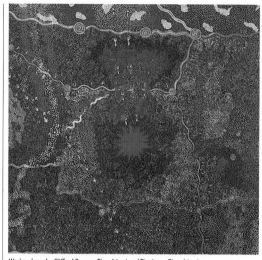

Warlugulong, by Clifford Possum Tjapaltjarri and Tim Leura Tjapaltjarri

Contemporary Art

The diversity and significance of contemporary art is reflected in the Gallery's collection of recent work by international and Australian artists, only a fraction of which can be displayed at any time. The collection highlights the artistic themes that have been central to art practice of the last three decades. Works by Australian artists, such as *Pataphysical Man* (Imants Tillers, 1984) and *Suspended Stone Circle II* (Ken Unsworth, 1988), are on display alongside pieces by notable international artists of the calibre of Cindy Sherman, Yves Klein, Philip Guston and Anselm Kiefer. The gallery also has a contemporary project space that features temporary experimental installations.

Yiribana Gallery

Devoted to the exhibition of Aboriginal and Torres Strait Islander artworks bought since the 1940s, traditional bark paintings hang alongside innovative works from both desert and urban areas, including stone and wood carvings, ceramics and weavings. The ability of contemporary artists to apply traditional ceremonial body and sand painting styles to new media forms, and the endurance of "Aboriginality", are repeatedly demonstrated. The significant early purchases are mainly natural pigment paintings on bark and card, often containing a simple, figurative motif of everyday life. Also of interest are two sandstone carvings by Queenslanders Linda Craigie and Nora Nathan, the only women artists in the collection until 1985. Topographical, geographical and cultural mapping of the land is displayed in a number of intricate landscapes. The qualities and forms of the natural world, and the actions and tracks of Ancestral Beings, are coded within the images. These paintings are maps of Ancestral journeys and events. The bark painting *Three Mimis Dancing* (1964) by Samuel Wagbara examines the habitation of the land by Spirits and the recurrence of the Creation Cycles.

Pukumani Grave Posts Melville Island (1958) is a solemn ceremonial work dealing with death, while the eminent Emily Kame Kngwarreye honours the land from which she comes. The canvases of her intricate dot paintings, created using new tools and technology, appear to move and shimmer, telling stories of the animals and food to be found there.

Mosaic replica of the Tasman Map in the State Library of NSW

❾ State Library of NSW

Macquarie St. **Map** 1 C4. **Tel** 9273 1414. ▦ Sydney Explorer, Elizabeth St routes. **Open** 9am–8pm Mon–Thu, 9am–5pm Fri, 10am–5pm Sat & Sun. **Closed** pub hols; Mitchell Library closed Sun. 🅿 🐾 🅱 🅲
Ⓦ sl.nsw.gov.au

The State Library is housed in two separate buildings connected by a passageway and a glass bridge. The older building, the Mitchell Library wing (1910), is a majestic sandstone edifice facing the Royal Botanic Garden. Huge stone columns supporting a vaulted ceiling frame the impressive vestibule. On the vestibule floor is a mosaic replica of an old map illustrating the two voyages made to Australia by Dutch navigator Abel Tasman in the 1640s. The original Tasman Map is held in the Mitchell Library as part of its large collection of historic Australian paintings, books, documents and pictorial records.

The Mitchell wing's vast reading room, with its huge skylight and oak panelling, is just beyond the main vestibule. The newest section, a modern structure facing Macquarie Street, houses the State Reference Library and a gourmet café.

Outside the library, also facing Macquarie Street, is a statue of explorer Matthew Flinders. Behind him on the windowsill is a statue of his co-voyager and faithful cat, Trim.

Malby's celestial globe, Parliament House

❿ Parliament House

Macquarie St. **Map** 1 C4. **Tel** 9230 2111. ▦ Sydney Explorer, Elizabeth St routes. 🚇 Martin Place. 🅿 book in advance 9230 3444. **Open** 9am–5pm Mon–Fri. **Closed** most public hols. 🅱
Ⓦ parliament.nsw.gov.au

The central section of this building, which houses the State Parliament, is part of the original Sydney Hospital built from 1811–16. It has been a seat of government since 1829 when the newly appointed Legislative Council first held meetings here. The building was extended twice during the 19th century and again during the 1970s and 1980s. The current building contains the chambers for both

---

Macquarie Street

Described in the 1860s as one of the gloomiest streets in Sydney, this could now claim to be the most elegant. A leisurely walk down this tree-lined street, open on the northeastern side to the harbour breezes and the greenery of The Domain, is one of the most pleasurable ways to view the architectural heritage of Sydney.

The new wing of the library was built in 1988 and connected to the old section by a glass walkway.

The Legislative Assembly, the lower house of state parliament, is furnished in the traditional green of the British House of Commons.

The Mitchell Library wing's portico (1906) has Ionic columns.

Parliament House was once the convict-built Rum Hospital's northern wing.

State Library of NSW *(1906–41)*

Parliament House *(1811–16)*

houses of state parliament, as well as parliamentary offices. Parliamentary memorabilia is on view in the Jubilee Room, as are displays showing Parliament House's development and the legislative history of New South Wales.

The corrugated iron building, with a cast-iron façade tacked on at the southern end, was a pre-fabricated kit from England. It was originally intended as a chapel for the gold fields, but was diverted from this purpose and sent to Sydney. In 1856, this dismantled kit became the chamber for the new Legislative Council. Its packing cases were used to line this chamber; the rough timber is still on view inside.

⓫ Sydney Hospital

Macquarie St. **Map** 1 C4. **Tel** 9382 7111. 🚌 Sydney Explorer, Elizabeth St routes. **Open** daily. 🕐 for tours. ♿ 📷 must be pre-booked by phone. 🌐 seslhd.health.nsw.gov.au

This imposing collection of Victorian sandstone buildings stands on the site of what was

Stained glass at Sydney Hospital

once the central section of the original convict-built Sydney Hospital – known as the Rum Hospital because the builders were paid by being allowed to import rum for resale. Both the north and south wings of the Rum Hospital survive as Parliament House and the Sydney Mint. The central wing, which was in danger of collapsing, was demolished in 1879 and the new hospital, which still functions today, was completed in 1894. The Classical Revival building boasts a Baroque staircase and elegant floral stained-glass windows in its entrance hall.

Florence Nightingale approved the design of the 1867 nurses' wing. In the inner courtyard, there is a brightly coloured Art Deco fountain (1907).

At the front of the hospital sits *Il Porcellino*, a brass boar. It is a copy of a 17th-century fountain in Florence's Mercato Nuovo. Donated in 1968 by an Italian woman whose relatives had worked at the hospital, the statue is an enduring symbol of the close friendship between Italy and Australia.

Like his Florentine counterpart, *Il Porcellino* is supposed to bring good luck to all those who rub his snout. All coins tossed in the shallow pool at his feet for luck and fortune are collected for the hospital.

Il Porcellino, the brass boar in front of Sydney Hospital

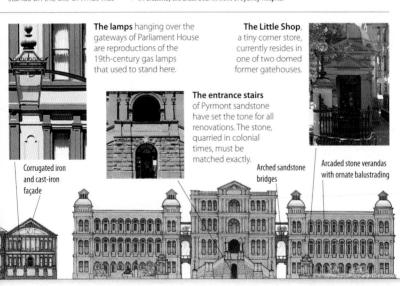

The lamps hanging over the gateways of Parliament House are reproductions of the 19th-century gas lamps that used to stand here.

The Little Shop, a tiny corner store, currently resides in one of two domed former gatehouses.

The entrance stairs of Pyrmont sandstone have set the tone for all renovations. The stone, quarried in colonial times, must be matched exactly.

Corrugated iron and cast-iron façade

Arched sandstone bridges

Arcaded stone verandas with ornate balustrading

Sydney Hospital (1868–94)

⑫ The Mint

10 Macquarie St. **Map** 1 C5.
Tel 8239 2288. ⛴ Sydney Explorer,
Elizabeth St routes. **Open** 9am–5pm
Mon–Fri. **Closed** Good Fri, 25 Dec.
🅿 ♿ ground floor only. 🆆 **sydney
livingmuseums.com.au/the-mint**

The gold rushes of the mid-
19th century transformed
colonial Australia. The Sydney
Mint opened in the 1816 Rum
Hospital's south wing in 1854 to
turn recently discovered gold
into bullion and currency.

It was the first branch of the
Royal Mint to be established
outside London. The Mint was
closed in 1927 as it was no

longer competitive with the
Melbourne and Perth Mints.
The Georgian building went
into its own decline after it was
converted into government
offices. In the 1950s, the front
courtyard was even used as a
car park. In 1982, it opened as
a branch of the Powerhouse
Museum *(see pp102–3)*, but the
collection moved to the main
museum in Harris Street.

This building is now the head
office of the Historic Houses
Trust of NSW and you can
wander through the front of
the building, or view the
small historical display near
the entrance.

Replica convict hammocks on the third
floor of Hyde Park Barracks

⑬ Hyde Park Barracks Museum

Queens Square, Macquarie St.
Map 1 C5. **Tel** 8239 2311. ♿ St
James, Martin Place. **Open** 10am–5pm
daily. **Closed** Good Fri, 25 Dec. 🈲 🅿
♿ level one only. 🎧 on request.
🆆 **sydneylivingmuseums.com.au/
hyde-park-barracks-museum**

Described by Governor
Macquarie as "spacious" and "well
aired", the beautifully proportioned barracks are the work of
Francis Greenway and are considered his masterpiece. They were
completed in 1819 by convict

Francis Greenway, Convict Architect

Francis Greenway (1777–1837)

Until the 1990s, Australian A$10 notes
bore the portrait of the early colonial
architect Francis Greenway, the only
currency in the world to pay tribute to a
convicted forger. Greenway was transported
to Sydney in 1814 to serve 14 years for his
crime. Under the patronage of Governor
Macquarie, who appointed him Civil Architect
in 1816, Greenway designed more than
40 buildings, of which only 11 remain
today. He received a full pardon in
1819, but soon fell out of favour as he
persisted in charging large fees while
still on a government salary. Greenway
died in poverty in 1837.

Macquarie Street

*Fine examples of Francis Greenway's Georgian style
are within an easy walk of one another at the Hyde
Park end of Macquarie Street. The brick and sandstone
of Hyde Park Barracks, St James Church and the Old
Supreme Court Building form a harmonious group on
the site the governor envisaged as the city's civic centre.*

The Mint, like its twin,
Parliament House, has an
unusual double-colonnaded,
two-storeyed veranda.

The roof of The Mint has
now been completely
restored to replicate the
original wooden shingles
in casuarina (she-oak).

The stone wall, of Hyde Park
Barracks' northwest pavilion
still bears the marks of the
convicts' chisels.

Hyde Park
Barracks Café

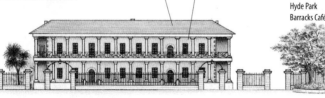

The Mint *(1816)*

labour and designed to house 600 convicts who had previously been forced to find their own lodgings after their day's work. The building later housed Irish orphans and then single female immigrants, before becoming courts and legal offices. Refurbished in 1990, it reopened as a museum with exhibits about the site and its occupants over the years.

The displays include a room reconstructed as convict quarters of the 1820s, as well as pictures, models and artifacts relating to this period of Australian history. Many of the objects now on display, recovered during archaeological digs at the site, had previously been dragged away by rats to their nests; the scavenging rodents are acknowledged as valuable agents of preservation.

The Greenway Gallery on the first floor holds temporary exhibitions on history, ideas and culture. From the Barracks Café, which incorporates the original confinement cell area, the visitor can enjoy refreshment, gazing out over the now serene courtyard, once the scene of brutal convict floggings.

Detail from the Children's Chapel mural in the St James' Church crypt

🄮 St James' Church

173 King St. **Map** 1 B5. **Tel** 8227 1300. 🚇 St James, Martin Place. **Open** 10am–4pm Mon–Fri, 9am–1pm Sat, 7:30am–4pm Sun. Free concerts: Mar–Dec: Wed 1:15pm. 🆆 sjks.org.au

This fine Georgian building, constructed with convict-made bricks, was designed as a courthouse in 1819. The architect, Francis Greenway, was forced to convert it into a church in 1820, when plans to build a grand cathedral on George Street were abandoned.

Greenway, unhappy about the change, designed a simple yet elegant church. Consecrated in 1824 by Samuel Marsden, the infamous "flogging parson", it is Sydney's oldest church. Many additions have been carried out, including designs by John Verge in which the pulpit faced towards high-rent pews, while convicts and the military sat behind the preacher where the service would have been inaudible. A Children's Chapel was added in 1930.

Prominent members of early 19th-century society, many of whom died violently, are commemorated in marble tablets. These tell the full and bloody stories of luckless explorers and shipwreck victims, among other untimely demises.

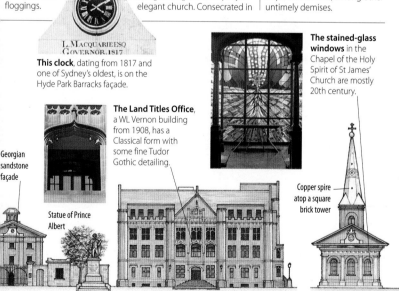

L. MACQUARIE ESQ GOVERNOR. 1817

This clock, dating from 1817 and one of Sydney's oldest, is on the Hyde Park Barracks façade.

The Land Titles Office, a WL Vernon building from 1908, has a Classical form with some fine Tudor Gothic detailing.

The stained-glass windows in the Chapel of the Holy Spirit of St James' Church are mostly 20th century.

Georgian sandstone façade

Statue of Prince Albert

Copper spire atop a square brick tower

Hyde Park Barracks *(1817–19)*

Land Titles Office *(1908–13)*

St James' *(1820)*

An elevated view of the Kings Cross area

Sights at a Glance

Historic Streets and Buildings
2 Victoria Street
3 Elizabeth Bay House
6 Old Gaol, Darlinghurst
7 Darlinghurst Court House

Museums and Galleries
5 Sydney Jewish Museum

Parks and Gardens
4 Beare Park

Monuments
1 El Alamein Fountain

*See also Street Finder,
maps 2, 3 & 5*

KINGS CROSS AND DARLINGHURST

Situated on the eastern fringe of the city, Kings Cross, known as "The Cross", and Darlinghurst are a couple of Sydney celebrities. Their allure is tarnished – or enhanced, perhaps – by trails of scandal and corruption. Kings Cross, particularly, is still regarded as a hotbed of vice; both areas still bear the taint of 1920s gangland associations. In fact, both are now cosmopolitan areas – among the most densely populated parts of Sydney, famed as much for their street life and thriving café culture as for their unsavoury features. Kings Cross exudes a welcome breath of bohemia, in spite of the sleaze of Darlinghurst Road and the flaunting of its red light district. Darlinghurst comes brilliantly into its own every March, when the flamboyant Gay and Lesbian Mardi Gras parade, supported by huge crowds of spectators, makes its triumphant way along Oxford Street.

☐ **Restaurants** *pp192–4*

1 A Tavola
2 Bar Coluzzi
3 Beppi's
4 Bill and Toni's
5 Bills
6 Billy Kwong
7 Casoni
8 The Fish Shop
9 Flour and Stone
10 Fratelli Paradiso
11 Fu Manchu
12 Govinda's
13 Harry's Café de Wheels
14 Jimmy Liks
15 Lucio Pizzeria
16 Macleay Street Bistrot
17 Ms G's
18 Phamish
19 Red Lantern on Crown
20 Riley Street Garage
21 Spice I Am
22 Tilbury Hotel
23 Yellow

Street-by-Street: Potts Point

The substantial Victorian houses filling the streets of this old suburb are excellent examples of the 19th-century concern with architectural harmony. New building projects were designed to enhance rather than contradict the surrounding buildings and general streetscape. Monumental structures and fine details of moulded stuccoed parapets, cornices and friezes, even the spandrels in herringbone pattern, are all integral parts of a grand suburban plan. (This plan included an 1831 order that all houses cost at least £1,000.) Cool, dark verandas extend the street's green canopy of shade, leaving an impression of cold drinks enjoyed on summer days in fine Victorian style.

The McElhone Stairs were preceded by a wooden ladder that linked Woolloomooloo Hill, as Kings Cross was known, to the estate far below.

Horderns Stairs

These villas, from the Georgian and Victorian eras, can be broadly labelled as Classical Revival and are fronted by leafy gardens.

❷ ★ Victoria Street
From 1972–4, residents of this historic street fought a sometimes violent battle against developers wanting to build high-rise towers, motels and blocks of flats.

Kings Cross Station

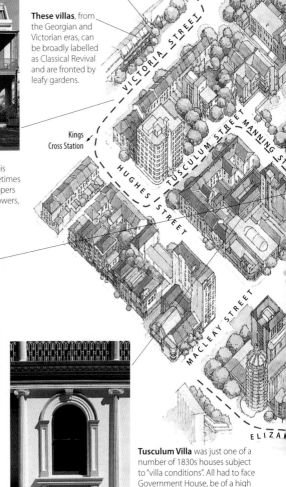

Werrington, a mostly serious and streamlined building, also has flamboyant Art Deco detailing, which is now hidden under brown paint.

Tusculum Villa was just one of a number of 1830s houses subject to "villa conditions". All had to face Government House, be of a high monetary value and be built within three years.

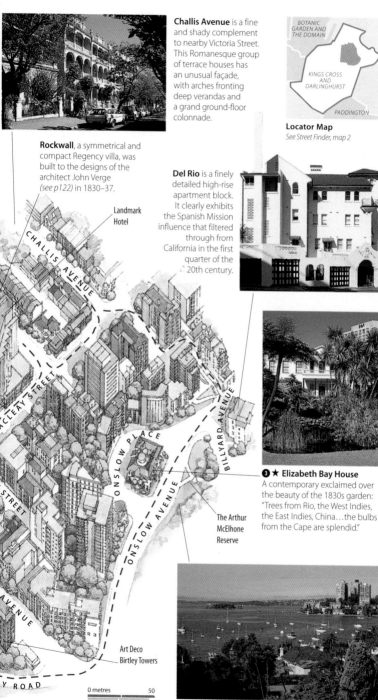

Challis Avenue is a fine and shady complement to nearby Victoria Street. This Romanesque group of terrace houses has an unusual façade, with arches fronting deep verandas and a grand ground-floor colonnade.

Locator Map
See Street Finder, map 2

Rockwall, a symmetrical and compact Regency villa, was built to the designs of the architect John Verge *(see p122)* in 1830–37.

Landmark Hotel

Del Rio is a finely detailed high-rise apartment block. It clearly exhibits the Spanish Mission influence that filtered through from California in the first quarter of the 20th century.

CHALLIS AVENUE

ACLEAY STREET

ONSLOW PLACE

ONSLOW AVENUE

BILLYARD AVENUE

STREET

AVENUE

Y ROAD

The Arthur McElhone Reserve

❸ ★ **Elizabeth Bay House**
A contemporary exclaimed over the beauty of the 1830s garden: "Trees from Rio, the West Indies, the East Indies, China…the bulbs from the Cape are splendid."

Art Deco Birtley Towers

| 0 metres | 50 |
| 0 yards | 50 |

Key

— Suggested route

Elizabeth Bay was part of the original land grant to Alexander Macleay *(see p122)*. He created a botanist's paradise with ornamental ponds, quaint grottoes and promenades winding all the way down to the harbour.

El Alamein Fountain, commemorating the World War II battle

❶ El Alamein Fountain

Fitzroy Gardens, Macleay St, Potts Point. **Map** 2 E5. 🚌 311.

This dandelion-shaped fountain in the heart of the Kings Cross district has a reputation for working so spasmodically that passers-by often murmur facetiously, "He loves me, he loves me not." Built in 1961, it commemorates the Australian army's role in the siege of Tobruk, Libya, and the battle of El Alamein in Egypt during World War II. At night, when it is brilliantly lit, the fountain looks surprisingly ethereal.

❷ Victoria Street

Potts Point. **Map** 2 E5. 🚌 311, 324, 325.

At the Potts Point end, this street of 19th-century terrace houses, interspersed with a few incongruous-looking high-rise blocks, is, by inner-city standards, almost a boulevard. This gracious street was once at the centre of a bitter conservation struggle, one which almost certainly cost a prominent heritage campaigner's life.

In the early 1970s, many residents, backed by the "green bans" (see p33) put in place by the Builders' Labourers' Federation of New South Wales, fought to prevent demolition of old buildings for high-rise development. Juanita Nielsen,

Juanita Nielsen

publisher of a local newspaper and heiress, vigorously took up the conservation battle. On 4 July 1975, she disappeared without trace. A subsequent inquest into her disappearance returned an open verdict.

As a result of the actions of the union and residents, most of Victoria Street's superb old buildings still stand. Ironically, they are now occupied not by the low-income residents who fought to save them, but by the well-off professionals who eventually displaced them.

❸ Elizabeth Bay House

7 Onslow Ave, Elizabeth Bay. **Map** 2 F5. **Tel** 9356 3022. 🚌 Sydney Explorer, 311. **Open** 11am–4pm Fri–Sun. **Closed** Good Fri, 25 Dec. 🅿 🆆 **sydney livingmuseums.com.au/elizabeth-bay-house**

Elizabeth Bay House (see pp26–7) has the finest colonial interior on display in Australia. It is a potent expression of how the 1840s depression cut short the 1830s prosperous optimism. Designed in the fashionable Greek Revival style by John Verge, it was built for Colonial Secretary Alexander Macleay, from 1835–9. The domed oval saloon with its cantilevered staircase is recognized as Verge's masterpiece. The exterior is less satisfactory, as the intended colonnade and portico were not finished owing to a crisis in Macleay's financial affairs.

The present portico dates from 1893. The interior is furnished to reflect Macleay's occupancy from 1839–45, and is based on inventories drawn up in 1845 for the transfer of the house to Macleay's son, William Sharp. He took the house in return for payment of his father's debts, leading to a rift never to be resolved.

Macleay's original 22-hectare (54-acre) land grant was subdivided for flats and villas from the 1880s to 1927. In the 1940s, the house itself was divided into 15 flats. In 1942, the artist Donald Friend, while standing on the balcony of his flat – the former morning room – saw the ferry *Kuttabul* hit by a torpedo from a Japanese midget submarine.

The house was restored and opened as a museum in 1977.

The sweeping staircase under the oval dome, Elizabeth Bay House

❹ Beare Park

Ithaca Rd, Elizabeth Bay. **Map** 2 F5. 🚌 311, 350.

Originally a part of the Macleay Estate, Beare Park is now encircled by a jumble of apartment blocks. A refuge from hectic Kings Cross, it is one of only a handful of parks serving a densely populated area. In the shape of a natural amphitheatre, the park puts Elizabeth Bay on glorious view.

The family home of J C Williamson, a famous theatrical entrepreneur who came to Australia from America in the 1870s, formerly stood at the eastern extremity of the park.

Star of David in the lobby of the Sydney Jewish Museum

❺ Sydney Jewish Museum

48 Darlinghurst Rd, Darlinghurst.
Map 5 B2. Tel 9360 7999.
Sydney Explorer, Bondi & Bay Explorer, 311, 388. Open 10am–4pm Sun–Thu, 10am–2pm Fri. Closed Sat, Jewish hols.
w sydneyjewishmuseum.com.au

Sixteen Jewish convicts were on the First Fleet and many more were to be transported before the end of the convict era. As with other convicts, most would endure and some would thrive, seizing all the opportunities the colony had to offer for those wishing to make something of themselves.

The Sydney Jewish Museum relates stories of Australian Jewry within the context of the Holocaust. The ground floor display explores present-day Jewish traditions and culture within Australia. Ascending the stairs to mezzanine levels 1–6, the visitor passes through chronological and thematic exhibitions which unravel the history of the Holocaust.

From Hitler's rise to power and *Kristallnacht*, through the evacuation of the ghettos and the Final Solution, to the ultimate liberation of the infamous death camps and Nuremberg Trials, the harrowing events are graphically documented. This horrific period is recalled using photographs and relics, some exhumed from mass graves, as well as audiovisual exhibits and oral testimonies.

Holocaust survivors act as volunteer guides. Their presence, bearing witness to the recorded events, lends considerable power and moving authenticity to the exhibits.

❻ Old Gaol, Darlinghurst

Cnr Burton & Forbes Sts, Darlinghurst.
Map 5 A2. Tel 9339 8744. 333, 378, 380, 389. Open 10:30am–5pm Mon–Fri. Closed public hols. 11am, 1pm, 2pm, 3pm.

Originally known as the Woolloomooloo Stockade and later as Darlinghurst Gaol, this complex is now part the National Art School. It was constructed over a 20-year period from 1822.

Surrounded by walls almost 7 m (23 ft) high, the cell blocks radiate from a central round-house. The jail is built of stone quarried on the site by convicts, which was then chiselled by them into blocks.

No fewer than 67 people were executed here between 1841 and 1908. Perhaps the most notorious hangman was Alexander "The Strangler" Green, after whom Green Park, outside the jail, is thought to have been named. Green lived near the park until public hostility forced him to live in relative safety inside the jail.

Some of Australia's most noted artists, including Frank Hodgkinson, Jon Molvig and William Dobell, trained or taught at the art school which was established here in 1921.

The former Governor's house, Old Gaol, Darlinghurst

❼ Darlinghurst Court House

Forbes St, Darlinghurst. Map 5 A2.
Tel 1300 679 272. 333, 378, 380.
Open Feb–mid-Dec: 10am–4pm Mon–Fri & Sun. Closed mid-Dec–Jan, public hols.

Abutting the grim old jail, to which it is connected by under-ground passages, and facing Taylor Square, this unlikely gem of Greek Revival architecture was begun in 1835 by Mortimer Lewis, the Colonial Architect of New South Wales from 1835 to 1843. He was only responsible for the central block of the main building with its splendid six-columned Doric portico. The balancing side wings were added in the 1880s.

The court house is still used by the state's Supreme Court mainly for criminal cases, and these are open to the public.

Beare Park, a quiet inner-city park with harbour views

A row of Victorian terrace houses in the suburb of Paddington

Sights at a Glance

Historic Streets and Buildings
❶ Paddington Street
❷ The Entertainment Quarter
❹ Five Ways
❺ Juniper Hall
❻ Paddington Town Hall
❼ Paddington Village
❽ Victoria Barracks

Parks and Gardens
❾ Centennial Park

Markets
❸ Paddington Markets

0 metres   500
0 yards   500

PADDINGTON

Paddington is justly celebrated for its handsome terraces, but this "village in the city", as it is often dubbed, is also famed for its interesting speciality shops full of oddities and collectables, fine restaurants, small hotels, fashionable art galleries and antique dealers' shops. Paddington boasts a lively street culture, especially on Saturdays when people from far and wide flock to the famous weekly Paddington Markets, spilling out into the streets, pubs and cafés of the surrounding area. Stretching from the Victoria Barracks at its western end, along Oxford Street to the green haven of Centennial Park, Paddington slopes away from this

bustling central thoroughfare into the narrow lanes and elegant, leafy streets. The suburb has undergone a series of quite radical transformations. The first Paddington was built in the 1830s as a Georgian weekend retreat for the moneyed class. These gracious homes had a short life, before being knocked down and subdivided. The terraces succeeding them fell into ruin by the 1920s, but are now admired as finely restored Victorian homes with their distinctive wrought-iron "lace" verandas. The glimpses of harbour found in the quiet streets make Paddington one of Sydney's most sought-after residential areas.

☐ **Restaurants** pp194–5

1 A10 William Street
2 Ampersand Café & Bookstore
3 The Bellevue
4 Big Mama's
5 Bistro Moncur
6 Buon Ricardo
7 Crème Café
8 Four in Hand
9 Guillaume
10 Hotel Centennial
11 La Scala on Jersey
12 The London Hotel
13 Lucio's
14 Paddington Inn
15 Pinbone
16 South Dowling Kitchen
17 Vamps Bistro
18 Vincent
19 Vino e Cucina
20 Wine Library

See also Street Finder, maps 5 & 6

For keys to symbols see back flap

Street-by-Street: Paddington

Paddington began to flourish in the 1840s, when the decision was made to build the Victoria Barracks. At the time much of it was "the most wild looking place… barren sandhills with patches of scrub, hills and hollows galore." The area began to fill rapidly, as owner builders bought into the area and built rows of terrace houses, many very narrow because of the lack of building regulations. After the Depression, most of the district was threatened with demolition, but was saved and restored by the large influx of postwar migrants.

❹ ★ Five Ways
This shopping hub was established in the late 19th century on the busy Glenmore roadway trodden out by bullocks.

Duxford Street's terrace houses in toning pale shades constitute an ideal of town planning: the Victorians preferred houses in a row to have a pleasingly uniform aspect.

"Gingerbread" houses can be seen in Broughton and Union streets. With their steeply pitched gables and fretwork barge-boards, they are typical of the rustic Gothic Picturesque architectural style.

The London Tavern opened for business in 1875, making it the suburb's oldest pub. Like many of the pubs and delicatessens in this well-serviced suburb, it stands at the end of a row of terraces.

Key

— Suggested route

The Sherman Gallery used to be housed in this strikingly modern building. It was designed to hold Australian and international contemporary sculpture and paintings. Suitable access gates and a special in-house crane enable the movement of large-scale artworks, including textiles.

Locator Map
See Street Finder, maps 5 & 6

Paddington's streets are a treasure trove of galleries, bars and restaurants. A wander through the area should prove an enjoyable experience.

Warwick, built in the 1860s, is a minor castle lying at the end of a row of humble terraces. Its turrets, battlements and assorted decorations, in a style somewhat fancifully described as "King Arthur", even adorn the garages at the rear.

Windsor Street's terrace houses are, in some cases, a mere 4.5 m (15 ft) wide.

Street-making in Paddington's early days was often an expensive and complicated business. A cascade of water was dammed to build Cascade Street.

NORFOLK LANE

NORFOLK STREET

HARGRAVE ST

CASCADE STREET

HOPETOUN STREET

WINDSOR ST

PADDINGTON STREET

DUDLEY STREET

0 metres   50
0 yards   50

❶ ★ Paddington Street
Under the established plane trees, some of Paddington's finest Victorian terraces exemplify the building boom of 1860–90. Over 30 years, 3,800 houses were built in the suburb.

A typical pretty terrace house on Paddington Street

❶ Paddington Street

Map 6 D3. 🚌 333, 378, 380.

With its huge plane trees shading the road and fine two-, three- and four-storey terrace houses on each side, Paddington Street is one of the oldest, loveliest, and at the same time most typical of the suburb's streets.

Paddington grew rapidly as a commuter suburb in the late 19th century and most of the terraces were built for renting to the city's artisans. They were cheaply decorated with iron lace (some of which had arrived in ships as ballast), as well as Grecian-style friezes, worked parapets, swagged urns, lions rampant, cornices, pilasters, scrolls and other fancy plastering. By the 1900s, these terraces had become unfashionable but in the 1960s, tastes changed again and Paddington experienced a renaissance.

Paddington Street now has a chic atmosphere where small art galleries operate out of quaint and grand shopfronts.

❷ The Entertainment Quarter

Lang Rd, Moore Park. **Tel** 8117 6700. **Map** 5 C5. 🚌 339, 355. **Open** most retail shops are open 10am–10pm. 🌐 eqmoorepark.com.au

There's a vibrant atmosphere at the Entertainment Quarter, which is located next door to Fox Studios, which produced

such well-known films as *The Matrix* and *Moulin Rouge*.

There are 16 cinema screens where you can watch the latest movies, and at the La Premiere cinema you can enjoy your movie with wine and cheese, sitting on comfortable sofas. There are four live-entertainment venues which regularly feature the latest local and international acts. You can also enjoy bungy trampolining, bowling or seasonal ice-skating, and children love the three, well-designed playgrounds.

In addition to shops there are plenty of restaurants, cafés and bars offering a range of meals, drinks and snacks.

Every Wednesday and Saturday you can sample fresh produce at the EQ Village Markets or try a gourmet delicacy from one of the dozens of stallholders. Sunday's market focuses on merchandise rather than food.

Shops are open until late, and there is a good selection offering fashion, books and homewares. There is plenty of undercover parking and the complex is a pleasant stroll from Oxford Street.

❸ Paddington Markets

395 Oxford St. **Map** 6 D4. **Tel** 9331 2923. 🚌 333, 378, 380. **Open** 10am–4pm Sat. **Closed** 25 Dec. ♿ *See Shops and Markets p203.* 🌐 paddingtonmarkets.com.au

This market, which began in 1973, takes place every Saturday, come rain or shine, in the grounds of Paddington Village Uniting Church and its neighbouring school. It is a place to meet and be seen as much as it is to shop. Stall-holders come from all over the world, and many young designers hoping to launch their careers display their wares. Among the offerings are jewellery, pottery, new and secondhand clothing, and an array of other arts and crafts. Whatever you are looking for, you are likely to find it here, from designer

bags to tarot reading, and from Oriental massages to handmade soaps.

❹ Five Ways

Cnr Glenmore Rd & Heeley St. **Map** 5 C3. 🚌 389.

There is a busy shopping hub at this picturesque junction by the tramline that once ran to Bondi Beach. On the five corners stand Victorian and early 20th-century shops, one now a restaurant.

On another corner is the impressive Royal Hotel, which was built in 1888. This mixed Victorian and Classical Revival building has a characteristic intricate cast-iron "lace"-screen balcony offering stunning harbour views.

❺ Juniper Hall

250 Oxford St. **Map** 5 C3. **Tel** 9258 0123. 🚌 333, 378, 380. **Open** see website for exhibition details and dates. 🌐 juniperhall.com.au

The emancipist gin distiller Robert Cooper built this superb example of Colonial Georgian architecture for his third wife, Sarah. He named it after the main ingredient of the gin that made his fortune.

Completed in 1824, it is the oldest building in Paddington still standing. It is probably also the largest and most extravagant. It had to be: he already had 14 children when he declared that Sarah would have the finest house in Sydney.

Juniper Hall was saved from demolition in the mid-1980s and fully restored. It is now home to the annual Moran Art Prize.

Balcony of the Royal Hotel in the heart of Paddington

❻ Paddington Town Hall

249 Oxford St (cnr Oatley Rd).
Map 5 C3. **Tel** 9265 9189.
🚌 333, 378, 380. **Closed** to the
public, except the cinema.
🌐 **palacecinemas.com.au**

The Paddington Town Hall was
completed in 1891. An international competition which,
in a spirit of Victorian self-
confidence, was intended to
produce the state's finest town
hall, was won by local architect
J E Kemp. His Classical Revival
building, to which a clock tower
was later added, still dominates
the surrounding area, although
it is no longer a centre of
local government.

The building now houses
Chauvel Cinema in the former
ballroom, which is managed by
the Australian Film Institute, as
well as the Paddington Library.

Paddington Town Hall, at the highest point
in the Oxford Street ridge

❼ Paddington Village

Cnr Gipps & Shadforth Sts. **Map** 5 C3.
🚌 333, 378, 380.

Paddington began its life as a
working-class suburb. The
community comprised the
carpenters, quarrymen and
stonemasons who supervised
the convict gangs that built
Victoria Barracks in the 1840s.

The artisans and their families
occupied a tight huddle of spar-
tan houses, a few of which still
remain, crowded into the narrow
streets nearby. Like the barracks,
these dwellings and surrounding
shops and hotels were built
mainly of locally quarried stone.

The lush green expanse of Centennial Park

❽ Victoria Barracks

Oxford St. **Map** 5 B4. **Tel** 8335 5330. 🚌
333, 378, 380. Museum: **Open** 10am–
1pm Thu (last adm noon), 10am–4pm
first Sun of month. **Closed** Dec–Jan.
♿ 📷 Parade & tour: 10am Thu.

Victoria Barracks is the largest
and best-preserved group of
late Georgian architecture in
Australia, covering almost 12 ha
(29 acres). It is widely
considered to be one of the
best examples of a military
barracks in the world.

Designed by the Colonial
Engineer, Lieutenant Colonel
George Barney, the barracks
were built between 1841 and
1848 using local sandstone
quarried by mainly convict
labour. Originally intended to
house 800 men, it has been in
continuous military use ever
since, and still operates as a
centre of military planning,
administration and command.

The main block is 225 m
(740 ft) long and has symmetrical two-storey wings with cast-
iron verandas flanking a central
archway. The perimeter walls,
which are designed to repel
surprise attacks, have

The archway at the Oxford Street entrance
to Victoria Barracks

foundations 10 m (40 ft) deep in
places. In a former jail block, a
museum traces New South
Wales' military heritage.

❾ Centennial Park

Map 6 E5. **Tel** 9339 6699. 🚌 Clovelly,
Coogee, Maroubra, Randwick, Bronte,
City, Bondi Beach & Bondi Junction
routes, Bondi Explorer Bus.
Open the park is open permanently;
cars are permitted from sunrise.
🚻 🚲 ♿ 📷 on request.
🌐 **centennialparklands.com.au**

Entering this 220-ha (544-acre)
park through one of its sandstone and wrought-iron gates,
the visitor may wonder how
such an extensive and idyllic
place has survived so close to
the centre of the city.

Formerly a common, it was
dedicated "to the enjoyment of
the people of New South Wales
forever" on 26 January 1888, the
centenary of the foundation of
the colony. On 1 January 1901,
more than 100,000 people
gathered here to witness the
birth of the Commonwealth of
Australia with the proclamation
of the Federation of Australia.
The striking Federation Pavilion
marks the site of this event.

Today picnickers, painters,
runners, horse riders, cyclists
and in-line skaters enjoy this
vast recreation area.

Once the source of Sydney's
water supply, the swamps are
now home to many waterbirds.
Within the park are ornamental
ponds, cultivated gardens, an
Avenue of Palms, a sports
ground and a café.

FURTHER AFIELD

Beyond the inner city, numerous places vie for the visitor's attention. Around the harbour foreshores are picturesque suburbs, secluded beaches, scenic outlooks and cultural and historic sights. Taronga Zoo is worth a visit as much for its incomparable setting as for its birds and animals. Manly, stretching between harbour and ocean, is the city's northern playground, while Bondi is its eastern counterpart. In Balmain, Glebe and Surry Hills, the visitor can experience the character of the inner suburbs. Still further afield, out west at Parramatta, there are sights that recall and evoke the first days of European settlement and the colony's initially unsteady steps towards agricultural self-sufficiency.

Sights at a Glance

Historic Districts and Buildings
- ❸ University of Sydney
- ❻ Balmain
- ❽ Kirribilli Point
- ⓬ North Head
- ⓭ Vaucluse House
- ⓯ Watsons Bay
- ⓰ Macquarie Lighthouse
- ⓲ Captain Cook's Landing Place
- ⓴ Elizabeth Farm
- ㉑ Hambledon Cottage
- ㉒ Experiment Farm Cottage
- ㉔ Old Government House

Parks and Gardens
- ⓮ Nielsen Park

Museums and Galleries
- ❶ Brett Whiteley Studio
- ❾ Nutcote

Entertainment
- ❼ Luna Park
- ❿ *Taronga Zoo pp136–7*
- ⓳ Sydney Olympic Park

Beaches
- ⓫ Manly
- ⓱ Bondi Beach

Restaurants and Pubs
- ❷ Dr Chau Chak Wing Building
- ❹ Glebe

Markets
- ❺ Sydney Fish Market

Cemeteries
- ㉓ St John's Cemetery

KEY

- ▓ Main sightseeing area
- ▢ Park or reserve
- ③ Metroad route
- ═ Freeway or motorway
- ═ Major road
- ═ Minor road

0 km   6
0 miles   3

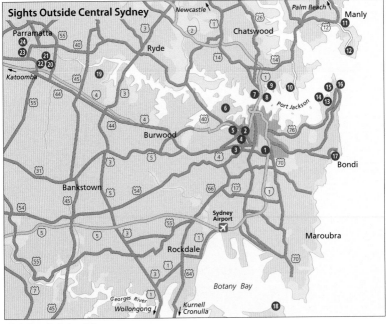

Sights Outside Central Sydney

◀ The Ferris wheel at Luna Park

Brett Whiteley Studio: former artist's studio, now a museum

❶ Brett Whiteley Studio

2 Raper St, Surry Hills. **Map** 5 A4.
Tel 9225 1881. 343, 372, 393.
Open 10am–4pm Sat & Sun, or by appointment on Thu & Fri.
Closed Easter Sun, 25 Dec.
partial access.

In June 1992, Brett Whiteley, *enfant terrible* of Australian contemporary art, died unexpectedly at the age of 53. An internationally acclaimed and prolific artist, he produced some of the most sumptuous images of Sydney and its distinctive harbour ever painted.

In 1985, Whiteley bought a former factory and converted it into a studio and residence. The studio is now a public museum and art gallery.

Very few changes have been made to the building since Whiteley was in residence. The furniture, lighting, collections of memorabilia, postcards, photographs and other objects are all as he arranged them.

The upstairs studio includes his unfinished paintings, art equipment, collections of reference books, and a graffiti wall covered with his quotes and images. Even the music that is played is from Whiteley's own collection.

The studio is under the administration of the Art Gallery of New South Wales (*see pp110–13*), and displays changing exhibitions of the artist's works borrowed from the Whiteley Estate, the Art Gallery of New South Wales and private collections.

❷ Dr Chau Chak Wing Building

14–28 Ultimo Road, University of Technology, Sydney, Ultimo. **Map** 4 D4.
Tel 9514 2000. Central Station.
Parramatta Rd & City Rd routes.
uts.edu.au

Named after the philanthropist who funded its construction, the Dr Chau Chak Wing Building is the first building in Australia designed by the renowned and influential architect, Frank Gehry.

Affectionately dubbed the "crumpled brown paper bag" building, this masterpiece of design and engineering is home to the Business School at the University of Technology (UTS).

Gehry described the design as a metaphorical tree house, a "growing, learning organism with many branches of thought".

The design is striking, both on the outside and the inside. The exterior features an east-facing, sandstone-coloured brick façade that undulates like fabric, and a western façade of angular glass shards that reflects the city back to itself. The "fluid" brickwork was a technical feat, with custom-made brick shapes laid by hand.

Visitors can enter the building and there is a café on the ground floor.

Statue of Hermes, Nicholson Museum

❸ University of Sydney

Parramatta Rd, Camperdown.
Map 3 B5. **Tel** 9351 2222. 343, Parramatta Rd & City Rd routes.
Open daily. phone 9351 2274 (book one week in advance).

Inaugurated in 1850, this is Australia's oldest university. The campus is a sprawling mix of buildings from different eras, often of dubious architectural merit. However, the original Victorian Gothic main building still stands on its elevated site, dominating its surroundings. The work of the Colonial Architect Edmund Blacket, it is scrupulously modelled on the architecture of Cambridge and Oxford. It features intricate stone tracery, a clock tower with carved pinnacles and gargoyles, and a cloistered main quadrangle.

The gem of the campus is the Great Hall at the main building's northern end. This sombre building, with its carved cedar ceiling and stained-glass windows depicting famous philosophers and scientists, is used for public concerts and university ceremonies.

The Nicholson Museum of antiquities, the Macleay Museum and the War Memorial Art Gallery are all within the grounds. They are open to the public on most weekdays.

The east-facing façade of the unusual Dr Chau Chak Wing Building

Badde Manors Café on Glebe Point Road, Glebe

❹ Glebe

Map 3 A4. 🚌 431, 433.
See Shops and Markets: p203.

The word "Glebe" means land assigned to a clergyman as part of his benefice. In 1789, Governor Phillip granted 162 ha (400 acres) to Richard Johnson, the First Fleet chaplain, and his wife Mary. Almost all of the present suburb was once part of that Glebe Estate. Many of its streets wind down to the working harbour and contain terrace houses with Sydney wrought-iron "lace" in varying states of repair.

The once-grand residences of the 19th-century élite were mostly towards the harbour end of Glebe Point Road, with workers' cottages clustered nearer Parramatta Road. Glebe is still partly a gentrified member of the café society, although its proximity to the Broadway shopping mall and its popularity with students from the nearby University of Sydney have given it a more bustling atmosphere.

It is densely populated and lively, with many restaurants and cafés in all price ranges, traditional and trendy pubs, good bookshops, an art-house cinema and shops selling everything from antique clocks

to New Age goods and chattels. Glebe Market, held every Saturday, sells an array of jewellery, secondhand clothing and bric-à-brac.

❺ Sydney Fish Market

Cnr Pyrmont Bridge Rd & Bank St, Pyrmont. **Map** 3 B2. **Tel** 9004 1100.
🚌 443, 501. 🚊 Fish Market. **Open** 7am–4pm daily. **Closed** 25 Dec. ♿
🍴 Mon, Thu & Fri. Booking essential; phone 9004 1143.
🌐 **sydneyfishmarket.com.au**
See Shops and Markets: pp202–3.

Every weekday, about 200 seafood retailers and dealers arrive at this market's private auction to bid for the previous day's catch. It is sold by Dutch auction, with prices starting high and decreasing. The volume and variety of the catch, including fish and seafood makes this the most diverse fish market after Tokyo.

A fair amount of this catch ends up, later in the morning, in the fish market's six large retail outlets which, for the general public, are its main attraction. As well as fresh fish, these retailers sell smoked salmon and roe, sushi, marinated baby octopus and many other ready-to-eat

delicacies. Visitors watch the experts as they tenderize octopus and squid in concrete mixers. As well as fishmongers, there are a number of fresh food shops, several restaurants and a seafood school – cost includes tuition, seafood and wine.

❻ Balmain

🚌 433, 434, 442. *See Shops and Markets p203 and Four Guided Walks pp144–5.*

Balmain was once one of Sydney's most staunchly working-class areas, with shipyards, a dry dock and repair yards, a coal mine, numerous rough-and-ready pubs and an intimidating criminal element. Its late 19th-century town hall, post office, court house and fire station in Darling Street reflect the civic pride of the suburb in the Victorian era.

The many stone and timber cottages of what had become a slum have transformed into a charming, bustling suburb that still retains its village character, with interesting shops, galleries, cafés, restaurants and pubs.

The proximity of the Balmain peninsula to the city and its bohemian ambience may explain why many prominent writers – including novelist Kate Grenville and playwright David Williamson – have lived and worked here.

The Saturday market, held at St Andrews Congregational Church in Darling Street, is one of Sydney's best. Antiques, estate jewellery and ingenious art and craft items are on sale.

Imposing entrance to Balmain court house on Darling Street

The Colourful Faces of Luna Park

The gateway to Luna Park is the gaping mouth of a huge laughing face, flanked by two 36-m (129-ft) Art Deco towers. Between 1935 and 1945, four successive canvas, wire and plaster faces fell to the ravages of time. Built in the 1950s, the fifth face was replaced in 1973 with one designed by the Sydney artist Martin Sharp. The seventh, made in 1982, is now at the Powerhouse Museum (see pp102–3). Today's face (1994) is made of polyurethane and fibreglass.

The gateway to Luna Park with its famous face

Ferris wheel at Luna Park, which is based on the Coney Island fair of the same name

● Luna Park

1 Olympic Drive, Milsons Point. **Tel** 9922 6644. **Open** 11am–4pm Mon, 11am–10pm Fri & Sat, 10am–6pm Sun (additional hours during school & pub hols). 🚇 Milsons Point. 🚢 Milsons Point. 🚻 🌐 lunaparksydney.com

This famous fun fair, built on the site of former Harbour Bridge construction workshops, was modelled on Luna Park at Coney Island, New York. It opened in 1935 using rides from a short-lived Luna Park in South Australia. For the next 43 years it was one of the most conspicuous landmarks on the harbour foreshores. Except during the compulsory blackouts of World War II, its brilliant illuminations were a feature of the city's night scene.

In 1979, seven people were killed in a ghost train fire, a tragedy that led to the park's immediate closure. The park has since reopened, and entry is free so you can just enjoy the atmosphere or buy a ticket and catch the views from the Ferris wheel. Las Vegas glitz and 1940s Futurism are just two of the styles at one of Sydney's most treasured icons. The old-style fun house Coney Island, Crystal Palace and the gateway face are all heritage listed. The Big Top, a 2,000-seat venue, hosts music, dance and comedy acts.

● Kirribilli Point

Kirribilli Ave, Kirribilli. 🚢 Kirribilli North Sydney.

The two houses occupying this prominent headland, in their delightful garden settings, are typical of the magnificent homes in sprawling grounds that once ringed the harbour. Most have been demolished

now and the land subdivided for apartment living. Kirribilli, meaning "place for fishing", is the most densely populated suburb in Australia.

The larger, more dominant of the two houses is Admiralty House, built as a single-storey residence in 1843. Between 1885 and 1913 it served as the residence of the commanding officer of Britain's Royal Navy Pacific Squadron, which was based in Sydney. Fortifications on the shoreline recall its military history. Now the official Sydney home of Australia's governor-general, it is said that even its shed could be considered the city's best address.

In 1855, the charming Gothic Kirribilli House, with its steep gables and decorative fretwork, was built in the grounds of Admiralty House. Today it is the official Sydney residence of Australia's prime minister.

● Nutcote

5 Wallaringa Ave, Neutral Bay. **Tel** 9953 4453. 🚢 Hayes St, Neutral Bay. **Open** 11am–3pm Wed–Sun. **Closed** some public hols. 🚻 🎫 🌐 nutcote.org

One of the classics of Australian children's literature, Snugglepot and Cuddlepie, was published in 1918. Since then, these two characters – known as the "gumnut" babies along with the cartoon characters Bib and Bub – have been loved by countless young Australians.

Nutcote was, for 44 years, the home of their creator, illustrator and author May Gibbs. Saved

Admiralty House and Kirribilli House, near Sydney Harbour Bridge

Shop façades featuring decorative gables along Manly's Corso

from demolition then restored and refurbished in the style of the 1930s, it opened in 1994 as an historic house museum. Visitors can view the author's painstakingly kept notebooks and other memorabilia (including the table at which she worked), as well as original editions of her books. There is a garden with views across the harbour and a shop that sells a range of May Gibbs' souvenirs.

May Gibbs' studio at Nutcote, where she lived for 44 years

❿ Taronga Zoo

See pp136–7.

⓫ Manly

🚢 Manly. Manly Sea Life Sanctuary: West Esplanade. **Tel** 1800 614 069. **Open** 9:30am–5pm daily. **Closed** 25 Dec. ♿ 🎫 *See Four Guided Walks: pp148–9.*
🌐 **manlysealifesanctuary.com.au**

Long after Australia's conversion to the metric system, the slogan "seven miles from Sydney and a thousand miles from care" is still current. It refers to Manly and the 7-mile (11-km) journey from Circular Quay by harbour ferry.

If asked to suggest a single excursion to enjoy during your time in the city, most Sydneysiders would nominate a ferry ride to Manly. This narrow stretch of land lying between the harbour and ocean was named by Governor Phillip, even before the township of Sydney got its name, for the impressive bearing of the Aboriginal men.

As the ferry pulls in to Manly wharf you will notice on the right many shops, restaurants and bars and on the left, the tranquil harbourside beach known as Manly Cove.

At the far end of Manly Cove is Manly Sea Life Sanctuary, where visitors can see reptiles, sharks and giant stingrays in an underwater viewing tunnel. You can also dive with sharks, and details of Shark Xtreme are on the sanctuary's website.

The Corso is a lively pedestrian thoroughfare of souvenir shops and fast food outlets, with a market held there on Sundays. The Corso leads to Manly's ocean beach, with its promenade lined by towering pines. Nearby is a monument to a local newspaper proprietor who, in 1902, defied bans on daytime bathing and was promptly arrested.

Every October Manly hosts a great jazz festival *(see p50)*.

⓬ North Head

🚢 Manly. Quarantine Station Ghost Tours: Bookings essential (starting times vary). **Tel** 9466 1500.
🌐 **qstation.com.au**

The majestic cliffs of North Head afford the finest views in Sydney Harbour National Park, providing vistas along the coastline, across to Middle Harbour and towards the city. North Head is also the ideal place for observing the movements of harbour and seagoing craft and especially for seeing off the yachts at the start of the annual Sydney to Hobart race *(see p51)*.

The Quarantine Station nestles just above Spring Cove within the national park. Here, between 1832 and the 1960s, many ships, with their crews and passengers, were quarantined to protect Sydneysiders from the spread of epidemic diseases. More than 500 people died here, leading some to believe the area is haunted.

Now a five-star hotel called Q Station, the site, including its hospital, shower block and morgue, can be explored on a guided "ghost" tour. Countless migrants spent their first months in Australia in this place of splendid isolation. Many of its internees left poignant messages carved in the sandstone.

First-class quarters at the Quarantine Station, North Head

⏱ Taronga Zoo

This famous harbourside zoo is home to almost 2,500 animals, with a special emphasis on unique Australian wildlife. Conspicuous bars and fences are absent, with moats used to separate the wandering public from the curious animal onlookers contained in environments closely resembling their natural habitat. The zoo is involved in the breeding of endangered animals, as well as in international efforts to ensure a sustainable future for wildlife.

Elephant Breeding Facility
Endangered Asian elephants have been bred at Taronga since a small collection were brought over from Thailand in 2006. The precinct features a rainforest habitat with pools, mud wallows and scratching posts.

Backyard to Bush

Athol Wharf Road

Bradleys Head Road

Lower entrance

Athol Wha

Bradleys Head Road

Sky Safari Cable Car

Capral seal theatre

Upper entrance

Common Wombat
This ground-dwelling animal is a powerful burrower able to move quickly if disturbed. It feeds on roots and has a pouch for carrying its young.

The platypus is one of only three species of egg-laying mammals.

0 metres   100
0 yards   100

Upper Entrance
This heritage-listed edifice has greeted visitors since the opening in 1916. By 1917, more than half of Sydney's population had paid a visit.

★ Orang-utan Rainforest
Threatened by widespread destruction of their natural habitat in the Sumatran and Borneo rainforests, these primates are on the world's endangered species list.

VISITORS' CHECKLIST

Practical Information
Bradleys Head Rd, Mosman.
Tel 9969 2777. **Open** 9:30am–5pm daily (May–Aug & 31 Dec: to 4:30pm). 🅿️ ♿ 📷 🚭 🖥️ 🏛️
W taronga.org.au

Transport
🚌 238, 247, 250. ⛴️ Taronga Zoo.

Ferry to
Circular Quay

Sky Safari
Cable Car

Taronga Zoo

★ QBE Free Flight Bird Show
In this spectacular display, birds fly free in an amphitheatre overlooking the harbour.

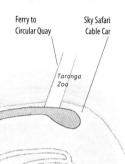

Meerkat
This southern African mongoose always forages in groups, with a guard alert for signs of danger.

African Waterhole
The zoo re-creates the environment of savannah waterholes for giraffes, zebras and pygmy hippopotami.

Reptile World has amphibians, invertebrates and reptiles.

★ Koala Walkabout
Visitors can see the koalas in their eucalypt habitat at tree level. The spiral ramp allows you to get close to feeding and sleeping animals.

Key to Animal Enclosures

① Wetlands
② Wild Australia
③ Platypus
④ Wombat
⑤ Koala Encounters
⑥ Australia's Nightlife
⑦ Rainforest Aviary
⑧ Bush birds
⑨ Saltwater crocodile
⑩ Creatures of the Wollemi
⑪ Yellow-footed rock wallaby
⑫ Tasmanian devil
⑬ Backyard to Bush
⑭ Penguin
⑮ Seals and sea-lions
⑯ Great Southern Oceans
⑰ Elephant Breeding Facility
⑱ Otter
⑲ Free Flight Bird Show
⑳ Bear
㉑ Meerkat
㉒ Snow leopard
㉓ Himalayan Tahr
㉔ Chimpanzee Park
㉕ African Waterhole
㉖ Reptile World
㉗ Koala Walkabout
㉘ Lion
㉙ Taronga International Food Market
㉚ Wild Asia
㉛ Gorilla Forest
㉜ Orang-utan Rainforest

For keys to symbols *see back flap*

Façade of Vaucluse House, with its garden and fountain

⓭ Vaucluse House

Wentworth Rd, Vaucluse. **Tel** 9388 7922. 🚌 325. **Open** 11am–4pm Fri–Sun (daily in Jan, NSW school hols & public hols). **Closed** Good Fri, 25 Dec. 🅿️ ♿ limited. 📷 🌐 **sydneyliving museums.com.au/vaucluse-house**

Tradition has it that the most riotous party colonial Sydney ever saw took place on the Vaucluse House lawns in 1831. W C Wentworth and 4,000 of his political cronies gathered there to celebrate the recall to England of Governor Ralph Darling, the arch-enemy.

W C Wentworth was a major figure in the colony, being one of the first three Europeans to cross the Blue Mountains *(see pp162–3)*. He was the son of a female convict and a physician forced to "volunteer" his services to the new colony in order to avoid conviction on a highway robbery charge.

The younger Wentworth became an author, barrister and statesman who stood for the Australian-born "currency" lads and lasses against the "sterling" English-born. He lived here with his family from 1829–53, during which time he drafted the Constitution Bill, giving self-government to the state.

Vaucluse House was begun in 1803 by Sir Henry Browne Hayes, a knight of the realm transported for kidnapping a Quaker heiress. Sitting in 11 ha (27 acres) of parkland, natural bush and cultivated gardens, this Gothic Revival house, with its many idiosyncratic additions, resembles a West Indian plantation house. The interior and grounds

have been restored to 1840s style and the house contains furniture that belonged to the Wentworth family. A popular tea house is in the grounds.

Greycliffe House, in the tranquil grounds of Nielsen Park

⓮ Nielsen Park

🚌 325. **Open** Sunrise–10pm daily.

Part of the Sydney Harbour National Park, Nielsen Park, with its grassy expanses, sandy beach and netted swimming pool, is the perfect spot for a family picnic. Here visitors can savour

the unusual peace that descends on many harbour beaches on an endless sunny day. It is also an ideal vantage point from which to enjoy a spectacular summer sunset or simply to observe the coming and going of ferries and the meandering harbour traffic.

In the midst of this tranquil setting, enhancing its charm, stands Greycliffe House with its decorative gables and ornate chimney stacks. This Victorian Gothic mansion was completed in 1852 for W C Wentworth's daughter.

⓯ Watsons Bay

🚌 324, 325. ⛴️ Watsons Bay. *See Four Guided Walks: pp150–51.*

As the base for the boats that take the pilots out to arriving ships, this pretty bay has long been a vital part of the working harbour. It is also the home of Doyle's famous waterfront seafood restaurant, long a magnet for Sydneysiders and visitors alike.

Just up the hill and almost opposite the bay on the ocean side is The Gap, a spectacular cliff with tragic associations. Many troubled people have taken a suicidal leap from this rugged cliff on to the wave-lashed rocks below.

It was here that the ill-fated ship *Dunbar* was wrecked in 1857, with the loss of all but one of its 122 passengers and crew. Treacherous conditions had led to miscalculation of the ship's distance from the Heads. All

View over Watsons Bay, looking southwest towards the city

The crescent-shaped Bondi Beach, Sydney's most famous beach, looking towards North Bondi

hands were ordered on deck as The Gap's rock walls loomed. The recovered anchor is now set into the cliff near the shipwreck site.

⑯ Macquarie Lighthouse

🚌 324, 325. ♿

This is the second lighthouse on this windswept site that is attributed to the convict architect Francis Greenway (see p116). He supervised the construction of the first tower, which was completed in 1818 and described by Governor Macquarie as a "noble magnificent edifice". The colony's first lighthouse, it replaced the previous system of bonfires lit up along the headland and earned Greenway a conditional pardon. When the sandstone eventually crumbled

The 1883 Macquarie Lighthouse overlooking the Pacific Ocean

away, the present lighthouse was built. Although designed by Colonial Architect James Barnet, it was based on Greenway's original and was illuminated for the first time in 1883.

⑰ Bondi Beach

🚌 333, 380, 381. *See Four Guided Walks: pp146–7.*

This long crescent of golden sand, so close to the city, has long been a mecca for the sun and surf set (see pp56–7). Throughout the year, surfing enthusiasts visit from far and wide in search of the perfect wave, and inline skaters hone their skills on the promenade. Despite a growing awareness of the dangers of sun exposure (see p223) and an expansion of other cultural preoccupations, beach life still defines the lives of many Australians, who regard it as healthier than ever.

People seek out Bondi for its trendy seafront cafés and cosmopolitan milieu as much as for the beach. The pavilion, built in 1928 as changing rooms, has been a community centre since the 1970s. Note that Bondi Beach itself is an alcohol-free zone.

Bondi Surf Bathers' Life Saving Club

The founding of the surf lifesaving club at Bondi Beach in 1906 gave impetus to the formation of other local clubs, and ultimately to a global movement. An early club member demonstrated his new lifesaving reel, designed using hair pins and a cotton reel. Now updated, it is standard equipment on beaches worldwide. In 1938, Australia's largest surf rescue was mounted at Bondi, when more than 200 people were washed out to sea by freak waves. Five died, but lifesavers rescued more than 180, establishing their highly dependable reputation.

Bondi surf lifesaving team at the Bondi Surf Carnival, 1937

⑱ Captain Cook's Landing Place

Captain Cook Drive, Kamay Botany Bay National Park, Kurnell. **Tel** 9668 2000. ▥ 987. Toll Gate: **Open** 7am–7:30pm daily (to 5:30pm Jun–Jul). Visitor Centre: **Open** 9:30am–4:30pm daily. **Closed** 25 Dec. 🅿️ ♿ 🌐 nationalparks.nsw.gov.au

Although it is difficult to get to, visitors will find this place worth the effort. It is, after all, one of Australia's most important European historic sites. Here James Cook, botanists Daniel Solander and Joseph Banks and the crew of HMS *Endeavour* landed on 29 April 1770. Aboriginal peoples with spears were shot at. One, hit in the legs, returned with a shield to defend himself.

Nowadays people can cast a fishing line from the rock where the Europeans stepped ashore. Nearby are the site of a well where, Cook recorded, a shore party "found fresh water sufficient to water the ship" and a monument which marks the first recorded European burial in Australia.

There are also monuments to Solander, Banks and Cook, but it is the peaceful ambience that is most impressive. Now part of Kamay Botany Bay National Park, Captain Cook's Landing Place has lovely walks, some accessible to wheelchairs, where visitors may roam and observe the flora which led to the naming of Botany Bay.

The Visitor Centre in the park focuses on a number of themes: the bay's wetlands and the

Cook's Obelisk, overlooking Botany Bay, Captain Cook's Landing Place

Pampas grass and banana plants in the garden at Elizabeth Farm

importance of their conservation; an interesting exhibition detailing Cook's exploration of the area; and an introduction to Aboriginal customs and culture.

⑲ Sydney Olympic Park

Homebush Bay. **Tel** 9714 7888. ▤ Olympic Park. Visitors Centre (1 Showground Rd). **Open** 9am–5pm daily. **Closed** 1 Jan, Good Fri, 25 & 26 Dec. 🚻 ♿ 🅿️ 🚌 🌐 sydneyolympicpark.com.au

Once host to the 27th Summer Olympic Games and Paralympic Games, Sydney Olympic Park is situated at Homebush Bay, 14 km (8.5 miles) west of the city centre. Visitors can follow a self-guided walk or buy a ticket for a guided tour to access venues such as the Showground and the AllPhones. The interactive "ANZ Stadium Explore Tour" gives a taste of some of the stadium's best-loved sporting moments. For nature lovers, there is a tour of the five wetlands of the Bicentennial Park. You can buy tickets for tours at the Visitor's Centre.

Other facilities at the park include the Aquatic Centre, with a kids' waterpark, and the Tennis Centre, where you can play in the footsteps of such greats as Lleyton Hewitt. There are picnic areas and cafés throughout the park that provide a welcome rest stop for those exploring the large precinct on its extensive bicycle paths.

⑳ Elizabeth Farm

70 Alice St, Rosehill. **Tel** 9635 9488. ▤ Parramatta. ▥ Parramatta or Granville. **Open** 10:30am–3:30pm Sat & Sun (daily in Jan, NSW school hols & pub hols). **Closed** Good Fri, 25 Dec. 🅿️ ♿ 🎦 📷 🌐 sydneylivingmuseums.com.au

The discovery of fertile land at Parramatta, and the harvesting of its first successful grain crop in 1790, helped save the fledgling colony from starvation and led to the rapid development of the area.

This zone was the location of several of Australia's first colonial land grants. In 1793, John Macarthur, who became a wealthy farmer and sheep breeder, was granted 40 ha (100 acres) of land at Parramatta. He named the property after his wife and this was to be Elizabeth's home for the rest of her life. Macarthur was often absent from the farm as the centre of his wool operations had moved to Camden.

Part of the house, a simple stone cottage built in 1793, still remains and it is the oldest

John Macarthur (1766–1834), architect of the house at Elizabeth Farm

European building in Australia. Over the next 50 years, it developed into a substantial home with many features of a typical Australian homestead. Simply furnished to the period of 1820–50, with reproductions of paintings and other possessions, it is now a museum that strongly evokes the original inhabitants' life and times.

The kitchen at Hambledon Cottage restored to how it was in the first half of the 1800s

㉑ Hambledon Cottage

Cnr of Hassall St & Gregory Place, Parramatta. **Tel** 9635 6924. 🚆 Parramatta. **Open** 11am–4pm Thu–Sun. **Closed** Good Fri, 25 & 26 Dec. 🅿️ 🚻 🅰️

This delightful cottage, with its walls of rendered and painted sandstock, was built in 1824 as the retirement home for Penelope Lucas, governess to the Macarthur daughters. It is set in a park containing trees brought to Australia from as early as 1817 by John Macarthur.

Visitors can see rooms restored to the period of 1820–50. An 1830 Broadwood piano is one of the furniture exhibits. The kitchen has walls of convict-made bricks and contains original appliances and utensils.

㉒ Experiment Farm Cottage

9 Ruse St, Parramatta. **Tel** 9635 5655. 🚆 Harris Park. **Open** 10:30am–3:30pm Wed–Sun. **Closed** Good Fri, 18–31 Dec. 🅿️ 🚻 🅰️ (groups must book in advance).
Ⓦ **nationaltrust.org.au**

When his sentence expired in 1789, convict farmer James Ruse was given 0.6 ha (1½ acres) of land at Parramatta on which to start a farm, along with a hut, grain for sowing, vital farming tools, two sows and six hens. He successfully planted and harvested a wheat crop with his wife Elizabeth's help. She was the first female convict to be emancipated in New South Wales. In 1791, they were rewarded with a grant of 12 ha (30 acres), the colony's first land grant. Arthur Phillip, governor of the day, called it Experiment Farm.

In 1793, Ruse sold this farm to surgeon John Harris for £40. The date of the cottage is not certain, but it is believed to be early 1830s. The woodwork is Australian red cedar and the cottage is furnished according to an 1838 inventory.

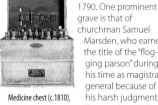

Medicine chest (c.1810), Experiment Farm

㉓ St John's Cemetery

O'Connell St, Parramatta. **Tel** 9891 0700. 🚆 Parramatta. 🚻

This walled cemetery – the oldest European cemetery in Australia – houses the graves of many convicts and settlers who arrived on the First Fleet in 1788. The oldest grave that can be identified is the flat sandstone slab simply inscribed, "H.E. Dodd 1791". Henry Edward Dodd, known to be Governor Phillip's butler, was the tenth person buried in the cemetery, but the location of the other nine graves is unknown.

The first recorded burial was of a child on 31 January 1790. One prominent grave is that of churchman Samuel Marsden, who earned the title of the "flogging parson" during his time as magistrate general because of his harsh judgments. The merchant Robert Campbell (see p68) and the father of explorer William Charles Wentworth (see p138), D'Arcy Wentworth, are also buried here.

㉔ Old Government House

Parramatta Park (entry by Macquarie St gates), Parramatta. **Tel** 9635 8149. 🚆 Parramatta. **Open** 10am–4:30pm Tue–Fri, 10:30am–4pm Sat, Sun & most public hols. **Closed** Good Fri, 25 Dec. 🅿️ 🚻 limited. 🅰️
Ⓦ **nationaltrust.org.au**

The central block of Old Government House is the oldest intact public building in Australia. This elegant brick structure, plastered to resemble stone, was built by Governor Hunter in 1799 on the site of a cottage constructed in 1790 for Governor Phillip. Wings to the side and rear were added between 1812 and 1818. The Doric porch, added in 1816, has been attributed to Francis Greenway (see p116).

Australia's finest collection of early 19th-century furniture is now housed inside.

The drawing room of Old Government House, Parramatta

FOUR GUIDED WALKS

Sydney's temperate climate and natural beauty make it an ideal city for walking. The following walks have been chosen for their distinct character; they all capture a view of the essential Sydney. You can follow the paths that trace the headlands and inlets around Watsons Bay; enjoy an invigorating clifftop walk at Bondi; catch glimpses of the original landscape in Manly's unspoilt bushland; or explore the narrow streets of historic Balmain. Three of the walks incorporate ocean or harbourside beaches, so be prepared in warmer weather by packing a swimsuit, towel and hat and wearing good-quality sunscreen. In Sydney's national parks and bushland all the indigenous flora and fauna are protected. The best sign of appreciation is to leave the bush as you found it. The *Tips for Walkers* provide practical information about each walk, listing accessibility by bus, train or ferry and the estimated distance of the walk, along with scenic rest areas, picnic spots, cafés and restaurants en route. There are some useful websites, such as www.imfree.com.au and www.sydneywalks.com.au, that give details of accompanied walking tours available throughout Sydney.

Key

••• Walk route

③ Metroad route

0 kilometres 3

0 miles 2

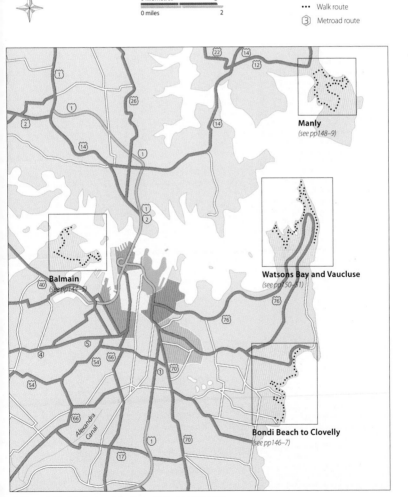

Manly
(see pp148–9)

Watsons Bay and Vaucluse
(see pp150–51)

Balmain
(see pp144–5)

Bondi Beach to Clovelly
(see pp146–7)

◄ The popular Bondi-to-Bronte coastal walk around Sydney's sandstone cliffs

A Two-Hour Walk Around Balmain

Historic Balmain village was named after William Balmain, a ship's surgeon on the First Fleet. In 1800, he was granted rights to 223 ha (550 acres) of the peninsula, which he later sold for a paltry 5 shillings in a dubious business transaction. From the mid-1800s, much of the land was subdivided for housing to support the then flourishing mining and maritime industries. Today, grand colonial and Victorian buildings stand side by side with tiny workers' cottages, adding variety to every street.

Colourful flower cart on Darling Street, Balmain

③ The Waterman's Cottage, made of locally sourced sandstone

East Balmain

Begin from the Balmain East Wharf at the bottom of Darling Street ①. By the 1840s, when the ferry service began, shipyards dotted these foreshores. The sandstone building at No. 10 Darling Street ②, once the Dolphin Hotel then the Shipwright's Arms, was a watering hole for sailors and ferrymen. Opposite is The Waterman's Cottage (1841) ③, home to Henry McKenzie, whose boat ferried residents to and from Sydney Town.

Turn left into Weston Street and walk through the Illoura Reserve for views of the city and Darling Harbour. Leave the park via William and Johnston Streets, stopping in the latter to view Onkaparinga ④, the colonial residence at No. 12. When building started in 1860, mussel shells from Aboriginal feasts stood in mounds upon the harbour foreshore beyond.

Turn left onto Darling Street then right into Duke Street. Gilchrist Place then leads down to Mort Bay Reserve ⑤. Ship's propellers stand as monuments to the area's working past. A path leads up to The Avenue's timber workers' cottages.

Back on Darling Street, turn left down Killeen Street. Take the path across Ewenton Park to Ewenton ⑥ (c.1854). Past the park, Hampton Villa ⑦ at 12B Grafton Street was home to state premier Henry Parkes.

Turn right into Ewenton Street and then left into Wallace Street, with its variety of early Australian architecture. The rough stone home at No. 1 is called the Railway Station as its narrow frontage makes it resemble one. The charming Clontarf ⑧ is at No. 4, while Maitland House ⑨ has a symmetry worth a second glance. Return to Darling Street.

The domestic grandeur of Louisa Road

Historic Links

Sydney's oldest extant lock-up, The Watch House (1854) ⑩ at No. 179 Darling Street, has been restored, but a ghostly female form remains. Further along, enjoy a drink at The London Hotel (1870) ⑪, where the balcony stools are made of old-fashioned tractor seats.

After the roundabout, visit St Andrew's Church ⑫ before losing yourself to the bookshops, cafés and delicatessens of Balmain. Every Saturday, Balmain Market fills the churchyard (see p203). At the shops' far end, the Victorian Post Office (1887) ⑬ and neighbouring Court House ⑭ reflect 1880s Sydney's prosperity. The Town Hall ⑮ dome was removed during World War II for fear of air raids. Across the street is the Fire Station ⑯ (1894). Set on the crest of a hill, its horse-drawn vehicles always travelled downhill on their outward journey.

Distant views of the city and Sydney Harbour Bridge from Snails Bay

Balmain to Birchgrove

Retrace your steps to Rowntree Street. Turn left and wander down to Birchgrove (about 10 minutes' walk). From Birchgrove shops ⑰, take Cameron Street left and Grove Street right, to Birchgrove Park ⑱ and Snails Bay. Walk down Rose Street to Louisa Road. Two of the most notable homes are Nos. 12 and 14, Keba (1878) and Vidette (1876) ⑲, where deep verandas and iron-lace balconies hint at colonial opulence. A poem in praise of the nearby park is inscribed on a plaque at Keba's entrance. Amid Vidette's formal greenery, a deep well is still fed by a natural spring. There is a wealth of interest in

Balmain War Memorial

the homes that follow: a tiny porch, Victorian entrance tiles, ornate iron lace – plus occasional glimpses of water frontage and private moorings. At the road's end, the reserve at Yurulbin Point ⑳ marks the mouth of Parramatta River. A fishing nook on its eastern corner is a perfect vantage point for taking in the city skyline and passing harbour traffic.

⑰ Shops nestled in the quiet Birchgrove village

Tips for Walkers

Starting point: Balmain East Wharf, end of Darling Street.
Length: 5.5 km (3¹/₂ miles).
Getting there: Ferries regularly leave Circular Quay for Darling Street's Balmain East Wharf. The 442 bus from the Queen Victoria Building stops in Darling Street. To return, there is a 15-minute ferry ride at hourly intervals from Birchgrove (pick up a schedule at Circular Quay). Alternatively, take Bus 441 from Grove Street (Snails Bay) back to the city (weekdays only).
Stopping-off points: Darling Street, in particular, has many good delicatessens, patisseries, restaurants and cafés. Places to picnic include Mort Bay Reserve, Gladstone Park, Birchgrove Park and Yurulbin Point.

Mort Bay

0 metres   250
0 yards   250

Key
···· Walk route

A Two-Hour Walk from Bondi Beach to Clovelly

This invigorating oceanside and clifftop walk explores the beautiful shoreline and surfing beaches of eastern Sydney. The local colour along this scenic trail is at its most vibrant at weekends, when people flock to the cafés and beaches. The Victorian cemetery at the walk's end bears witness to Sydney's multicultural heritage.

Icebergs Ocean Pool, one of two swimming-pools on Bondi Beach

A Seaside Community
Walk north along Campbell Parade ①, passing a colourful array of hotels, beachwear shops and lively cafés that give the street a raffish atmosphere. The stylish Gelato Bar at No. 140 makes an indulgent pit-stop. Keep walking until the Hotel Bondi ②, the parade's most significant building and easily spotted by its pretty clock tower. Opened as a first-class hotel in 1920, it initially stood quite alone by what was then a bush-fringed beach. Turn right,

Statue of lifesaver near Bondi Pavilion

crossing the road in front of the hotel, and walk down to Queen Elizabeth Drive leaving the traffic and noise of Campbell Parade behind as you reach Sydney's most famous beach, Bondi.

Bondi's popularity dates back to the 1880s. Although daylight bathing was banned at the time, the beach was considered a fashionable place to stroll. Bondi trams came into use shortly after and, by the time bathing restrictions were lifted in 1902, the red and white trams were filled with beachgoers. Just ahead you will see Bondi Pavilion ③. Built in 1928 to replace a modest timber building, it was designed on a grand scale and originally housed a ballroom, gymnasium, restaurant, café, Turkish baths and open-air theatre. Although decidedly less glamorous today, the complex is still a thriving local community centre hosting cultural events. Photographs inside recall the romance of Bondi Beach in earlier times.

Next to the Pavilion is the home of arguably Australia's oldest surf life saving club, the Bondi Surf Bathers ④ (see p139). Follow the sweep of the beach to its southern end.

Climb a flight of steps to continue on Notts Avenue, above Bondi Baths ⑤ and alongside the Bondi Icebergs clubhouse. Members of the Swimming Club swim every Sunday during the winter regardless of the weather.

Bronte's swimming baths, a safe alternative when the sea is rough

Bondi to Bronte
Veer left off Notts Avenue as the path drops down and skirts sharp rock formations, the result of years of erosion. Take the steep steps to Mackenzies Point lookout ⑥ on the headland. The magnificent view stretches for 180 degrees from Ben Buckler in the north to Malabar in the distant south.

Tips for Walkers
Starting point: Campbell Parade, southern end.
Length: 4 km (2½ miles).
Getting there: Take the train to Bondi Junction, then Bus 380 to Bondi Beach. Bus 339 runs from Clovelly Beach to Circular Quay. Waverley Cemetery is open from 8am to dusk every day.
Stopping-off points: Public toilets, showers and food and refreshments are available at Bondi, Tamarama and Bronte Beaches. Take-away cuisine can be bought along Bondi's Campbell Parade as the walk begins. Tamarama's beach café serves refreshing drinks. In warm weather, make the most of four of Sydney's best beaches by packing your swimming gear.

Tamarama Surf Life Saving Club, at the beach's northern end

Key
••• Walk route

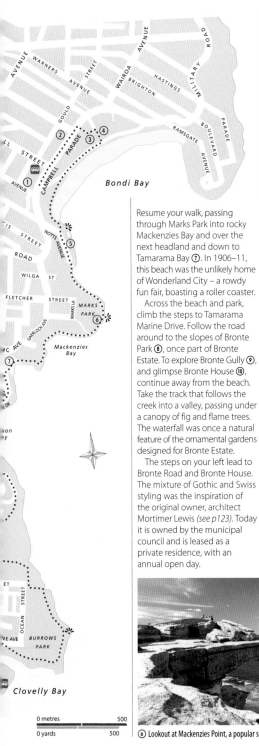

Irish Memorial, Waverley Cemetery,
a popular filming location

Bronte to Waverley

Continue down Bronte Road
towards the southern end of
Bronte Beach. After passing
Bronte's cafés, walk through
the car park and follow the
road uphill, through a cutaway
originally dug for trams. As the
road winds through the cutting
and veers right, take the steps
through Calga Reserve. Walk
down Trafalgar Street to the
Waverley Cemetery ⑪.

In grand displays of Edwardian
and Victorian monumental
masonry, English, Italian and Irish
residents have been laid to rest.
Among notable Australians buried
here are writers Henry Lawson
and Dorothea Mackellar; Fanny
Durack, the first woman to win an
Olympic gold medal (in 1912), and
do the Australian crawl swimming
stroke; and aeronautical pioneer
Lawrence Hargrave.

The Irish Memorial honours
the 1798 Irish Rebellion and its
leader Michael Dwyer, who was
transported to Australia for his
part in the uprising.

Leave the cemetery at the
southern end. Walk through
Burrows Park, hugging the
coast, to Eastbourne Avenue,
which leads to the walk's end
at Clovelly Beach ⑫.

Resume your walk, passing
through Marks Park into rocky
Mackenzies Bay and over the
next headland and down to
Tamarama Bay ⑦. In 1906–11,
this beach was the unlikely home
of Wonderland City – a rowdy
fun fair, boasting a roller coaster.

Across the beach and park,
climb the steps to Tamarama
Marine Drive. Follow the road
around to the slopes of Bronte
Park ⑧, once part of Bronte
Estate. To explore Bronte Gully ⑨,
and glimpse Bronte House ⑩,
continue away from the beach.
Take the track that follows the
creek into a valley, passing under
a canopy of fig and flame trees.
The waterfall was once a natural
feature of the ornamental gardens
designed for Bronte Estate.

The steps on your left lead to
Bronte Road and Bronte House.
The mixture of Gothic and Swiss
styling was the inspiration of
the original owner, architect
Mortimer Lewis (see p123). Today
it is owned by the municipal
council and is leased as a
private residence, with an
annual open day.

⑥ Lookout at Mackenzies Point, a popular spot for watching surfers

0 metres 500
0 yards 500

For keys to symbols see back flap

A Three-Hour Walk Around Manly

This walk takes in the holiday atmosphere of downtown Manly and its splendid surf beach, before passing along quieter shorelines and clifftop streets, and through unspoilt bushland replete with native flora and fauna. It features marvellous views, the commanding architecture of the historic building that was formerly St Patrick's Seminary, and the charm of Collins Beach and Fairy Bower.

Houses rising above Fairy Bower

Brass band plays in The Corso that links the harbour cove to the ocean beach

From Harbour to Ocean

Start at Manly Wharf ①. This suburb was little more than a cosy fishing village until 1852, when entrepreneur Henry Gilbert Smith's vision of a resort similar to fashionable Brighton in his native England started to take shape. The ferry service began in 1855, operating from the same spot in use today.

Leaving Manly Cove, cross The Esplanade and walk down The Corso, a pedestrian mall. At the end of The Corso, to the left, stands the New Brighton Hotel ② in striking Egyptian Classical

Revival Style. In 1926, it replaced the original New Brighton, built in 1880 as the resort's first attraction.

Head towards the rolling surf and sweeping sands of Manly Beach ③ then continue south along the promenade. From the 1950s-style Surf Pavilion, follow Marine Parade walkway around to Cabbage Tree Bay. The pretty area around the rock pool was named Fairy Bower ④ for the delicate wildflowers and maidenhair ferns that once grew on the hillside. Beyond the rock pool, continue on the pathway around to Shelly Beach ⑤, a secluded scuba diving and snorkelling spot, which is also ideal for child swimmers. The 1920s beach kiosk has been restored and converted into a smart restaurant.

Shelly Beach to the former St Patrick's Seminary

Across the park, take the steps to your left to Shelly Beach Headland. A path further left loops around the headland. Viewing platforms ⑥ overlook the vast South Pacific Ocean.

Take the car park exit into Bower Street. Follow the road as it rounds high above Fairy Bower,

passing by homes of diverse architectural styles, from Spanish Mission to Neo-Georgian. Turn left into College Street, then right into Reddall Street, and left again into Addison Road. Opposite the Victorian

1926

Detail on the New Brighton Hotel

Manly Wharf

Manly Cove

THE CORSO

WENTWORTH S

VICTOR

②

①

EAST WOOD

ESPLANADE

COVE AVENUE

ROAD

ADDISON

STUA

⑩

Little Manly Cove

MANLY POINT PEACE PARK

Little Manly Point

Tips for Walkers

Starting point: Manly Wharf
Length: 7.5 km (4¹/₂ miles).
Getting there: Regular ferry and Manly Fast Ferry services depart from Circular Quay.
Stopping-off points: The wide range of fresh food counters at Manly Pier make it an ideal place to stock up on picnic fare. Restaurants and cafés line The Corso and Manly Beach Promenade. The Boathouse at Shelly Beach offers the choice of a smart restaurant, barbecue or snack bar. In warm weather, come prepared with a swimsuit, hat, towel and sunscreen.

⑤ The clear waters of sheltered Shelly Beach

buildings at Nos. 97–99 and 95, a lane into Fairy Bower Road leads to views of the former St Patrick's Seminary, now the International College of Tourism and Hotel Management ⑦. Both Romanesque and Neo-Gothic architecture are in evidence in this 1885 edifice, built only after much deliberation by an essentially Protestant government.

Leave Fairy Bower Road by Vivian Street to turn left into Darley Road and arrive at the seminary building. Just opposite, is the site of the former Archbishop's House, once known as the Cardinal's Palace, which is being redeveloped.

⑦ The former St Patrick's Seminary, now the International College of Tourism

North Head Reserve

At the top of Darley Road, turn right beneath the Parkhill Sandstone Arch ⑧ into North Head Reserve. Follow the right-hand fork (leading to the Institute of Police Management) onto Collins Beach Road down through bushland alive with bird calls and native lizards. Paperbarks, smooth-barked apple trees and banksias are some of the native flora growing in abundance.

At the road's end, follow the track to your right across two footbridges, then down steps to Collins Beach ⑨. A stone cairn between the second footbridge and the beach marks where Governor Arthur Phillip was speared by the Aboriginal Wil-ee-ma-rin after a misunderstanding. The quiet waterfall and dense bushland make it possible to imagine this beach in pre-colonial days.

Leave via a small set of stone steps at the right-hand end of the beach which lead to a footpath, then out into Stuart Street.

Back to the Present

For memorable harbour views, follow the direction of Stuart Street through Little Manly Point Reserve, passing by the baths of Little Manly Cove ⑩. If you are reluctant to end this charming walk, turn left from Stuart Street and proceed to the end of Addison Road. Manly Point Peace Park offers a quiet place to take in a panorama of the distant city.

Return down Addison Road, making your way back to the wharf via Stuart Street and the East Esplanade. With its boat sheds and timber yacht clubs, the East Esplanade Park has a nautical atmosphere and is a relaxing place to meander. Continue past the attractions of the amusement pier to Manly Wharf, which was your starting point.

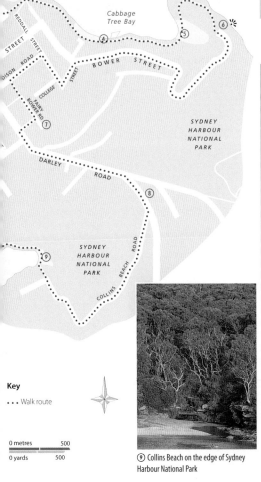

Key

••• Walk route

0 metres 500
0 yards 500

⑨ Collins Beach on the edge of Sydney Harbour National Park

For keys to symbols *see back flap*

A Three-Hour Walk in Watsons Bay and Vauclus

Tracing the perimeters of spectacular South Head, this walk touches on the area's colonial connections and takes in a variety of ocean and harbourside terrain, from headlands with sweeping views and crashing waves, to secluded coves, white sandy beaches and the streets of one of Sydney's most desirable neighbourhoods.

② Signal Station built in 1848, looking out over Dunbar Head

Macquarie Lighthouse to Camp Cove

The start of this walk is majestic Macquarie Lighthouse (1883) ①. A copy of the country's first lighthouse built in 1818 *(see p139)*, it stands on the same site.

Take the walk northwards, passing by the Signal Station ② following Old South Head Road. Before the station was built in 1848, a flag was hoisted to warn the colony of ships entering the harbour.

Continue along the footpath, where a plaque marks the location of Australia's worst maritime disaster. It was here that the migrant ship *Dunbar* crashed onto the rocks in a gale in 1857 *(see pp138–9)*. The only survivor was hauled to safety up the treacherous cleft in the cliff face known as Jacob's Ladder ③. From here, follow the descending path, arriving at the jutting stony ledges of The Gap ④.

① Bust, Macquarie Lighthouse

The *Dunbar's* anchor is here set into concrete, while salvaged personal effects are displayed at the Australian National Maritime Museum *(see pp96–7)*.

Taking the steps down from The Gap, bear right into the entrance of Sydney Harbour National Park. This single-lane roadway leads through natural bushland into HMAS *Watson* Military Reserve. Follow the road up to visit the Naval Memorial Chapel ⑤. A large clear window inside the chapel offers spectacular views of North Head and the Pacific Ocean. Resume your walk by taking the road out of the reserve, and then turn right into Cliff Street. Passing a row of

weatherboard cottages on your left, follow the street to its end and onto Camp Cove Beach ⑥. It was here in 1788 that Captain Arthur Phillip first stepped ashore after leaving Botany Bay to explore the coastline.

Camp Cove to Watsons Bay

Take the wooden steps at the northern end of the cove to make the 40-minute return walk to South Head. Above the steps are signs of colonial defences: a firing wall with rifle

Nudist Lady Bay beach, also known as Lady Jane beach

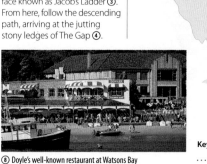

⑧ Doyle's well-known restaurant at Watsons Bay

Key

··· Walk route

⑩ Suspension bridge across Parsley Bay

slots; a cannon lying further along. After passing Lady Bay Beach, you will reach Hornby Lighthouse ⑦, which marks the harbour's entrance. Retrace your steps to Camp Cove Beach. Climb the western-end stairs to Laings Point, a defence post in World War II. A net stretching across the harbour mouth was anchored here to prevent enemy ships entering.

Follow Pacific Street to Cove Street, then along to Marine Parade and Wharf Beach in Watsons Bay ⑧ (*see pp138–9*). Named after Robert Watson of the First Fleet's *Sirius*, this was once first port of call for ships entering the harbour. Nearby, Doyle's restaurant offers seafood with a view. Follow the parade past the baths and tea rooms. Pilot boats ⑨ moored close by guide cruise and container ships into the harbour.

Watsons Bay to Vaucluse

Continue to secluded Gibsons Beach, taking the footpath left through native shrubbery, then right onto Hopetoun Avenue. Turn into The Crescent, tracing the curve of this exclusive street around to Parsley Bay Reserve. A short descent opens onto a suspension bridge hung across

the waters of tranquil Parsley Bay ⑩. Crossing the bridge, follow the pathway between two houses to arrive on Fitzwilliam Road. Continue right along Fitzwilliam Road, turning left into Wentworth Road to reach the extravagant Vaucluse House ⑪, surrounded by exotic gardens (*see p138*).

To finish your walk, make your way along Coolong Road to Nielsen Park (*see p138*) and Shark Bay ⑫. Protected from its namesake by a netted enclosure, the natural setting and safe waters of this beach make it a favourite for picnics.

③ Dramatic rock cleft known as Jacob's Ladder near The Gap

Tips for Walkers

Starting point: Macquarie Lighthouse.
Length: 8 km (5 miles).
Getting there: Take Bus 324 from Circular Quay, or Bus 387 from Bondi Junction. Return by Bus 325 from Nielsen Park.
Stopping-off points: There are public toilets and showers at Camp Cove, Watsons Bay, Parsley Bay and Nielsen Park. Food and refreshments are available throughout the walk at Watsons Bay, Parsley Bay, Vaucluse and Nielsen Park. The tea rooms at Vaucluse House offer views of the gardens, and the café at Nielsen Park sells homemade fare. The walk covers several harbour beaches where you can swim safely. In warm weather, bring a swimsuit, towel, hat and sunscreen, and allow time for swimming, sunbathing and picnicking.

⑪ Children's bedroom, one of the exhibits at Vaucluse House

BEYOND
SYDNEY

Exploring Beyond Sydney **154–155**

Pittwater and Ku-ring-gai
   Chase **156–157**

Hawkesbury Tour **158–159**

Hunter Valley **160–161**

Blue Mountains **162–163**

Southern Highlands Tour **164–165**

Royal National Park **166–167**

Exploring Beyond Sydney

To the east, Sydney is bounded by the Pacific Ocean; to the west, by the Great Dividing Range. To the north and south, within easy distance of the city, are superb beaches and stretches of coastal scenery, while inland, you will encounter waterfalls, deep valleys and fascinating flora and wildlife. On the Hawkesbury River, to the north and west of the city, are settlements of historical as well as scenic interest while, further north, the Hunter River meanders through sloping vineyards. The excursions on pages 156–67 offer the visitor the chance to sample the rich variety of Sydney landscapes from the exhilarating to the tranquil.

Three Sisters towering over the Jamison Valley

Façade of Hope Estate in the Hunter Valley

Sights at a Glance

❶ Pittwater and Ku-ring-gai Chase National Park
❷ Hawkesbury Tour
❸ Hunter Valley
❹ Blue Mountains
❺ Southern Highlands Tour
❻ Royal National Park

```
0 kilometres          50
0 miles          25
```

Getting Around

All the areas covered in these excursions can be easily reached by road from Sydney. Freeways and motorways take travellers part of the way to the Southern Highlands, Blue Mountains and Hunter Valley, while the other areas are accessible on sealed, well-signposted major roads. A number of tour operators offer guided one-day, or longer, tours to the Blue Mountains, Hunter Valley, Southern Highlands and South Coast, and parts of the Hawkesbury region. Sydney Trains has regular train services to the Blue Mountains, Royal National Park and to parts of the area covered by the Southern Highlands Tour. Ferries offer access to some parts of the Hawkesbury River.

Grand old house in Kiama, near the Southern Highlands

◀ Three Sisters at sunset, Blue Mountains

Mudgee
Glen Davis
86
Cullen Bullen
Portland
Bathurst
Meadow Flats
Orange, Dubbo
Walang
32 Lithgow
Zig Zag Railway
Tarana
Beram
Mount Victoria
Hampton
Blackheath
Oberon
BLUE MOUNT
MOUNT
Kato
Black Springs
Jenolan Caves
Porters Retreat
Richlands
Bullio
Taralga
Myrtleville
Bo
Chatsbury
Moss Val
Tarlo
Brayton
SOUT
31
Canberra
Morto
Bungonia
Nation
Park
Nerriga
Sass
Co
Beg

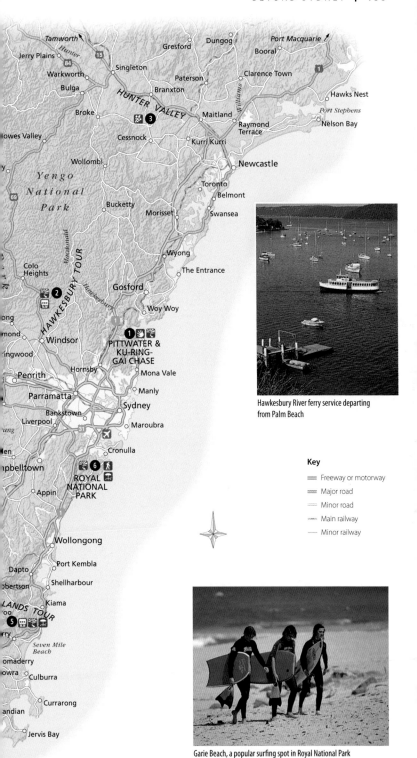

Tamworth

Jerry Plains

Hunter

Warkworth

Bulga

Broke

owes Valley

Singleton

Gresford

Dungog

Booral

Port Macquarie

Paterson

Branxton

Clarence Town

Hawks Nest

HUNTER VALLEY

Maitland

Williams

Raymond
Terrace

Port Stephens

Nelson Bay

Cessnock

Kurri Kurri

Wollombi

Yengo
National
Park

Bucketty

Morisset

Swansea

Newcastle

Toronto

Belmont

Wyong

The Entrance

Colo
Heights

HAWKESBURY TOUR

Macdonald

Hawkesbury

Gosford

Woy Woy

Windsor

ichmond

ringwood

Penrith

Parramatta

Bankstown

Liverpool

Hornsby

PITTWATER &
KU-RING-
GAI CHASE

Mona Vale

Manly

Sydney

Maroubra

Cronulla

ampbelltown

Appin

ROYAL
NATIONAL
PARK

Wollongong

Dapto

Port Kembla

Shellharbour

obertson

LANDS TOUR

Kiama

Seven Mile
Beach

omaderry

owra

Culburra

Currarong

andian

Jervis Bay

Hawkesbury River ferry service departing
from Palm Beach

Key

Freeway or motorway

Major road

Minor road

Main railway

Minor railway

Garie Beach, a popular surfing spot in Royal National Park

For keys to symbols *see back flap*

❶ Pittwater and Ku-ring-gai Chase

Pittwater and the adjacent Ku-ring-gai Chase National Park
lie on Sydney's northernmost outskirts. They are bounded
to the north by Broken Bay, at the mouth of the Hawkesbury
River *(see pp158–9)*. Sparkling waterways and golden beaches
are set against the unspoiled backdrop of the national
park. Picnicking, bushwalking, surfing, boating, sailing and
windsurfing are popular pastimes with visitors. The Hawkesbury River system curls around an ancient sandstone
landscape rich in Aboriginal rock art, and flora and fauna.

**Coal and
Candle Creek**
The pretty inlet is
typical of eroded
valleys formed during
the last Ice Age. Water
that melted from the
ice caps flooded the
valleys to form the
bays and creeks of
Broken Bay.

*Brisbane
Nationc*

Patonga

Hawkesbury River

*Juno
Point*

*Gunyah
Beach*

*Hungry
Beach*

*Challenger
Head*

Cowan Creek

Refuge Bay

West Head R...

*Cowan
Point*

*Ku-ring-gai Ch
National Par*

*Cottage
Point*

Coal and Candle Creek

Smiths Creek

Akuna Bay
The isolated marina, general store
and café serve the Hawkesbury
River boating fraternity.

*Akuna
Bay*

General San Martin Drive

McCarrs Creek Road

*Ryde,
Chatswood*

Aboriginal Art in Ku-ring-gai Chase

Ku-ring-gai Chase has literally
hundreds of Aboriginal rock art
sites, providing an insight into
one of the world's oldest cultures.
The most common are rock
engravings, generally made in
groups with as many as 100
individual figures. They include
whales up to 8 m (26 ft) long,
fish, sharks, wallabies, echidnas
and Ancestral Spirits such as
Daràmulan, who created the
land, its people and animals.

Aboriginal rock art near the Basin,
Ku-ring-gai Chase

```
0 kilometres          2

0 miles         1
```

Key

▬▬ Major road

═══ Secondary road

═══ Minor road

▢ National Park

- - Ferry route

– – Walk route

Palm Beach Wharf

Palm Beach, a haven for sea birds such as pelicans, is popular with sun-seekers. It is also the base for the boats that visit and deliver supplies to the isolated communities on Pittwater and the Hawkesbury.

Pittwater

This graceful finger of water separates Palm Beach from Ku-ring-gai Chase. Pittwater boasts secluded beaches, picnic areas and several hamlets that can only be reached by water.

Whale Beach

Spectacular houses seem to hug the cliffs overlooking this fine surf beach. The Palm Beach Peninsula's beaches are often less congested than those closer to the city.

Tips for Travellers

Distance from Sydney: About 30 km (19 miles). **Duration of journey:** About 45 minutes to Mona Vale Beach. **Getting there:** Take Military Rd on the city's North Shore and cross the Spit Bridge. Follow Pittwater Rd to Mona Vale Beach. **When to go:** The Christmas holiday period is the peak season and beaches can be crowded. Ku-ring-gai Chase offers everything from shoreline to bushwalks and can be enjoyed year round. **Where to stay and eat:** Contact the visitors' information centre for full details of facilities. **Tourist information:** Bobbin Head Info Centre. **Tel** 9472 8949. **Open** 9am–4pm Mon–Fri. **Closed** Christmas Day. W npws.nsw.gov.au

Bilgola Beach

A small community of residents backs this patrolled surf beach set against a pretty rainforested valley. Wooden steps lead down from the ridge above through coastal heathland.

Map labels:

Broken Bay

Lion Island

Barrenjoey Head

West Head

Palm Beach

Mackerel Beach

Pittwater

Whale Beach

Careel Bay

Longnose Point

...lers Bay

Barrenjoey Road

Bilgola Plateau

Avalon Beach

Bilgola Beach

Scotland Island

Newport Beach

Church Point

...eek

Bungan Beach

Mona Vale Road

Mona Vale Beach

Pittwater Road

...yde, ...hatswood

Dee Why, Manly ↓

❷ Hawkesbury Tour

Australia's longest eastward-flowing river, the Hawkesbury-Nepean, forms Sydney's northern and western boundaries. It was at first thought to be two separate rivers until further exploration revealed that they were in fact one. The section known as the Hawkesbury runs from the Colo River Valley to Broken Bay in the north *(see pp156–7)*.

Settled in 1794, by 1799 the Hawkesbury Valley's small farms produced three-quarters of the colony's grain. Its riverscape is little changed since then and much of the area remains a quiet backwater. It is an area rich in relics of the early colonial period, including towns and villages established during the Macquarie era of 1810–19 *(see p26)*. It is also a place of great scenic grandeur, with magnificent vistas of one of Australia's most beautiful rivers.

⑤ Tizzana Winery
A touch of Tuscany on the banks of the Hawkesbury, this sandstone winery was built in 1887 by Dr Thomas Fiaschi. It is open to visitors on weekends and public holidays.

④ Ebenezer Uniting Church
Built in 1809, the church and its 1817 schoolhouse have been superbly restored. The tree under which services were first held still stands.

③ Colo River Drive
This pretty route travels along the Putty Road to Colo, then follows the river to Lower Portland.

⑥ Portland Reach
On the river, pleasure craft have replaced the grain barges of the past, but the area's farming community survives.

Singleton

Colo River

Kurranjong heights

Ebenezer

Pitt Town

Parramatta

② Tebbutts Observatory
John Tebbutt (1834–1916), an early amateur astronomer, built this observatory in Windsor in 1854, where he studied the solar system and discovered a comet in 1861.

⑦ Sackville Ferry
It only takes a few minutes to cross the river by cable ferry.

① Windsor
Built in 1815, the Macquarie Arms Hotel is just one of Windsor's fine early colonial buildings. Many others, including several by architect Francis Greenway *(see p116)*, remain from the town laid out in 1810.

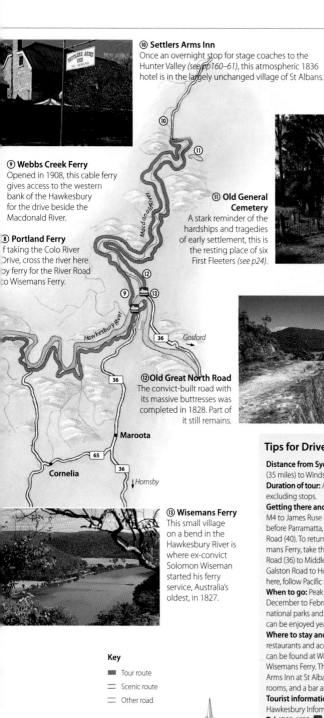

⑩ Settlers Arms Inn
Once an overnight stop for stage coaches to the Hunter Valley *(see pp160–61)*, this atmospheric 1836 hotel is in the largely unchanged village of St Albans.

⑨ Webbs Creek Ferry
Opened in 1908, this cable ferry gives access to the western bank of the Hawkesbury for the drive beside the Macdonald River.

⑧ Portland Ferry
If taking the Colo River Drive, cross the river here by ferry for the River Road to Wisemans Ferry.

⑪ Old General Cemetery
A stark reminder of the hardships and tragedies of early settlement, this is the resting place of six First Fleeters *(see p24)*.

⑫ Old Great North Road
The convict-built road with its massive buttresses was completed in 1828. Part of it still remains.

Gosford

Maroota

Cornelia

Hornsby

⑬ Wisemans Ferry
This small village on a bend in the Hawkesbury River is where ex-convict Solomon Wiseman started his ferry service, Australia's oldest, in 1827.

Tips for Drivers

Distance from Sydney: 55 km (35 miles) to Windsor.
Duration of tour: About 3½ hours, excluding stops.
Getting there and back: Follow M4 to James Ruse Drive (53) just before Parramatta, then Windsor Road (40). To return from Wisemans Ferry, take the Old Northern Road (36) to Middle Dural, then Galston Road to Hornsby. From here, follow Pacific Highway south.
When to go: Peak season is from December to February. The river, national parks and small towns can be enjoyed year round.
Where to stay and eat: Cafés, restaurants and accommodation can be found at Windsor and Wisemans Ferry. The Settlers Arms Inn at St Albans has a few rooms, and a bar and restaurant.
Tourist information: Hawkesbury Information Centre. **Tel** 4560 4620. **W** hawkesbury tourism.com.au

Key

▬ Tour route
═ Scenic route
═ Other road

0 kilometres   5
0 miles   5

❸ Hunter Valley

Some of the earliest vineyards to be planted in Australia were on the fertile flats of the Hunter River in the 1830s, developing a thriving industry in fortified wine. Since the 1970s, it has evolved into a premium wine district *(see pp184–5)*. With some 90 wineries, the area is a great weekend trip from Sydney. Hot air ballooning, golf and horse riding are other popular activities in the region. The Jazz in the Vines festival takes place in October. Many wineries open daily but it is best to phone ahead and check.

Brokenwood
Under the ownership of Ian Riggs, this medium-sized winery has produced some of the region's finest Shiraz from the Graveyard vineyard, as well as an excellent Sémillon.

Lindemans
In 1842, Dr Henry John Lindeman resigned his naval commission to establish a vineyard in the Hunter Valley. His company has been a major producer in the Australian wine industry ever since.

Personalities of the Hunter Valley

The wine industry seems to attract or create larger-than-life characters. Among the legends was the great Len Evans, writer, wine judge, *bon vivant* and founder of the ambitious Hope Estate and Evans Family Wines, as well as Tower Estate. His contemporaries included Max Lake, a Sydney surgeon who started Lake's Folly as a weekend winery, and the late Murray Tyrrell, patriarch of a wine-making family that produced its first Hunter vintage in 1864 and proudly retains its independence.

Len Evans checking grape vines

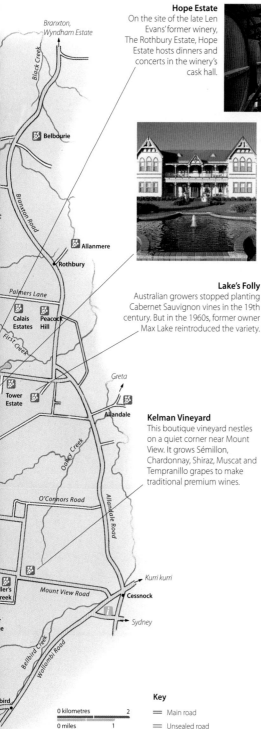

Hope Estate
On the site of the late Len Evans' former winery, The Rothbury Estate, Hope Estate hosts dinners and concerts in the winery's cask hall.

Pepper's Convent
A restored 1909 convent is now an elegantly appointed guest house, with the Pepper Tree vineyard and winery and Robert's Restaurant only a short walk away.

Lake's Folly
Australian growers stopped planting Cabernet Sauvignon vines in the 19th century. But in the 1960s, former owner Max Lake reintroduced the variety.

Kelman Vineyard
This boutique vineyard nestles on a quiet corner near Mount View. It grows Sémillon, Chardonnay, Shiraz, Muscat and Tempranillo grapes to make traditional premium wines.

Tips for Travellers

Distance from Sydney: 160 km (100 miles).
Duration of journey: About 2 hours from the centre of Sydney.
Getting there and back: Take the Sydney–Newcastle F3 freeway north of Sydney and follow the signs to Cessnock. Another route is through the picturesque Wollombi Valley. Allow about 3 hours as there are unsealed roads.
When to go: Year round. The best grapes are harvested between January and March.
Where to stay and eat: There is a wide variety of motels, guest-houses, self-catering cottages and cabins, cafés and restaurants.
Visitor information: Hunter Valley Wine Country Tourism, 455 Wine Country Drive, Pokolbin. **Tel** 4990 0900.
W winecountry.com.au
Further afield: The Upper Hunter vineyards are about 40 minutes by car northwest of Pokolbin.

Key
0 kilometres 2
0 miles 1
═ Main road
═ Unsealed road

For keys to symbols *see back flap*

⊙ Blue Mountains

The Blue Mountains, now a UNESCO World Heritage Site, prevented westward expansion of the European colony until 1813, when explorers Gregory Blaxland, William Lawson and William Charles Wentworth found a way across. The magnificent scenery, characterized by rugged cliffs and rock formations, ravines and waterfalls, is best appreciated on the bushwalks that wind along cliff tops and through valleys. The restaurants, cafés and antique shops in the centre of Katoomba will tempt the less energetic. The mountains are named for the blue haze, caused by light striking eucalyptus oil particles in the air.

Zig Zag Railway
Steam trains travelled this railway until fire destroyed the historic carriages in 2013; services are due to resume in 2015.

KEY

① **Mount York**

② **Victoria Falls**

③ **The Grose River** flows between the two roads crossing the mountains.

④ **The Cathedral of Ferns** is a remnant of the temperate rainforest that once covered this area.

⑤ **Mount Banks**

⑥ **Kings Tableland**

⑦ **Jamison Valley**

⑧ **Leura village** is listed by the National Trust. Nearby are Leura Cascades, floodlit at night and one of the prettiest sights in the mountains.

Zig Zag railway

Jenolan caves

Grose Valley from Govetts Leap
Considered by many to be the most imposing view in the Blue Mountains, a great panorama with a series of ridges stretches into the far distance.

Three Sisters
This giant rock formation near Echo Point takes its name from an Aboriginal legend. The story tells of three sisters turned to stone by their witch-doctor father to keep them safe from an evil bunyip or monster.

Jenolan Caves

About 55 km (34 miles) south-west of Mount Victoria is a magical series of spectacular underground limestone caves with icy blue rivers and fleecy limestone formations. They are surrounded by an extensive wildlife reserve. People have been making the trek here since the caves were discovered in 1838, staying originally in the Grand Arch cave and later in the Edwardian splendour of Jenolan Caves House, which still operates today.

The vividly coloured Pool of Cerberus at Jenolan Caves

Key

— Major road

Other road

•• Suggested walk

Mount Wilson

A picturesque village with cultivated gardens and exotic trees, it has been called a "little corner of the northern hemisphere". Some gardens are open to the public in spring and autumn.

Mount Tomah Botanic Gardens

This superbly landscaped garden, specializing in cool-climate plants, has sweeping views over the Grose Valley.

Richmond

Norman Lindsay Gallery and Museum

The stone cottage is home to a collection of works by artist and writer Norman Lindsay (1879–1967).

Wentworth Falls

An impressive double waterfall is the starting point for the National Pass track, a challenging four-hour return walk to the next valley.

0 kilometres 5
0 miles 3

Tips for Travellers

Distance from Sydney: About 105 km (65 miles).
Duration of journey: About 90 minutes to Wentworth Falls.
Getting there and back: Follow Metroad route 4 and the Great Western Highway. Return by Bells Line of Road to Windsor. State Rail has regular services to the area. An Explorer Bus runs from Katoomba train station at 9:30am on weekends and public holidays.
When to go: Year round. Always be prepared for the cold, especially when hiking, as the weather can change rapidly in all seasons.
Where to stay and eat: Contact the Visitor Information Centre.
Tourist information: Blue Mountains Visitors' Information Centre, Echo Point, Katoomba. **Tel** 1300 653 408. **W** **visitblue** **mountains.com.au**

For keys to symbols *see back flap*

❺ Southern Highlands Tour

This easily accessible area to the south of Sydney is often said to be more typical of Great Britain than Australia. It is actually a delightful combination of both: Australian high country and coastal hinterland with many European qualities. It is a land of abrupt hills and valleys, waterfalls and streams; of quaint villages, cosy restaurants, antique shops and elegant places to stay. The tour takes in spectacular Seven Mile Beach and the pretty town of Berry before heading to Kangaroo Valley, sleepy Bundanoon and the antique shops and wineries of Berrima and Bowral. An exhilarating adjunct to the tour is nearby Minnamurra Falls with its boardwalk through rainforest.

⑧ **Bowral**
This highlands town holds a famous spring tulip festival every year and is home to cricket's Bradman Museum.

⑦ **Berrima**
By-passed by the railway in the 19th century, the only Georgian village in the highlands remains one of the most picturesque.

⑥ **Bundanoon**
Romantic guesthouses and a glow-worm cave make this town a popular weekend destination.

⑤ **Fitzroy Falls**
Part of Morton National Park, the falls plunge 80 m (262 ft) into the subtropical rainforest below. The falls lookout has access for the disabled and walking trails with stunning views.

0 kilometres   10
0 miles   5

Key

▬▬ Tour route
═ Scenic route (alternative)
═ Other roads

④ **Kangaroo Valley**
Hampden Bridge, a castellated suspension bridge, crosses the Kangaroo River at this small village. The river idyllic place for canoei

Berrima Gaol

Completed in 1839 by convict labour, this Georgian sandstone jail is featured in Rolf Boldrewood's classic 1888 bushranging novel, *Robbery Under Arms*. The fictitious character Captain Starlight, who escapes from Berrima, describes it as "the largest, most severe, the most dreaded of all prisons in New South Wales".

① Kiama
The historic town began life in the 1820s as a port for shipping cedar. Its blowhole can spurt water as high as 60 m (200 ft).

② Seven Mile Beach
Part of a national park and best seen from Gerroa's Black Head, the beach is flanked by dunes and hardy coastal vegetation, including forest and swamp. It is a great fishing, swimming and picnicking spot.

Tips for Drivers

Distance from Sydney: 120 km (75 miles).
Duration of tour: About 3½ hours, excluding stops.
Getting there and back: Take Metroad route 1, then follow the F3 freeway and Princes Hwy (1) to Kiama. Return via the F5 freeway (31) from Mittagong, then Metroad route 5 into the city.
When to go: Year round.
The beaches are best in summer, and the gardens are at their peak in spring and autumn.
Where to stay and eat: Eating places, hotels and guesthouses are found all over the area.
Tourist information:
Kiama Visitors Centre, Blowhole Point, Kiama. **Tel** 4232 3322.
🆆 **kiama.com.au**
Southern Highlands Visitors Information Centre, 62–70 Main St, Mittagong. **Tel** 4871 2888.
🆆 **visitsouthern highlands. com.au**

③ Berry
This town, surrounded by lush dairy country, is well known for its main street lined with shady trees, antique and craft shops, tea rooms and historic buildings. The Berry Museum, built in 1886, is in a former bank.

❻ Royal National Park

Designated as a national park in 1879, the "Royal" is the oldest national park in Australia. It covers 16,000 ha (37,100 acres) of landscape typical of the Sydney Basin sandstone. To the east, waves from the Pacific Ocean have undercut the sandstone and produced majestic coastal cliffs broken occasionally by small creeks and some spectacular beaches. Streams flowing north and east have incised deep river valleys. Heath vegetation on the plateaux merges with woodlands on the upper slopes. The park is ideal for bushwalking, picnicking, camping, swimming and birdwatching.

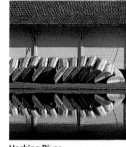

Hacking River
Boating, fishing and canoeing are common water sports.

Audley
A popular picnic area since the Edwardian era, it has a pavilion that was built in 1901. Look out for the 1920s dance hall also in the park.

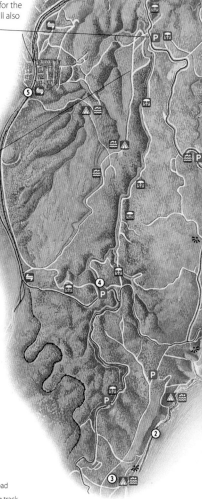

Lady Carrington Drive
Named after a governor's wife and now closed to vehicles, the road is crossed by 15 creeks and is delightful to walk or cycle. It also leads to the track to Palona Cave.

KEY

① **Garie Beach** is a popular surf beach accessible by road.

② **Figure Eight Pool**

③ **Werrong Naturist Beach**

④ **The Forest Path** follows a circular route, passing through subtropical rainforest.

⑤ **Heathcote**

⑥ **Cronulla**

⑦ **Jibbon Lagoon**

⑧ **Little Marley Beach**

Key

— Main road

Walking track

Bundeena
Enclosed by national park on three sides, the small settlement at the mouth of the Hacking River may be reached by ferry from Cronulla or by road through the national park.

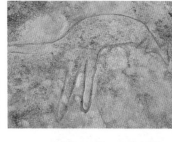

Jibbon Head
Guided tours of the Jibbon Head Aboriginal rock engravings site may be arranged.

Deer Pool
One of many fresh-water pools in the park, this sheltered spot is on the track from Bundeena Drive to Marley and Little Marley.

Wattamolla Lagoon
This pretty picnic spot has a lagoon with a waterfall at its edge and a protected ocean beach.

```
0 kilometres        4
0 miles        2
```

Curracurrang
This rock formation is about halfway along the two-day Coast Walk. Sea eagles and terns nest in caves at the base of this rocky cove which also has a secluded swimming hole and waterfall.

Tips for Travellers

Distance from Sydney: 34 km (21 miles).
Duration of journey: About 1 hour from the centre of Sydney.
Getting there: Follow Metroad route 1 south to Sutherland, then the signs to Heathcote and Wollongong. The turn-off to Farnell Avenue and the park entrance is shortly after Sutherland.
When to go: Year round, but conditions for walking in summer can be hot so allow for this. If bushwalking, carry fresh water at all times and check on the fire danger at the Visitors' Centre.
Where to stay and eat: There are kiosks at Audley, Garie Beach and Wattamolla. Camping details can be obtained at the Visitors' Centre.
Tourist information: Royal National Park Visitors' Centre, Farnell Ave, Audley. **Tel** 9542 0648. **W** npws.nsw.gov.au
Guided Walks, Adventure Tours and Kayak Hire: **Tel** 9544 5294.
W bundeenakayaks.com.au

For keys to symbols *see back flap*

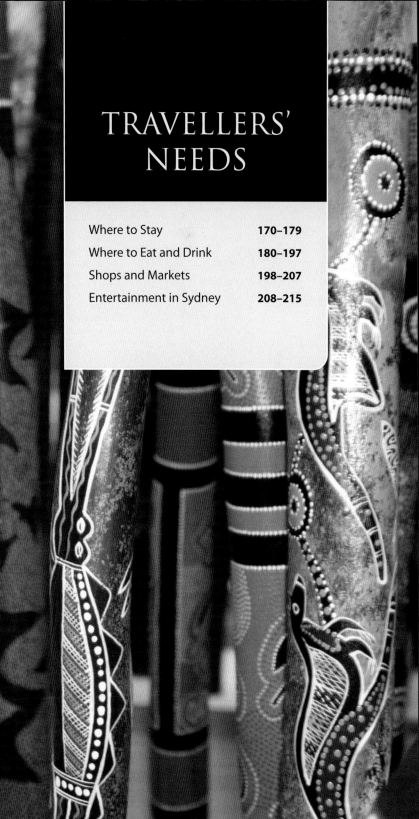

TRAVELLERS' NEEDS

Where to Stay   170–179
Where to Eat and Drink   180–197
Shops and Markets   198–207
Entertainment in Sydney   208–215

WHERE TO STAY

Australia's emergence as a major tourist destination, coupled with a building boom in the lead-up to Sydney hosting the 2000 Olympic Games, resulted in a large pool of quality and value accommodation choices for visitors, ranging from five-star luxury to the homeliness of a small, unpretentious hotel. In addition to hotels, Sydney has self-catering apartments, homestay accommodation and back-packer hostels for those travelling on a budget. History buffs can find a range of accommodation in buildings with interesting post-European-settlement heritage, particularly from colonial times to the early 1900s, in the "older" parts of Sydney – the Rocks, the finger wharves at Walsh Bay and Woolloomooloo, and Paddington and Darlinghurst. The hotels listed on pages 174–9 are among the best in Sydney and cater to a variety of different budgets and requirements.

Where to Look

Most of the expensive hotels are in or near the city centre and by the harbour, but it is possible to find accommodation within most price ranges throughout Sydney. The city centre has the advantage of having many of the larger theatres, museums, galleries and shops at hand, as well as easy transport access to more distant sights.

Cheaper accommodation can be found in the vibrant Kings Cross and Darlinghurst district. Choices here range from backpacker hostels to small "boutique" hotels where the emphasis is on quality and personal service. Many of these low-rise buildings may be three storeys but do not have lifts due to heritage regulations. Ask about stairs and ground-floor rooms if mobility is a problem.

In The Rocks area, with its beautifully restored colonial buildings, you can opt for a bed and breakfast in a traditional Sydney pub or the opulence of a five-star luxury hotel with harbour views.

The hotels around Darling Harbour, Chinatown and Surry Hills offer good value for shoppers and are also within easy reach of the city centre. Quaint Paddington has fewer options, mostly smaller boutique and bed-and-breakfast offerings.

Just beyond the city fringe, the vibrant, scruffy and arty inner west suburbs of Newtown, Enmore and Glebe are home to numerous affordable accommodation choices, while still being close to the city.

Eating alfresco at the Admiral Collingwood Lodge (see p177)

The popular beachside suburbs of Bondi, Coogee and Manly are a little way out of the centre of Sydney but provide the opportunity to enjoy beach life, particularly in spring and summer, and yet still be reasonably near to the city.

Many pubs provide basic accommodation, usually on the floor above the ground-floor bar areas. Bear in mind it can be noisy at night, especially at weekends and if live music is playing. Check closing times and entertainment before booking if you are a light sleeper.

How to Book

It is advisable to book well in advance, especially for December and January, the Gay and Lesbian Mardi Gras Festival in February to early March, Easter, the school holidays and when major sporting events are held.

Bookings can be made online, by phone or email, or through your local international travel agent. A credit card number is usually required to secure your booking. Some providers will accept bank cheques in Australian dollars. Check cancellation requirements, and reconfirm before you arrive in Sydney.

The **Sydney Visitors Centre** books certain hotels and has a wealth of options on its website. **Australian Accommodation Services** arranges bookings for all styles of accommodation.

The stunning Full Harbour View junior suite at the Four Seasons Hotel Sydney (see p177)

◀ Detail of hand-painted didgeridoos

you belong to a motoring association, ask your travel agent to check which hotels affiliated with the NRMA (National Roads and Motorists' Association) offer a discount. **NSW TrainLink** travel centres at major railway stations offer a comprehensive service, and AFTA travel agencies will book most major hotels. Tourist information centres can also offer valuable advice about where to stay in Sydney.

Discount Rates

The best way to secure discount rates is by booking directly on the accommodation providers' website. Virtually all accommodation styles, from hostels to luxury, offer online booking. Most will show their best online flexible rate – a sensible choice if there is a chance you may need to cancel or change the booking. The best rates are usually for those with "no cancellation" clauses attached, so beware if your plans may change. It is always worth asking for the corporate rate at which hotels give discounts for group or company bookings.

At the weekend there are fewer business clients in the city centre, so this is the time when prices are frequently cheaper in the top hotels. Smaller operators often reduce the daily rate for bookings of five and seven days or longer. Asking

The opulence and understated elegance of The Langham *(see p179)*

for a room without a harbour or ocean view is another good way of reducing the costs. (You may still be able to secure an upgrade at check-in if the hotel isn't full.)

The **Travellers Information Service** in the city can often arrange discounts off the price of regular hotel accommodation rates (this does not normally apply to budget hotels) to those who book in person on the day a room is required.

Hidden Extras

Breakfast is usually charged on top of the room rate in the more expensive hotels. It is best to avoid consuming any of the contents of the mini-bar until you have checked the price. Alcohol and snacks are usually much more expensive here than in shops. While free Wi-Fi is increasingly offered (at least in the shared areas of the accommodation), many hotels still impose hefty charges for in-room Wi-Fi. Also, be wary of telephone charges. There will almost certainly be a considerable mark-up on any calls you make from your room. In general, tipping is not widespread, but it is expected in the more expensive hotels. You should make a note of the check-out time when you arrive, or negotiate a late check-out, since a surcharge may be incurred if you stay later.

Special Offers

Hotels promote special deals heavily on their own websites, so check regularly before your trip for any deals. They also often cooperate with airlines, theatres and entertainment and sporting event promoters to provide package deals that include discounted accommodation. "Special occasion" packages (such as for anniversaries or honeymoons) are available at the top end of the market.

Disabled Travellers

Most new hotels now provide special wheelchair access and toilets for the disabled, but many older establishments will have more limited facilities.

Spinal Cord Injuries Australia's website provides information for disabled travellers, including transport (public transport, driving and hiring) and public toilet locations. Its online publication *RollAwayz* opens in Google Earth to show the location of wheelchair-accessible accommodation across Australia.

Sydney-based **Time Flys Travel** focuses on planning travel, including hotels and specialized transport for the disabled.

Travelling with Children

It is worth inquiring about special rates or deals that allow children to stay in their parents'

The stunning 1850s sandstone façade of the Radisson Blu Plaza Hotel *(see p178)*

Bet's B&B, a self-contained studio in the suburb of Annandale *(see p175)*

room for no extra cost. Most hotels in Sydney welcome children, although you should ask about special facilities before booking.

Self-Catering Flats

Accommodation including full kitchen and laundry facilities offers the traveller greater independence. In addition to comfort, they also provide good value because the living space is larger than standard hotel rooms and the prices are competitive.

All the "apartment" hotels in the listings on pages 174–9 offer self-catering facilities. In addition, Sydney has several agencies that can help visitors to arrange self-catering accommodation *(see p173)*.

Private Homes

European-style bed-and-breakfast accommodation in a private home can be an ideal way to experience a city. It is fast becoming a popular alternative to more impersonal hotel rooms for many people who choose to visit Sydney. Most, but not all, bed-and-breakfast-type accommodation includes breakfast, so it is wise to check when booking.

People from all walks of life offer rooms in a variety of house styles and locations. Agencies such as **Bed and Breakfast NSW** and the **Homestay Network** make it easy to search for suitable accommodation from centralized listings.

Budget Accommodation

As a favoured destination for many young travellers, Sydney has a large number of hostels that cater specifically to their needs. Standards vary widely, but, at their best, hostels offer excellent value.

It is best to book in advance or call hotels ahead of arriving to make sure a room or bed is available. Kings Cross and the southern end of the city near Central Station have the largest concentration of cheap accommodation.

G'day Backpackers and **Pink House** are smaller hostels offering good facilities in restored buildings close to Kings Cross. Pink House also provides help if you need to find work in Sydney.

Blue Parrot Backpackers is situated in a converted mansion in the quieter end of Potts Point, with a sunny garden courtyard and large, cosy common room complete with fireplace.

YHA Australia is a useful source of information when planning your trip, offering advice about travel deals, as well as helping you decide on your itinerary and find places to stay. Two other useful online sources that provide lists of budget hostels in Sydney are hostels. com and hostelworld.com.

Halls of Residence are another good option for travellers on a budget. Student rooms with shared bathroom facilities are available at the **University of Sydney** over the summer break from late November to mid-February. The university is conveniently close to the city

and to public transport, and the moderate price usually includes breakfast.

Gay and Lesbian Accommodation

Lesbian and gay visitors are welcome in all of Sydney's hotels. In fact, quite a number of places cater primarily to same-sex couples, particularly in small hotels in the inner-city areas of Darlinghurst, Paddington, Newtown and Surry Hills.

At the **IGLTA** (International Gay and Lesbian Travel Association) and the **Gay and Lesbian Tourism Australia** websites, you can search for gay or gay-friendly travel-related businesses, including hotels, guest-houses and tours.

Camping

Although not an option in the city itself (other than on the harbour at Cockatoo Island, *see p108*), camping is available in several national parks close to Sydney.

The Royal National Park *(see pp166–7)* has a camp site with facilities at Bonnie Vale, just outside Bundeena. Free bush or "walk-in" camping is allowed in several other places, but you should ring the park in advance to obtain the necessary camping permit.

At The Basin camp site in **Ku-ring-gai Chase National Park** *(see pp156–7)*, there are toilets, cold showers, barbecue facilities and a phone.

There are basic camp sites near Glenbrook, Woodford, Blackheath and Wentworth Falls in the **Blue Mountains National Park** *(see pp162–3)*. **Jenolan Caravan Park** in Oberon has cabins and caravans for hire, as well as camping pitches with and without electric hook-ups. You will need to book if you want to camp at the Euroka Clearing near Glenbrook, but this is not necessary for the other sites. Bush camping is also permitted in the park, but there are some restrictions. Contact the national park for more details before you visit.

Recommended Hotels

The accommodation options featured in this guide have been selected for their excellent facilities and unique appeal. They have been divided into a number of categories to help you make the best choices for your trip.

There are a wide range of apartments available to rent for short stays in Sydney. Some are privately owned and others are maintained by bigger companies. All have been furnished to a high standard and offer independent living in the centre of the city.

B&Bs are dotted throughout the city. Accommodation can range from no-frills digs to luxurious rooms in beautiful heritage buildings.

The cosiness of a roaring fire at The Lord Nelson Brewery Hotel *(see p178)*

Basic hotels, hostels and chain hotels may lack character, but those listed in this guide offer great value for money, with good quality rooms and excellent service.

Boutique hotels place an emphasis on chic design. They generally offer the same facilities and services as larger hotels, but in a more intimate setting.

There are a number of historic hotels to choose from in Sydney. These are situated in places with a unique history and are often decked out with period features.

Luxury hotels provide five-star facilities, most with stunning views and beautifully decorated rooms.

Outstanding hotels are highlighted as a DK Choice. These hotels offer something really special, be it excellent service, opulent decor, a huge range of amenities, or something entirely unique.

DIRECTORY

Discount Agencies

Travellers Information Service – coach bookings
Sydney Coach Terminal, Eddy Ave, NSW 2000.
Map 4 E5.
Tel 9281 9366.
Fax 9281 0123.

Useful Booking Addresses

Australian Accommodation Services
Tel 9974 4884.
Fax 9974 1692.
w tourist.net

NSW TrainLink
Central Railway Station.
Map 4 E5. **Tel** 132 829.

Sydney Visitors Centre
Cnr Argyle & Playfair Sts, The Rocks, NSW 2000.
Map 1 A2.
Tel 1800 067 676.
w sydney.com

Disabled Assistance

Ideas Incorporated
81 Caper St, Tumut, NSW 2720.
Tel 1800 029 904 or 6947 3377.
w ideas.org.au

Spinal Cord Injuries Australia
1 Jennifer St, Little Bay, NSW 2036. **Tel** 9661 8855 or 1800 819 775.
Postal address: PO Box 397, Matraville, NSW 2036.
w scia.org.au

Time Flys Travel
577 Sydney Rd, Seaforth, NSW 2092.
Tel 9949 5099.
w timeflystravel.com.au

Self-Catering Agencies

Medina
359 Crown St, Surry Hills, NSW 2010. **Map** 5 A3.
Tel 1300 633 462.
w medina apartments.com.au
Also nine other locations.

Pacific International Hotels
Sydney, Chatswood and Parramatta.
Tel 1300 987 604.
w pacificinthotels.com

Homestay Agencies

Bed and Breakfast NSW
Tel 1300 888 862.
w bbfaccommodation.com.au

Oz Bed & Breakfast
w ozbedand breakfast.com

Homestay Network
PO Box 270, Beecroft, NSW 2119. **Tel** 9412 3100.
w homestaynetwork.com.au

Hostels

Backpackers World Travel
477 Kent St, NSW 2000.
Tel 9262 7277.

Hostel World
w hostelworld.com

Blue Parrot Backpackers
87 Macleay St, Potts Point, NSW 2011.
Tel 9356 4888.
w blueparrot.com.au

G'day Backpackers
153 Forbes St, Woolloo-mooloo, NSW 2011.
Map 5 B1. **Tel** 9358 4327.

Pink House
6–8 Barncleuth Sq, Kings Cross, NSW 2011.
Map 5 C1.
Tel 1800 806 385.
w pinkhouse.com.au

University of Sydney
International House
Tel 9950 9800.
St John's College.
Tel 9394 5200.

Sancta Sophia.
Tel 9577 2100.
Wesley College.
Tel 9565 3333.
Women's College.
Tel 9517 5000.

YHA Australia
Level 3/9 Castlereagh St, NSW 2000. **Map** 1 B4.
Tel 9261 1111.
w yha.com.au

Gay and Lesbian Accommodation

Gay and Lesbian Tourism Australia
w galta.com.au

IGLTA
PO Box 20891, World Square, NSW. **Tel** 9575 4869. w iglta.org

Camping

Blue Mountains National Park
Tel 4787 8877.

Jenolan Caravan Park
Tel 6336 0344.

Ku-ring-gai Chase National Park
Tel 9472 8949.

Royal National Park
Tel 9542 0648.

Where to Stay

Apartments

The Rocks and Circular Quay

Rendezvous Hotel Sydney $$
75 Harrington St, The Rocks
Tel *9251 6711*   **Map** 1 B2
W tfehotels.com/brands/rendezvous-hotels/rendezvous-hotel-sydney-the-rocks
Good-sized apartments with kitchenettes in an excellent location. Some rooms come with harbour views. There is also a lovely outdoor pool with a café.

The York Apartment $$
5 York St
Tel *9210 5000*   **Map** 1 A3
W theyorkapartments.com.au
Sizable and well-appointed rooms are available here. The standard rooms have older-style decor but are still perfectly acceptable. Can be noisy on the lower floors.

City Centre

Fraser Suites Sydney $$
488 Kent St
Tel *8823 8888*   **Map** 4 E3
W sydney.frasershospitality.com
Comfortable accommodation with all mod cons in an edgy 42-storey tower with a striking glass façade designed by architect Sir Norman Foster.

Meriton Pitt Street $$
329 Pitt St
Tel *8263 7400*   **Map** 4 E3
W meritonapartments.com.au/sydney/pitt-street
Immaculate, clean and well-managed modern apartments in the heart of the city. There is an on-site pool, spa, sauna and gym. A large supermarket is just a block away.

Darling Harbour and Surry Hills

Adina Apartment Hotel Crown Street $$
359 Crown St, Surry Hills
Tel *8302 1000*   **Map** 5 A3
W tfehotels.com/brands/adina-apartment-hotels/adina-apartment-hotel-sydney-crown-street
Functional, clean and comfortable accommodation, if lacking a bit of natural light. Lovely palm-fringed pool and room service from the wonderful Bill's restaurant next door.

Meriton Serviced Apartments Campbell Street $$
6 Campbell St
Tel *9009 7000*   **Map** 4 F4
W meritonapartments.com.au/sydney/campbell-street
Spacious and modern apartments with helpful extras such as free Wi-Fi and a washer/dryer.

Meriton World Tower $$
95 Liverpool St
Tel *9263 7500*   **Map** 4 E3
W meritonapartments.com.au/sydney/world-tower-sydney
Outstanding modern apartments in Sydney's tallest residential tower. Floor-to-ceiling windows offer stunning views.

Zara Tower Serviced Apartments $$
61–65 Wentworth Ave
Tel *8228 7659*   **Map** 4 F4
W zaratower.com.au
Spacious apartments on the city fringe, with gourmet kitchen appliances and a choice of pillows. Although this is a convenient location, it is not especially pretty.

DK Choice

Adge Boutique Apartment Hotel $$$
222 Riley St, Surry Hills
Tel *8093 9888*   **Map** 4 F4
W adgehotel.com.au
Daring design and colourful, bold styling – think pink fridges and gaudy striped carpet. These two-bedroom urban apartments sit in the heart of the inner city's best café and dining area. Includes quality amenities and extras, such as a complimentary welcome drink.

The entrance to Meriton Serviced Apartments Campbell Street

Price Guide
Prices are based on one night's stay in high season for a standard double room, inclusive of service charges and taxes.

$	up to A$150
$$	A$150 to A$350
$$$	over A$350

Kings Cross and Darlinghurst

Regent's Court Apartments $$
18 Springfield Ave, Potts Point
Tel *9331 2099*   **Map** 2 E1
W regentscourtsydney.com.au
A character Art Deco building with warmth and charm in a pretty, tree-lined street. There are 25 self-contained studios, all with access to a gorgeous rooftop garden.

Woolloomooloo Waters Apartment Hotel $$
88 Dowling St, Woolloomooloo
Tel *8837 8000*   **Map** 2 E5
W waldorf.com.au/serviced-apartments/woolloomooloo-waters-apartment-hotel.html
Not waterfront despite the name – it's a block back from the bay (although it does have a small indoor pool). Basic, no frills apartment with a good light breakfast included.

Further Afield

Balmain Wharf Apartments $$
10 Darling St, Balmain
Tel *4455 3044*
W balmainwharf.com.au
You're not in the city here, but you get great views of it from this charming sandstone building. A ferry service right outside can take you to the city centre.

Meriton Bondi Junction $$
97 Grafton St, Bondi Junction
Tel *8305 7600*
W meritonapartments.com.au/sydney/bondi-junction
Halfway between the city and Bondi Beach, and surrounded by shopping choices from luxury to markets. Here you will find clean, spacious, well-equipped rooms with great views.

Adina Apartment Hotel Bondi Beach $$$
69–73 Hall St, Bondi
Tel *9300 4800*
W tfehotels.com/brands/adina-apartment-hotels/adina-apartment-hotel-bondi-beach
These small, modern but pricey apartments with a beachhouse feel are in the hip Hall St strip that runs down to the beach.

B&Bs

The Rocks and Circular Quay

Sydney Harbour B&B $$
140–142 Cumberland St, The Rocks
Tel 9247 1130   **Map** 1 B2
W bbsydneyharbour.com.au
An restored historic mansion with
communal lounge, garden and
nine clean, comfortable rooms.
The pretty colonial-style furniture
is in keeping with the location.

Darling Harbour and Surry Hills

Brickfield Hill $$
403 Riley St, Surry Hills
Tel 9211 4886   **Map** 4 F5
W brickfieldhill.com.au
Four rooms (only one with a
private bathroom) in a vibrant
neighbourhood. Breakfast is not
included, but some of Sydney's
best cafés can be found nearby.

Kings Cross and Darlinghurst

Victoria Court $$
122 Victoria St, Potts Point
Tel 9357 3200   **Map** 2 E5
W victoriacourt.com.au
Basic, old-style rooms and a
generous continental-style
breakfast served by a bubbling
fountain in the courtyard
conservatory. Friendly hosts.

Paddington

Hart's Home Stay $$
91 Stewart St, Paddington
Tel 9380 5516   **Map** 6 D4
W bbbook.com.au
A 19th-century, Gothic-style
cottage with a central courtyard
in a quiet residential street. It is
just a short stroll away from the
cafés and shops of Oxford Street.

DK Choice

Kathryn's on Queen $$
20 Queen St, Woollahra
Tel 9327 4535   **Map** 6 E4
W kathryns.com.au
Tranquil, luxurious accom-
modation in a National Trust-
listed home with a secluded
courtyard in one of Sydney's
finest streets for antiques and
designer shopping. Of the two
rooms, opt for Le Grand, with
French doors opening to a
balcony that overlooks the leafy
street below.

Unique interiors at Adge Boutique Apartment Hotel *(see p174)*

Further Afield

Australia Street Guesthouse $
146 Australia St, Newtown
Tel 9557 0702
W australiastreetguesthouse.
com.au
A large, older-style two-storey
house filled with retro furniture
and Aboriginal and contem-
porary art. No breakfast, but there
is a kitchenette, and it's also just a
short walk to King St cafés.

Dadirri Church Street Apartment $
238 Church St, Newtown
Tel 0430 883 067
W dadirri.com.au
A split-level apartment opposite
a park, with a master bedroom
and small loft-style child's room.
No breakfast, but there is an eat-
in kitchen for preparing meals.

Windermere $
31 Cliff St, Manly
Tel 9977 7363
W windermeremanly.com.au
Two spacious bedrooms with
bathrooms in a pretty building
just a short stroll from the ferry
and beach. Continental breakfast
provisions are provided.

101 Addison Rd B&B $$
101 Addison Rd, Manly
Tel 9977 6216
W bb-manly.com
Character-filled property in a quiet
street close to the beach. Warm
host Jill shares local knowledge
and serves a great breakfast in
your private living room.

Bet's B&B $$
176 Johnston St, Annandale
Tel 9660 8265
W betsbandb.com.au
Self-contained two-level studio in
the quaint suburb of Annandale,
with good cafés, boutiques and
parks. There are regular buses to
the city (a 20-minute ride away).

Bundeena Beach B&B $$
75 Bundeena Drive, Bundeena
Tel 9527 9977
W beachbedandbreakfast.com.au
Step off the front lawn and on to
the beach at this self-contained
luxury accommodation with
breakfast. Explore the nearby
Royal National Park, or relax in the
double spa bath and open shower.

Forsyth B&B $$
3 Forsyth St, Glebe
Tel 9552 2110   **Map** 3 A3
W forsythbnb.com
Outstanding hospitality and
breakfast, just a minute's walk
from Blackwattle Bay. Quick bus
or Light Rail to the city. Hosts do
airport pick-up and drop-off for a
very reasonable charge.

Golden Grove B&B $$
30 Golden Grove St,
Cnr Abercrombie St, Darlington
Tel 8003 7333
W bedbreakfastsydney.com.au
Two large, fully self-contained
apartments between the city
fringe and vibrant Newtown.
Breakfast provisions provided.
Art installations feature in the
old shopfront window.

Manly Harbour Loft B&B $$
12 George St, Manly
Tel 9949 8487
W manlyloft.com.au
Well-appointed, well-located, and
with a private entrance through a
courtyard, this lovely room has
a tiny balcony with water views.
Clean and comfortable.

Tara Guesthouse $$
12 Edgeware Rd, Enmore
Tel 9519 4809
W taraguesthouse.com.au
Think Soho, Bohemia and artists'
digs. This is a gracious place to
stay in a busy area that is full of
character – just like the owners.
Free airport transfers.

For more information on types of hotels *see pages 172–3*

Basic Hotels

The Rocks and Circular Quay

The Mercantile Hotel $
25 George St, The Rocks
Tel *9247 3570*   **Map** 1 B2
W themercantilehotel.com.au
Spacious rooms (some with Jacuzzi baths), with period fittings and marble fireplaces. A continental breakfast is included. Basic-rate rooms share a bathroom.

City Centre

Travelodge Wynyard $$
7–9 York St
Tel *9274 1222*   **Map** 1 A4
W tfehotels.com/brands/travelodge-hotels/travelodge-wynyard-york-street
No fancy extras, just good, clean rooms and a central location that is ideal for exploring the city. Rooms near the old lifts tend to be noisiest.

Y Hotel Hyde Park $$
5–11 Wentworth Ave
Tel *9264 6288*   **Map** 4 F3
W yhotels.com. au/y-hotel-hyde-park
Excellent-value accommodation in a prime spot in the city, with basic continental breakfast and clean, functional rooms. Opt for a courtyard-facing room, as street-facing rooms can be noisy.

Darling Harbour and Surry Hills

Aaron's Hotel Sydney $$
37 Ultimo Rd, Haymarket
Tel *9281 5555*   **Map** 4 D4
W aaronssydney.com.au
No bells and whistles here – just good-value, well-kept digs in an ideal location for exploring the southern end of the city. It is also very close to transport links for exploring the rest.

DK Choice

Vibe Sydney $$
111 Goulburn St
Tel *8272 3300*   **Map** 4 E4
W tfehotels.com/brands/vibe-hotels/vibe-hotel-sydney
Neat and clean, simple yet comfortable, this hotel has almost 200 rooms and is located in the heart of the city. It is within easy walking distance of most major attractions. Facilities include a bar and café, and there is also a small but attractive pool on the roof.

Kings Cross and Darlinghurst

The Bayswater $
17 Bayswater Rd, Kings Cross
Tel *8070 0100*   **Map** 5 B1
W sydneylodges.com/lodges/the-bayswater-sydney/
Great-value rooms in a convenient spot for transport, shops and restaurants. There's a nice guest lounge area with kitchenette.

Hotel 59 $
59 Bayswater Rd, Rushcutters Bay
Tel *9360 5900*   **Map** 5 C1
W hotel59.com.au
Great-value, family-run place with just nine rooms. Complimentary breakfast is served in the property's street-front café.

Mariners Court $$
44–50 McElhone St, Woolloomooloo
Tel *9320 3888*   **Map** 2 E5
W marinerscourt.com.au
Clean, comfortable rooms in a great location. The place is reasonably quiet for a busy area, and there are plenty of good dining choices nearby.

Sydney City Lodge $$
146 Crown St, Darlinghurst
Tel *8354 1001*   **Map** 5 A1
W sydneycitylodge.com.au
This pleasant hotel is within easy walking distance of the city and airport train. Rooms at the back and on higher floors are quietest.

Paddington

Arts Hotel $$
21 Oxford St, Paddington
Tel *9361 0211*   **Map** 5 B3
W artshotel.com.au
Friendly, family-run hotel with small basic rooms. The decor is starting to date a little. Quieter garden rooms face a central courtyard with a small pool.

Further Afield

Alishan Guesthouse $
100 Glebe Point Rd, Glebe
Tel *9566 4048*   **Map** 3 A5
W alishan.com.au
Functional, no frills accommodation with a communal kitchen for preparing meals. Convenient location on Glebe's main street.

The Merton Hotel $$
38 Victoria Rd, Rozelle
Tel *8065 9577*
W themertonhotel.com.au
A pub on a main road with clean rooms and breakfast included. It also has a good bistro and offers live music in the evenings. Some rooms can be a little noisy.

Central courtyard and pool at the friendly, family-run Arts Hotel

Boutique Hotels

The Rocks and Circular Quay

Harbour Rocks Hotel $$
34 Harrington St, The Rocks
Tel *8220 9999*   **Map** 1 B2
W harbourrocks.com.au
This hotel offers very small, basic rooms in a heritage building located in a central location. The staff are friendly.

City Centre

Park8 $$
185 Castlereagh St
Tel *9283 2488*   **Map** 1 B5
W park8.com.au
Small, stylish, somewhat dark rooms, with a 24-hour, guests-only espresso bar. Rooms vary.

DK Choice

QT Sydney $$$
49 Market St
Tel *8262 4000*   **Map** 1 B5
W qtsydney.com.au
Kooky, cutting edge and a little over the top, this designer hotel, set within the Art Deco historical State Theatre and Gowings building, is one of a kind. It has an in-house "design and art curator", and customer-service staff wear red wigs.

Darling Harbour and Surry Hills

1888 Hotel Pyrmont $$
139 Murray St, Pyrmont
Tel *8586 1888*   **Map** 3 C2
W 1888hotel.com.au
This is a vibrant, stylish converted wool store that has been meticulously restored with recycled wooden beams.

Pensione Hotel $$
631–635 George St
Tel 9265 8888 **Map** 4 E4
ⓦ pensione.com.au
Convenient hotel in a busy area.
A bit of a maze to get through the
corridors, but the rooms are clean
and generally well maintained.

Botanic Gardens and The Domain

Sir Stamford at Circular Quay $$
93 Macquarie St
Tel 9252 4600 **Map** 1 C3
ⓦ stamford.com.au/sscq
Character and charm from a
historic hotel offering gracious,
old-fashioned service and good
modern amenities.

Kings Cross and Darlinghurst

Larmont Sydney $$
2–14 Kings Cross Rd, Kings Cross
Tel 9295 8888 **Map** 5 B1
ⓦ diamant.com.au
Modern, stylish rooms close to
lots of eateries and transport.
Lovely staff, and there is free Wi-Fi
and iPads for guests' use.

Medusa $$
267 Darlinghurst Rd, Darlinghurst
Tel 9331 1000 **Map** 5 B1
ⓦ medusa.com.au
A labyrinth of 18 rooms, styled to
maximize comfort and privacy.
There is also a pretty courtyard
with a reflection pool.

Simpsons of Potts Point $$
8 Challis Ave, Potts Point
Tel 9356 2199 **Map** 2 E4
ⓦ simpsonshotel.com
A peaceful and elegant property.
Relax in the character-filled
drawing room with a fireplace,
books and sherry or port. Breakfast
is in a charming conservatory.

Further Afield

Admiral Collingwood Lodge $$
5 Collingwood St, Drummoyne
Tel 9181 3881
ⓦ admiralcollingwoodlodge.com.au
A lovely 1880s Italianate mansion
with well-kept rooms near waterfront parklands. There are regular
buses and ferries to the city.

Ravesi's $$$
118 Campbell Parade, Bondi
Tel 9365 4422
ⓦ ravesis.com.au
Beachside glamour and elegance.
Stay in one of 12 chic, individually
styled rooms. The iconic beach is
right across the road.

Chain Hotels

The Rocks and Circular Quay

Four Seasons Hotel Sydney $$$
199 George St
Tel 9250 3100 **Map** 1 B3
ⓦ fourseasons.com/sydney/
Harbour views, a handy location
and top-notch facilities for
business and leisure travellers.
The service is excellent.

Holiday Inn Old Sydney $$$
55 George St, The Rocks
Tel 9252 0524 **Map** 1 B2
ⓘ ihg.com/holidayinn/hotels/
us/en/sydney/sydgs/hoteldetail
A step back in time to colonial
Sydney. Old-world charm complemented by modern facilities.

City Centre

Hilton Sydney $$
488 George St
Tel 9266 2000 **Map** 1 B5
ⓦ hiltonsydney.com.au
There are no waterfront views
here, but it is right in the pulsing
city centre. Pop into the historic
Marble Bar downstairs.

Swissotel Sydney $$
68 Market St
Tel 9238 8888 **Map** 4 E2
ⓦ swissotel.com/hotels/sydney
The colourful kids rooms – stocked
with age-appropriate toys and
facilities – are great for families.

Darling Harbour and Surry Hills

Travelodge Wentworth Ave $
27–33 Wentworth Ave
Tel 9267 1700 **Map** 4 F4
ⓦ tfehotels.com/brands/
travelodge-hotels/travelodge-
sydney
Basic, simply furnished rooms.
Surprisingly quiet despite its
size and central location, this is a
handy base from which to explore.

Novotel Sydney on Darling Harbour $$
100 Murray St, Pyrmont
Tel 9934 0000 **Map** 3 C2
ⓦ noveldarlingharbour.com.au
Lovely location and views.
The lobby, dining and meeting
areas have all been renovated,
but the rooms would also
benefit from a bit of a revamp.

Rydges World Square $$
389 Pitt St
Tel 8268 1888 **Map** 4 E3
ⓦ rydges.com/accommodation/
sydney-nsw/world-square-sydney-
cbd/
Good hospitality and service, a
terrific central location, and neat
and tidy rooms. Furnishings could
do with some updating.

Kings Cross and Darlinghurst

Ibis Budget Sydney East $
191–201 William Street, Kings Cross
Tel 9326 0300 **Map** 5 B1
ⓦ accorhotels.com.au/hotel/ibis-
budget-sydney-east
Lives up to low-cost expectations.
Very basic rooms. Street-facing
ones can be noisy due to traffic
and nightlife. Cheerful staff.

Further Afield

Novotel Manly Pacific $$
55 N Styne, Manly
Tel 9977 7666
ⓦ novotelmanlypacific.com.au
Opposite the beach with plenty
of on-site dining and entertainment options, as well as a lovely
rooftop pool.

Quest Bondi Junction $$
28 Spring St, Bondi Junction
Tel 9078 1700
ⓦ questapartments.com.au
Three train stops from the city,
a short bus ride to the beach
and shopping of every kind
at your doorstep, here you will
find pleasant, modern well-
appointed rooms and facilities.

Bright and spacious room at the Admiral Collingwood Lodge

For more information on types of hotels *see pages 172–3*

Historic Hotels

The Rocks and Circular Quay

The Lord Nelson Brewery Hotel $$
19 Kent St, The Rocks
Tel *9251 4044* **Map** 1 A2
🔣 lordnelsonbrewery.com
This venue is brimming with history and personality. The top floor of this celebrated pub, Australia's oldest pub brewery, offers cosy rooms with stone walls and rustic decor.

Pier One Sydney Harbour $$
11 Hickson Rd, Walsh Bay
Tel *8298 9999* **Map** 1 A2
🔣 pieronesydneyharbour.com.au
The 1912 Pier One wharf played a role in Sydney's early shipping and cargo history. This beautiful hotel has revived and preserved this historic landmark.

The Russell Hotel $$
143a George St, The Rocks
Tel *9241 3543* **Map** 1 B2
🔣 therussell.com.au
The site of the colony's "movable hospital" in 1790, this charming hotel sits above the historic Fortune of War pub. Lovely staff, a quaint sitting room, a well-stocked library and a rooftop garden.

City Centre

The Grace $$
77 York St
Tel *9272 6888* **Map** 1 A4
🔣 gracehotel.com.au
Built by Grace Bros in the 1920s as a showpiece department store, this place is a fine example of Neo-Gothic architecture with a contrasting Art Deco interior.

Radisson Blu Plaza Hotel $$$
27 O'Connell St
Tel *8214 0000* **Map** 1 B4
🔣 radissonblu.com/plazahotel-sydney
With its stunning 1850s sandstone façade, this was once home to John Fairfax & Sons' newspaper empire and the Bank of NSW. Today, you'll find exceptional comfort and service.

Paddington

The Hughenden $$
14 Queen St, Woollahra
Tel *9363 4863* **Map** 6 E4
🔣 thehughenden.com.au
A restored grand mansion with a colourful history: it has been a masonic hall, a nurses' home and a dance hall.

Further Afield

DK Choice

Cockatoo Island $$
Cockatoo Island
Tel *9700 4100*
🔣 cockatooisland.gov.au
Why stay by the harbour when you can stay on it? This is the only harbour island where you can stay overnight, just a short ferry ride from the city. Embrace your sense of adventure and explore its convict and shipbuilding history, then relax on the balcony or deck of a self-contained apartment.

Q-Station $$
North Head Scenic Drive, Manly
Tel *9466 1500*
🔣 qstation.com.au
Stay in Sydney Harbour National Park and take history or ghost tours of the 1830s North Head Quarantine Station *(see p135)*.

Beyond Sydney

The Carrington $$
15–47 Katoomba St, Katoomba
Tel *4782 1111*
🔣 thecarrington.com.au
This 1883 grand old lady was a magnet for Sydney's elite, and the southern hemisphere's most popular retreat from the early 1900s. Bags of old-world charm.

The Hydro Majestic $$$
Great Western Highway, Medlow Bath
Tel *4782 6885*
🔣 hydromajestic.com.au
Stretching 1.1 km (0.7 miles) along the escarpment overlooking the Megalong Valley, this magnificent property's Art Deco-styled 54 guest rooms reflect its rich heritage and the glitz and glamour of yesteryear.

Modern fittings and a stunning view at Pier One Sydney Harbour

Hostels

The Rocks and Circular Quay

DK Choice

Sydney Harbour YHA $$
110 Cumberland St, The Rocks
Tel *8272 0900* **Map** 1 B2
🔣 yha.com.au
Private rooms with harbour views here cost slightly more than standard hostels – but less than a meal in a nearby fine-dining restaurant. Clean double, family and dormitory rooms, and just a short walk to major attractions and transport. Incredible views to the Opera House from the relaxing, expansive rooftop deck.

Darling Harbour and Surry Hills

Big Hostel $
212 Elizabeth St
Tel *9281 6030* **Map** 4 E4
🔣 bighostel.com
Clean place, attracting less of the party crowd than other hostels. Free basic breakfast – toast, cereal, coffee, tea. Slow Wi-Fi in the common areas.

Railway Square YHA $
8 Lee St
Tel *2981 9666* **Map** 4 D5
🔣 yha.com.au
Next to Central Station, stay in a private room in the historic 1904 main building or a funky, shared railway carriage.

Wake Up! $
509 Pitt St
Tel *9288 7888* **Map** 4 E5
🔣 wakeup.com.au
Fun, modern backpacker accommodation in a convenient location with shared and private rooms. There are free activities like barbecues, pool competitions and guided city orientation tours. Good on-site café and bar.

Kings Cross and Darlinghurst

Eva's Backpackers $
6 Orwell St, Potts Point
Tel *9358 2185* **Map** 2 E5
🔣 evasbackpackers.com.au
Small, clean rooms, with little extras like free Wi-Fi on the ground floor. (High-speed Internet in your room for a small charge.) A rooftop terrace for barbecues.

Luxury Hotels

The Rocks and Circular Quay

The Langham $$$
89–113 Kent St, Millers Point
Tel *8248 5220* **Map** 1 A2
W sydney.langhamhotels.com.au
This is a charming, bright, impossibly pretty hotel that strikes a wonderful balance between opulence and understated elegance. It also has a magnificent indoor pool, with a sky-dappled star ceiling.

DK Choice

Park Hyatt $$$
7 Hickson Rd, The Rocks
Tel *9256 1234* **Map** 1 B1
W sydney.park.hyatt.com
Impeccable attention to detail in the best harbourfront location, with views straight across the water to the Opera House. This intimate, low-rise hotel has just 155 spacious guest rooms and suites, contemporary interiors and floor-to-ceiling glass doors that open to private balconies. The rooftop pool area is lovely, too.

Pullman Quay Grand Sydney Harbour $$$
61 Macquarie St
Tel *9256 4000* **Map** 1 C3
W pullmanquaygrandsydney harbour.com
Get a room with a spectacular view at this spacious, upscale, all-suite property on the edge of Circular Quay, with the Opera House as your next-door neighbour.

Quay West Suites $$$
98 Gloucester St, The Rocks
Tel *9240 6000* **Map** 1 A3
W quaywestsuitessydney.com.au
Enjoy a swim with a view of the Harbour Bridge in the stunning, sunken, Roman-style heated pool on level 24 of this truly opulent apartment hotel.

City Centre

Establishment Hotel $$$
5 Bridge Lane
Tel *9240 3100* **Map** 1 B3
W merivale.com.au/accommodation/ establishmenthotel/
The effortlessly cool Establishment is tucked away in a hidden lane. It has beautifully appointed rooms, access to a private gym, and a handful of Sydney's best restaurants, bars and clubs all under one roof.

Guests sunning themselves on the terrace at Big Hostel *(see p178)*

Sheraton on the Park $$$
161 Elizabeth St
Tel *9286 6000* **Map** 1 B5
W sheratonontheparksydney.com
Michael Jackson got married in this hotel, which is set in an idyllic spot opposite Hyde Park. There is also a lovely indoor rooftop pool.

Westin $$$
1 Martin Place
Tel *8223 1111* **Map** 4 E1
W westinsydney.com
Soaring above the historic GPO building at 1 Martin Place – the true heart of the city – this property mixes old-fashioned service with modern comforts.

Darling Harbour and Surry Hills

The Darling $$$
80 Pyrmont St, Pyrmont
Tel *9777 9000* **Map** 3 B1
W thedarling.com.au
Floor-to-ceiling windows give stunning views in this opulent property, which is part of The Star complex, with its casino, theatres, bars and first-class restaurants.

Botanic Gardens and The Domain

Blue Sydney $$$
6 Cowper Wharf Roadway, Woolloomooloo
Tel *9331 9000* **Map** 2 D4
W bluehotel.com.au
Relaxed, over-the-water accom-modation in a restored, century-old wool warehouse set on a historic wharf.

Hotel InterContinental $$$
117 Macquarie St
Tel *9253 9000* **Map** 1 C3
W sydney.intercontinental.com
This is a real meeting of style and history – from the grand sandstone exterior beauty of the restored former 1851 Treasury Building, to the rooftop view from Club Continental.

Further Afield

InterContinental Sydney Double Bay $$$
33 Cross St, Double Bay
Tel *8388 8388*
W ihg.com/intercontinental/hotels/ gb/en/sydney/sydic/hoteldetail
This is an exclusive sanctuary, the lavish jewel in the crown of picturesque Double Bay village. The whole place is pure luxury – from the Italian marble floors in the foyer, to the swanky rooftop pool bar.

Jonah's $$$
69 Bynya Rd, Palm Beach
Tel *9974 5599*
W jonahs.com.au
A sumptuous and discreet ocean retreat on Sydney's northern beaches, just a 50-minute drive from the city or scenic 20-minute flight by seaplane.

Beyond Sydney

Lilianfels $$$
5–19 Lilianfels Ave, Katoomba
Tel *4780 1200*
W lilianfels.com.au
A short walk from the iconic Three Sisters at Echo Point in the Blue Mountains, this graceful and elegant resort is a throwback to yesteryear.

One & Only Wolgan Valley Resort & Spa $$$
2600 Wolgan Rd, Wolgan Valley
Tel *9290 9733*
W wolganvalley.com
Luxury and seclusion abound at this exclusive, conservation-based retreat with stunning views of the valley and the rugged sandstone escarpments in the Greater Blue Mountains.

For more information on types of hotels *see pages 172–3*

WHERE TO EAT AND DRINK

Sydneysiders are justifiably proud of their dining scene. Australia's largest city has been populated by successive waves of migrants who have added to the communal table. These influences have inspired contemporary adaptations of a variety of international cuisines, often called "Modern Australian". This term, coined in 1994 and affectionately shortened to "Mod Oz", covers just about any ethnic style a chef may take inspiration from. The result is that, in terms of ethnic diversity, Sydney offers many dining options.

A detailed guide to the best restaurants in the city can be found on pages 186–97. These cover a variety of different types of restaurant across all price brackets, ranging from some of the world's best fine dining establishments to inexpensive casual cafés.

Where to Eat

Circular Quay, The Rocks, Darlinghurst, Potts Point, Surry Hills and Paddington are the areas where you will find the widest choice of places to eat. Many restaurants at Darling Harbour, Cockle Bay and King Street Wharf also have outside tables, so diners can enjoy the atmosphere of the lights, the water and the boats.

Just outside the city centre, and not covered in depth in these listings, are the inner-city "eat streets" of Glebe Point Road, Glebe (see p133), and King Street, Newtown and Enmore.

On the lower North Shore, you will find the food hub of Willoughby Road, Crows Nest, while the beach suburbs of Bondi, Coogee and Manly are awash with dining choices. It would be difficult to walk around any of these precincts and not find a café or restaurant to suit your taste and budget.

All of the major hotels offer at least one restaurant, usually open even on public holidays.

How Much to Pay

The cost of dining out in Sydney has steadily climbed, putting it on a par with other major world capitals. The cost of a three-course meal in an average restaurant is roughly equivalent to similar offerings in New York or London. The cost can be reduced if you choose a BYO (bring your own) restaurant, where you can avoid paying the marked-up price of restaurant wine by taking your own wine, and sometimes beer. However, there will usually be a corkage cost per drinker or per bottle.

Opening Times

Most restaurants serve lunch from noon to 3pm and dinner from 6pm to about 10:30pm, though last orders are often at 10pm. Outside the city centre, restaurants may close one day a week, usually Monday. Many restaurants close on public holidays (see p53), and those that open usually add a 10 per cent surcharge to the bill.

Reservations

Booking is recommended for most restaurants – earlier in the day or the day before is usually adequate. However, if you want to secure a table for Friday or Saturday in a top-end or very popular restaurant, you may need to make a reservation at least one week, and sometimes up to one month, in advance. Some top restaurants require credit card details, which may incur a charge in the event of a "no show". Many casual brasseries and bistros are open throughout the day and do not take bookings. You may have to wait for a table at busy times, particularly weekend breakfast and brunch.

Licensing Laws

Sydney restaurants must be licensed to sell food, but when a place is described as licensed, this usually refers to its licence to sell alcohol. BYO restaurants are not licensed to sell liquor, and you will need to buy it beforehand if you want to drink alcohol with your meal.

Tax and Tipping

A 10 per cent GST is inclusive in prices, although it can be listed separately on the receipt. While tipping is not compulsory, most customers leave 10 to 15 per cent of the total bill as a reward for good service in restaurants. You can leave a cash tip after you have paid or add it to the total if paying your bill by credit card. Cafés often have a tip jar at the counter.

Paddington's Four in Hand pub, which has great food and a reputation to match (see p195)

Dress Codes and Smoking

Dress standards in Sydney restaurants are really quite relaxed, even in the more up-market establishments. Most restaurants will draw the line, however, at patrons in swimwear and flip-flops.

Smart-casual dress is the safest option when considering what to wear. Jackets and ties are a rare sight unless the wearer has come straight from the office or is conducting a business meeting over a meal.

Non-smoking legislation is in place for indoor dining areas of all restaurants, pubs and clubs. However, venues can provide a separate, designated outdoor area for smokers.

Eating with Children

Most restaurants accept children who can sit still throughout a meal, although you may feel more comfortable in one of the numerous cafés, Chinese, Thai or noodle bar restaurants, or the cheap pasta eateries like Bill and Toni's *(see p192)* in East Sydney, where children are always welcome. Harry's Café de Wheels *(see p193)* next to the Finger Wharf is a cheap-and-cheerful roadside pie cart. Many restaurants offer good-value children's menus, usually featuring burgers, fish and chips, and pasta, a drink and ice cream.

Many shopping centres have inexpensive food halls, including The Galeries on

A simple eatery offering authentic Indian food – Maya, in Surry Hills *(see p196)*

George St *(see pp198–9)* or Market City food court in Haymarket, Darling Harbour. They offer a variety of casual eating places featuring a range of cuisines in one complex, with a central seating area. For families who prefer to dine out rather than snack, casual pub bistros offer menus with plenty of choices for children and also serve alcohol for the adults.

Wheelchair Access

Most restaurants in Sydney provide wheelchair access and toilet facilities for the disabled. However, it is always best to check the facilities available in advance.

Vegetarians

It is rare for a restaurant in Sydney not to feature at least one dish for vegetarians; a variety of choices is the norm.

There are also a number of specialist vegetarian restaurants and cafés across the city.

Credit Cards

Many restaurants will accept credit cards, but you should ask if in doubt. Visa, MasterCard and Japanese Credit Bureau are widely accepted; Amex and Diners Club are less commonly accepted, so always check before ordering a meal. Some restaurants also now offer EFTPOS transactions (electronic money transfers direct from your bank account), which may be more convenient for some diners.

Recommended Restaurants

The restaurants listed in this guide are among the best in Sydney. They have been carefully selected for their reliably good food, location, service, value or a combination of these. The listings cover a vast variety of eateries, from simple pubs, bistros and cafés to top gourmet restaurants. Whether you are looking for authentic "bush tucker", fresh sushi, or a pub meal, the pages that follow offer lots of choice.

Establishments labelled DK Choice have been selected because they are outstanding in some way. They may offer superb cuisine, a stunning setting, excellent value or a combination of these.

Decorative saucers on the walls at Lucio's Italian restaurant, in Paddington *(see p195)*

The Flavours of Sydney

The city of Sydney surrounds its famous harbour, and countless bars, restaurants and cafés have views of sparkling sunlit water. Taking advantage of the mild climate, outdoor eating – from morning coffee to dinner – is the norm. The cutting-edge food scene is often categorized with New York, London and Paris, and Sydney's top-class chefs are admired the world over. Sydney is cosmopolitan, multicultural and vibrant, with the laid-back atmosphere of the beach always nearby. Sydneysiders are passionate about socializing and, whether eating out or cooking at home, food is always central to a good time.

Wattleseed, pepperberry and lemon myrtle

Fresh seafood dishes at one of the city's many upmarket restaurants

Native Ingredients

There are many native foods in Australia that have been used by aborigines for thousands of years, and which are now becoming widely popular. Fruits and vegetables with distinctive colours, flavours and textures include quandong, munthari, bush tomato, wild limes, warrigal greens and rosellas. All of them are still primarily wild-harvested by aboriginal communities. Although native Australians never used seasonings in their campfire cooking, modern Australians have discovered the exciting flavours of such indigenous herbs and spices as lemon myrtle, wattleseed, mountain pepperleaf, pepperberry, forest berry and akudjura. Native meats such as kangaroo and emu are also being used more frequently, although don't expect to see witchity grubs on many menus. These native meats sit alongside a vast and impressive array of beef, lamb and, of course, seafood. Fish native to Australia include barramundi, trevalla and blue eye trevalla. The popular native shellfish, yabbies and moreton bay bugs are similar to, but smaller than, lobster. Also worth a mention are the lovely fragrant honeys that are produced out of native Australian forests.

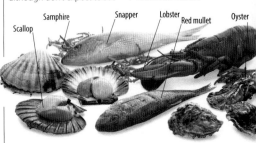

Scallop · Samphire · Snapper · Lobster · Red mullet · Oyster

Selection of seafood available in Sydney's restaurants and food shops

Local Dishes and Specialities

Kangaroo pizza This Italian classic is given a modern Australian spin with the addition of seared lean fillet.

There's nowhere better in the world to enjoy fish and chips than sitting on a Sydney beach. As well as the standard choice of hake fillets, you may find more unusual fish on offer, such as wild barramundi or John Dory. Alongside traditional Asian restaurants serving yum cha, dim sum curries and noodles, there is plenty of modern cuisine, fusing Asian flavours with local produce, such as a Thai-style salad of kangaroo with peanuts and lime. And you can rest assured that just about every other cuisine in the world will be represented in Sydney in some way.

Anzac biscuits

Sandwiches and burgers are often made with Sydney's favourite "Turkish" bread – light and fluffy, and great toasted with Vegemite or for dipping in olive oil.

Diners enjoying an outdoor meal on the harbour at Circular Quay

The World on a Plate

Having one of the most eclectic populations on earth means great things for food (or "tucker"). Australians are happy with olive oil in one hand and fresh chilies in the other, so no rules apply – you can be sure of great flavours and the best produce.

Farming plays a very important role in Australia, the world's largest producer of beef. The lush pastures on the coast are particularly good for farming, and milk-fed lamb from New South Wales is as wonderful as the brie produced in South Australia. King Island, off the coast of Victoria, is dedicated to dairy produce, selling their amazing cheeses and creams all around the country. Alongside the rapidly growing wine industry is olive oil and balsamic vinegar production, examples of which you are likely to find at the cellar door of many vineyards.

Australia has one of the most diverse marine faunas in the world, due to its range of habitats, from the warm tropical northern waters to the sub-Antarctic Tasman sea, as well as its geographical isolation. A total of 600 marine and freshwater species are caught in Australian waters, providing chefs with plenty of inspiration (see p202).

Every kind of fruit and vegetable is grown in Australia. Pineapples and mangoes are widely grown in Queensland, apples in Victoria, strawberries in New South Wales and rambutans in the Northern Territory. Exotic and notoriously hard to farm, truffles are cultivated in several areas, including Tasmania, highlighting the versatility of Australia's land.

Fresh fruit on sale at Paddy's Market in Chinatown

FOOD ON THE RUN

Sushi The city is dotted with tiny counters offering fresh sushi to grab on the go.

Juice bars This booming industry is found on most city streets, serving delicious, cool blends of fruits.

Milk bars As well as milk-shakes, ice creams and salads, these sell a wide range of deep-fried foods.

Coffee & cake Little cafés everywhere also sell Italian-style cakes and pastries.

Pubs Most pubs serve a decent steak sandwich.

Pies An Aussie institution, pies are readily available. Look out for gourmet versions.

Grilled barramundi Served on ginger and bok choy risotto, this is a great mix of local seafood and Asian flavours.

Prawn Laksa This spicy coconut noodle soup can be found all over the country in noodle bars, cafés and pubs.

Lamingtons These little Victoria sponge cakes are coated in chocolate icing and shredded coconut.

What to Drink in Sydney

Australia offers some of the world's finest cuisine and part of its enjoyment is the marriage of the country's wine with great food. Australians have a very relaxed attitude to food and wine mixes, so red wine with fish and a cold, dry Riesling as an apéritif can easily be the order of the day. In addition, many of the restaurants in the wine regions offer exclusive brands, or offer rare wines that are worth seeking out. Australians also enjoy some of the best good-value wine in the world. It is estimated that there are 10,000 different Australian wines on the market at any one time. Australians love their beer, too, and it remains a popular drink, with a wide range of choices available. Imported wines, beers and spirits are readily available, and the health-conscious can choose from a variety of bottled waters and select-your-own, freshly squeezed fruit juices.

Sparkling Wine

Australia is justly famous for its sparkling wines, from Yalumba's Angas Brut to Seppelts Salinger. Tasmania has showed considerable promise in producing some high quality sparkling wines, particularly Pirie from Pipers Brook. However, the real hidden gems are the sparkling red wines – the best are made using the French *méthode champenoise*, matured over a number of years and helped by a small drop of vintage port. The best producers of red sparkling wines are Rockford and Seppelts. These sparkling wines are available throughout Sydney from "bottle shops", which sell alcohol.

Domaine Chandon in the Yarra Valley produces high-quality sparkling wines

Angus Brut premium

White Wine

The revolution in wine making in the 1970s firmly established dry wines made from international grape varieties on the Australian table. Chardonnay, Sauvignon Blanc, and more recently Viognier and Pinot Gris are all popular. However, there has also been a renaissance and growing appreciation for Riesling, Marsanne and Sémillon, which age very gracefully. Australia's other great wines are their fortified and dessert wines. Australian winemakers use *Botrytis cinerea*, or noble rot, to make luscious dessert wines such as De Bortoli's "Noble One".

Australian Riesling

Botrytis Sémillon

Some of the vines in Australia are the oldest in the world.

Grape Type	State	Best Regions	Best Producers
Chardonnay	VIC	Geelong, Beechworth	Bannockburn, Giaconda, Stoniers
	NSW	Hunter Valley	Lakes Folly, Rosemount, Tyrrell's
	WA	Margaret River	Leeuwin Estate, Pierro, Cullen
	SA	Barossa Valley, Eden Valley	Penfolds, Mountadam
Sémillon	NSW	Hunter Valley	Brokenwood, McWilliams, Tyrrell
	SA	Barossa Valley	Peter Lehmann, Willows, Penfolds
	WA	Margaret River	Moss Wood, Voyager, Evans & Tate
Riesling	SA	Clare Valley and Adelaide Hills	Grosset, Pikes, Petaluma, Mitchells
	SA	Barossa Valley	Richmond Grove, Leo Buring, Yalumba
	TAS	Tasmania	Piper's Brook
Marsanne	VIC	Goulburn Valley	Chateau Tahbilk, Mitchelton

Red Wine

Vineyards of Leeuwin Estate, Margaret River

Australia's benchmark red is Grange Hermitage, the creation of the late vintner Max Schubert in the 1950s and 1960s. Due to his work, Shiraz has established itself as Australia's premium red variety. However, there is also plenty of diversity with the acknowledged quality of Cabernet Sauvignon produced in the Coonawarra. Recently, there has also been a re-appraisal of traditional "old vine" Grenache and Mourvedre varieties in the Barossa Valley and McLaren Vale.

Shiraz

Pinot Noir

Grape Type	State	Best Regions	Best Producers
Shiraj	NSW	Hunter Valley	Brokenwood, Lindmans, Tyrrells
	VIC	Great Western, Sunbury	Bests, Seppelts, Craiglee
	SA	Barossa Valley	Henschke, Penfolds, Rockford, Torbreck
	SA	McLaren Vale	Hardys, Coriole, Chapel Hill
	WA	Margaret River, Great Southern	Cape Mentelle, Plantagenet
Cabernet Sauvignon	WA	Margaret River	Cape Mentelle, Cullen, Moss Wood
	SA	Coonawarra	Wynns, Lindemans, Bowen Estate
	SA	Barossa, Adelaide Hills	Penfolds, Henschke, Petaluma
	VIC	Yarra Valley, Great Western	Yarra Yering, Yerinberg, Bests
Merlot	VIC	Yarra Valley, Great Western	Bests, Yara Yering
	SA	Adelaide Hills, Clare Valley	Petaluma, Pikes
Pinot Noir	VIC	Yarra Valley	Coldstream Hills, Tarrawarra
	VIC	Gippsland, Geelong	Bass Philip, Bannockburn, Shadowfax

Beer

Most Australian beer is vat fermented, or lager, and consumed chilled. Full-strength beer has an alcohol content of about 4.8 per cent, mid-strength beers have around 3.5 per cent while "light" beers have less than 3 per cent. Traditionally heat sterilized, cold filtration is now popular. Fans of real ale should seek out one of the city's pub breweries. Beer is ordered by glass size and brand: a schooner is a 426 ml (15 fl oz) glass and a middy is 284 ml (10 fl oz).

Bluetongue Lager   Cascade Premium Lager

Middy

Schooner

Fruit Juices

With the fabulous fresh fruit at their disposal year round, cafés concoct an astonishing array of fruit-based non-alcoholic drinks. They include frappés of fruit pulp and juice blended with crushed ice; smoothies of fruit blended with milk or yoghurt; and pure juices, extracted from everything from carrots to watermelons.

Pear and kiwi frappé

Banana smoothie

Strawberry juice

Other Drinks

Tap water in Sydney is fresh and clean, but local and imported bottled water is fashionable. The cola generation has graduated to alcoholic soft drinks and soda drinks. One brand, Two Dogs alcoholic lemonade, was born when a glut of lemons flooded the fruit market.

Spring water

Coffee

Sydney's passion for coffee means that short black, macchiato, caffe latte, cappuccino and flat white (with milk) are available at every neighbourhood café.

Flat white coffee

Caffe latte

Where to Eat and Drink

The Rocks and Circular Quay

Cabrito Coffee Traders $
Café **Map** 1 B3
10–14 Bulletin Place, Circular Quay
Tel *8065 8899* **Closed** *Sat, Sun*
Tucked away in a tiny alley, this
friendly place is favoured by city
workers looking for a takeaway
caffeine fix. Once the morning
rush hour has passed, sit in and
enjoy the aroma of in-house
roasted beans with a toasted
sandwich or lamington.

Ground Control Café $
Café **Map** 1 B3
Shop W4, Alfred St, Circular Quay
Tel *9247 4330*
Located under Circular Quay
railway station, this spot has
limited seating and is therefore
primarily a grab-and-go
destination. The coffee is
excellent, and there is a small
selection of delicious cakes,
pastries, wraps and sandwiches.

Vintage Café $
Mediterranean **Map** 1 B2
3 Nurses Walk, The Rocks
Tel *9252 2055*
Set in a cobblestoned courtyard,
this hidden gem is a great pit
stop for refuelling while out
exploring by day. In the evening,
it's an excellent place to enjoy a
romantic dinner for two,
accompanied by live jazz
several nights a week.

The Australian Heritage Hotel $$
Pub **Map** 1 B2
100 Cumberland St, The Rocks
Tel *9247 2229*
Pizza features here, with toppings
given a local twist – try the
kangaroo, emu or saltwater
crocodile. Other options on the
menu include Aussie beef-and-
beer pies, salads, pasta dishes
and burgers. An interesting range
of suggested beers complements
the menu.

Café Nice $$
French **Map** 1 C3
Level 3, 2 Phillip St, Circular Quay
Tel *8248 9600* **Closed** *Sun*
A charming light, bright and
airy space featuring honest, rustic
Provençal-style cooking and with
views to the Harbour Bridge.
A great place to enjoy a meal
before a show at the Opera
House. Service can be slow
during busy periods, so let your
waiter know if you are in a hurry.

The East Chinese Restaurant $$
Chinese **Map** 1 C2
Shop 8, 1 Macquarie St,
East Circular Quay
Tel *9252 6868*
Subtle, pungent, hot, mild –
there is something for every
palate here. Contrasting tastes,
colours and textures appeal to
the eye and the taste buds.
Dishes include stir-fried kangaroo
and crocodile tail fillet.

Heritage Belgian Beer Café $$
Belgian **Map** 1 A3
135 Harrington St, The Rocks
Tel *8488 2460*
Atmospheric restaurant set in a
historic building. The menu
boasts its Belgian mussels are a
"dish the world is jealous of".
Enjoy them cooked one of eight
ways, or try Flemish beef stew
washed down with an array of
artisan beers.

Hickson Road Bistro $$
Modern Australian **Map** 1 A2
22 Hickson Rd, Walsh Bay
Tel *9250 1990* **Closed** *Sun*
Next door to the Sydney Theatre
Company's Roslyn Packer Theatre,
this is the ideal location for pre-
or post-show dining, with fast,
friendly service. The menu often
features dishes created to reflect
the current theatre productions.

Lotus Dumpling Bar $$
Chinese **Map** 1 A1
16 Hickson Rd, Dawes Point
Tel *9251 8328*
Dumplings are served almost as
quickly as they are made here,
making this a great fast-food
choice. Enjoy dim sum at the
bar with a delicious variety of
side dishes.

The bright and airy Café Nice, ideal for
a pre-show meal

DK Choice

MCA Café $$
Café **Map** 1 B2
Level 4, 140 George St, The Rocks
Tel *9259 8443*
It's all about the million-dollar
harbour views from the open
sculpture terrace on the fourth
floor of the Museum of
Contemporary Art. Grab a seat
and enjoy a cup of coffee or
glass of wine with a light bite
on the expansive deck that
overlooks the Harbour Bridge
and Opera House.

The Morrison Bar & Oyster Room $$
Seafood **Map** 1 B3
225 George St
Tel *9247 6744* **Closed** *Sun*
There is a setting for every
occasion here – from the quiet
of the conservatory, to the
communal dining area and the
party atmosphere of the Oyster
Room. Enjoy breakfast, bar
snacks, a diverse mains menu or
oysters "shucked to order".

Nelson's Brasserie $$
Pub **Map** 1 A2
19 Kent St, The Rocks
Tel *9251 4044* **Closed** *Sun, Mon*
This eatery is on the first floor
above the Lord Nelson Brewery
Hotel. Enjoy a drink downstairs,
then head up for innovative
food in a historic 18th-century
sandstone-walled building.

Neptune Palace $$
Chinese and Malaysian **Map** 1 B3
Level 1, Gateway Building, Cnr of Pitt &
Alfred Sts, Circular Quay
Tel *9241 3338*
Popular with the business crowd
for more than two decades,
Neptune Palace serves award-
winning fare including salt-and-
pepper king prawns, wasabi beef,
and Kapitan chicken.

Opera Bar $$
Modern Australian **Map** 1 C2
Lower Concourse, Sydney Opera
House, Bennelong Point
Tel *9247 1666*
This is a great place to stop on
the way to the Opera House –

or just settle in, relax and watch the ferries over a drink and choice of bar food, light meals and sharing plates.

Sailors Thai $$
Thai Map 1 B2
106 George St, The Rocks
Tel *9251 2466* **Closed** *Sun, Mon*
This is the formal option of the twin Thai restaurants in this historic sandstone building. A pioneer in all things spice since the early 1990s, it features betel leaves in many starters.

Sailors Thai Canteen $$
Thai Map 1 B2
Level 1, 106 George St, The Rocks
Tel *9251 2466*
Tuck into bowls of traditional authentic Thai street food from the open kitchen here. Sit on the sunny balcony, or join fellow diners at the informal, long zinc communal table in this historic Sailors' Home building.

Saké Restaurant & Bar $$
Japanese Map 1 B2
12 Argyle St, The Rocks
Tel *9259 5656*
Set within an impressive designer space featuring dark wood, low light and loud music, Saké has a resident sushi master who serves up an authentic mix of new and classic sushi dishes.

Tapavino $$
Spanish Tapas Map 1 B3
6 Bulletin Place, Circular Quay
Tel *9247 3221* **Closed** *Sat, Sun*
It's like Barcelona by the harbour at this wine and sherry bar with an extensive menu. There is a strong "sip a little bit of this and eat a little bit of that" philosophy.

Young Alfred $$
Italian Map 1 B3
31 Alfred St, Circular Quay
Tel *9251 5192* **Closed** *Sun*
From the former owners of one of Sydney's all-time favourite pizza places comes modern Italian fare with flair. Enjoy fabulously named pizzas dished up in the historic Customs House building near the harbour.

Altitude $$$
Modern Australian Map 1 A3
Level 36, Shangri-La Hotel, 176 Cumberland St, The Rocks
Tel *9250 6123* **Closed** *Sunday*
Floor-to-ceiling windows maximize the dramatic harbour views, especially at night. Service can be slow, but at least that gives you more time to enjoy the stunning panorama.

Nelson's Brasserie, with its original 18th-century sandstone walls *(see p186)*

Ananas Bar & Brasserie $$$
French Mediterranean Map 1 A2
18 Argyle St, The Rocks
Tel *9259 5668* **Closed** *Sun*
This avant-garde brasserie puts a modern spin on traditional French favourites in a sassy space with 1920s-inspired decor. There are generous portions here, but make sure you save room for the inventive, decadent desserts.

ARIA $$$
Modern Australian Map 1 C2
1 Macquarie St, East Circular Quay
Tel *9252 2555*
An intimate, elegant dining experience on the edge of the harbour with stunning views, with a choice of set-price menus from one to four courses, a seasonal tasting menu and pre- and post-theatre dining. There is an exceptional wine list and very helpful sommeliers on hand.

The Bridge Room $$$
Modern Australian Map 1 B3
44 Bridge St, Sydney
Tel *9247 7000* **Closed** *Sun*
Come here for a unique take on Asian and European dishes, some cooked over a charcoal grill and slow-smoked in the Japanese *robata* style. Try the New England lamb with Jerusalem artichoke butter and black Russian tomatoes. With just 66 seats, the service is as flawless as the food.

Café Sydney $$$
Modern Australian Map 1 B3
Level 5, Customs House, 31 Alfred St, Circular Quay
Tel *9251 8683*
Enjoy picture-postcard harbour views from the covered terrace of this prime rooftop location above Circular Quay. Warm and friendly service and an ever-changing menu of consistently excellent dishes.

The Cut Bar & Grill $$$
Steak Map 1 A2
16 Argyle St, The Rocks
Tel *9259 5695*
Meat-lovers rejoice! The four-hour slow-roast Wagyu standing rib here is served straight from the carving trolley. There's also sustainable seafood for those wanting something lighter, as well as a tasting menu in the bar.

Quay $$$
Modern Australian Map 1 B2
Upper level, Overseas Passenger Terminal, West Circular Quay
Tel *9251 5600*
Another spectacular view with food to match. Star chef Peter Gilmore makes magic out of the best and freshest produce, combining ingredients in surprising ways, reworking old favourites and creating new dishes each season.

Yoshii $$$
Japanese Map 1 A3
115 Harrington St, The Rocks
Tel *9247 2566* **Closed** *Sun*
Dinner is a degustation affair, served in the *kaiseki* style, with a series of small dishes designed to warm the stomach gradually. Set lunch menus offer a more affordable way to try the excellent food.

City Centre

Baker Bros Espresso Bar $
Café Map 4 E2
Shop 1, 56–58 York St
Tel *9262 3884* **Closed** *Sat, Sun*
Get a spot at the small bench at this café that becomes a bar on Thursday and Fridays evenings. Sample smooth espresso and superb-tasting sandwiches and salads with Italian-inspired fillings.

Bodhi in the Park
Vegetarian   **Map** 1 C5
Cook & Phillip Park, 2–4 College St
Tel *9360 2523* $
A wonderful place for lunch on
a sunny day, with its peaceful,
park location, or to have dinner
outside on a summer's night.
Awesome pan-Asian cuisine
in the *yum cha* (tea with dim
sum) tradition.

GPO Pizza by Wood
Italian   **Map** 1 B4
Lower ground floor, GPO,
1 Martin Place
Tel *9229 7722*   **Closed** *Sun*
This pizzeria brings a tasty slice of
Italy to the heart of Sydney.
The light and crispy traditional
thin-crust pizzas feature delicately
balanced toppings and are
cooked in wood-fired ovens.

Indochine Café
Vietnamese   **Map** 4 F2
Shop 14, 111 Elizabeth St
Tel *9233 1088*   **Closed** *Sat, Sun*
Authentic-tasting Vietnamese
food. The menu includes all the
classics, simply done well. Watch
the rush on the busy street
below from the pleasant first-
floor location. A very popular
weekday lunch spot.

Madame Nhu
Vietnamese   **Map** 4 E2
Shop 5, Lower ground floor,
The Galeries, 500 George St
Tel *9283 3355* $
Simple and delicious modern
Vietnamese street food just as it
should be – fresh and fuss-free.
Ideal for a fast, filling, flavoursome
lunch at food-court prices.
The pho noodle soup and stir
fries are delicious.

Mother Chu's Vegetarian Kitchen
Asian Vegetarian   **Map** 4 E3
367 Pitt St
Tel *9283 2828* $
Overlook the decor and join the
regulars enjoying big helpings of
hearty food blending the flavours
of Taiwan, China and Japan – all
served with warm hospitality.
There is also a great-value
takeaway menu.

Pablo & Rusty's
Café   **Map** 4 E2
161 Castlereagh St
Tel *9807 6293*   **Closed** *Sun*
Warm service in an inviting,
buzzy, industrial space, but it's
the coffee, tea and food menu
that shines here at breakfast and
lunch. Helpful, friendly service,
but there can be a wait for a
table at peak times.

Sushi Hotara
Japanese   **Map** 4 E2
Level 1, The Galeries, 500 George St
Tel *9264 9917* $
A bustling setting with Japanese-
inspired interiors offering up
a fresh, authentic, reasonably
priced sushi conveyer belt –
which explains why there's often
a queue at the door.

Workshop Espresso
Café   **Map** 4 E2
The Galeries, 500 George St
Tel *9264 8836*   **Closed** *Sun*
It would be easy to miss this
hole-in-the-wall spot were it not
for the regulars lining up for their
coffee fix. Great for a simple, tasty
breakfast or lunch on the go.

York Lane
Café   **Map** 1 A4
56 York Lane, Wynyard
Tel *9299 1676*   **Closed** *Sun*
Stop by for tasty quick meals,
sandwiches, breakfasts, cakes and
coffee by day. By night, the place
becomes a bar and restaurant.
Split-level seating and a backing
track of vinyl records.

Bambini Trust
European   **Map** 4 F2
Ground floor, 185 Elizabeth St
Tel *9283 7098*   **Closed** *Sun*
A sophisticated spot. The elegant
wood-panelled interiors, crisp
white linen and excellent service
complement the well-executed
menu. This is a great place for a
stylish breakfast, working lunch
or leisurely dinner.

Barrafina
Spanish Tapas   **Map** 1 B4
2 Bligh St
Tel *9231 2551*   **Closed** *Sat, Sun*
A wide selection of sharing plates
and grazing boards here include
produce from the restaurant
gardens, Spanish cheeses and
artisan cured meats. A genuine
taste of Spain, from light starters
to more substantial offerings.

Bistrode CBD
Modern bistro   **Map** 4 E1
Level 1, Hotel CBD, 52 King St
Tel *9240 3000*   **Closed** *Sat, Sun*
Modern British cuisine with a
focus on local produce from
English expat chef Jeremy Strode.
Wide-arched windows give the
first-floor location an elegance
that matches the food.

Bridge Street Garage
American Diner   **Map** 1 B3
17–19 Bridge St
Tel *9251 9392*   **Closed** *Sun*
This former car garage has been
transformed into a burger bar

Madame Nhu – the place to go for
reasonably priced Vietnamese street food

and a bistro at the back,
accessible by a hand-cranked
garage door. Retro finishes,
including recycled car headlights,
add to the raw industrial space.

Chophouse
Steak   **Map** 1 B4
25 Bligh St
Tel *1300 246 748*   **Closed** *Sun*
Reminiscent of the fine
steakhouses of old New York,
here you can settle into the
leather and dark wood booths
and tuck into a steak with house
sauces, or opt for lighter salad
and seafood options.

Danjee
Korean   **Map** 4 E3
1–7 Albion Place
Tel *8084 9041* $$
Taking Korean BBQ into the fine-
dining arena, the quality and
presentation at this spot attracts
a cool crowd eager to try new
tastes. The lunch-box specials are
great value.

Diethnes
Greek   **Map** 1 B5
336 Pitt St
Tel *9267 8956*   **Closed** *Sun*
A Sydney institution, Diethnes
has been in the same basement
location for almost four decades.
The decor might show its age,
but the big portions of hearty
Greek fare still satisfy.

Encasa
Spanish   **Map** 4 E4
423 Pitt St
Tel *9211 4257* $$
This casual Spanish restaurant
offers great tapas, paella and
sangria. Let them know in
advance if you want to order
the *romesco de peix*, a Catalan
seafood stew with a traditional
hazelnut sauce.

Felix $$
French Bistro **Map** 1 B4
2 Ash St
Tel 9240 3000
Designed as a romantic homage
to the quintessential French
brasserie, Felix offers classic fare
and an extensive wine list in an
elegant room, with white-tiled
walls, mounted bread baskets
and red table lamps.

Gowings Bar & Grill $$
Modern European **Map** 4 E2
QT Hotel, 49 Market St
Tel 8262 0062
European brasserie style with
an edgy contemporary design
featuring dark wood and
exposed bricks. The menu takes
its cues from around the world
and across generations, but the
grill is the star. Save room for
the decadent retro desserts.

Machiavelli $$
Italian **Map** 1 A4
123 Clarence St
Tel 9299 3748 **Closed** *Sat, Sun*
A Sydney institution, this is
where politicians, lawyers and
business leaders come to eat
and be seen, doing deals over
hearty Italian food. Rustic decor,
with air-dried meats hanging
from the ceiling.

Mr Wong $$
Chinese **Map** 1 B3
3 Bridge Lane
Tel 9240 3000
Sprawled over two stylish
levels, Mr Wong pays tribute
to classic Chinese influences
with a Cantonese-based menu.
A choice of more than 60 dishes
is listed on one of the best dim
sum menus in town.

Rockpool Bar & Grill $$
Steak **Map** 1 B4
66 Hunter St
Tel 8078 1900 **Closed** *Sun*
The grand Art Deco interior
would not be out of place in
Manhattan. Steak is the main
attraction, but there's much
more to enjoy here, with a crowd
drawn from the big business
end of town.

Sushi e $$
Japanese **Map** 1 B3
Level 4, Establishment, 252 George St
Tel 9240 3000 **Closed** *Sunday*
Exceptionally fresh fish served
up in stunning surroundings.
A good way to experience a
range of delicious tastes is by
ordering a selection of small
pieces from the sashimi menu or
a mix of items from the sushi
nigiri menu. Excellent service.

est. $$$
Modern Australian **Map** 1 B3
Level 1, Establishment, 252 George St
Tel 9240 3000 **Closed** *Sun*
Head chef Peter Doyle is
widely regarded as a founding
father of "Modern Australian"
cuisine. Attention to detail
reigns here: every dish is
prepared to perfection and
exquisitely presented.

Glass Brasserie $$$
Modern Australian **Map** 1 B5
Level 2, Hilton Sydney, 488 George St
Tel 9265 6068
Celebrity chef Luke Mangan's
large, bright and light space
(thanks to the floor-to-ceiling
windows) gets diners arguing
over what was better – dishes
from the grill, or the desserts.
The best way to settle the score
is to try both.

Rockpool $$$
Modern Australian **Map** 1 B3
11 Bridge St
Tel 9252 1888 **Closed** *Sun*
The pinnacle in fine Australian
dining for two decades, chef
Neil Perry's iconic restaurant
has a new home in a grand
sandstone heritage building.
The very stylized, dark interiors
complement an amazing menu
and dining experience – from
indulgent set-menu "snacks" to
full courses – and an even more
indulgent wine list.

Spice Temple $$$
Chinese **Map** 4 F1
10 Bligh St
Tel 8078 1888 **Closed** *Sun*
Open the video screen door and
enter a modern Chinese marvel.
Chilies feature – fresh, dried,
salted, pickled, brined and
fermented – all served in a dark,
moody basement with Chinese
lanterns and red table lamps.
Exceptional service.

Tetsuya's $$$
Japanese/French **Map** 4 E3
529 Kent St
Tel 9267 2900 **Closed** *Sun, Mon*
Internationally recognized
as one of the best restaurants
in Australia, this serene space
features a ten-course degustation
menu that fuses Japanese
flavours with French technique.
A vegetarian version is available
on request.

Darling Harbour and Surry Hills

Bar Zini $
Café **Map** 3 B1
78 Harris St, Pyrmont
Tel 9660 5718 **Closed** *Sun*
A cosy café by day, and a great
place for a filling breakfast. When
the sun goes down, it transforms
into a relaxed restaurant and
wine bar, serving delicious pizzas,
risottos and pasta dishes. A little
piece of Italy in Pyrmont.

BBQ King $
Chinese **Map** 4 E4
18–20 Goulburn St
Tel 9267 2586
Basic decor at best and abrupt
service, but this is still the go-to
destination for many of the
city's night owls in search of a
late meal of barbecued duck,
pork and Chinese beer. Great
vegetable dishes and sides, too.

Caysorn Thai $
Thai **Map** 4 D4
Level 1, 8 Quay St, Haymarket
Tel 9211 5749
Challenge your taste buds'
heat tolerance here, where the
speciality is Southern Thai food –
known as the spiciest in Thailand.
The chicken *larb* is highly recommended. The food is hot, but the
service is warm and gracious.

Coffee – and food – that is worth the wait, at Pablo & Rusty's *(see p188)*

For more information on types of restaurants *see pages 180–81*

Chat Thai $
Thai   **Map** 4 E4
20 Campbell St, Haymarket
Tel *9211 1808*
A standout among a sea of
Chinese restaurants, with an
interesting menu featuring daily
specials. Food is prepared in the
shop-front window, which helps
entertain those who are waiting
in line for a table.

Devon $
Café
76 Devonshire St, Surry Hills
Tel *9211 8777*
One of Sydney's best breakfast
spots, with only seasonal
produce used – much of it
picked from the café's own
walled garden. If you're in luck,
you'll be there when truffle-
infused eggs are on the menu.

Din Tai Fung $
Chinese   **Map** 4 E3
World Square, 644 George St
Tel *9264 6010*
A haven for dumplings and pork-
bun aficionados. Locals can't get
enough of the steamed *xiao long
bao* – soupy pork dumplings that
ooze flavour. The pork and
vegetable buns are fabulous, too.

El Loco at Slip Inn $
Pub   **Map** 1 A4
111 Sussex St
Tel *8295 9999*   **Closed** *Sun*
Tuck into tacos, Mexican-style
pork or grilled fish burgers, or try
one of the weekly specials in
colourful surroundings. If you're
after a change, there's a Thai menu
on the pub's ground floor, too.

Mamak $
Malaysian   **Map** 4 D4
15 Goulburn St, Haymarket
Tel *9211 1668*
Be prepared to wait outside for a
table, where you can watch the
chefs at work. Once inside, enjoy
the buzz of the crowd and staff
as you tuck into tasty street food.

Pasteur $
Vietnamese   **Map** 4 E4
709 George St, Haymarket
Tel *9212 5622*
Fast service in a no-frills setting,
but locals and students come
for great-value authentic tastes,
not the ambience. Try a hearty
bowl of *pho bo* (beef and rice
noodle soup).

Reuben Hills $
Café   **Map** 4 F5
61 Albion St, Surry Hills
Tel *9212 3603*
There's hot coffee, warm service
and a cool atmosphere in this
industrial-style warehouse
conversion. Worth waiting for a
table for breakfast at weekends.
The salted-caramel milkshake is
always a hit.

Taste Baguette on Sussex Lane
Vietnamese   **Map** 4 D1   **$**
275 Kent St
Tel *9299 0888*   **Closed** *Sat, Sun*
You can really smell the freshly
baked bread here. Don't miss the
signature baguettes, baked on-
site and stuffed with your choice
of fillings – from traditional
Vietnamese lemongrass beef
to Portuguese chicken.

Berta $$
Italian   **Map** 4 F4
17–19 Alberta St
Tel *9264 6133*   **Closed** *Sun, Mon*
The menu here changes daily
to deliver simple, seasonal fare
including dishes designed for
sharing, with a sustainable
philosophy to use the whole
animal. Big focus on Italian
wines, most directly imported.

Bodega $$
Tapas
216 Commonwealth St, Surry Hills
Tel *9212 7766*   **Closed** *Sun, Mon*
The dishes at Bodega celebrate
Spanish and South American
cuisine. Savour the flavours with
a giant mural of a matador and
large bull looking down at you.
There's an excellent selection of
matching wines, too.

Café Morso $$
Café   **Map** 3 B1
*Jones Bay Wharf, 26–32 Pirrama Rd,
Pyrmont*
Tel *9692 0111*
A fabulous place to enjoy a
delicious breakfast or lunch
by the water's edge on a rustic

Sepia – named Restaurant of the Year
several times, including 2015 *(see p191)*

heritage wharf. Sit outside
and enjoy the breeze, or dine
inside with the soaring
industrial ceilings.

Home Café & Thai Restaurant $$
Thai   **Map** 4 E3
39 Liverpool St
Tel *9261 3011*
This place gets crowded, and no
wonder – with great food, great
value and very fast service.
Big portions, too, so if you order
too much, ask for a takeaway
container to enjoy later.

King Street Brewhouse $$
Pub   **Map** 4 D1
22 The Promenade, King St Wharf
Tel *8270 7901*
A diverse menu with all the pub
favourites – burgers, wings,
grilled steaks, steamed mussels
and seafood platters. Wash it
down with a cold beer at this
micro-brewery and restaurant.

Longrain $$
Asian
85 Commonwealth St, Surry Hills
Tel *9280 2888*
Top Thai in a big space that fills
quickly. The bar occupies a whole
separate floor; ask about the
famous "drink sticks" during the
inevitable wait for a spot on the
long communal dining table.

Mahjong Room $$
Chinese
312 Crown St, Surry Hills
Tel *9361 3985*   **Closed** *Sun*
This is a low-profile restaurant
that lets the food do the talking.
A creative spin on Chinese
cuisine attracts a young crowd,
with dishes served at mahjong
tables in a series of small rooms.

The Malaya $$
Malaysian   **Map** 4 D1
39 Lime St, King Street Wharf
Tel *9279 1170*   **Closed** *Sunday*
A Sydney institution for 50 years,
originally in George St but now
by the water. It's noisy, but the
cooking packs a punch, with
a feisty, flavour-filled range
covering all the favourites, as
well as some surprises.

Marigold $$
Chinese   **Map** 4 E4
*Level 4 & 5, Citymark Building,
683–689 George St*
Tel *9281 3388*
An enormous restaurant,
spread over two floors above
a shopping arcade, is home to
one of Sydney's best *yum cha*
offerings. Banquet menus make
ordering easy when you can't
decide what to choose.

Mohr Fish $$

Seafood
202 Devonshire St, Surry Hills
Tel *9318 1326*
A humble, classy, small fish-and-chip shop, where you can enjoy your order fresh, steamed, grilled or fried. You can wait for a table or eat your takeaway order in the pub next door.

DK Choice

MoVida $$
Tapas **Map** 4 F5
50 Holt St, Surry Hills
Tel *8964 7642* **Closed** *Sun*
The stylish interior and open kitchen adds to the theatre here. The first Sydney outpost of Frank Camorra's popular Melbourne tapas empire, it attracts a crowd for both the people-watching and fabulous flavours. The service is as good as the menu; the hardest part is deciding what *not* to order.

Nick's Bar & Grill $$

Seafood and Steak
The Promenade, Cockle Bay Wharf
Tel *9279 0122*
A delicious menu and a fabulous spot to enjoy the sunshine or night lights on the water. Keep little ones happy with a value kids' meal of pasta, fish, calamari or chicken, with salad, chips and dessert.

Steersons Steakhouse $$

Steakhouse **Map** 4 D1
17 Lime St, King Street Wharf
Tel *9295 5060*
Huge choice of succulent steaks served in a surprisingly swish dining room, with menus carrying over the theme – they are bound in cow hide. There are lighter chicken, seafood and vegetarian dishes on offer, too.

Zaafran $$

Indian **Map** 3 C2
Level 2, 345 Harbourside Shopping Centre, Darling Harbour
Tel *9211 8900*
This is the pick of the eateries on this side of the Darling Harbour tourist strip, with good-value set menus and a range of delicious dishes to satisfy vegetarians and meat-lovers alike.

Café del Mar $$$

Mediterranean Seafood **Map** 4 D2
Rooftop Terrace, Cockle Bay Wharf, Darling Harbour
Tel *9267 6700*
Suited to a quick bite or a long meal, the menu pays homage to the Mediterranean basin with an

Cocktails, style and the open kitchen all help draw crowds to MoVida

Aussie accent. The interior features a contemporary dining room, lounge bar and massive sun deck.

Golden Century $$$

Chinese **Map** 4 E4
393–399 Sussex St
Tel *9281 1598*
The menu is huge, the staff friendly and the selection of live seafood enormous. With the kitchen open until 4am, it's not unusual to find it full of other chefs relaxing after work.

Kobe Jones $$$

Japanese **Map** 4 D1
29 Lime St, King Street Wharf, Darling Harbour
Tel *9299 5290*
Stylishly decorated in black and red, this restaurant puts a Californian twist on traditional Japanese and teppanyaki. Helpful staff can guide you through the extensive and tantalizing offerings to suit all palates.

Marque $$$

French **Map** 5 A3
355 Crown St, Surry Hills
Tel *9332 2225*
Dishes with complexity and flavours you could not imagine. Works of art, as much as food for consuming, they are all cooked to perfection by a true master craftsman. Choose from the degustation or à la carte menus. The Friday set lunch is tremendous value.

Momofuku Seiobo $$$

Japanese **Map** 3 B1
The Star, 80 Pyrmont St, Pyrmont
Tel *9777 9000* **Closed** *Sun*
This first off-shoot of the renowned New York original has a set-price tasting menu, or you can arrive early for one of the five bar seats for walk-ins and try the limited bar menu.

DK Choice

Sepia $$$
Modern Japanese Fusion
Map 4 D2
201 Sussex St
Tel *9283 1990* **Closed** *Sun, Mon*
Lauded with titles including Restaurant of the Year, Sepia offers a unique take on Japanese flavours, artfully done, set in an upscale, uptown New York-style bar and diner. There is a choice of four set menus or a degustation menu, while a separate bar offering includes a selection of Japanese charcoal-grill dishes. First-class service from the waiting staff and sommelier.

Botanic Garden and The Domain

Botanic Garden Café $

Café **Map** 2 D4
Royal Botanic Garden, Mrs Macquaries Rd
Tel *9241 2419*
Set in the lush gardens overlooking the duck pond, this place serves gourmet sandwiches, salads, baked goods and coffee. There's also the option to pre-order a picnic basket to enjoy at leisure as you explore the Garden.

Café at the Gallery $

Café **Map** 2 D4
The Art Gallery of NSW, Art Gallery Rd, The Domain
Tel *9225 1744*
Head to the Gallery's lower level 1 for a casual dining experience in a relaxed environment, with freshly prepared light snacks, sandwiches, salads and baked goods. Stays open late on Wednesday for Art After Hours.

For more information on types of restaurants *see pages 180–81*

Charlie's $
Café   Map 2 D5
7–41 Cowper Wharf Roadway,
Woolloomooloo
Tel *9358 4443*
A no-fuss, long-established café
serving up a big selection of hot
and fresh fast food, including
burgers, sandwiches, rolls,
barbecue chicken, hot chips
and salads. This is the perfect
way to fuel the troops on a
family outing.

The Pavillion Kiosk $
Café   Map 2 D4
1 Art Gallery Rd, The Domain
Tel *9232 1322*
Tucked in The Domain across
from the Art Gallery. Order from
light refreshments including
sandwiches, soup and freshly
baked pastries and muffins, and
find a spot on the green to enjoy it.

Aki's $$
Indian   Map 2 D4
6 Cowper Wharf Road,
Woolloomooloo
Tel *9332 4600*
Masterful modern Indian food,
combining tandoori flavours
from the north, classics from
the chef's native Chennai and
seafood dishes from Goa. Get an
outside table and dine during
sunset, or enjoy the cool, split-
mezzanine interior.

Botanic Garden Restaurant $$
Modern Australian   Map 1 C3
Royal Botanic Garden,
Mrs Macquaries Rd
Tel *9241 2419*
An enchanting venue in the
middle of the picturesque
Botanic Garden, featuring the
original 19th-century façade and
offering beautiful leafy views.
Enjoy an open-air lunch any day
or a lazy breakfast at weekends.

China Doll $$
Modern Asian   Map 2 D4
4/6 Cowper Wharf Road,
Woolloomooloo
Tel *9380 6744*
Another wharf eatery with
spectacular views, but this would
be a gem anywhere. A favourite
with celebrities and those who
want to be, it offers generous
portions of delectable dishes and
a well-priced banquet menu.

Chiswick at the Gallery $$
Modern Australian   Map 2 D4
The Art Gallery of NSW,
Art Gallery Rd, The Domain
Tel *9225 1819*
Head to the contemporary
dining room and grab a bite to
eat at the large communal table,

or have a drink in the casual bar
area before or after enjoying
the exhibitions.

The Hyde Park Barracks Café $$
Modern Australian   Map 1 C5
Queen's Square, Hyde Park Barracks,
Macquarie St
Tel *9222 1815*
This quiet retreat is within the
sandstone walls of the historic
Hyde Park Barracks. Modern takes
on Italian and French food are
well crafted, and a children's
menu will keep little ones happy.

Kingsleys Sydney $$
Steak and Crab   Map 2 D4
10/6 Cowper Wharf Road,
Woolloomooloo
Tel *1300 546 475*
No need to decide between
steak or seafood, enjoy both
with surf and turf options –
from Wagyu rib-eye scotch fillet,
to yellow-fin tuna sashimi and
Singapore chilli crab.

The Pavilion Restaurant $$
Modern Australian   Map 2 D4
1 Art Gallery Rd, The Domain
Tel *9232 1322*
In The Domain, just across the
road from the Art Gallery, this
elegant restaurant's uniquely
shaped curved building serves
up breakfast and lunch with
beautiful garden views from
the terrace and deck.

Poolside Café $$
Café   Map 2 E3
Andrew (Boy) Charlton Pool,
1C Mrs Macquaries Rd, The Domain
Tel *8354 1044   Closed* June, July
Perched above the Olympic-
sized Andrew (Boy) Charlton
swimming pool with views
across Woolloomooloo Bay.
Enjoy a swim and a snack – from
healthy salads, to fish and chips
and ice-cream sandwiches.

Sienna Marina $$
Italian   Map 2 D5
6/7-41 Cowper Wharf Roadway,
Woolloomooloo
Tel *9358 6299*
Stop by and choose from the
breakfast, lunch, dinner, pizza or
kids' menus – there's something
for every time of day. Take a spot
on the leather loungers in front
of the fireplace and relax.

Manta $$$
Seafood   Map 2 D4
6 Cowper Wharf Road, Woolloomooloo
Tel *9332 3822*
Another delightful destination
best enjoyed from a prime
position outside, with fish so
fresh they could have jumped

Classic Italian dishes with a stylish twist
at Otto Ristorante

from the harbour waters below
straight onto the plate. Good-
quality and value house wine.

DK Choice

Otto Ristorante $$$
Italian   Map 2 D4
Area 8, 6 Cowper Wharf Rd,
Woolloomooloo
Tel *9368 7488*
The Finger Wharf is great for
people watching and celebrity
spotting, but Otto is the real
star among stars on this
waterfront, reinventing the
flavours of Italy in stylish
new forms, with dishes that
delight and superb service.
The food somehow tastes even
better if you can get a seat on
the alfresco terrace.

Kings Cross and Darlinghurst

Bar Coluzzi $
Café   Map 5 B1
322 Victoria St, Darlinghurst
Tel *9380 5420*
Established in 1957, this small
old-school original has stood
the test of time. Locals from
politicians to art students get
their morning coffee fix sitting on
the little stools on the footpath.

Bill and Toni's $
Italian   Map 5 A1
74 Stanley St, East Sydney
Tel *9360 4702*
A stalwart loved for its great-
value, no-frills Italian food,
strong coffee, free cordial and
old-fashioned red tablecloths.
Upstairs, enjoy basic but tasty
and filling pasta dishes, then
head downstairs for gelato.

Bills $
Café   **Map** 5 B2
433 Liverpool St, Surry Hills
Tel 9360 9631
Regulars would be up in arms if owner-chef Bill Granger's famous ricotta hotcakes were ever taken off the menu here. They make breakfast or brunch the best time to visit.

Flour and Stone $
Café   **Map** 5 A1
53 Riley St, Woolloomooloo
Tel 8068 8818   **Closed** *Sun*
There are savoury offerings including gourmet tarts, pies and sandwiches, but it's the sweet treats that get customers salivating. The delights range from lamingtons and lemon drizzle cake, to more healthy bran muffins if you must.

Govinda's $
Vegetarian Buffet   **Map** 5 B1
112 Darlinghurst Rd, Darlinghurst
Tel 9380 5155   **Closed** *Mon, Tue*
Pile up a plate of curries, breads and salads from the opulent buffet, then, for a little extra, lie on floor cushions or couches and watch a movie at the boutique cinema upstairs.

Harry's Café de Wheels $
Pie Cart   **Map** 2 E4
Cnr Cowper Wharf Roadway & Brougham St, Woolloomooloo
Tel 8346 4100
Now at several locations, but this is the original and best, serving meat pies topped with mashed potato, peas and gravy to sailors, taxi drivers, celebrities, tourists and locals since the Great Depression in 1938.

Phamish $
Vietnamese   **Map** 5 B2
50 Burton St, Darlinghurst
Tel 9357 2688
A small, intimate place with moody red-and-black interiors. It can get very crowded, but service is swift. Seating is on small stools, so don't come expecting to recline after a fresh, flavoursome and filling meal.

A Tavola $$
Italian
348 Victoria St, Darlinghurst
Tel 9331 7871
Join fellow diners at the 10-m-(32-ft-) long pink-marble table, the centrepiece of this stylish trattoria's long, narrow dining room. The menu changes daily and is determined by the fresh seasonal produce that is available. Delicious, authentic Italian cuisine.

Billy Kwong $$
Chinese
Shop 1, 28 Macleay Street, Potts Point
Tel 9332 3300
Celebrity chef Kylie Kwong puts her unique spin on Chinese food, featuring locally grown, organic and biodynamic produce, with a strong focus on Australian native bush foods.

Casoni $$
Italian   **Map** 5 A2
371–373 Bourke St (cnr Foley St), Darlinghurst   **Closed** *Mon, Tue*
Be surprised, as the chef creates a new pasta dish daily – it's on the menu until sold out. Plenty of other choices, too, at a place that puts the emphasis on shared dishes, fun times and fresh food.

The Fish Shop $$
Seafood   **Map** 2 E4
22 Challis Ave, Potts Point
Tel 9326 9000
A little piece of The Hamptons in Potts Point, with its white-washed walls and fun East Coast American seaside feel. Grab a stool and enjoy fresh, locally caught fish and delicious seafood dishes.

Fratelli Paradiso $$
Italian   **Map** 2 E4
12–16 Challis Ave, Potts Point
Tel 9357 1744
This spot morphs from breakfast and lunch café to sassy wine bar and restaurant. No bookings, so arrive early. Go for the fab breakfasts or, later, for the pasta, tiramisu and Italian cheeses.

Fu Manchu $$
Asian   **Map** 5 B1
229 Darlinghurst Rd, Darlinghurst
Tel 9360 9424
A smart dining room with carved timber screens and silk cushions on the chairs. Portions are small, but there is a wide choice of dishes, with *gow gee* and Nonya chicken among the best.

Jimmy Liks $$
Southeast Asian   **Map** 2 E5
186–188 Victoria St, Potts Point
Tel 8354 1400
A seductively lit, buzzy Asian eatery, wine and cocktail bar. Enjoy an Asian-inspired beverage before dinner. The traditional hawker-style lunch with small dishes to share is great on Friday to Sunday afternoons.

Lucio Pizzeria $$
Italian   **Map** 5 A2
248 Palmer St, Darlinghurst
Tel 9332 3766   **Closed** *Tue*
A superb slice of Naples in the corner of a piazza, with relaxed indoor or outdoor dining in the pretty courtyard. Antipasti to start and indulgent desserts – but really, it's all about perfect pizza.

Ms G's $$
Modern Asian   **Map** 2 E5
155 Victoria St, Potts Point
Tel 8313 1000
Four levels of fabulous fun. This place is styled like no other: there's a pink neon-bathed entrance, graffiti wall, rows of jars on the ceiling and veggie garden courtyard. And the food? Mouth-wateringly excellent. Don't miss the spicy squid ink *nasi goreng* (Indonesian stir-fried rice).

Red Lantern on Crown $$
Vietnamese   **Map** 5 A1
60 Riley St, Darlinghurst
Tel 9698 4355   **Closed** *Sun, Mon*
Go on a flavour journey to old Saigon with a focus on shared dishes from celebrity chef Luke Nguyen and his team, in a designer setting that evokes French-colonial Vietnam. Try the Burrawong chicken with strands of poached jellyfish.

Dine in the most relaxing of surroundings at the Poolside Café *(see p192)*

For more information on types of restaurants *see pages 180–81*

Riley Street Garage $$
Modern Australian   **Map** 5 A1
55 Riley St, Woolloomooloo
Tel 9326 9055   **Closed** *Sun*
This former 1930s car depot,
garage and machine shop pays
homage to its heritage with a
fun, stylish fit-out and food
"for all your gastronomic service
and repairs". Decadent dishes
designed for sharing.

DK Choice

Spice I Am $$
Thai   **Map** 5 B1
296–300 Victoria St, Darlinghurst
Tel 9332 2445
Spices are at the heart of Thai
cuisine, and here they take
centre stage. The end result is
bold, innovative, authentic –
and hot – dishes that will make
you feel you're in bustling
Bangkok. You can even book a
private cooking class to learn
how to recreate classic Thai
dishes at home.

Tilbury Hotel $$
Pub   **Map** 2 D5
12–18 Nicholson St, Woolloomooloo
Tel 9368 1955   **Closed** *Mon*
(restaurant; café open daily)
Try breakfast or a light bite from
the small but tasty selection in the
café, or enjoy a more substantial
meal in the restaurant dining
room looking out on a courtyard.

Yellow $$
Modern Australian   **Map** 2 E4
57 Macleay St, Potts Point
Tel 9332 2344
Formerly the Yellow House and
once home to artist Martin Sharp
and his artists' collective that
brought bohemia to Potts Point.
Not much yellow here now, but
there is wonderful food and an
informal atmosphere.

Beppi's $$$
Italian   **Map** 4 F3
21 Yurong St, East Sydney
Tel 9360 4558   **Closed** *Sun*
Delivering Italian hospitality and
fine food that's all about taste not
trends since 1956. Ask for a table
in the magnificent cellar room.
Old-fashioned charm at its best.

Macleay Street Bistro $$$
Modern French   **Map** 2 E5
73a Macleay St, Potts Point
Tel 9358 4891
A small seasonal menu and
weekly specials board, all dishes
artfully prepared, raising it above
typical bistro fare. This is a touch
of France in an area known as the
Paris end of Potts Point.

Paddington

Ampersand Café & Bookstore $
Café   **Map** 5 B3
78 Oxford St, Paddington
Tel 9380 6617
Soap up the tranquillity at this
charming café in a quaint
second-hand bookstore. There's
a lovely selection of breakfast
items, baked goods, sandwiches,
pastas and salads – and more
than 30,000 books.

Crème Café $
Café   **Map** 6 E4
101–103 Queen St, Woollahra
Tel 9327 6543
Stroll one of the prettiest streets
in Paddington, then enjoy
breakfast, lunch or a sweet treat
at the outdoor tables on the
footpath, shaded by giant
trees. Dine alfresco Friday and
Saturday evenings – if the
weather permits.

Paddington Inn $
Pub   **Map** 6 D4
338 Oxford St, Paddington
Tel 9380 5913
A perennially popular pub in the
heart of the Paddington strip.
It attracts a buzzy crowd at
weekends and is great for a
casual lunch of modern pub
classics like fish and chips, light
meals or a long, lazy three-
course affair.

South Dowling Kitchen $
Café   **Map** 5 A3
354 South Dowling St, Paddington
Tel 8964 9700
Friendly staff, tasty food and
good coffee create a fun vibe
here. All the usual suspects are
present for breakfast: eggs,
smoked salmon, sourdough
toast, muffins, fresh juice. Good-
quality lunch salads and rolls, too.

Stylish fine dining and service at Guillaume
(see p195)

A10 William Street $$
Italian   **Map** 6 D4
10 William Street, Paddington
Tel 9360 3310   **Closed** *Sun*
A great vibe at this small wine
bar and restaurant that oozes
style. Servings are small, so don't
come hungry. Order tapas-style
dishes, and enjoy a matching
drink recommended by the
helpful bar staff.

The Bellevue $$
Pub   **Map** 6 E3
159 Hargrave St, Paddington
Tel 9363 2293
A relaxed, light and airy restaurant
tucked away at the back of the
Bellevue. More upmarket
offerings than most pubs, with
dishes like Queensland spanner
crab with young coconut and
fresh chamomile.

Big Mama's $$
Italian   **Map** 6 E4
51 Moncur St, Woollahra
Tel 9328 7629   **Closed** *Mon*
A long-established, old-style
trattoria with a large menu for
those lengthy, relaxed dinners.
Generous portions of
uncomplicated but delicious
food and friendly service mean
you'll feel like one of the family.

Bistro Moncur $$
French   **Map** 6 E4
*The Woollahra Hotel, 116 Queen St,
Woollahra*
Tel 9327 9713
A stylish spot that's more
Paris than pub, delivering
a consistently good menu
of French bistro classics,
complemented using the best available
Australian seasonal produce.

Hotel Centennial $$
Pub   **Map** 6 E5
88 Oxford St, Woollahra
Tel 9362 3838
On a main road overlooking
Centennial Park, the relaxed,
expansive dining area is
beautifully fitted out for dining
in style. The menu offers a
modern take on comfort food,
using fresh, seasonal produce.

La Scala on Jersey $$
Italian   **Map** 6 D4
2a Oxford St, Woollahra
Tel 9357 0815   **Closed** *Sun*
A modern restaurant located
above the Light Bridge Hotel.
Start with a drink downstairs,
then head upstairs for dinner,
where the true Italian feasting
and sharing style is encouraged.
The *ragù* of pork cheeks, onions
and Pecorino is particularly good

The London Hotel
Pub   **$$**   **Map** 6 D3
85 Underwood St (cnr William St), Paddington
Tel *9331 3200*
You will not go hungry at this historic pub nestled in the winding back streets. There's an array of classics available here – pasta, steaks and fish – as well as a separate pizza menu. Warm, friendly service.

Pinbone
Modern Australian   **$$**   **Map** 6 D4
3 Jersey Rd, Woollahra
Tel *9328 1600*   **Closed** *Mon, Tue*
The menu features intriguingly named snacks: a potato "thing", "chicken poppers" and "fairy bread" that is actually topped with caviar. The sharing plates, desserts and brunch are less quirky but equally delicious.

Vamps Bistro
Italian   **$$**   **Map** 5 B3
227 Glenmore Rd, Paddington
Tel *9331 1032*   **Closed** *Sun*
Operated by the same husband-and-wife team since 1993 and housed in a cosy Victorian terrace with a charming garden courtyard. Enjoy classical French fare with Australian and Asian influences.

Vincent
French   **$$**   **Map** 6 E4
14 Queen St, Woollahra
Tel *8039 1500*   **Closed** *Mon*
This is an effortlessly relaxed and stylish bistro tucked inside the Hughenden Hotel that puts its own spin on French classics. Eat at the inside or outdoor dining room areas, or at the bar.

Vino e Cucina
Italian   **$$**   **Map** 5 C3
211 Glenmore Rd, Paddington
Tel *9331 7389*   **Closed** *Tue*
Pasta, pizza and traditional dishes – fresh produce, simple flavours, friendly service. It can get loud and raucous during busy periods, but it's quieter if you request a seat out the back. A good Italian wine list, too.

Wine Library
European   **$$**   **Map** 6 D4
18 Oxford St, Woollahra
Tel *9360 5686*
An array of small dishes is offered to share here from a menu that spans charcuterie, items "from the sea", meats, salads, cheeses and desserts. There's also a 29-page wine list, in what must be Sydney's loudest library.

Beppi's – serving fine Italian fare for sixty years *(see p194)*

Buon Ricardo
Italian   **$$$**   **Map** 5 C2
108 Boundary St, Paddington
Tel *9360 6729*   **Closed** *Sun, Mon*
Owner-chef Armando Percuoco has been serving up the fine flavours of Italy at its best for almost 30 years. It's delicious, and made to order; the truffled-egg fettuccine is tossed at the table.

Four in Hand
Pub   **$$$**   **Map** 6 E3
105 Sutherland St, Paddington
Tel *9362 1999*
A favourite with locals, the dining room here is the ideal setting for a long, lazy lunch or dinner. Or stay in the bar and order from the extensive grazing menu.

DK Choice

Guillaume
French   **$$$**   **Map** 6 E3
92 Hargrave St, Paddington
Tel *9302 5222*   **Closed** *Mon*
A true fine-dining experience, with exquisite food and attention to detail from the chef who ran his namesake restaurant at the Sydney Opera House for many years. Guillaume Brahimi – and his famous Paris mash – now brings joy to foodies in Sydney's east, with this elegant restaurant in the historic three-level Darcy's building.

Lucio's
Italian   **$$$**   **Map** 6 D3
47 Windsor St, Paddington
Tel *9380 5996*   **Closed** *Sun, Mon*
An art gallery in a fine-dining restaurant – the walls are adorned with works by Australian artist Tim Storrier, and the menu covers are designed by John Olsen. The artistry also extends to the food; the pesto is even freshly ground at the table.

Further Afield

AB Hotel
Pub Bistro   **$**
225 Glebe Point Rd, Glebe
Tel *9660 1417*
A basic cheap-and-cheerful old-style pub bistro serving up big portions at low prices. Daily and happy-hour specials make this hunger-buster even more of a money saver.

Badde Manors
Café   **$**
37 Glebe Point Rd, Glebe
Tel *9660 3797*
Keeping the locals happy and nourished since 1992. Quirky decor – from the twin angels on the awning outside, to the retro fittings inside. The food is simple and reliable café fare.

Il Baretto
Italian   **$**   **Map** 5 A4
496 Bourke St, Surry Hills
Tel *9361 6163*   **Closed** *Sun, Mon*
Simple Italian cooking with home-made pasta served in a crowded space that can mean queues for a table. The signature pappardelle duck *ragù* is a menu stalwart.

Bean Drinking
Café   **$**
1/13 Ernest Place, Crows Nest
Tel *9436 1678*
Speciality coffee and espresso bar with a grass area out the front for the kids to run around on while grown-ups choose from the mostly organic all-day menu.

Brewtown
Café   **$**
6-8 O'Connell St, Newtown
Tel *9519 2920*
This micro roaster and brew bar takes its coffee seriously – and it's seriously good. The breakfast and lunch menus feature seasonal, organic and pasture-fed produce.

For more information on types of restaurants *see pages 180–81*

Café Mint
Middle Eastern $
579 Crown St, Surry Hills
Tel *9319 0848*
If the small cosy space doesn't warm your heart, the quality of the food will. Mediterranean and Lebanese classics pack a flavour punch – from hot breakfasts to lunch meze plates, with salad, dips and bread. Be sure to try the hummus and lamb mince.

The Crabbe Hole
Café $
1 Knotts Ave, Bondi Beach
Tel *0450 272 223*
A tiny spot but big on views and value. Perched above the Bondi Icebergs ocean pool, here you can grab a coffee, breakfast roll, sandwich or ice cream after swimming and see the beach life unfold. Great for people watching.

Fika Swedish Kitchen
Café $
5b Market Lane
Tel *9976 5099*
A bright space with splashes of blue and yellow. Enjoy traditional Swedish breakfast offerings like Kalles cod roe on crispbread, washed down with Scandinavian hot chocolate or, later in the day, Swedish beer.

Luxe Bakery
Café $
195 Missenden Rd, Camperdown
Tel *9409 713 818*
Loyal locals flock for takeaway coffee and sweet and savoury treats at this place. Sit at a communal table and enjoy a quality coffee with a decadent tart or a hot chocolate and healthy salad.

Maya
Indian Vegetarian $
470 Cleveland St, Surry Hills
Tel *9699 8663*
Join the diverse crowd of students, taxi drivers and foodies at this humble purveyor of authentic treats. Try *thali* plates of assorted curries and breads and the famous *masala dosa*. Finish with Indian fudge. A simple setting offering fabulous food.

Shenkin Kitchen
Middle Eastern Café $
129 Enmore Rd, Enmore
Tel *9519 7463*
Awarded Sydney's best breakfast. It's worth the wait for the *shakshuka*, served in a copper pan with a thick, rich tomato sauce and soft-boiled eggs, with wads of bread to soak it up.

Stunning view of the Sydney Harbour Bridge and Opera House, at Aqua Dining

Sonoma
Café $
215a Glebe Point Rd, Glebe
Tel *9660 2116*
Small in space but big on flavour – from the must-try breakfast rolls, which will keep you fuelled for hours, to a selection of wonderful artisan breads.

Square Peg
Café $
Cnr Carr and Arden Streets, Coogee
Tel *0425 304 862*
Any closer to the water and you'd be in it. The outdoor seating is a great spot to wash down sourdough toast with a smoothie, juice, coffee or tea.

Tom Yum Tum Gang
Thai $
249 Glebe Point Rd, Glebe
Tel *8065 0859*
It's always busy here, but the prompt, courteous service means you won't wait long to taste the home-style Thai that keeps locals coming back for more.

X74 Café
Café $
10 Bream St, Coogee
Tel *9665 2222*
This eatery draws a crowd away from the beach with classic breakfast choices on its all-day menu, including goodies like fried eggs, caramelized onions, potato rosti, or banana bread for something sweeter.

A3 Weeds Restaurant
Modern Australian $$
197 Evans St, Rozelle
Tel *9818 2788*   **Closed** *Mon*
Start with a drink at the bar at this pub-restaurant off Balmain and Rozelle's main drag, where the vibe is casual and comfortable. The food served in the stylish dining room is top notch.

Aqua Dining
Italian $$
Cnr Paul and Northcliff Sts, Milson's Point
Tel *9964 9998*
Perched above the North Sydney Olympic Pool, with a sweeping view from Luna Park across the harbour to the Bridge and Opera House. Good, if pricey, food, but it's all about that view.

Barzura
Modern Australian $$
62 Carr St, Coogee
Tel *9665 5546*
A café, restaurant and bar, so come for breakfast, lunch, dinner or a drink, with spectacular views over Coogee Beach. There's even a healthy menu for the kids.

Bondi Trattoria
Italian $$
34 Campbell Parade, Bondi
Tel *9365 4303*
A long-time favourite on the strip opposite the beach, with some of the best pizza and gelato in the city. Get the day off to a great start with a filling "Bondi Trat" breakfast.

Mouthwatering Indian *thali*, as served at Maya, in Surry Hills

China Beach
$$
Modern Asian
43–45 N Styne, Manly
Tel *9976 0500*
This welcoming beachfront spot serving mostly Thai and Chinese flavours is always busy, and the staff are friendly. The crispy soft-shell crab is a standout choice.

Chiswick
$$ **Map** 6 F3
Modern Australian
65 Ocean St, Woollahra
Tel *8388 8688*
A delightful white, bright, cheerful casual dining venue in a small park with fresh produce from the kitchen garden. The menu includes a range of dishes for sharing – or just indulge yourself.

Coogee Pavillion
$$
Modern Australian
169 Dolphin St, Coogee
Tel *9664 2900*
Family-friendly and fun, there's something for everyone in this multi-level, beachfront pavilion, from breakfast to oysters, burgers, grills and wood-fired pizza. There's even a nostalgic games arena, barbershop and flower stand.

Fish Face
$$
Seafood and Japanese
346 New South Head Rd, Double Bay
Tel *9328 9599*
Not your everyday fish and chippery, this is a noisy, casual diner with stools and tall tables at the front and a quieter rear dining room with daily specials, sushi and sashimi.

Garfish
$$
Seafood
2/21 Broughton St, Kirribilli (off Burton St)
Tel *9922 4322*
The menu promises the best seafood from each season – you choose how you'd like it prepared. Try the locals' favourite, snapper pie, or go early for a breakfast of smoked salmon and eggs.

Glebe Point Diner
$$ **Map** 3 A4
Modern Australian
407 Glebe Point Rd, Glebe
Tel *9660 2646*
Come here for wholesome hearty food from a seasonal menu, with the bread, butter and pasta all made from scratch and served in a relaxed space. A "local" feel, with friendly staff.

Hugo's Manly
$$
Italian
Manly Wharf, East Esplanade, Manly
Tel *8116 8555*
Hip Sydney at its lazy, waterfront best. Contemporary Italian, signature pizzas and decadent desserts are served at lunch or dinner, or try the Afternoon Deck menu (3–6pm) for light snacks, more pizza and sweet treats.

Icebergs Bistro
$$
Bistro
Bondi Icebergs, 1 Notts Ave, Bondi
Tel *9130 3120*
An old-school club bistro: find a table, order hearty pub-style meals at the counter, and choose from a wide selection of drinks at the bar. Enjoy the same view as the very expensive restaurant upstairs. The place is packed at weekends, so come early to secure your spot.

Manly Wharf Hotel
$$
Pub
Manly Wharf, 21 East Esplanade, Manly
Tel *9977 1266*
Steaks, burgers, chicken, salads, pizza, seafood and a kids' menu to keep the little ones happy – it's all on offer at this relaxed spot with harbour views that are worth the price alone. A friendly place with excellent staff.

The Boathouse on Blackwattle Bay
$$$ **Map** 3 A3
Modern Australian
End of Ferry Rd, Glebe
Tel *9518 9011*   **Closed** *Mon*
On the upper level of a boat shed, with views across the working harbour, here you will find a changing menu, but seafood dominates – which is not surprising, with the fish markets across the water. There's even a dedicated oyster menu.

Catalina
$$$
Modern Australian
1 Sunderland Ave, Lyne Park, Rose Bay
Tel *9371 0555*
Seafood is the speciality here, befitting the harbourside location of this gastronomic icon. If you don't have the time – or wallet – for a long lunch or dinner, a bar menu provides a casual, affordable alternative.

Pilu at Freshwater
$$$
Italian
End of Moore Rd, Freshwater
Tel *9938 3331*
You will wish you could move in to this gorgeous cottage by the beautiful Freshwater Beach. There are whitewashed walls, crisp white linen, attentive staff and food that will leave you very satisfied.

Sean's Panorama
$$$
Modern Australian
270 Campbell Pde, Bondi
Tel *9365 4924*   **Closed** *Mon, Tue*
The tiny dining room here makes for an intimate experience – and means booking is essential. Sean's been serving artful meals cooked with care for more than 20 years, and the iconic handmade nougat is still the best.

Beyond Sydney

True to the Bean
$
Café
123 Katoomba St, Katoomba
Tel *0438 396 761*
Coffee and waffles are the dynamic duo everyone raves about for breakfast – or any time, really. Come for enough caffeine and sugar to fuel a day exploring "the mountains" or for a post-adventure afternoon tea break.

Ashcrofts
$$$
European
18 Govetts Leap Rd, Blackheath
Tel *4787 8297*   **Closed** *Sun, Mon*
A cosy mountain hideaway with warm lighting, village hospitality and personal touches that whet the appetite for the meal ahead.

A stunning setting for a friendly dining experience – Manly Wharf Hotel

For more information on types of restaurants *see pages 180–81*

SHOPS AND MARKETS

The range of goods on offer in Sydney is enormous and the quality of merchandise is usually good. The inner city has innumerable elegant arcades and shopping galleries, with plenty of nooks and crannies to explore. Most international labels, such as Gucci, Louis Vuitton and Chanel, are imported and local talent in many fields, notably jewellery, fashion and indigenous arts and crafts, is promoted. The most interesting shopping does not stop at the city centre; there are several "satellite" alternatives. Some of the best shopping areas are highlighted on pages 200–1.

A typical junk-shop-cum-café in Balmain *(see p133)*

Shopping Hours

Most shops are open from 10am–5:30pm each day of the week, though some may close early on Sundays. High-end boutiques open from 10am–6pm. On Thursdays, most shops stay open until 9pm. Most shops in Chinatown are open late every evening and on Sundays.

How to Pay

Major credit cards are accepted almost everywhere. You will need identification, such as a passport or driver's licence, when using traveller's cheques. Department stores will exchange goods or refund your money if you are not satisfied, provided you have kept your receipt. Other stores will only refund if an item is faulty. There is also a 10 per cent Goods and Services Tax (GST) which by law must be displayed in the marked price.

Sales

Many shops conduct sales all year round. The big depart-ment stores of **David Jones** and **Myer** have two gigantic and chaotic clearance sales each year. The post-Christmas sales start on 26 December, lasting into January. The other major sale time is during June, in the lead up to the end of the financial year.

Tax-Free Sales

Duty-free shops are found in the city centre as well as at Kingsford Smith Airport *(see p228)*. You can save 10 per cent on goods such as perfume, jewellery, watches and perhaps up to 30 per cent on alcohol at duty-free shops but you must show your passport and onward ticket. Some stores will also deliver your goods to the airport to be picked up on departure. Duty-free items must be kept in their sealed bags until you leave the city.

You can claim back the GST paid on most goods, purchased for (or in a single transaction of) A$300 or more, at the airport.

Chifley Tower, with the Chifley Plaza shopping arcade at its base

Arcades and Malls

The **Queen Victoria Building** *(see p84)* is Sydney's most palatial shopping space. Four levels contain more than 200 shops. The top level, Victoria Walk, is devoted to merchandise such as silver, antiques, designer knitwear and high-quality souvenirs. The **Strand Arcade** *(see p86)* was originally built in 1892. Jewellery, chocolates, coffee shops and tea rooms are its stock in trade.

Pitt Street Mall has several shopping centres. **Westfield Sydney** features numerous local and international designer brand stores, including Zara, Escada, Gucci and Gap.

Next door to the Hilton, **The Galeries** houses the fantastic

Inside Gleebooks, popular with students and locals in Glebe *(see p133)*

Kinokuniya bookstore, which sells a variety of both Australian and American imprints as well as Chinese and Japanese language, anime art books and stationery. The Monsterthreads store mixes folk and street art with contemporary graphic design on clothing, accessories, homeware, stationery, bags and jewellery lines and also sells brands like Bucketfeet and MOMOT paper toys.

Further down George Street, **World Square** shopping centre houses more than 90 speciality stores, from electronics to Australian menswear label Jack London.

The **MLC Centre**, which faces onto Castlereagh Street, and **Chifley Plaza** also cater to the prestige shopper. Cartier, Tiffany & Co., MaxMara and Kenzo are among the shops here.

The **Harbourside Shopping Centre** has dozens of shops, as well as waterfront restaurants. The atmosphere is festive and the merchandise includes fine arts, jewellery, duty-free shopping, beachwear and Australiana.

Department Stores

The **David Jones** and **Myer** chains compete fiercely, each snaring exclusive rights to stock various local design talents and international labels. The David Jones in Sydney, or DJs, is legendary for its spring floral displays, as well as for its luxurious perfumery and cosmetics hall on the ground

Greengrocer's display of fresh fruit and vegetables

floor. The magnificent store spreads out in two buildings, across the road from each other on Market and Elizabeth streets. The food hall on the lower ground floor is famous for its gourmet fare and fine wines. The first David Jones store opened in 1838, and they claim to have the oldest department store in the world still trading under its original name. Myer now operates 60 stores across Australia, and their first store opened in 1900. The Myer store here in Sydney has a ground floor packed with make-up and accessories, including a large MAC counter. Both the Sydney stores of these famous chains sell women's clothing, lingerie, menswear, baby goods, children's clothes, toys, stationery, kitchenware, furniture, china, crystal and silver.

Shopping Further Afield

Good shopping areas outside central Sydney are Balmain, for village-style shopping; Double Bay, with its chic, though pricey, boutiques; the enormous mega-mall **Westfield Bondi Junction** which is only a short train journey away; and Left Bank-style student haunts of Newtown and Glebe. Bargains can be found at the factory outlets in Redfern, **Market City** and at Birkenhead Point. **Shop & Save Tours** arrange shopping day trips, while *DFO*, near Sydney Olympic Park, has outlet stores selling luxury and popular brands.

Part of the spring floral display, David Jones department store

DIRECTORY

Chifley Plaza
2 Chifley Square. **Map** 1 B4.
Tel 9229 0165.

David Jones
Cnr Elizabeth St & Market St.
Map 1 B5. **Tel** 9266 5544.
Also: Cnr Market St & Castlereagh
St. **Map** 1 B5. **Tel** 9266 5544.

DFO
3–5 Underwood St, Homebush.
Tel 9748 9800.

The Galeries
500 George St. **Map** 1 B5.
Tel 9265 6800.

**Harbourside Shopping
Centre**
Darling Harbour. **Map** 3 C2.
Tel 8204 1888.

Market City
9–13 Hay St, Haymarket.
Map 4 D4. **Tel** 9288 8900.

MLC Centre
19–29 Martin Place. **Map** 1 B4.
Tel 9224 8333.

Myer
436 George St. **Map** 1 B5.
Tel 9238 9111.

Queen Victoria Building
455 George St. **Map** 1 B5.
Tel 9265 6800.

Shop & Save Tours
Tel 9672 2992.

Strand Arcade
412–414 George St. **Map** 1 B5.
Tel 9232 4199.

Westfield Bondi Junction
500 Oxford St, Bondi Junction.
Map 4 F3. **Tel** 9947 8000.

Westfield Sydney
Pitt St Mall. **Map** 4 E2.
Tel 8236 9200.

World Square
680 George St. **Map** 4 E3.
Tel 8669 6900.

Sydney's Best: Shopping Streets and Markets

Sydney's best shopping areas range from galleries, arcades and department stores selling expensive gifts and jewellery *(see pp198–9)*, to boutiques of extroverted cutting-edge fashion. The range of styles is impressive – both international couture brands and acclaimed local designer labels *(pp204–5)*. The city's hip fringe areas, such as Glebe and Surry Hills, are alive with street fashion and accessories.

Colourful markets are a delight for collectors and bargain-hunters alike *(p203)*. Those who seek out quirky and one-off items are well catered for, as are those looking to take home quality craft and indigenous art as mementos of their visit. Specialist browsers will find a tempting selection of book and music shops *(pp206–7)*.

The Rocks Market
At weekends, the stalls offer affordable arts and crafts and jewellery. *(See p203.)*

THE RO
AND
CIRCUL
QUAY

Queen Victoria Building
This elegant shopping gallery offers four floors of designer wear, gifts, and speciality stores amid cafés.

Darling Harbour
Quality Australiana, surf and beach wear, souvenir ideas, children's clothes, colourful knits and art and craft shops abound.

CIT
CENT

DARLING
HARBOUR
AND
SURRY HILLS

Sydney Fish Market
You can buy fresh seafood daily in the colourful fishmongers' halls or order from the cafés that spill out on to the sunny terrace alongside the marina. *(See p202.)*

| 0 metres | 500 |
| 0 yards | 500 |

Chinatown
This is the place to find discounts on watches, gold jewellery, opals and even fabrics. There are also Chinese butchers' shops, herbalists and supermarkets.

City Centre
Dazzling shopping arcades and smart malls are dotted throughout the city centre, notably Pitt Street Mall, Strand Arcade and Westfield Sydney.

Castlereagh Street
The city's designer row is home to Chanel, Gucci, Hermès and others. The most exclusive names cluster near the King Street intersection.

BOTANIC GARDEN AND THE DOMAIN

Darlinghurst and Surry Hills
These suburbs are the youth culture barometer: young designers, leather à la mode, gay fashion, hot music and gifts for those who love quirky collectables.

KINGS CROSS AND DARLINGHURST

PADDINGTON

Paddington Markets
Considered by many to be Sydney's best market and a showcase for up-and-coming fashions, it is held every Saturday. *(See p203.)*

Paddington and Woollahra
Upmarket clothing, shoes, homeware and gourmet food are on show here, while cafés and galleries add to the allure. Queen Street, Woollahra, is the antique shop strip.

Sydney Fish Market

Each day, 65 tonnes (tons) of fresh fish and other seafood are sold at the Fish Market's Dutch Clock auction. According to this system, prices start high, and gradually descend on a computerized "clock", until a buyer puts in a bid. At this point, no other bids are accepted, and the deal is made. This unusually quiet auction starts at 5:30am every Monday to Friday, and runs for two to three hours until all the seafood is sold. Members of the public can follow the auction proceedings from a viewing area.

The waterfront cafés offering fine seafood at reasonable prices make dining here a rare treat.

Blue swimmer crabs have a mild flavour and are found all around the Australian coastline.

About 30 wholesalers, many of them family businesses, buy bulk quantities of the day's catch; some also have retail outlets at the market itself.

Local fishermen send their fish to the market anytime between 4pm the previous day and 8am on the day of the auction. Most of the catch is from the far coasts of New South Wales.

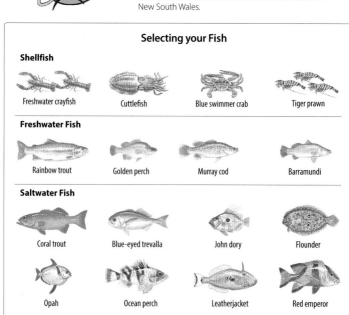

Selecting your Fish

Shellfish

Freshwater crayfish

Cuttlefish

Blue swimmer crab

Tiger prawn

Freshwater Fish

Rainbow trout

Golden perch

Murray cod

Barramundi

Saltwater Fish

Coral trout

Blue-eyed trevalla

John dory

Flounder

Opah

Ocean perch

Leatherjacket

Red emperor

Markets

Scouring markets for the cheap, the cheerful and the chic has become a popular weekend pastime in Sydney. Weekly or monthly markets that suit both the bargain-hunter and the serious shopper have sprung up all over the suburbs. Souvenir T-shirts, leather jackets, high-class art – there is something to suit every taste. Even more popular are the Sydney Fish Market and the produce markets, which teem with people from early in the morning and have turned shopping into a big event.

Balmain Market

Cnr Darling St and Curtis Rd, Balmain. 442, 434. **Open** *8:30am–4pm Sat.*

Held in the grounds of St Andrews Congregational Church in the shade of a fig tree said to be more than 150 years old, this compact market attracts both locals and tourists. Fees from stallholders contribute to the ongoing restoration of the church, which was built in 1853. As well as stalls selling children's wear, second-hand books, contemporary and antique jewellery, stained-glass mobiles and Chinese healing balls, there is a food hall where you can find fresh and aromatic Japanese, Thai, Indian and specialist vegetarian dishes in the making.

Bondi Beach Market

Bondi Beach Public School, Campbell Parade, North Bondi. 333, 380. **Open** *10am–5pm Sun in summer; 4pm in winter.*

Many Sydney fashion labels start off here, as did current darlings **Sass & Bide** *(see p204).* There are also lots of second-hand clothing buys; funky 1970s gear is particularly popular. Arrive early as some of the stalls are all set up by 9am. The best bargain clothes are near the back of the market. Expect to see the odd actor or rock star among the browsers.

The Entertainment Quarter

Lang Rd, Moore Park. **Map** *5 C5.* Oxford St or Anzac Pde routes. **Open** *10am–3:30pm Wed, Sat, 10am–4pm Sun. (See p128.)*
There is plenty of fresh produce and gourmet delicacies to sample at the EQ Village Markets every Wednesday and Saturday, located next to the working Fox Studios, where films such as *Mission: Impossible II* and the *Star Wars* prequels were shot. There is a Merchandise Market on Sunday.

Glebe Market

Glebe Public School, Glebe Point Road, Glebe. **Map** *3 B5.* 431, 433. **Open** *10am–4pm Sat.*
A treasure trove for the junk shop enthusiast and canny scavenger, this market is popular with the inner-city grunge set. Best buys are bric-à-brac and crafts made from recycled wood, metal and glass. Arrive early for bargain porcelain and, perhaps, the odd undervalued lithograph. A few fashion students also sell their work. You will also find handmade bags, hats and jewellery. Second-hand clothes are a good buy here, as are rings and pendants, books, CDs and records.

The Sydney Morning Herald Growers' Market

Pyrmont Bay Park, opposite The Star Casino. **Map** *3 C1.* light rail from Central. **Open** *7–11am first Saturday of every month.*

Get in early; by 8am there are long lines for coffee, bread and pastries. This is the place for native Australian bushfoods, such as dried bush tomatoes, nutty wattleseed and pepperberries. There is everything you will need for a gourmet feast, such as poultry, beef, pork and venison from around NSW; lesser-found vegetables such as wild mushrooms, cavolo nero and golden beetroot; and delicacies such as honey, cheese and fudge. Fresh flowers are available, too.

Paddington Markets

(See p128.)

From nouveau to novelties, there is always something tempting here, and it is unlikely you will come away empty-handed. Silver jewellery is abundant, so prices are very competitive; there are also children's clothes, leather goods, unusual buckles, belts and accessories, stationery, candles, and oddities such as babies' baseball caps and rubbery novelty masks.

Paddy's Markets

(See p101.)

In the 19th century, Paddy's in the Haymarket was the city's fringe market and also the location of fairgrounds and circuses. Today, it has between 500 and 1,000 stalls under one roof. Early birds will get the best flowers, fruit, vegetables and seafood. There are also good buys in caneware, luggage, leather goods, tools, homewares, ornaments, souvenirs and toys.

The Rocks Market

George St, The Rocks. **Map** *1 B2.* 431, 432, 433, 434. **Open** *10am –5pm Sat & Sun.*

At weekends, rain or shine, a sail-like canopy is erected at the top end of George Street, transforming the area into an atmospheric marketplace. Get there early to beat the afternoon crowds. There are about 140 stalls, whose wares are unique rather than inexpensive. Quality is a priority here. Look out for wind chimes, pewter picture frames, pub poster prints, oils, leather goods, wooden toys, gold-plated bush leaves, and jewellery made from wood, shell, silver or crystal. Every Friday in November the Rocks Market hosts "Markets by Moonlight", a combination of night markets, live music and outdoor bars and food stalls.

Sydney Fish Market

(See p133.)

Sydney is famous for its fresh seafood and the Sydney Fish Market is the ideal place to buy it. The displays of seafood are arresting, with coral reds, marble pinks, greys, blacks and iridescent yellows to take your mind off the sloshy floors and the smell of the sea. The market also has a sushi bar, fish cafés, a bakery, a gourmet deli, a poultry and game specialist, a bottle shop, and a vegetable shop. The Sydney Seafood School operates above the market, offering lessons in preparing and serving seafood.

Eveleigh Markets

245 Wilson St, Eveleigh. 352, 370, 423, 426, 442. **Open** *8am–1pm Sat.*

These farmers' and artisans' markets, with a focus on fresh local produce and creative arts and crafts, are held in a historic railway workshop a short walk from Redfern train station.

Clothes and Accessories

Australian style was once an oxymoron. Sydney now offers a plethora of chic shops as long as you know where to look. Top boutiques sell both men's and women's clothing, as well as accessories. The city's "smart casual" ethos, particularly in summer, means there are plenty of luxe but informal clothes available.

Australian Fashion

A number of Sydney's fashion designers have attained a global profile, including **Akira Isogawa**. Japanese-born Isogawa makes artistic clothing for women and men. Some of the most interesting fashion is from young emerging designers like **Kaliver**, who began designing at age 12.

Young jeans label **Sass & Bide** (women only) has also shot to fame, with celebrities wearing their denims. **Scanlan & Theodore** is another stalwart of the Australian fashion scene, as is **Country Road**, known for its stylish office- and weekend-wear.

For retro women's and children's clothes head to **Dragstar**. **Jack London** stocks upscale, trendy menswear; their suits are particularly popular. The quirky **Capital L** boutique houses the hottest names in Aussie fashion, while **Zimmermann** offers women's and girls' clothes and is famous for its swimwear. **Camilla** is known for its flamboyant, colourful print kaftans and dresses. Head to **Farage Women** for classic tailored suits and shirts.

High-street clothing can be found in and around Pitt Street Mall and Bondi Junction. Here you will find both international and homegrown fashion outlets. **Sportsgirl** sells funky clothes that appeal to both teens and adult women. The **Witchery** stores are a favourite among women for their stylish designs. **Just Jeans** doesn't just sell jeans; it stocks the latest trends for men and women.

General Pants has funky street labels like One Teaspoon and Just Ask Amanda. Surry Hills is the place for discount and vintage clothing; check out **Zoo Emporium**. New designers try out their wares in Bondi, Glebe and Paddington markets.

International Labels

Many Sydney stores sell designer imports. For the best ranges, visit **Belinda** – a men's and women's boutique – as well as others in Double Bay, and the MLC Centre. In **Robby Ingham Stores** you will find women's and men's ranges including Chloé, Paul Smith and Comme des Garçons. For shoe addicts, **Cosmopolitan Shoes** stocks labels such as Dolce & Gabbana, Sonia Rykiel, Dior and Jimmy Choo. **Hype DC** also offers all the latest ranges. New Zealand designers **Zambesi** offer their own designs for women and men as well as a range of Martin Margiela pieces.

Luxury Brands

Many visitors like to shop for international labels such as **Louis Vuitton**, which you will find located in Castlereagh Street, along with **Chanel**. The Queen Victoria Building is home to **Bally**, and Martin Place has resident A-listers such as **Prada** and **Giorgio Armani**. **Girls With Gems** is further afield in Double Bay.

Surf Shops

For the latest surf gear, look no further than Bondi where the streets are lined with shops selling clothing, swimwear and boards of all sizes to buy and hire. Serious surfers and novices should check out **Between the Flags** and **Bondi Surf Co**. Besides stocking its own beachwear label, **Rip Curl** also sells Australian brands such as Tigerlily and Billabong. **Surfection** and **Surf Dive 'n' Ski** are hugely popular surf- and skatewear shops packed with the latest fashion and performance brands and accessories.

Clothes for Children

Department stores, **David Jones** and **Myer** (see pp198–9), are one-stop shops for children's clothes, from newborn to teenage. Look out for good quality Australian labels such

Size Chart

Women's clothes

Australian	6	8	10	12	14	16	18	20
American	4	6	8	10	12	14	16	18
British	6	8	10	12	14	16	18	20
Continental	38	40	42	44	46	48	50	52

Women's shoes

Australian	6–6½	7	7½–8	8½	9–9½	10	10½–11	
American	5	6	7	8	9	10	11	
British	3	4	5	6	7	8	9	
Continental	36	37	38	39	40	41	42	

Men's suits

Australian	44	46	48	50	52	54	56	58
American	34	36	38	40	42	44	46	48
British	34	36	38	40	42	44	46	48
Continental	44	46	48	50	52	54	56	58

Men's shirts

Australian	36	38	39	41	42	43	44	45
American	14	15	15½	16	16½	17	17½	18
British	14	15	15½	16	16½	17	17½	18
Continental	36	38	39	41	42	43	44	45

Men's shoes

Australian	7	7½	8	8½	9	10	11	12
American	7	7½	8	8½	9½	10½	11	11½
British	6	7	7½	8	9	10	11	12
Continental	39	40	41	42	43	44	45	46

as Fred Bare and Gumboots. Mambo, Dragstar and Zimmermann *(see above)* also sell fun and unusual kidswear.

Accessories

The team behind **Dinosaur Designs** are some of Australia's most celebrated designers. They craft chunky bangles, necklaces and rings, and also bowls, plates and vases, from jewel-coloured

resin. **Chilli Coral** sells home decor and gifts, including Australian-made Samantha Ronson bowls, Bison tableware, vintage bottles and handmade jewellery. At trendy **Family Jewels**, unique silver creations feature Australian pearls, nautilus shell and crystals. They also showcase international designers. In her plush store, **Jan Logan** sells exquisite jewellery, using precious

and semi-precious stones. Australian hat designer **Helen Kaminski** uses fabrics, raffia, straw, felt and leather to make hats and bags. In a different style, **Crumpler** uses high-tech fabrics to make bags that will last a century. And in a street of designer names, **Andrew McDonald**'s little studio shop doesn't cry for attention, but he does sell handcrafted shoes for men and women.

DIRECTORY

Australian Fashion

Akira Isogawa
12A Queen St, Woollahra. **Map** 6 E4. **Tel** 9361 5221. Level 2, Strand Arcade. **Map** 1 B4. **Tel** 9232 1078.

Camilla
132A Warners Ave, Bondi. **Tel** 9130 1430.

Capital L
100 Oxford St, Paddington. **Map** 5 B3. **Tel** 9361 0111.

Country Road
Ground level, Queen Victoria Building. **Map** 1 B5. **Tel** 9261 2009.

Dragstar
535a King St, Newtown. **Tel** 9550 1243.

Farage Women
Shops 54 & 79, Level 1 Strand Arcade. **Map** 1 B5. **Tel** 9233 1272.

General Pants
Ground level, Mid City Shopping St, Pitt St Mall. **Map** 4 E2. **Tel** 8275 5111.

Jack London
World Square Shopping Centre, 680 George St. **Map** 4 E3. **Tel** 9261 2012.

Just Jeans
Ground floor, Westfield Sydney *(see p199)*. **Map** 1 B5. **Tel** 9231 2297.

Kaliver
448 Oxford St, Paddington. **Map** 6 D4. **Tel** 8283 8542.

Sass & Bide
132 Oxford St, Paddington. **Map** 5 B3. **Tel** 9360 3900.

Scanlan & Theodore
122 Oxford St, Paddington. **Map** 5 B3. **Tel** 9380 9388.

Sportsgirl
Street level, Westfield Sydney, Pitt St Mall. **Map** 1 B5. **Tel** 9223 8255.

Witchery
Shop 3, Met Centre, 273 George St. **Map** 1 B4. **Tel** 9252 8450.

Zimmermann
Shop 2, 2–16 Glenmore Rd, Paddington. **Map** 5 B3. **Tel** 9357 4700.

Zoo Emporium
180b Campbell St, Surry Hills. **Map** 5 A2. **Tel** 9380 5990.

International Labels

Belinda
8 Transvaal Ave, Double Bay. **Tel** 9328 6288.

Cosmopolitan Shoes
Cosmopolitan Centre, Knox St, Double Bay. **Tel** 9362 0510.

Hype DC
Shop 50, Queen Victoria Building, 455 George St. **Map** 1 B5. **Tel** 9262 7444.

Robby Ingham Stores
424–428 Oxford St, Paddington. **Map** 6 D4. **Tel** 9332 2124.

Zambesi
5 Glenmore Rd. **Tel** 9331 1140.

Luxury Brands

Bally
Ground floor, Queen Victoria Building, 455 George St. **Map** 1 B5. **Tel** 9267 3887.

Chanel
70 Castlereagh St. **Map** 1 B5. **Tel** 9233 4800.

Giorgio Armani
4 Martin Place. **Map** 1 B4. **Tel** 8233 5888.

Girls With Gems
Shop 15, 28–34 Cross St, Double Bay. **Tel** 0413 488 823.

Louis Vuitton
365 George St. **Map** 1 B4. **Tel** 1300 883 880.

Prada
Level 5, Westfield Sydney, Castlereagh St. **Map** 1 B5. **Tel** 9231 3929.

Surf Shops

Between the Flags
152–158 Campbell Parade, Bondi Beach. **Tel** 9365 5611.

Bondi Surf Co.
80 Campbell Parade, Bondi Beach. **Tel** 9365 0870.

Rip Curl
82 Campbell Parade, Bondi Beach. **Tel** 9130 2660.

Surf Dive 'n' Ski
Westfield Bondi Junction, 500 Oxford St. **Tel** 9458 4982.

Surfection
31 Hall St, Bondi Beach. **Tel** 9130 1051.

Clothes For Children

David Jones
Cnr Elizabeth & Market sts. **Map** 1 B5. **Tel** 9266 5544.

Myer
436 George St. **Map** 1 B5. **Tel** 9238 9111.

Accessories

Andrew McDonald
Ground floor, Strand Arcade. **Map** 1 B5. **Tel** 8084 2595.

Chilli Coral
401 Crown St, Surry Hills. **Map** 5 A3. **Tel** 8021 7869.

Crumpler
The Strand Arcade. **Map** 1 B5. **Tel** 9222 1300.

Dinosaur Designs
See pp206–7.

Family Jewels
48 Oxford St, Paddington. **Map** 6 E4. **Tel** 9331 6647.

Helen Kaminski
Shop 3, Four Seasons Hotel, 199 George St. **Map** 1 B3. **Tel** 9251 9850.

Jan Logan
36 Cross St, Double Bay. **Tel** 9363 2529.

Specialist Shops and Souvenirs

Sydney offers an extensive range of gift and souvenir ideas, from unset opals and jewellery to Aboriginal art and hand-crafted souvenirs. Museum shops, such as at the Museum of Sydney *(see p87)* and the Art Gallery of NSW *(see pp110–13)*, often have specially commissioned items that make great presents or reminders of your visit.

One-Offs

Specialist shops abound in Sydney – some practical, some eccentric, others simply indulgent. **R M Williams'** stockman's gear includes its signature cowboy-style boots, belts, clothes and accessories.

Wheels & Doll Baby is a powder-room, with 1950s chic, a mix of rock 'n' roll and Hollywood glamour. **The Hour Glass** stocks traditional-style watches, while sunglasses from the likes of Armani and Gaultier can be found at **The Looking Glass**.

For celebrity glamour, **Napoleon Perdis Cosmetics** sells a huge array of make-up and bears the name of Australia's leading make-up artist to the "stars". Or, for some eclectic fashion and homewares, try a branch of **Orson & Blake**, the one in Surry Hills has a good café.

Australiana

Australiana has become more than just a souvenir genre; it is now an art form in itself.

Artist Ken Done's distinctive prints feature on posters, scarves, books and more are available in the shop at his small **Ken Done Gallery**, while the **Australian Geographic** store sells novelty and educational products, including soft toys, boomerangs, calendars and tea towels. The shop at the **Art Gallery of New South Wales** stocks art books, posters, prints and gifts. The Queen Victoria Building's Victoria Walk *(see p84)* is dominated by Australiana: souvenirs, silver, antiques, art and crafts.

The **Australian Museum** *(see pp90–91)* has a shop that sells unusual gift items such as native flower presses, bark paintings and Australian animal puppets, puzzles and games.

Books

The large **Dymocks** chain has a good range of guide books and maps on Sydney. For more eclectic browsing, try **Abbey's Bookshop, Ariel** and **Gleebooks**, while **Berkelouw Books** has three floors of new, second-hand and rare books. **The Bookshop Darlinghurst** specializes in gay and lesbian fiction and non-fiction. The **State Library of NSW** *(see p114)* bookshop has a good choice of Australian books, particularly on history. The **ABC Shop** stocks TV tie-in titles, many of them on cookery and music.

Music

Several specialist music shops of international repute can be found in Sydney. **Red Eye Records** is for the streetwise, with its stock of collectables, rarities, alternative music and concert tickets. **Suzie Q Coffee + Records** has an eclectic mix of LPs and offers a good caffeine hit. **Mojo Record Bar** has a great selection of rock, blues, country and psychedelia. **The Record Store** offers music from jazz to electronica and also sells turntables, needles, and other accessories for vinyl-lovers, while **Utopia Records** has an impressively comprehensive stock of hard rock and heavy metal. **Fish Fine Music** specializes in classical music.

Aboriginal Art

Traditional paintings, fabric, jewellery, boomerangs, cards and carvings can be bought at the **Aboriginal and Pacific Art**. You can find tribal artifacts from Aboriginal Australia at several shops in the Harbourside Shopping Centre, Darling Harbour. The **Coo-ee Aboriginal Art Gallery** boasts a large selection of limited edition prints, hand-printed fabrics, books and Aboriginal music. The **Kate Owen Gallery & Studio** in Rozelle features a wide range of contemporary Aboriginal art displayed over three floors. With works by numerous indigenous artists, it has been voted one of Sydney's best Aboriginal art galleries. Works by urban indigenous artists are found at the **Boomalli Aboriginal Artists' Cooperative**.

Opals

Sydney offers a variety of opals in myriad settings. **Flame Opals** is a family-run store, selling stones from all the major Australian opal fields. At **Opal Fields** you can view a museum collection of opalised fossils, before buying from the wide range of gems. **Giulian's** has unset opals, including blacks from Lightning Ridge, whites from Coober Pedy and boulder opals from Quilpie.

Jewellery

Long-established Sydney jewellers with 24-carat reputations include **Fairfax & Roberts, Hardy Brothers** and **Percy Marks**. World-class pearls are found in the waters off the northwestern coast of Australia. Rare and beautiful examples can be found at **Paspaley Pearls**.

Bill Hicks Jewellery's award-winning owner can create unique one-off pieces according to your designs. Alternatively, browse their ready-made collection. **Dinosaur Designs** made its name with colourful, chunky resin jewellery, while at **Love & Hatred**, jewelled wrist cuffs, rings and crosses recall lush medieval treasures. **Jan Logan** is an iconic Australian jewellery designer, with stores in Melbourne, Hong Kong, and London. Choose from beautiful and unusual contemporary pieces, otherwise the shop also carries antiques.

DIRECTORY

One-Offs

The Hour Glass
142 King St. **Map** 1 B5.
Tel 9221 2288.

The Looking Glass
Queen Victoria Building.
Map 1 B5. **Tel** 9264 3696.

Napoleon Perdis Cosmetics
74 Oxford St, Paddington.
Tel 9331 1702. **Map** 5 A2.
w napoleoncosm
etics.com

Orson & Blake
388 Pacific Highway,
Crows Nest. **Tel** 8399 2525.
Also at: Gallery level,
Supa Centa Moore Park,
Cnr South Dowling St,
Todman and Dacey Aves.
Tel 9622 2926.
w orsanandblake.
com.au

R M Williams
Level 3, Westfield Sydney,
Pitt St. **Map** 4 E2.
Tel 8246 9136.

Wheels & Doll Baby
259 Crown St,
Darlinghurst. **Map** 5 A2.
Tel 9361 3286.

Australiana

Art Gallery of New South Wales Shop
Art Gallery Rd. **Map** 2 D4.
Tel 9225 1700.

Australian Geographic
Shop 100, Westfield Bondi
Junction, 500 Oxford St.
Tel 9257 0600.

Australian Museum Shop
6 College St. **Map** 4 F3.
Tel 9320 6150.

Ken Done Gallery
1 Hickson Rd, The Rocks.
Map 1 B1. **Tel** 8274 4599.
w kendone.com.au

Books

Abbey's Bookshop
131 York St. **Map** 1 A5.
Tel 9264 3111.

ABC Shop
Shop 48, Queen Victoria
Building. **Map** 1 B5.
Tel 9286 3726.

Ariel
42 Oxford St, Paddington.
Map 5 B3. **Tel** 9332 4581.

Berkelouw Books
19 Oxford St, Paddington.
Map 5 B3. **Tel** 9360 3200.
Also at: 70 Norton St,
Leichhardt. **Tel** 9560 3200.
w berkelouw.com.au

The Bookshop Darlinghurst
207 Oxford St,
Darlinghurst. **Map** 5 A2.
Tel 9331 1103.

Dymocks
424 George St. **Map** 1 B5.
Tel 9235 0155. One of
many branches.

Gleebooks
49 Glebe Point Rd, Glebe.
Map 3 B5. **Tel** 9660 2333.

State Library of NSW Shop
Macquarie St. **Map** 1 C4.
Tel 9273 1611.

Music

Fish Fine Music
Shop 40, Level 2, Queen
Victoria Building.
Map 1 B5. **Tel** 9264 6458

Mojo Record Bar
Basement level,
73 York St. **Map** 1 A4.
Tel 9262 4999.

The Record Store
255 Crown St,
Darlinghurst. **Map** 5 A4.
Tel 9380 8223.

Red Eye Records
66 King St, Sydney.
Map 1 B5. **Tel** 9299 4233.

Suzie Q Coffee + Records
1/18 Hutchinson St,
Surry Hills. **Map** 5 A3.
Tel 9332 2739.

Utopia Records
233 Broadway, Broadway.
Map 3 C5. **Tel** 9571 6662.

Aboriginal Art

Aboriginal and Pacific Art
2 Danks St, Waterloo.
Tel 9699 2211.

Boomalli Aboriginal Artists' Cooperative
55–59 Flood St,
Leichhardt. **Tel** 9560 2541.

Coo-ee Aboriginal Art Gallery
31 Lamrock Ave, Bondi
Beach. **Tel** 9300 9233.

Kate Owen Gallery & Studio
680 Darling St, Rozelle.
Tel 9555 5283.

Opals

Flame Opals
119 George Street,
The Rocks. **Map** 1 B2.
Tel 9247 3446.

Giulian's
Level 3, Four Seasons
Hotel, 199 George St.
Map 1 B3. **Tel** 9252 2051.
Also at: 198 Harrington St,
The Rocks.

Opal Fields
Queen Victoria Building,
George St, The Rocks.
Map 1 B5. **Tel** 9247 6800.
One of two branches.

Jewellery

Bill Hicks Jewellery
Suite 1005/155 King St.
Map 4 E1. **Tel** 9231 0994.

Dinosaur Designs
Strand Arcade. **Map** 1 B5.
Tel 9223 2953.
One of two branches.

Fairfax & Roberts
44 Martin Place.
Map 1 B4. **Tel** 9232 8511.

Hardy Brothers
60 Castlereagh St.
Map 1 B5. **Tel** 8262 3100.

Jan Logan
36 Cross St, Double Bay.
Tel 9363 2529.

Love & Hatred
Strand Arcade. **Map** 1 B5.
Tel 9233 3441.

Paspaley Pearls
2 Martin Place. **Map** 1 A4.
Tel 9232 7633.

Percy Marks
60–70 Elizabeth St.
Map 1 B4. **Tel** 9233 1355.

ENTERTAINMENT IN SYDNEY

Sydney has the standard of entertainment and nightlife you would expect from a cosmopolitan city. Everything from opera and ballet at Sydney Opera House to open-air productions in the Botanic Garden is on offer. Venues such as the Capitol and the Theatre Royal play host to the latest musicals, while Sydney's many smaller theatres are home to interesting fringe theatre, modern dance and rock and pop concerts. Pub rock thrives in the inner city and beyond; and there are many nightspots for jazz, dance and alternative music. Movie buffs are well catered for with film festivals, art-house films and foreign titles, as well as the latest Hollywood blockbusters. One of the features of harbourside living is the free outdoor entertainment, so children will find that a visit to Sydney can be especially memorable.

Sydney Theatre *(see p210)* on Hickson Road, Walsh Bay

Information

For details of events in the city, you should check the daily newspapers first. They carry cinema, and often arts and theatre, advertisements daily. The most comprehensive listings appear in the *Sydney Morning Herald*'s "Metro" guide every Friday and its "Spectrum" section on Saturdays. The *Daily Telegraph* has a gig guide on daily, with opportunities to win free tickets to special events. The *Australian*'s main arts pages appear on Fridays and all the papers review new films in weekend editions.

Tourism NSW information kiosks have free guides and the quarterly *What's on in Darling Harbour*. Kiosks are at Town Hall, Circular Quay and Martin Place. *Where Magazine* is available at the airport and the **Sydney Visitor Centre** at The Rocks. Hotels offer free guides, or try **True Local**.

Music fans are well served by the free weekly guides *Drum Media* and *3-D World* and *Brag*, found at video and music shops, pubs and clubs. Many venues have leaflets about forthcoming attractions, while the major venues have information telephone lines and websites.

Buying Tickets

Some of the most popular operas, shows, plays and ballets in Sydney are sold out months in advance. While it is better to book ahead, many theatres do set aside tickets to be sold at the door on the night.

You can buy tickets from the box office or by telephone. Some orchestral performances do not admit children under seven, so check with the box office before buying. If you make a phone booking using a credit card, the tickets can be mailed to you. Alternatively, tickets can be collected from the box office half an hour before the show. The major agencies will take overseas bookings.

Buying tickets from touts is not advisable; if you are caught with a "sold on" ticket you will be denied access to the event. If all else fails, hotel concierges have a reputation for being able to secure hard-to-get tickets.

Choosing Seats

If booking in person at either the venue or the agency, you will be able to look at a seating plan. Be aware that in the State Theatre's stalls, row A is the back row. In Sydney, there is not as much difference in price between stalls and the dress circle as in other cities.

If booking by phone with one of the agencies, you will only be able to get a rough idea of where your seats are. The computer will select the "best available" tickets.

The annual New Mardi Gras Festival's Dog Show *(see p51)*

Booking Agencies

Sydney has two main ticket agencies: **Ticketek** and **Ticketmaster**. Between them, they represent all the major entertainment and sporting events. Ticketek has more than 30 outlets throughout NSW and the ACT, open from 9am to 5pm weekdays, and Saturdays from 9am to 4pm. Opening hours vary between agencies and call centres, so check with Ticketek to confirm. Phone bookings: 9am–9pm, Monday to Saturday, and 9am–7pm Sundays. For Internet bookings, visit their website.

Ticketmaster outlets are open 9am–5pm Monday to Friday – some are open later. Phone bookings: 9am–9pm Monday to Saturday and 10am–5pm Sunday. A booking fee applies, plus a postage and handling charge if tickets are mailed out. There are generally no refunds (unless a show is cancelled) or exchanges. The easiest way to buy tickets is online, on the ticket agencies' websites. You will be able to see availability by date, choose your seat and have electronic tickets delivered via email or to a mobile phone.

A busker at Circular Quay

Discount Tickets and Free Entertainment

Tuesday is budget-price day at most cinemas. Some independent cinemas have special prices throughout the week. The Sydney Symphony Orchestra and Opera Australia *(see p212)* offer a special Student Rush price to full-time students under 28 but only if surplus tickets are available. These can be bought on the day of the performance, from the box office at the venue.

Outdoor events are especially popular in Sydney, and many are free *(see pp50–53)*.

The Spanish firedancers Els Comediants at the Sydney Festival

Sydney Harbour is a splendid setting for the fabulous New Year's Eve fireworks, with a display at 9pm for families as well as the midnight display.

The Sydney Festival in January is a huge extravaganza of performance and visual art. Various outdoor venues in the Rocks, Darling Harbour and in front of the Opera House feature events to suit every taste, including musical productions, drama, dance, exhibitions and circuses. The most popular free events are the symphony and jazz concerts held in the Domain. Also popular are Darling Harbour's Hoopla over Easter and the food and wine festival held in June at Manly Beach.

The highly respected Australian Chamber Orchestra *(see p212)*

Disabled Visitors

Many older venues were not designed with the disabled visitor in mind, but this has been redressed in most newer buildings. It is best to phone the box office beforehand to request special seating and other requirements, or call **Ideas Inc**, who can provide a list of Sydney's most wheelchair-friendly venues. The **Sydney Opera House** has disabled parking, wheelchair access and a loop system in the Concert Hall for the hearing impaired. A brochure, *Services for the Disabled*, is also available.

DIRECTORY

Useful Numbers

Ideas Inc
Tel 1800 029 904.

Sydney Opera House
Information Desk:
Tel 9250 7111.
Disabled Information:
Tel 9250 7175.

Sydney Visitor Centre
Tel 8273 0000 or 9281 2244.
W sydney.com

Tourism NSW
W visitnsw.com.au

True Local
W truelocal.com.au

Ticket Agencies

Ticketek
Tel 132 849.
W ticketek.com.au

Ticketmaster
Tel 136 100.
W ticketmaster.com.au

Theatre and Film

Sydney's theatrical venues are well known for their atmosphere and quality. There is a stimulating range of productions, from musicals, classic plays and Shakespeare by the Sea to contemporary, fringe and experimental theatre. Comedy is also finding a strong niche as a mainstream performance art. Prominent playwrights include David Williamson, Debra Oswald, Brendan Cowell, Stephen Sewell and Louis Nowra.

Australian film-making has also earned an excellent international reputation. A rich variety of both local and foreign films is screened throughout the year, as well as during the city's film festivals.

Theatre

Sydney's larger, mainstream musicals, such as those of Andrew Lloyd Webber, are staged at the **Theatre Royal**, the opulent **State Theatre** *(see p84)* and the **Capitol Theatre** *(see p101)*. **The Star** entertainment and casino complex boasts two theatres, the Showroom, and the first-rate Lyric Theatre for musical productions and stage shows.

Smaller venues also offer a range of interesting plays and performances. These include the **Seymour Theatre Centre**, which has three theatres; the **Belvoir Street Theatre**, which has two; the **Ensemble Theatre**, a theatre-in-the-round by the water; and the **Footbridge Theatre**. The **Griffin Theatre** specializes in works by new Australian playwrights, while the **Parade Theatre** at the National Institute of Dramatic Arts (NIDA) show-cases work by NIDA's acting, directing and production students throughout the year. It also hosts shows by other theatre groups and is part of the Festival of Sydney *(see p51)*. The well-respected **Sydney Theatre Company** (STC) has introduced an ensemble of actors, employed full time, who perform a minimum of two plays each season. Most STC productions are at **The Wharf** or the **Sydney Theatre's** Roslyn Packer Theatre at Walsh Bay, though some are staged in the Drama Theatre of the Sydney Opera House *(see pp76–9)*.

The **Bell Shakespeare Company** interprets the Bard with an innovative slant without tampering with the original text. Its productions are ideal for young or wary theatre-goers. While venues vary, there are two seasons in Sydney – one at the beginning of summer and one in autumn.

Street performances and open-air theatre are popular during the summer months when life in Sydney moves outdoors. **Shakespeare Australia** puts on open-air productions in the Botanic Garden in January.

For the adventurous, the **Festival of Sydney** *(see p51)* offers a celebration of original, often quirky, Australian theatre, dance, music and visual arts. Once considered somewhat frivolous, it has developed the reputation of having serious artistic depth.

Children's Theatre

Sydney thrives on spectacles that delight children, and their parents. You will often find jugglers, mime artists, buskers and magic shows at Circular Quay and around Darling Harbour *(see p93)*. The Sydney Opera House regularly has performances for children.

In the suburb of Killara, the **Marian St Theatre for Young People** stages the occasional theatrical production. With luck, you may even be able to see a performance by the incredibly athletic **Flying Fruit Fly Circus**. This troupe of boys and girls, aged from eight to 18, excels in aerial gymnastics.

Film

The city's largest cinema complex, the **Event Cinemas** multiplex is in George Street, just one block south of Town Hall, and screens the most recent film releases. Similar multiplexes, such as **Hoyts at Broadway**, can be found in the Entertainment Quarter on Driver Avenue, and in Bondi Junction in the Westfield Shopping Centre. The **IMAX Theatre** *(see p100)* in Darling Harbour has a giant, 8-storey screen and shows 2-D and 3-D films made specifically for the large screen. Many of these are suitable for children.

Cinephiles flock to the **Palace Norton St Cinema** at Norton Street, and to the **Dendy Cinemas** at Newtown and Opera Quays. **Cinema Paris** shows arthouse and indie films, and often screens Bollywood movies as well. The **Chauvel Cinema** at Paddington Town Hall screens the best of independent and world movies in a lovely space with proscenium-arched stage.

For a movie and a meal, **Govinda's** *(see p193)*, which is also an Indian restaurant, screens films that have just finished their run at the cinemas. The admission price includes a tasty vegetarian buffet dinner.

The latest screenings are usually at 9:30pm, although most major cinema complexes run shows up to as late as midnight. Commercial cinema houses offer reduced-price tickets on Tuesday, while Palace and Dendy do so on Monday.

Film Censorship Ratings

G For general exhibition
PG Parental guidance recommended for those under 15 years
M 15+ Recommended for mature audiences aged 15 and over
MA 15+ Restricted to people 15 years and over
R 18+ Restricted to adults 18 years and over

Film Festivals

The **Sydney Film Festival** is a highlight of the city's calendar (see p53), screening some 200 new features, shorts and documentaries from all over the globe. Tribute sessions and retrospectives are also presented. The main venue is the State Theatre but other venues hold satellite screenings.

The **Flickerfest International Short Film Festival** (see p51) is held at the Bondi Pavilion Amphitheatre at Bondi Beach in early January. It screens shorts and animation films from around the world. In December, **Tropfest** (see p51) shows local short films that can be no longer than seven minutes. Each must feature the special Tropfest signature item, which in past years has included a rock, a pickle and a match.

Run by Queer Screen, the **Mardi Gras Film Festival** (see p51), starts mid-February and continues for 15 days. Films dealing with issues relevant to the lesbian, gay and transgender community are shown at various inner-city venues.

Comedy

Sydney's most established comedy venue, the **Comedy Store** is known for performances by the best of the touring comedians and is owned by the same people who organise the Sydney Comedy Festival. Monday is comedy night at **The Old Manly Boatshed**, where both local and visiting comics perform. The **Roxbury Hotel** hosts comedy several nights a week. Newcomers to the stage mix with seasoned professionals.

DIRECTORY

Theatre

Bell Shakespeare Company
Tel 8298 9000.
W bellshakespeare.com.au

Belvoir Street Theatre
25 Belvoir St, Surry Hills.
Tel 9699 3444.
W belvoir.com.au

Capitol Theatre
13 Campbell St,
Haymarket. Map 4 E4.
Tel 9320 5000.
Box Office: Tel 1300 558 878. W capitoltheatre.com.au

Ensemble Theatre
78 McDougall St, Kirribilli.
Tel 9929 8877.
Box Office: Tel 9929 0644.
W ensemble.com.au

Footbridge Theatre
University of Sydney,
Parramatta Rd, Glebe.
Map 3 A5. Tel 9351 2222.

Griffin Theatre
10 Nimrod St, Kings Cross.
Map 5 B1. Tel 9361 3817.

Parade Theatre
215 Anzac Parade,
Kensington. Map 5 B4.
Tel 9697 7613.
W nida.edu.au

Seymour Theatre Centre
Cnr Cleveland St and
City Rd, Chippendale.
Tel 9351 7940.
W seymourcentre.com

Shakespeare Australia
Tel 1300 122 344.
W shakespeare australia.com.au

The Star
80 Pyrmont St, Pyrmont.
Map 3 B1. Tel 9777 9000.
Lyric Theatre Box Office:
Tel 9777 9000.
W starcity.com.au

State Theatre
49 Market St. Map 1 B5.
Tel 9373 6852.
W statetheatre.com.au

Sydney Festival
Tel 8248 6500.
W sydneyfestival.org.au

Sydney Theatre
22 Hickson Rd, Walsh Bay.
Map 1 A2. Tel 9250 1999.

Sydney Theatre Company
Tel 9250 1777.
W sydneytheatre.com.au

Theatre Royal
MLC Centre, King St.
Map 1 B5. Tel 9224 8444.
W theatreroyal.net.au

The Wharf
Pier 4, Hickson Rd,
Walsh Bay. Map 1 A1.
Tel 9250 1777.

Children's Theatre

Flying Fruit Fly Circus
Tel 6021 7044.
W fruitflycircus.com.au

Marian St Theatre for Young People
2 Marian St, Killara.
Tel 9498 7671.
W mstyp.org.au

Film

Chauvel Cinema
Paddington Town Hall,
249 Oxford St. Map 5 C3.
Tel 9361 5398.

Cinema Paris
Entertainment Quarter,
Driver Ave, Moore Park.
Map 5 C5. Tel 9332 1633.

Dendy Cinemas
Newtown
261–263 King St,
Newtown. Tel 9550 5699.
Opera Quays
Shop 9/2, East Circular
Quay. Tel 9247 3800.

Event Cinemas
505–525 George St.
Map 4 E3. Tel 9273 7300.
W eventcinemas.com

Govinda's
112 Darlinghurst Rd.
Map 5 A2. Tel 9380 5155.
W govindas.com.au

Hoyts at Broadway
Broadway Shopping
Centre, 3 Bay St.
Map 3 C5. Tel 9211 1911.
W hoyts.com.au

IMAX Theatre
Southern Promenade,
Darling Harbour.
Map 4 D3. Tel 9281 3300.
W imax.com.au

Palace Norton St Cinema
99 Norton St, Leichhardt.
Tel 9550 0122.
W palacecinemas.com.au

Film Festivals

Flickerfest International Short Film Festival
Tel 9365 6888.
W flickerfest.com.au

Mardi Gras Film Festival
Tel 9332 4938.
W queerscreen.org.au

Sydney Film Festival
Tel 9318 0999.
W sff.org.au

Tropfest
Tel 9368 0434.
W tropfest.com

Comedy

Comedy Store
Entertainment Quarter,
Driver Ave, Moore Park.
Map 5 C5. Tel 9357 1419.
W comedystore. com.au

The Old Manly Boatshed
40 The Corso, Manly.
Tel 9977 4443.

The Roxbury Hotel
182 St Johns Rd, Glebe.
Tel 9692 0822.
W roxbury.com.au

Opera, Classical Music and Dance

Music buffs cannot possibly visit Sydney without seeing an opera or hearing the city's premier orchestra perform in the Sydney Opera House. And that is just the start. The wide range of music on offer in Sydney includes influences from Asia, Europe and the Pacific, as well as local compositions. For the visitor, there is a wealth of orchestral, choral, chamber, contemporary and traditional aboriginal music to choose from.

Opera

Australia has produced a number of world-class opera singers, including Joan Sutherland, and eminent conductors such as Sir Charles Mackerras, Simone Young and Stuart Challender. The first recorded performance of an opera in Sydney was in 1834. For 120 years, most opera was performed by visiting international companies.

In 1956, the Australian Opera (now called **Opera Australia**) was formed. It presented four Mozart operas in its first year. But it was the opening of the **Sydney Opera House** (see pp76–9) in 1973 that heralded a new interest in the art form. Opera Australia's summer season is held from early January to early March; the winter season from June to the end of October. Each season usually includes one accessible opera in English as well as more challenging shows. Every year at the hugely popular Opera in The Domain (see p51), members of Opera Australia perform excerpts from famous operas.

Orchestral Music

Much of Sydney's orchestral music and recitals are the work of the famous **Sydney Symphony Orchestra** (SSO). Numerous concerts are given, mostly in the Opera House Concert Hall, the **City Recital Hall** and the **Sydney Town Hall** (see p89). A Tea and Symphony series is held mid-year on Friday mornings at the Sydney Opera House.

The renovated Conservatorium of Music (see p108), set in the Royal Botanic Garden, provides a wonderful atmosphere and location. It holds a number of concerts, where you can enjoy symphony and chamber orchestras, or jazz big bands.

Formed in 1973, the **Sydney Youth Orchestra**, is praised for its talent, enthusiasm and impressive young soloists. With a loyal following, it stages several performances in major concert venues throughout the year. Aficionados of Baroque and classical music should try to catch a performance by the **Australian Brandenburg Orchestra**. Australia's first period instrument orchestra, this popular group appears regularly in Sydney's major concert halls.

Contemporary Music

The first concert held by **Musica Viva** was in 1945, at the NSW Conservatorium of Music. Originally specializing in chamber music, it now also presents string quartets, jazz, piano groups, percussionists, soloists and international avant-garde artists. Concerts take place at the Opera House and the City Recital Hall.

Synergy is one of Australia's foremost percussion quartets. The group commissions works from all over the world and gives its own concert series at the Sydney Opera House and at Sydney Town Hall. It also collaborates with dance and theatre groups.

Eastside Arts, held, like Paddington Markets (see p128), in the Uniting Church, hosts Café Carnivale every Friday night, showcasing some of the best world music, including rembetika, Indian, African, percussion, gypsy, salsa and tango music.

Fourplay is a group of classically trained musicians who play electric string quartet versions of popular music at various venues.

Chamber Music

Under director Richard Tognetti, the **Australian Chamber Orchestra** has won acclaim for its creativity and interesting choice of venues, including museums, churches and even wineries. Its main concerts are held at the Opera House and the City Recital Hall, Angel Place.

The **Australia Ensemble** is the resident chamber music group at the University of New South Wales. It performs six times a year at the Sir John Clancy Auditorium and also appears for Musica Viva. Many choral groups and ensembles like to book **St James' Church** because of its atmosphere and acoustics.

Free Concerts

Throughout the year, festivals (see pp50–53) provide free live music. These are mostly held outdoors, to take advantage of Sydney's warm weather. During the Sydney Festival the city's favourite outdoor concerts take place, including Opera in the Park, Symphony in the Domain and the Australia Day Concert, all held in The Domain, as well as Latin music in the Aquadome at Darling Harbour and events in the Sydney Opera House forecourt.

The Conservatorium of Music holds a weekly series of inexpensive concerts in their Verbrugghen Hall (see p108) at 1:10pm each Wednesday during the university semester, entry is by gold coin (A$1 or A$2) donation. Staff and students present classical, modern and jazz music in ensemble, soloist and chamber performances. Each January the renowned choir of St James' (see p117 and p213) presents two orchestral masses to the congregation and entry to these events is free.

Choral Music

Comprised of four choirs: the 300-member Festival Chorus, the 100-member Symphony Chorus, the 32-member Chamber Singers and the 25-member Vox, the **Sydney Philharmonia Choirs** are the city's finest. They perform at the Opera House. December is the focal point of Sydney's choral scene, with regular massed choir performances of Handel's *Messiah*.

The **Australian Youth Choir** is booked for many private functions, but if you are lucky, you may catch one of their major annual performances.

One of Sydney's most impressive vocal groups is the **Café of the Gate of Salvation**, described as an "Aussie blend of a capella and gospel."

The choir of St James' Church is an excellent choral group. The orchestral masses performed in January, such as those by Mozart, Haydn and Schubert, usually fill the church to capacity so arrive early. Former choir members who are now professional soloists also occasionally perform.

Dance

There is an eclectic variety of dance on offer in Sydney. The **Australian Ballet** has two seven-week Sydney seasons at the Opera House: one in March/April, the other in November/December. The company's repertoire spans traditional through to modern, although it is perhaps most noted for classical ballets such as *Swan Lake* and *Giselle*.

Sydney Dance Company is the city's leading modern dance group, often combining its vigorous productions with innovative musical scores. The company has performed in Italy, New York, London and China. Productions are mostly staged at the Sydney Opera House, but are, on occasion, held at The Wharf or the new Sydney Theatre *(see pp210–11)*. Rafaela Bonachela was appointed artistic director in 2009.

The **Performance Space**, which is now located at the CarriageWorks, is very popular for its experimental dance and movement theatre. Artists with backgrounds in dance, mime, circus work, Butoh or performance art are likely to appear here.

Bangarra Dance Theatre uses traditional Aboriginal and Torres Strait Islander dance and music as its inspiration, infused with contemporary elements. It makes outback interstate and international tours, but is based in Sydney.

The startling and original **Legs on the Wall** are a physical theatre group who work all over the world, combining circus and aerial techniques with dance and narrative to form a heady mix. Their spectacular performances take place in intimate theatres or use dramatic settings such as skyscrapers from which the performers are suspended.

Golden Oldies

Seniors are treated to concerts by well-known Australian performers, including tenor David Hobson, several times a year through **The Good Old Days** series. There are morning and afternoon performances at the Sydney Town Hall.

DIRECTORY

Opera

Opera Australia
Tel 9318 8200.
W opera.org.au

Orchestral Music

Australian Brandenburg Orchestra
Tel 9328 7581. W brandenburg.com.au

Sydney Symphony Orchestra
Tel 8215 4600. W sydneysymphony.com

Sydney Youth Orchestra
Tel 9251 2422.
W syo.com.au

Contemporary Music

Eastside Arts
395 Oxford St, Paddington.
Tel 93312646. W paddingtonuca.org.au

Fourplay
W fourplay.com.au

Musica Viva
W mva.org.au

Synergy
W synergypercussion.com

Chamber Music

Australian Chamber Orchestra
W aco.com.au

Australia Ensemble
Tel 9385 4872.
W ae.unsw.edu.au

Choral Music

Australian Youth Choir
W niypaa.com.au

Café of the Gate of Salvation
W cafeofthegateofsalvation.com.au

Sydney Philharmonia Choirs
Tel 9251 2024.
W sydneyphilharmonia.com.au

Dance Companies

Australian Ballet
Tel 9252 5500.
W australianballet.com.au

Bangarra Dance Theatre
Tel 9251 5333.
W bangarra.com.au

Legs on the Wall
Tel 9560 9479.
W legsonthewall.com.au

Sydney Dance Company
W sydneydancecompany.com

Concert and Dance Venues

City Recital Hall
Angel Place. Map 1 B4.
Tel 8256 2222. W cityrecitalhall.com

Performance Space
245 Wilson St, Everleigh.
Tel 8571 9111.
W performancespace.com.au

St James' Church
173 King St. Map 1 B5. Tel 9232 3022. W sjks.org.au

Sydney Opera House
Bennelong Point.
Map 1 C2. Tel 9250 7111.
W sydneyoperahouse.com

Sydney Town Hall
483 George Street. Map 4 E2. Tel 9265 9333.

Golden Oldies

The Good Old Days
W goodolddays.com.au

Music Venues and Nightclubs

Sydney attracts some of the biggest names in modern music all year round. Venues range from the cavernous Sydney Entertainment Centre to small and noisy back rooms in pubs. Visiting international DJs frequently play sets at Sydney clubs. Some venues cater for a variety of music tastes – rock and pop one night, jazz, blues or folk the next. There are free online gig guides, including themusic.com.au, thebrag.com.au and inthemix.com.au, where you can find out what is on.

Getting In

Tickets for major shows are available through booking agencies such as Ticketek and Ticketmaster *(see p209)*. Prices vary considerably, depending on the type of show. You may pay from $30 to $70 for a gig at the Metro, but over $150 for seats for a Rolling Stones concert. Moshtix also sells tickets for smaller venues across Sydney and their website gives a good idea of the line up at various venues. Buying online also prevents you from having to queue early for tickets on the door.

You can pay at the door on the night at most places, unless the show is already sold out. Nightclubs often have a cover charge, but some venues will admit you free before a certain time in the evening or on weeknights.

Most venues serve alcohol, so shows are restricted to those at least 18 years of age. This is the usual case unless a gig is specified "all ages". It is advisable that people under 30 years old carry photo identification, such as a passport or driver's licence, because entry to some venues is very strict. You are also not allowed to carry any kind of bottle into most nightclubs or other venues. Similarly, any cameras and recording devices are usually banned.

Dress codes vary, but generally, shorts (on men) and flip-flops are not welcome. Wear thin layers that you can remove when you get hot instead of a coat, and avoid carrying a big bag because many venues do not have a cloakroom.

Rock, Pop and Hip Hop

Pop's big names and famous rock groups perform at the **AllPhones Arena**, **Hordern Pavilion**, and sports grounds such as the ANZ Stadium at **Sydney Olympic Park** *(see p140)* in Homebush Bay. More intimate locations include the **State Theatre** *(see pp210–11)*, **Enmore Theatre** and Sydney's best venue, **The Metro Theatre**. Hip hop acts usually play in rock venues rather than in nightclubs. You are almost as likely to find a crew rapping as a band strumming and drumming at the Metro Theatre, the **Gaelic Club**, the **Bridge Hotel** and **The Merton** in Rozelle. It is not unusual to catch a punk, garage or electro-folk band at **Spectrum** or the **Annandale Hotel** on Parramatta Road.

Pub rock is a constantly changing scene in Sydney. Weekly listings appear on Fridays in the "Metro" section of the *Sydney Morning Herald* and in the street press *(see p208)*. Music stores are also full of flyers. Note that gigs by international acts and popular Australian bands, on every week at the Metro Theatre and Gaelic Club, usually sell out.

Jazz, Folk and Blues

For many years, the first port of call for any jazz, funk, groove or folk enthusiast has been **The Basement**. Visiting luminaries play some nights, talented but struggling local musicians others, and the line-ups now also include increasingly popular world music and hip hop bands. **Slide**, in a converted Art Deco bank building on Oxford Street, is a combination of a Parisian-style nightclub and a New York-style lounge bar. It plays host to both local and international performers. Experimental jazz is offered on Fridays and Saturdays at the **Seymour Theatre Centre** *(see pp210–11)*. **The Vanguard** also offers dinner and show deals, as well as show-only tickets, and has been drawing an excellent roster of jazz, blues and roots talent. The **Fitzroy Hotel** in Windsor, north-west of Sydney, holds a blues festival in October, and the **Cat & Fiddle Hotel** in Balmain offers acoustic music and folk.

House, Breakbeats and Techno

Sydney's only super club, **Home Sydney** in Cockle Bay features three levels and a gargantuan sound system. Friday night is the time to go, as the DJs present house, trance, drum and bass, and breakbeats. A mainstream crowd flocks to the nearby **Bungalow 8** on King Street Wharf with its fresh seafood dishes and great views of the Harbour. Once the sun has set, house DJs turn the place into a club. **The Marquee**, at The Star, hosts international DJs in the venue's three distinct spaces, while **Cargo Bar** showcases a diverse mix of performers in its mainstream house club.

For something a little more hip, try the underground **Candy's Apartment** with its bunker-style bar on Bayswater Road, or the buzzy **World Bar** on the same street. Based in a converted Victorian terrace, World Bar is known for serving its cocktails in teapots designed for sharing. Down the road, **Q Bar** on Oxford Street, Darling-hurst, has arcade games for when you need a breather. Or try the low-ceilinged **Chinese Laundry** on Sussex Street tucked under the gentrified pub, Slip Inn *(see El Loco, p190)*.

Gay and Lesbian Pubs and Clubs

Sunday night is the big night for many of Sydney's gay community, although there is plenty of action throughout the week. A number of venues have a gay or lesbian night on one night of the week and attract a mainstream crowd on the other nights. Wednesday is lesbian night at the stylish **Bank Hotel** in Newtown and some Sundays are queer nights at Darling Harbour's Home Sydney.

ARQ on Flinders Street is the largest of the gay clubs, with pounding commercial house music. The main dance floor is overlooked by a mezzanine for watching the writhing mass of bodies below. This is a world-class venue with great facilities, from the cutting-edge sound systems to the state-of-the-art lighting shows. **Midnight Shift** on Oxford Street is for men only, and **Stonewall** plays camp anthems and is patronized mostly by men and their straight female friends.

The **Colombian** is the best and one of the most popular of the Oxford Street bars. It has a mock-Central American jungle decor, self-styled as "South American chic", and large windows that open out to the street. The **Oxford Hotel** and its upper-level cocktail bars are popular too. Some of Sydney's most entertaining drag shows can be found in the Cabaret Bar of the **Imperial Hotel** where shows are staged most nights of the week.

DIRECTORY

Rock, Pop and Hip Hop

AllPhones Arena
Edwin Flack Ave,
Sydney Olympic Park.
Tel 8765 4321.

Annandale Hotel
17–19 Parramatta Rd,
Annandale. **Tel** 9550 1078.
W annandalehotel.com

The Bridge Hotel
119 Victoria Rd, Rozelle.
Tel 9810 1260.

Enmore Theatre
130 Enmore Rd, Newtown.
Tel 9550 3666. W enmoretheatre.com.au

The Gaelic Club
64 Devonshire St, Surry
Hills. **Tel** 9211 1687.
W thegaelic.com

Hordern Pavilion
Driver Ave, Moore Park.
Map 5 C5. **Tel** 9921 5333.
W playbillvenues.com

The Merton
38 Victoria Rd, Rozelle.
Tel 8065 9577.

The Metro Theatre
624 George St. **Map** 4 E3.
Tel 9550 3666. W metrotheatre.com.au

Moshtix
Tel 1300 438 849.
W moshtix.com.au

Spectrum
34 Oxford St, Darlinghurst.
Map 4 F4. **Tel** 9360 1375.
W spectrum.exchange
sydney.com.au

State Theatre
49 Market St. **Map** 1 B5.
Tel 9373 6852.
W statetheatre.com.au

Sydney Olympic Park
Homebush Bay.
Tel 9714 7888.
W sydneyolympicpark.
nsw.gov.au

Jazz, Folk and Blues

The Basement
29 Reiby Place. **Map** 1 B3.
Tel 9251 2797.
W thebasement.com.au

Cat & Fiddle Hotel
456 Darling St, Balmain.
Tel 9810 7931.
W catandfiddle.com.au

Fitzroy Hotel
161 George St, Windsor.
Tel 4577 3396.

Seymour Theatre Centre
Cnr Cleveland St and City
Rd, Chippendale.
Tel 9351 7940.
W seymourcentre.com

Slide
41 Oxford St, Darlinghurst.
Map 4 F4. **Tel** 8915 1899.
W slide.com.au

The Vanguard
42 King St, Newtown.
Tel 9557 7992.
W thevanguard.com.au

House, Breakbeats and Techno

Bungalow 8
The Promenade, King St
Wharf. **Tel** 9299 4660.
W bungalow8sydney.com

Candy's Apartment
22 Bayswater Rd, Kings
Cross. **Map** 5 B1. **Tel** 9380
5600. W candys.com.au

Cargo Bar
52–60 The Promenade,
King St Wharf, Darling
Harbour. **Tel** 8070 2424.
W cargobar.com.au

Chinese Laundry
Slip Inn, 111 Sussex St.
Map 1 A3. **Tel** 8295 9999.

Home Sydney
Wheat Rd, Cockle Bay,
Darling Harbour. **Map** 4
D2. **Tel** 9266 0600.
W homesydney.com

The Marquee
The Star, Pyrmont.
Map 3 C1. **Tel** 9777 9000.
W marqueesydney.com

Q Bar
Level 2, 44 Oxford St,
Darlinghurst. **Map** 4 F4.
Tel 9360 1375.
W qbar.exchange
sydney.com.au

The World Bar
24 Bayswater Rd, King's
Cross. **Map** 5 C1.
Tel 9357 7700.
W theworldbar.com

Gay and Lesbian Clubs and Pubs

ARQ
16 Flinders St, Taylor
Square. **Map** 5 A2.
Tel 9380 8700.
W arqsydney.com.au

Bank Hotel
324 King St, Newtown.
Tel 8568 1900.
W bankhotel.com.au

Colombian
Cnr Oxford & Crown sts,
Surry Hills. **Map** 5 A2.
Tel 9360 2151.
W colombian.com.au

Imperial Hotel
35 Erskineville Rd,
Erskineville. **Tel** 9519
9899.

Midnight Shift
85 Oxford St, Darlinghurst.
Map 5 A2. **Tel** 9358 3848.
W themidnight
shift.com.au

Oxford Hotel
134 Oxford St,
Darlinghurst. **Map** 5 A2.
Tel 9331 3467.
W theoxfordhotel.com.au

Stonewall
175 Oxford St,
Darlinghurst. **Map** 5 A2.
Tel 9360 1963.
W stonewallhotel.com

SURVIVAL
GUIDE

Practical Information   218–227
Travel Information   228–237

PRACTICAL INFORMATION

Sydney has become a popular destination for international tourists. Located on one of the world's most beautiful harbours, the city offers exciting nightlife, excellent sporting activities, interesting culture and the opportunity to just relax and enjoy the spectacular views. As expected of a major city, Sydney has first-rate facilities, good service and a comprehensive range of hotels and restaurants to suit most budgets and requirements. Public transport is reliable and inexpensive, especially if you take advantage of the composite travel cards that offer combined bus, ferry, train and light rail (tram) travel *(see p230)*. Cash dispensers (ATMs) are plentiful, with bureaux de change found in the more tourist-frequented areas *(see pp224–5)*, and credit cards are accepted in most hotels, restaurants and shops. Visitors will find Sydney a safe, clean and welcoming city. They should encounter few practical problems as long as they follow a few common-sense guidelines about personal security *(see pp222–3)*.

When to Go

The best times to travel are during autumn (March–May) and spring (September–November), when the weather is warm to mild. The summer months tend to be hot and humid, particularly in February. However, if you can stand the heat then some of the best deals often occur during this period when children are back at school. Winter (June–August) is rarely very cold, and temperatures can be as high as 20° C (68° F).

Visas and Passports

All visitors to Australia must hold a valid passport and, with the exception of New Zealand, must either have an Electronic Travel Authority (ETA) or a tourist visa (depending on your country of origin). Citizens of the UK, the USA, France, Spain, Ireland, Germany, Denmark and several other countries qualify for an ETA, which allows entry to Australia for up to three months. The ETA can be applied for online or through a travel agent, airline or an Australian Visa Office, and has a service fee of A$20. Visitors who are not eligible for an ETA, want to stay longer or enter on a working holiday, should check the requirements through the **Department of Immigration and Citizenship**. All visitors must also have an onward ticket and proof they have sufficient funds for their visit.

Customs Information

The customs allowance per person over 18 entering Australia is up to the value of A$900 plus 2.25 litres (3.75 pints) of alcohol and a carton of 250 cigarettes or 250 grams (0.5 pounds) of cigars/tobacco.

Australia's quarantine regulations are strict and all people entering the country at Sydney Airport will be given a customs form to fill in on the plane. Visitors must declare all foods – it is illegal to bring in fruit, vegetables, seeds, live plants and plant products, and any endangered species or animal products. Packaged food such as biscuits and chocolates are usually allowed but must still be declared. There are severe penalties for bringing in illegal drugs. Because of these restrictions, personal luggage and hand luggage may be X-rayed before you can leave the baggage reclaim area and often customs officers with sniffer dogs will check luggage both near the baggage carousel and along the queues of exiting passengers from the airport.

Australia levies a departure tax on all passengers aged 12 or over. This is included in the cost of your airline ticket.

Tourist Information

To obtain information about Sydney and the rest of Australia before leaving home, travellers should look at the **Tourism Australia** website, where there are lists of specialist Australian travel agents, who can provide the latest information.

Once in Australia, Sydney's principal tourist information points are the **Sydney Visitor Centres** at The Rocks and Darling Harbour. Both centres can book tours as well as accommodation at certain listed hotels. Information booths can also be found at **Central Railway Station**, **Circular Quay** and **Town Hall**, as well as at Sydney's major attractions

Visitor information kiosk inside Central Railway Station

◄ Surfers and beachgoers on Bondi Beach

and main beaches. These booths have free maps, brochures and entertainment listings (see p208).

For visitors arriving by air, there are free Sydney visitor booklets available on stands just before the duty free shops and customs area. Once in the arrivals hall (Terminal 1) you will see the **Travel Concierge** desk (see p228). As part of this complimentary service, staff can make accommodation, car hire, restaurant and event bookings. They also sell shuttle bus tickets to the domestic airport and international phone cards, and can provide additional travel information. Visitors have access to a bank of self-help computers where they can browse for themselves.

The striking sandstone entrance to the Art Gallery of New South Wales

Admission Prices

Most of Sydney's museums, galleries and historic houses charge an admission fee, usually from A\$8–12. The Art Gallery of New South Wales (see pp110–13) is free but charges for special exhibitions. Family attractions such as zoos, aquariums and wildlife parks are more expensive, often A\$20–60. However, cheaper family passes are usually available on the company's website, and combination attraction deals may be offered. A multi-attraction pass offers big savings for those planning to visit Sea Life Sydney Aquarium, Wild Life Sydney, Sydney Tower Eye and other **Merlin Entertainment Group** venues. Buy tickets in advance online for further discounts.

Student and senior concessions are available at many attractions on presentation of an official international ID card.

Public toilets with a colourful exterior

The **Sydney Living Museums** Pass gives access to four of the city's best museums – Museum of Sydney, Hyde Park Barracks, Justice and Police Museum, and Susannah Place Museum – at a saving of more than 50 per cent.

Opening Hours

Although opening hours vary, the majority of museums and galleries are open 10am–5pm daily, except on Good Friday and Christmas Day. Smaller galleries are usually closed on Mondays. Museums, galleries and other attractions are often at their busiest at weekends.

Etiquette and Smoking

While Sydney society is generally laid back, there are a few rules to follow. Eating and drinking is prohibited on public transport, and is also frowned upon when travelling in taxis. Dress codes are generally smart casual, but are more relaxed in summer – although people do go all out for formal occasions. Topless bathing is accepted on many beaches, but not at public swimming pools.

Smoking is banned in all public venues, restaurants, pubs and bars, but many clubs have covered outdoor areas (often accessed via corridors) where smoking is allowed.

Accessibility to Public Conveniences

Free public toilets can be found in Sydney's galleries and museums, department stores and all bus and railway stations. They are generally well serviced and clean. Baby changing facilities are also quite common, particularly in department stores and major museums and galleries.

Clean drinking fountains can be found throughout the city. Spring or distilled water is also often freely available from dispensers in waiting areas of chemist shops, travel agents and offices.

Taxes and Tipping

Sydney has a 10 per cent Goods and Services Tax (GST), but it is often included within the price, especially for clothing and restaurant bills. If travellers spend more than A\$300 in one store and get a single tax invoice, they can claim back the GST when they leave Australia – this is known as the Tourist Refund Scheme (TRS). Refunds are available at the airport and at cruise line terminals. All goods must either be carried as hand luggage or worn (unless they are liquids, which must be packed in your checked baggage). It is advisable to allow extra time at the airport or port to make your claim. For more information, check the **Australian Customs and Border Protection** website.

Although tipping is optional, it is the custom to leave about 10 per cent for good service in restaurants (see p181), to tip hotel porters (see p171) and to leave any small change for bartenders and taxi drivers. Most small cafés have a tip jar on the counter for gratuities.

Travellers with Special Needs

Sydney has made much-needed advances in catering for the disabled. As old buses go out of service, Transport NSW (the government body that manages buses and ferries) is purchasing new buses with doors at pavement level and ramps that allow people in wheelchairs access to the vehicle. There is also priority seating for those with a disability, and bus handrails and steps are marked with bright yellow paint to assist visually impaired passengers.

Many of the Sydney Trains stations, including Circular Quay railway station, are completely accessible to wheelchair users, while several other stations have wide entrance gates and most have ramps installed.

Light Rail stations are all wheelchair accessible. The **Transport Infoline** (see p233) has details on disabled access at each station and bus stop.

Museums, many hotels and some major sights cater to the less mobile, including those in wheelchairs, as well as people with other disabilities. You are strongly advised to phone all sights in advance to check on facilities.

For detailed information on accessible services and venues, *Access Sydney* is available from Spinal Cord Injuries Australia (see p173). A map and directory for those with limited mobility can be obtained from the

Sydney Time

Sydney is in the Australian Eastern Standard Time zone (AEST). Daylight saving in New South Wales starts on the last Sunday in October and finishes on the last Sunday in March. The Northern Territory, Queensland and Western Australia do not observe daylight saving, so check time differences when you are there.

City and Country	Hours + or − AEST
Adelaide (Australia)	−½
Brisbane (Australia)	same
Canberra (Australia)	same
Darwin (Australia)	−½
Hobart (Australia)	same
Melbourne (Australia)	same
Perth (Australia)	−2
London (UK)	−9
Los Angeles (USA)	−17
Singapore	−2
Toronto (Canada)	−14

Sydney City Council One-Stop Shop behind Sydney Town Hall.

Travelling with Children

Sydney is an easy city to explore with children. There are many beaches, several wildlife parks (two either in or very near the city centre) and plenty of fun attractions to keep families entertained. Public transport and most attractions offer cheaper tickets for children and many offer discount family tickets. There are numerous free festivals and events held in the city and tourist areas, like The Festival of Sydney (see p51) and Sculpture by the Sea (see p50), that appeal to families. Details can be obtained from the **Sydney Visitors Centre** (see p218) and are often publicised

in the *Sydney Morning Herald* newspaper and the free publication, *Sydney's Child*.

Student Travellers

Student travellers carrying the International Student Identity Card (ISIC) are eligible for discounts in many museums, theatres and cinemas, as well as a 40 per cent reduction on internal air fares and 15 per cent off interstate coach travel. Students receive cheaper fares on Great Southern Rail trips – The Ghan and Indian Pacific trains – when booking the budget "red service".

Overseas visitors who are full-time students in Australia can buy an ISIC card (which comes with a guide book) for $25 from Sydney branches of **STA Travel**.

Gay and Lesbian Travellers

Sydney is an ultra gay-friendly city with many gay bars and nightclubs. It also hosts the annual Gay Mardi Gras festival which attracts thousands of international visitors and a vast TV audience. The hub of Sydney's gay community is Oxford Street, Darlinghurst (on the city's eastern fringe, see pp118–23). There are several gay newspapers including the *Sydney Star Observer* and *Lesbians on the Loose*, with online editions found at starobserver.com.au and

Entrance gates with wheelchair access at Circular Quay railway station

Gay pride event, Sydney harbour

LOTL.com. A well known gay travel agency is **Out Travel** in Elizabeth Bay.

Electricity

Australia's electrical current is 240–250 volts AC. Electrical plugs can have either two or three pins. Most good hotels will provide 110-volt shaver sockets and hair dryers, but a flat, two- or three-pin adaptor will be necessary for other appliances. These can be bought from electrical stores and also from airports.

Conversion Table

Imperial to Metric
1 inch = 2.54 centimetres
1 foot = 30 centimetres
1 mile = 1.6 kilometres
1 ounce = 28 grams
1 pound = 454 grams
1 pint = 0.6 litres
1 gallon = 4.6 litres

Metric to Imperial
1 centimetre = 0.4 inches
1 metre = 3 feet, 3 inches
1 kilometre = 0.6 miles
1 gram = 0.04 ounces
1 kilogram = 2.2 pounds
1 litre = 1.8 pints

Responsible Tourism

Many Sydney hotels have adopted power-saving and recycling practices. At least 10 city hotels have been bench-marked by the **EarthCheck** organization for their efficient energy plans, including the Hotel InterContinental (see p179). The purpose-built Sydney Harbour YHA (youth hostel) also has a strong eco focus (see p178).

Increasing numbers of restaurants are making a point of using produce from local growers or their own farms. **Farmers' Markets** have sprung up in the city and main tourist areas, including Eveleigh (near Redfern railway station), the Sydney Morning Herald Growers' Market at Prymont Bay Park and the Bondi Beach Farmers' Market. These offer an opportunity to buy fresh, local produce, which can make a delicious, cheap picnic with less packaging.

DIRECTORY

Embassies and Consulates

Canada
Level 5, 111 Harrington St.
Map 1 B3. **Tel** 9364 3000.
W canada
international.gc.ca

New Zealand
Level 10, 55 Hunter St.
Map 1 B4.
Tel 1300 559535.
W nzembassy.
com/australia

Republic of Ireland
Level 26, 1 Market St.
Map 4 E2. **Tel** 9264 9635.
W irishconsulate
sydney.net

United Kingdom
Level 16, Gateway Building, 1 Macquarie Place. **Map** 1 B3.
Tel 9247 7521.
W gov.uk/government/
world/australia

USA
Level 10, MLC Centre,
19–29 Martin Place.
Map 1 B4. **Tel** 9373 9200.
W sydney.usconsulate.
gov

Visas and Passports

Department of Immigration and Citizenship
W immi.gov.au

Tourist Information

Central Railway Station
Sydney Terminal.
Map 4 E5.
Open 6am–10pm daily.

Circular Quay
Cnr of Pitt & Alfred Sts,
Circular Quay. **Map** 1 B3.
Open 9am–5pm daily.

Darling Harbour Sydney Visitor Centre
Next to IMAX Theatre,
Darling Harbour.
Map 3 C2. **Tel** 9281 2244.
Open 9:30am–5:30pm
daily. W visitnsw.com

Sydney Airport International
Tel 9667 9111.

Sydney Visitor Centre
Cnr Argyle & Playfairs Sts,
The Rocks. **Map** 1 B2.
Tel 8273 0000. **Open**
9:30am–5:30pm daily.
W sydney.com

Tourism Australia
W tourism.australia.com

Town Hall
George St, Sydney. **Map** 4
E2. **Open** 9am–5pm daily.

Travel Concierge Sydney Airport
Tel 1300 402060.
W gnconcierge.com

Admission Prices

Merlin Entertainment Group
W merlinannualpass.
com.au

Sydney Living Museums
W sydneyliving
museums.com.au

Taxes and Tipping

Australian Customs & Border Protection
W customs.gov.au

Travellers with Special Needs

Sydney City Council One-Stop Shop
Town Hall House, Sydney
Square. **Map** 4 E3.
Tel 9265 9333. W cityof
sydney.nsw.gov.au

Student Travellers

STA Travel
W statravel.com.au

Gay and Lesbian Travellers

Out Travel
47 Elizabeth Bay Road.
Map 2 F5. **Tel** 8667 3336.
W out-travel.com.au

Pride Centre
W pridecentre.com.au

Responsible Tourism

EarthCheck
W earthcheck.org

Farmers' Markets
W farmersmarkets.
org.au

Personal Security and Health

Street crime in Sydney is less prevalent than in many other large cities, but it does exist, particularly late at night in some popular entertainment areas. You can minimize any risks by exercising reasonable caution and following the advice given below. Members of Sydney's police patrol the city's streets and public transport system in pairs. Mobile police stations are set up at crowded tourist areas and at public events. Further afield, the surf beaches and natural bushland can present dangers of their own, and the following information offers some practical advice for coping with environmental hazards.

Police officers patrolling the streets of Sydney on motorbikes

Police

Sydney has a strong police force with more than 700 officers stationed in the city centre, The Rocks and Kings Cross. To report emergencies, major crimes and fires call 000 from any phone. Victims of non-life threatening crimes such as personal theft, car theft, breaking and entering, and malicious damage should call the Police Assistance Line on 131 444. There are 24-hour police stations at **The Rocks**, **Kings Cross** and **Day Street**, Sydney.

What to Be Aware of

Leave valuables and important documents in your hotel safe, and don't carry large sums of cash. Try to avoid carrying all of your credit and debit cards with you. Leave one of your cards in the hotel safe as a backup if your wallet is stolen. It is also worth photocopying vital documents in case of loss or theft.

Be on guard against purse snatchers and pickpockets in big crowds. Prime places for theft are tourist areas, beaches, markets, sporting venues and on public transport.

Never carry your wallet in an outside pocket and wear shoulder bags and cameras with the strap across your body and the bag or camera in front. Park cars in well-lit, reasonably busy streets, and don't leave any valuables or property visible inside the car.

Sydney has no definite off-limit areas during the day, but try to avoid the more unsavoury side streets and lanes of areas such as Kings Cross. At night, stay clear of deserted, poorly lit streets and toilets in parks.

When travelling by train at night, travel in the carriage near the guard's compartment, which is marked with a blue light. Nightsafe buses run from major train stations to the suburbs when trains stop running from midnight to dawn.

Taxis are probably the safest means of travel at night, especially for shorter journeys or for women on their own. Ten secure taxi ranks in the city centre are manned by security guards on Friday and Saturday nights.

Two secure bus services run between Circular Quay and Parramatta suburb, and between The Rocks and Town Hall at weekends.

In an Emergency

The number to call for all emergencies – police, fire and ambulance – is 000. If you witness suspicious activity, report it to the National Security Hot Line 1800 123400.

Lost and Stolen Property

If you lose anything on public transport or in a taxi you should report it immediately, providing the transport route you were travelling on. **NSW Trains** and **Sydney Trains** have one number. **Sydney Ferries** has a separate number, while bus passengers should call the individual **Sydney Buses** depots. For anything left in a taxi, call the taxi company.

If your passport is stolen report it to your embassy or consulate (see p221). Lost or stolen credit or debit cards should also be reported to your card provider so that your account can be blocked.

Hospitals and Pharmacies

Sydney has excellent medical services. If you are in need of urgent medical attention, dial 000 for an ambulance or go to

Police car

Fire engine

Intensive care ambulance

Surf lifesaving sign indicating a dangerous undertow or "rip"

the emergency department of the nearest main public hospital. **Sydney Hospital** and **St Vincent's Hospital** both have emergency departments. For less urgent treatment, look under "Medical Centres" in the Yellow Pages of the Sydney telephone directory or at www.yellowpages.com.au.

The **King's Cross Travellers' Clinic** and the **International Travel Vaccinations Centre** offer treatment for travel-related illnesses and vaccinations.

For non-urgent dental treatment, look under "Dentists" in the Yellow Pages. **The Gentle Dentist** can be contacted after hours for urgent cases. The **Dental Hospital** is open from 8am–4:30pm Mon–Fri.

Pharmacies are generally known as "chemists" and can be found throughout the city and suburbs. They sell a wide range of drugs and medical supplies over the counter. A handful of city, Kings Cross and Bondi Beach chemists stay open until around 10pm.

Travel and Health Insurance

It is a good idea to buy travel insurance before arriving in Australia. Most overseas visitors are not covered by Australia's "Medicare" government health scheme, and medical, dental and ambulance costs are expensive.

British and New Zealand passport holders (and nationals from eight other European countries) are entitled to free basic emergency medical and hospital treatment.

Environmental Hazards

When swimming at an ocean beach, check that there are lifesavers on patrol and swim within the "flagged" areas. In their red and yellow caps, volunteer surf lifesavers keep an eye out for changing surf conditions, people in difficulty and surfers close to areas set aside for swimmers only. Lifeguards from district councils are dressed in blue *(see p56)*. Look out for signs on the beach indicating that it is dangerous to swim, and do not go in under any circumstances.

If you plan to bushwalk, do not hike alone. Always tell someone where you are going and when you will be back. Take a map, a basic first-aid kit, food and fresh water, and warm, waterproof clothing. It is very unlikely that you will encounter any poisonous snakes or spiders, but you should wear substantial footwear, keep a close eye on where you step, and check around logs and rocks before sitting on them.

Protecting Your Skin

Australia has the world's highest rates of skin cancer, caused by the harmful effects of ultraviolet rays. The risk of skin damage is high, even on cloudy days, and particularly between 10am and 2pm (11am and 3pm in daylight saving). Always wear a good SPF 30+ sunscreen and cover up with protective clothing, hat and sunglasses. The **Cancer Council** has more information.

Banking and Local Currency

Sydney is Australia's financial capital. In the central business district (CBD) are the imposing headquarters of several of the country's leading banks, as well as the Australian head offices of major foreign banks. Visitors will find local, state and national bank branches dotted at convenient intervals throughout the city and suburbs.

There is no limit to the amount of personal funds that visitors can bring into Australia, but they must declare amounts over A$10,000 on their entry form. Most currencies can be exchanged on arrival at the airport. Banks generally offer the best exchange rates, but money can also be changed at bureaux de change and hotels.

High street bank logos of three major Australian banks

Banks and Bureaux de Change

Bank trading hours are usually from 9:30am–4pm Monday to Thursday, and 9:30am–5pm on Fridays. Some branches are also open to midday on Saturdays. Major city banks open 8:30am–5pm on weekdays.

Most bureaux de change are open Monday to Saturday, 9am–5:30pm, and some are open Sundays. Many state they don't charge commissions or fees, but their exchange rates may be lower than at banks. The current exchange rates, which can vary considerably day to day, are shown in the windows or foyers of banks and bureaux de change.

Traveller's cheques are a safe way to carry large sums of money, but they are rarely accepted by hotels or shops; if stores take them, they will display a sign. A valid passport or another form of ID is usually needed if you are cashing traveller's cheques.

ATMs

Automatic teller machines (ATMs) can be found in most bank lobbies or on an external wall near the bank's entrance. They are also found in the foyers of some clubs and pubs, and at some convenience stores in tourist areas. Ask your home bank or credit card provider which Sydney banks and cash dispensers will accept your debit and credit cards, and what the transaction charges will be. Using an ATM is not only convenient, but may also provide a better exchange rate than cash transactions.

Automatic cash dispenser

Credit and Debit Cards

All well-known international credit cards are widely accepted in Australia, as well as debit cards issued by major foreign banks. Use your card to book and pay for hotel rooms, airline tickets, car hire and entertainment tickets. Visa and MasterCard (Access) are the most widely accepted cards, and American Express is also taken by many retailers and travel providers. You can use credit cards to withdraw cash from ATMs at most banks.

Credit cards are a convenient way to make phone bookings and avoid the need to carry large sums of cash. They can be very useful in emergencies or if you need to fly home at short notice.

Carry the phone number of your credit card issuer in case your card is lost or stolen.

Wiring Money

Money can only be transferred to a person travelling in Australia if that person has set up a bank account in Australia. Transfer fees, which may average around £10, are charged by UK banks and the Australian bank may also charge a fee. The **ANZ Bank** has a branch in London where travellers can set up an Australian account before they leave home. It can take up to five days for the money to arrive. A quicker way is via **Western Union** and other similar operators.

DIRECTORY

Banks and Bureaux de Change

American Express
60 Martin Place. **Map** 1 B4.
50 Pitt St. **Map** 1 B3.
275 & 341 George St. **Map** 1 B4.
296 & 673 George St. **Map** 1 B3.
Tel 1300 132 639.

ANZ Bank
68 Pitt St. **Map** 1 B4.

The Change Group
Jetty 6, Circular Quay. **Map** 1 B3.
Tel 9247 2082. **Open** 9am–7pm daily.

Citibank
2 Park St. **Map** 4 E2.
55–57 Pitt St. **Map** 1 B3. 695 George St. **Map** 4 E4.
Tel 9978 2871.

Commonwealth Bank
48 Martin Place. **Map** 1 B4.

National Australia Bank
343 George St. **Map** 1 B4.

Travelex
330 George St. **Map** 1 B4.
570 George St. **Map** 1 B5.

Westpac Bank
341 George St. **Map** 1 B4.

Wiring Money

ANZ Bank UK
40 Bank St, Canary Wharf, London, E14 5EJ, UK.
Tel 0203 229 2121

Western Union
w westernunion.co.uk

Currency

The Australian currency is the Australian dollar ($ or A$), which breaks down into 100 cents (c).

Single cents may still be used for some prices, but as the Australian 1c and 2c coins are no longer in circulation, the total amount to be paid will be rounded up or down to the nearest five cent amount.

It can be difficult to get A$50 and A$100 notes changed, so avoid using them in smaller shops and cafés and, more particularly, when paying for taxi fares. If you do not have change, it is always wise to tell the taxi driver before you start your journey to avoid any misunderstandings. Otherwise, when you arrive at your destination, you may have to find change at the nearest shop or automatic cash dispenser.

To improve security, as well as increase their circulation life, all Australian bank notes have now been plasticized.

Bank Notes

Australian bank notes are produced in denominations of A$5, A$10, A$20, A$50 and A$100. All bank notes are made of plastic. Paper notes have been phased out and are no longer legal tender.

A$100 note

A$50 note

A$20 note

A$5 note

A$10 note

5 cents (5c)

10 cents (10c)

20 cents (20c)

50 cents (50c)

1 dollar (A$1)

2 dollars (A$2)

Coins

Coins currently in use are 5c, 10c, 20c, 50c, A$1 and A$2 (shown here actual size). There are several 20c, 50c and $1 coins in circulation; all are the same shape, but have different commemorative images. The 10c and 20c coins are useful for local telephone calls (see p226).

Media and Communications

The rise in mobile-phone ownership means there are fewer public payphones in Sydney than there used to be, but they are generally well maintained. Alternatively, hire a mobile phone or bring your own and buy an Australian SIM card for it on arrival. Internet cafés are easily found and offer another means of communication. Australia's postal service is efficient, and there's an express delivery option. Several different newspapers and magazines are also readily available.

Telstra public telephone booths

International and Local Phone Calls

Local calls (those with the 02 area code) are untimed and cost 50 cents. Credit card public phones have a minimum charge of A$1.20 making them uneconomical for local calls. It's better to find a public phone that takes phonecards.

Long-distance calls are cheaper if you dial without the help of an operator. **Telstra** sells pre-paid phonecards in denominations of A$5, A$10 and A$20. You can buy cards from newsagents, chemists and other retail outlets. A cheaper option is to buy an international calling card for the country you will be calling. These are available at newsagents and supermarkets.

Mobile Phones

Mobile phones are used extensively in Australia. You can rent one from **Vodafone** at their shop in the airport international arrivals hall (open 6am–10pm). It costs A$4–10 a day to rent the phone and calls are extra. You'll need a credit card and your passport. Other rental companies are listed in the Yellow Pages telephone directory under "Mobile Telephones".

Another option is to buy an Australian SIM card to use in your mobile phone – the rates are much cheaper than roaming charges using your own service plan. SIM cards are available from **Optus**, **Telstra**, **Virgin** and Vodafone. You must have an unlocked compatible international phone; if in doubt, ask your service provider about whether your mobile phone will work in Australia. Online companies such as **Telestial** sell Australian SIM cards for about $9 each.

Public Telephones

Most payphones accept coins and phonecards, although some operate solely with phonecards and credit cards. Phonecards can be bought from selected newsagents and news kiosks displaying the Telstra sign. All public telephones have a hand receiver and 12-button keypad, though they may vary in shape and colour, as well as instructions (in English only). They are easy to use: lift the receiver, wait for the dial tone and then insert coins, a phonecard or a credit card. Dial the number. When finished any unused coins will be refunded. Only put 50 cents in for a local call – if you insert a A$2 coin you won't receive change. If making an international call or a call to a mobile using coins, don't overload the phone with change; just insert your money when the phone prompts you to do so. If using a pre-paid phone-card, the amount to be debited will appear on the phone screen.

Internet

Internet cafés provide relatively cheap Internet access and can be found throughout the city; one of the most popular is **Global Gossip**, which also offers fax and scanning services. Wireless (Wi-Fi), which allows you to connect to the Internet using your own laptop, is increasingly common in Sydney and is available for free in many public places, including Gloria Jean's cafés and McDonalds. Hotels also provide Wi-Fi and broadband Internet, but often charge for it, although some boutique hotels offer Wi-Fi for free. A list of free Wi-Fi hotspots is available at www.freewifi.com.au.

Postal Services

All domestic mail is first class and usually arrives within one to four days, depending on distance. Be sure to include the postcode in the address to avoid delays in delivery.

Computer terminals at a Global Gossip Internet café

Reaching the Right Number

- To ring Sydney from the UK, dial 0061 2, then the local number.
- To ring Sydney from the USA and Canada, dial 011 61 2, then the local number.
- For long-distance direct-dial calls outside your local area code, but within Australia (STD calls), dial the appropriate area code, then the number, e.g. for Melbourne dial 03 first.
- For international direct-dial calls (IDD calls): dial 0011, followed by the country code (USA and Canada: 1; UK: 44; New Zealand: 64), then the city or area code (omit initial 0) and then the local number.
- International directory enquiries: dial 1225.
- Local directory enquiries: dial 1223.
- Call Connect: dial 12455 (call connection charges apply).
- International operator assistance: dial 1225.
- International reverse charge call 1800 801 800 to access operator in home country.
- Numbers beginning with 1800 are toll-free numbers.
- Ten-digit numbers beginning with 04 are mobile phones.
- See also Emergency Numbers, p223.

Standard postboxes are red (for normal post) and yellow (for Express Post)

parcel, use Registered Post International where the recipient signs for the item on delivery.

Sydney has red and yellow postboxes. The red boxes are for the normal postal service; the yellow boxes are for Express Post within Australia.

Post offices are open 9am–5pm week days. Almost all post offices offer a wide range of services, including fax, money orders, money transfer and telegrams, as well as stamps, envelopes, packaging, stationery and postcards. Stamps can also be bought from hotels and shops where postcards are sold, and from some newsagents.

Address **Poste Restante** letters to c/- Poste Restante, GPO Sydney, NSW 2000, but collect them from 310 George St, Hunter Connection Building, opposite Wynyard Station. You will need to show your passport or other proof of identity.

Newspapers and Magazines

Sydney's chief daily morning newspaper is the *Sydney Morning Herald*. It includes a comprehensive listing of local entertainment on Fridays and Saturdays. The other Sydney daily is the *Daily Telegraph*.

The *Australian* is the country's only daily national paper with the most comprehensive coverage of overseas news; the *Australian Financial Review* largely reports on business and international monetary matters. Some newspapers require a subscription for access to online editions. Others, including news.com.au, thenew daily.com.au and national broadcaster abc.net.au, are free.

Major foreign newspapers and magazines are available at many newsstands.

Television and Radio

Sydney has two state-run television networks, ABC (Channel 2) and SBS. There are also commercial networks: Channels 7, 9 and 10. ABC provides news and current affairs coverage, children's programmes and local and international dramas. The Special Broadcasting Service (SBS) caters to Australia's many cultures with foreign-language programmes. Commercial channels offer a variety of entertainment from sport and news to soap operas.

Sydney has several AM and FM radio stations and 20 digital stations. ABC stations cater for various musical tastes, as well as providing news and magazine-style programmes.

DIRECTORY

International and Local Phone Calls

Telstra
W telstra.com

Mobile Phones

Optus
W optus.com.au

Telestial
W telestial.com

Virgin
W virginmobile.com.au

Vodafone
W vodafone.com.au

Internet

Global Gossip
790 George St. **Map** 4 E5.
W globalgossip.com

Postal Services

General Post Office (GPO)
1 Martin Place. **Map** 4 E1.
Tel 131 318.
Open 8:30am–5:30pm Mon–Fri, 10am–2pm Sat.
Poste Restante: 310 George St, Level 2a Hunter Connection Building. **Map** 4 E1. **Tel** 9244 3732.
Open 9am–5:30pm Mon–Fri.

Express Post, for which you need to buy one of the special yellow and white envelopes sold in post offices, guarantees next-day delivery in designated areas of Australia. International airmail takes from 5 to 10 days to reach most countries.

There are two types of international express mail. Express Courier International is the fastest service and will reach nearly all overseas destinations within two to four days, with its delivery tracked from door-to-door. Alternatively, items sent via Express Post International will reach most destinations throughout the world in three to seven days.

If you want to ensure the addressee receives the letter or

TRAVEL INFORMATION

Travelling to Sydney can involve a long and tiring flight. Visitors from Europe can take advantage of stopovers in Asia; those from the United States could break their journey in Hawaii or one of the other Pacific Islands. A break can mean the difference between arriving in Sydney jet-lagged or stepping off the plane refreshed and ready to take in the sights. Sydney is linked to Australia's other state capitals by efficient air, rail and coach connections. Long-distance coach travel is comfortable and relatively inexpensive; interstate trains are more expensive, but they are generally a great deal faster. People travelling by coach should consider taking one of the scenic routes with stopovers offered by some coach companies. Car travellers can also plan their journey to Sydney to pass through scenic areas.

Arriving by Air

The main gateway to the city is **Sydney Airport**, which has three terminals. T1 is the international terminal, and is 3 km (2 miles) from the two domestic terminals – T2 and the Qantas-only T3. The international and domestic terminals are connected by a shuttle bus (fare A$5.50) and train line (fare A$5). Taxis are also available.

T1 can get busy at peak times (usually early morning), which can sometimes result in delays in immigration and baggage collection. There is a large duty-free shop for arriving passengers and a stand with free Sydney guidebooks. The arrivals lounge has a concierge desk whose staff can book hotels, tours and other tourist services *(see p219)*. T1 also has a range of shops, a bureau de change, Internet facilities, ATMs and several car hire desks.

Qantas Airways, **Virgin Australia** and **Jetstar**, which are Australia's major international and domestic carriers, link Sydney with other cities and tourist destinations in Australia from T2 and T3. Other regional carriers, including **REX**, which connects Sydney to New South Wales, also use T2.

Tickets and Fares

International flights to Sydney are expensive and are often heavily booked, especially from December to February. December is the pinnacle of peak season, and therefore the most expensive time to fly. From February to mid-April tickets are much cheaper.

APEX fares are often the best priced. Some stipulate set arrival and departure dates, or carry penalties if you cancel your flight. Round-the-world fares can offer good value and are popular, as are flight comparison websites such as **skyscanner.com**.

On Arrival

International airline passengers are issued with an Incoming Passenger Card to be filled in before passport control. This card, along with your passport, is presented to immigration and customs officials, who will mark and return it. Keep the

Taxis lining up to take passengers at Sydney Airport

card safe, because you must hand it to another customs officer once you have collected your luggage and are exiting the customs area. Packaged food, wooden items and other goods deemed to be a risk must be declared *(see p218)*.

Getting into the City

Sydney airport is about 9 km (5 miles) from the central business district. The **Airport Link** rail line (a private line that links with CityRail), takes 15 minutes to get into the city and costs A$15.80 from T1. Shuttle bus companies, such as **KST Sydney Airporter**, run from the airport to hotels in the city, Darling Harbour and Kings Cross. Tickets cost around A$12 one way.

Catch buses and taxis from outside the terminals or take the train from the underground station at each terminal. A State Transit bus (Metro route 400) stops at the airport. It travels to Bondi Junction and the western suburb of Burwood (but not the city). A taxi from the airport to the city costs A$25–30.

Qantas flight arriving at Sydney Airport

A passenger ship berthed at Circular Quay

Arriving by Sea

Undoubtedly, the most delightful way to arrive in Sydney is by ship. Passenger ships berth at terminals at **Circular Quay** and **White Bay** at Rozelle. The Circular Quay site (known as the Overseas Passenger Terminal) is in The Rocks, with the information booths, tour booking centres, buses, trains, ferries, taxis and water taxis all close at hand. White Bay caters predominantly to the domestic cruise market, since most international cruise ships are too tall to cross under the Sydney Harbour Bridge to reach White Bay. The terminal is a 5–15-minute taxi trip across Anzac Bridge to or from the city, although at peak hours it may take longer. There are ATM facilities, short-term parking and a taxi rank at the terminal, and it is also wheelchair accessible.

Arriving by Train

All interstate and regional trains arrive at **Central Railway Station**. Australia's nationwide rail network is known by a different name in each state, but it still operates cohesively. **NSW Trains** is the New South Wales regional rail network. Its reservations line answers queries and takes bookings (6:30am–10pm daily) for train services throughout Australia.

The city train operator, Sydney Trains (see p232), also has slower but cheaper services to some country areas such as Newcastle and Wollongong, but seats cannot be booked in advance.

The Transport Infoline (see p236) has details about NSW Trains' services beyond Greater Sydney.

Arriving by Coach

Most long-distance bus or coach services arrive at the **Sydney Coach Terminal** at Central Railway Station. The terminal has left-luggage facilities but will not store anything overnight. Competition between the coach companies is fierce, so shop around to get the best price.

Arriving by Car

The four major routes into Sydney are the Pacific Highway from the north; the Great Western Highway from the west; the Princes Highway, following the coast from Melbourne; and the Hume Highway, which runs inland from Melbourne.

As these routes approach Sydney, they feed into freeways or motorways, which either link to other motorways or lead towards the city centre. Some include tunnels, such as the Sydney Harbour Tunnel, an alternative to the Sydney Harbour Bridge. All exits are clearly marked with green and white signs, as are connecting roads.

DIRECTORY

Arriving by Air

Airport Information
Tel 9667 9111.
Ⓦ sydneyairport.com.au

Air Canada
Reservations:
Tel 1300 655 767.

Air New Zealand
Reservations: Tel 132 476.

British Airways
Reservations:
Tel 1300 767 177.

Emirates
Reservations and flight information:
Tel 1300 303 777.

Japan Airlines
Reservations and flight information:
Tel 1800 802 228.

Jetstar
Reservations: Tel 131 538.

Qantas Airways
Reservations:
Tel 131 313.
Arrivals and departures:
Tel 131 223.

REX – Regional Express Airlines
Tel 131 713.

Singapore Airlines
Reservations: Tel 131 011.
Arrivals: Tel 1300 654 475.

Thai Airways
Reservations:
Tel 1300 051 960.

United Airlines
Reservations, arrivals and departures: Tel 131 777.

Virgin Australia
Tel 136 789.

Getting into the City

Airport Connect
Tel 9557 7615.
Ⓦ airportconnect. com.au

Airport Link (Train)
Tel 8337 8417.

KST Sydney Airporter
Tel 9666 9988.
Ⓦ kst.com.au

Arriving by Sea

Circular Quay
West Circular Quay, Sydney. **Map** 1 B3.

White Bay Cruise Terminal
off James Craig Rd, Rozelle.

Train Information

Central Railway Station
Tel 131 500.

Lost property
Tel 9379 3341.

NSW Trains
Tel 1300 038 500.

Long-Distance Coach Station

Sydney Coach Terminal
Cnr of Eddy Ave & Pitt St.
Map 4 E5. Tel 9281 9366.

Getting Around Sydney

In general, the best way to see Sydney's many sights and attractions is on foot, coupled with use of the public transport system. Buses, trains and the Metro Light Rail system (modern trams) will take visitors to within easy walking distance of anywhere in the inner city. They also serve the suburbs and outlying areas. Passenger ferries provide a fast and scenic means of travel between the city and harbour-side suburbs. The best selection of maps, plus fascinating aerial and satellite views and historical maps, can be found at **Map World**.

Cycling is an eco-friendly way to explore the city

Green Travel

The best way to reduce your carbon footprint in Sydney is to travel on foot, by bicycle and on public transport. You can also take the train from Sydney Airport – cutting down on vehicle traffic on this busy corridor. To encourage car-pooling, there are several transit lanes (T2 or T3 lanes), which can only be used in peak hours by cars carrying two, three or more passengers.

Several operators, including **Sydney Electric Bikes**, sell and rent these bikes, which are powered by a battery and make cycling up hills and long distances easy.

Finding Your Way Around Sydney

Sydney is a sprawling metropolis, however, the Central Business District (CBD) is quite small. The city centre lies on the south side of the harbour; the Sydney Harbour Bridge connects it with the north of Sydney. The main shopping area is an easy walk south from the harbour's edge. Darling Harbour is on the city's western edge; the closest beaches, including Bondi are about 9 km (6 miles) to the east of the city and Manly is 11 km (7 miles) northeast (and over the Bridge).

Walking

Take care when walking around the city. Vehicles are driven on the left and often move quickly. It is wise to use pedestrian crossings; there are two types. Push-button crossings are found at traffic lights. Wait for the green man signal and do not cross at lights if the red warning sign is on or flashing. Zebra crossings are marked by yellow and black signs. Make sure vehicles are stopping before you cross.

Guided Tours

Tours and excursions offer the visitor many different ways of exploring the city and its surroundings – from bus tours for food-lovers to jaunts on the back of a Harley Davidson, guided nature or history walks, cruises on replica tall ships, guided bicycle tours and aerial adventures by hot-air balloon, seaplane or helicopter. As well as being an easy way to take in the sights, a tour can help you to get a feel for your new surroundings.

Perhaps the most flexible and economical introduction to Sydney's attractions are the unregimented hop-on-hop-off tours in an open-top double decker bus organised by **Sydney and Bondi Explorer**.

In addition, visitors can use commuter ferries (see pp234–5) as a less costly alternative to commercial harbour cruises, of which there are many.

Tickets and Travel Passes

Sydney's public transport system has paper and electronic tickets. Colour-coded MyBus (blue), MyTrain (red), MyFerry (green) and MyMulti (gold) paper tickets are available for a number of distance-based travel zones. MyMulti includes unlimited travel on buses, trains, ferries and light rail, but it does not cover travel on the Airport Link train (see p228) and Explorer sightseeing buses.

MyTrain and MyFerry tickets are for both single and return journeys. MyBus offers single-journey tickets or ten-trip TravelTen passes. Light Rail offers single, return, day, week and family day tickets.

Opal electronic tickets can be used on all modes of public transport. Customers pre-load value onto an Opal card, with a starting value of A$10 for adults and A$5 for children.

To use an Opal card, riders "tap on" by placing the card on the Opal touchpad as they board, and "tap off" in the same way when they disembark. The fare is calculated based on distance travelled. Daily fare caps of A$15, weekly fare caps of A$60 and A$2.50 unlimited travel on Sundays apply.

Opal cards are available from the domestic and international airport train stations, airport terminal retailers, the Circular Quay Transport Information Centre, newsagents and convenience stores.

Driving in Sydney

If you are planning to use a car to drive around greater Sydney, you will need a good street directory or an in-car Global Positioning System (GPS), which is usually offered as an option when you hire a car.

It is best to avoid the peak-hour traffic periods (about 7:30–9:30am and 4–7:30pm),

Traffic crossing Johnstons Bay on Sydney's Anzac Bridge

if possible. Regular traffic update reports are broadcast on many radio stations.

Petrol is a little more expensive than in North America, but about half the price of petrol in Europe. Most petrol stations are self-service and will accept major credit cards.

Overseas visitors can use their usual driver's licence to drive in New South Wales, but must have proof that they are only visiting. If your licence is not in English, however, you must carry a translation. Make sure you keep your licence on you at all times when driving.

Australians drive on the left-hand side of the road and over-take on the right. Drivers and passengers must wear seatbelts. In the city and suburbs the speed limit is between 40–60 km/h (25–37 mph), and 100–110 km/h (60–65 mph) on motorways, freeways and highways. The maximum speed in a school zone is 40 km/h (25 mph). You must obey the signs relating to these zones as well as bus lanes and T2 and T3 lanes for cars carrying two, three or more passengers.

Kerbside Traffic Signs

Always pay strict attention to Sydney's parking and traffic signs as fines for infringements can be very expensive.

The 0.05 per cent maximum blood alcohol level for drivers is enforced by random breath tests. A driver found to be over the legal limit will incur a heavy fine, loss of licence and even a prison sentence.

Parking

Parking in Sydney is strictly regulated with fines for any infringements. In certain areas, particularly along clearways (indicated by signposts), vehicles are towed away if parked illegally. Contact the **Transport Management Centre** to find out where your vehicle has been taken if this happens.

Car parks in the city area charge fees from A$4 to A$25 an hour on weekdays. Look out for the blue and white "P" signs. On-street parking meters vary in price, depending on the time and area.

Taxis

Taxis are plentiful in Sydney in the city and inner suburbs, although they can be scarce "between shifts" at 2:30–3:15pm. There are taxi ranks at many city locations and taxis are often found outside large hotels. Meters indicate the fare plus any extras, such as booking fees and waiting time. Fares and extra charges are regulated and are more expensive after 10pm.

Taxis designed to accommodate disabled passengers can be booked through any of the major companies.

Cycling

Visitors should restrict their cycling to designated bicycle tracks, or to areas where motor traffic is likely to be light. They should also remember that wearing a helmet is compulsory. Centennial Park *(see p55)* is a popular biking spot.

Bicycle New South Wales publishes a handbook, *Bike It, Sydney*, which has a map of good cycling routes. The company also provides advice to cyclists. **Bonza Bike Tours** and **Manly Bike Tours** offer entertaining guided cycling tours.

Travelling by Sydney Trains and Light Rail

Sydney's railway network (operated by Sydney Trains) connects the suburbs with the city and serves a large part of the central business district. Sydney Trains also operates services to the Blue Mountains, Central Coast and Southern Highlands. A convenient alternative for exploring the museums and shops of Darling Harbour, as well as Chinatown, The Star casino and some inner west suburbs, is the Sydney Light Rail (tram).

Sydney Trains train at a platform,
Central Railway Station

Travelling by Sydney Trains

The **Sydney Trains** network covers a vast area and is the quickest way to get into the city from most suburbs, as well as to and from the airport. The City Circle loop runs through the city centre stopping at Central, Town Hall, Wynyard, Circular Quay, St James and Museum stations.

All suburban lines connect with the City Circle at Central Station. The western, northern and southern suburbs are well covered by the network, but it does not extend to the eastern or northern beaches (note: Bondi Junction is covered by the eastern suburb trains but not Bondi Beach).

Fares start at A$4 per ticket. Discounts on return fares apply after 9:30am. Trains run from 4:30am to about midnight. After midnight, NightSafe buses travel along rail routes, and all routes pick up from George St and Town Hall, providing long-haul

services to many suburban areas. The bus drivers are in contact with taxi firms and can organise a pick up for you.

Using the Sydney Light Rail Trams

The **Sydney Light Rail** is both a tourist and commuter service. The environmentally friendly trams offer a quicker and quieter way of visiting places of interest between Glebe and Darling Harbour.

The trams travel from Central Station to the inner western suburb of Dulwich Hill on a disused goods line, calling at several stations, including stops at the The Star casino, the Sydney Fish Markets and Jubilee Park.

Buy tickets on board from the conductor or use MyMulti tickets (see p230), which can be bought from newsagents and convenience stores. The Light Rail has two zones: Zone 1 from Central to Convention, and Zone 2 from Pyrmont Bay to Dulwich Hill. A return ticket for Zone 1 or Zone 2 costs A$5.20, and a return for Zones 1 and 2 costs A$6.40.

Using the Sydney Trains Route Map

The different Sydney Trains lines are colour-coded and route maps are displayed at all Sydney Trains stations and inside train carriages. Distances shown on the map are not to scale and the routes that lines are seen to take may not be geographically correct.

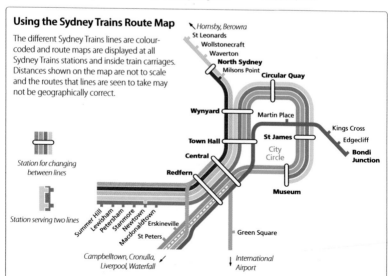

Station for changing between lines

Station serving two lines

Hornsby, Berowra
St Leonards
Wollstonecraft
Waverton
North Sydney
Milsons Point
Circular Quay
Wynyard
Martin Place
Kings Cross
Edgecliff
Town Hall
St James
Bondi Junction
Central
City Circle
Redfern
Museum
Summer Hill
Lewisham
Petersham
Stanmore
Newtown
Macdonaldtown
Erskineville
St Peters
Green Square
Campbelltown, Cronulla, Liverpool, Waterfall
International Airport

A tram on the Light Rail network leaves Central Railway Station

It is significantly more cost effective to buy a return ticket than two single tickets. For those intending to take three or more trips in a day, a day pass can be bought for less than A$10. A day pass makes the Light Rail a good sightseeing option for those who want to venture out of the main city areas. The Jubilee Park stop is in a vibrant and beautiful park filled with interesting wetlands, bridges and a delightful walking path around Rozelle Bay, with plaques pointing out some of the area's history. The path leads around to the Sydney Fish Market, where there is another Light Rail stop, from which you can head back to the city.

Another pleasant excursion from Jubilee Park station is a stroll through the park to Glebe Point Road, a long stretch filled with cool cafés, cheap eateries, bookshops, and antiques and second-hand stores.

DIRECTORY

Useful Information

Central Railway Station
Map 4 E5.
Tel 9379 1777.

Circular Quay Railway Station
Map 1 B3.
Tel 9224 3553.

Sydney Light Rail
Tel 131 500.
w transportnsw.info

Sydney Trains Information
w sydneytrains.info

Transport Infoline
Tel 131 500.
w transportnsw.info

Late-night gamblers can take advantage of the Central–The Star–Central trams that run along this limited-stop route 24 hours a day. The all-stops service between Central and Dulwich Hill operates from 6am–11pm daily (until midnight on Fridays and Saturdays). The daily service runs every 10–15 minutes at peak times, and every 30 minutes between midnight and 6am.

Making a Journey by Sydney Trains

1 Study the Sydney Trains route map. Route lines are distinguished by colour, so simply trace the line from where you are to your destination, noting where you need to change and make connections.

2 Buy tickets from ticket dispensing machines or ticket booths at stations. (Single and return tickets can only be bought at stations.) To obtain your ticket from a dispensing machine, press the button to indicate destination, then the ticket type (single, return, etc). Insert money into the slot, then collect your ticket and any change.

3 To pass through the ticket barrier, insert your ticket (arrow side up) into the slot at the front of barrier machines (indicated by green arrows). Take your ticket as it comes out of the machine and the barrier gates or turnstile will open.

4 To find the right platform, follow the signs with the same colour code as the line you need and the name of the line's final station.

Platform 20   City Circle via Museum
Platform 21   City Circle via Museum

5 On the platform, display signs show all the stations the line travels through. Stations at which the next train will stop are lit up and are announced as the train arrives at the station.

Travelling by Ferry and Water Taxi

Travelling by ferry is a great way to commute between the harbour suburbs. State-owned, privately managed Sydney Ferries provides the majority of services, but it competes with a second private operator on the Manly run. The government privatized the entire fleet in 2012 but retains control of fares and routes, as well as ownership of the ferries. Water taxis are a convenient but expensive alternative, and there are numerous sightseeing cruises.

Captain Cook ferry approaching the Sydney Opera House

Using Sydney's Ferries

There is a constant procession of **Sydney Ferries** traversing the harbour between 6am and midnight daily. The boats cover most of Sydney Harbour and several stops along the Parramatta River. Frequent services run to and from Manly, Darling Harbour, Balmain, Parramatta, Taronga Zoo, Neutral Bay, Pyrmont Bay, Balmain/Woolwich, Mosman, Rose Bay and Watsons Bay, with numerous stops en route. Sydney Buses *(see p236)* provide convenient connections at most wharves.

Staff at the **Sydney Ferries Information Office** can answer queries and provide ferry timetables. You can also call the **Sydney Ferries Infoline** for advice about connections, destinations and fares.

Making a Journey by Ferry

All ferry journeys start at the Circular Quay Ferry Terminal. Electronic destination boards at the entrance to each wharf indicate the wharf from which your ferry will leave, and also give departure times and all stops made en route.

Tickets can be bought from ticket booths located on the wharves at Circular Quay and from vending machines. MyMulti tickets (for unlimited travel on buses, trains, ferries and MLR trams) can be purchased at several outlets, including newsagents and convenience stores *(see p230)*.

At Circular Quay and Manly Wharf there are automatic ticket barrier machines. To board your ferry, insert the ticket into the slot with the arrow side up and the arrow pointing into the slot.

Manly's ferry terminal is serviced by regular ferries and the faster, privately run Manly Fast Ferry. Tickets and information can be obtained from the ticket windows in the centre of the terminal. No food or drink is permitted on the fast ferries. Most, but not all, wharves have wheelchair access.

Types of Vessel

Sydney Ferries operates six types of vessel: the SuperCats serving Watsons Bay, the RiverCats that travel up river to Parramatta, the HarbourCats, the First Fleet Class for short inner suburb routes, the Lady Class and the large and elegant Freshwaters that pass by the North and South Heads on their way to Manly.

Private Ferries

The **Manly Fast Ferry** is owned by a private company; the journey to Manly takes 17 minutes rather than the 30 minutes by Sydney Ferries. The service runs regularly between Circular Quay and Manly in the morning and afternoon peak times, and every hour from 10:50am–3:50pm Monday to Friday. While the peak hour fares are more expensive than Sydney Ferries, fares decrease at non-peak times of the day. The ferry is primarily used by Manly residents who work in the city,

A Sydney Ferries SuperCat

The Freshwater *Collaroy* en route to Manly

A Sydney Ferries RiverCat

but it does run at the weekend and there's also a service that connects Circular Quay and Darling Harbour with Manly. Timetables change, so check the website. Ferries depart from Wharf 6; tickets can be bought from Wharf 3 at Circular Quay, on board the vessel and at booths at Manly. Passengers can buy individual tickets at around A$8.50 each, or a Smartcard that offers discounted fares.

Sightseeing by Ferry and Commercial Operators

Catching a commuter ferry is a great way to discover the harbour, and no visit to Sydney is complete without seeing the skyline from the water. Close-up views of the Opera House and Fort Denison can be had from any of the North Shore commuter routes, while the Balmain/Woolwich ferry and the RiverCat ferry make a stop at Cockatoo Island *(see p108)*. As well as providing a fascinating glimpse of Sydney's convict history, this island offers perhaps the best vantage point for views of Harbour Bridge and the city skyline.

Other harbour islands can also be visited: the **National Parks and Wildlife Service** runs tours of Fort Denison and Goat Island, while **Captain Cook Cruises** and **Matilda Cruises** operate the hop-on-hop-off Harbour Explorer, which is a 24-hour cruise pass that allows visits to seven harbour

sights including Fort Denison and Shark Island.

Numerous commercial sightseeing cruises cover all budgets, themes and time constraints; most last around 90 minutes. **Australian Travel Specialists** has information on all harbour cruises from Circular Quay and Darling Harbour and they do not charge a booking fee. Many of these leave from Wharf 6 (Circular Quay) so it is worth checking out the day's departures there.

Water Taxis

Small, fast taxi boats carry passengers to any number of destinations on the harbour, including harbour islands. You can flag them down like normal cabs if you spot one cruising for a fare. Try Circular Quay near the Overseas Passenger Terminal or King Street Wharf. You can also telephone for a water taxi or book them over the Internet. They will pick up and drop off at any navigable pier. Rates vary, but expect to pay a charge of around A$90–110 for a short journey from Darling Harbour to the Opera House for up to six people.

A water taxi on Sydney Harbour – a convenient but pricey ride

DIRECTORY

Using Sydney's Ferries

Sydney Ferries Infoline
Tel 131 500.
🌐 transportnsw.info

Sydney Ferries Information Office – Harbour City Ferries
Tel 8113 3002.
🌐 beyondthewharf.com.au

Private Ferries

Manly Fast Ferry
Tel 9583 1199.
🌐 manlyfastferry.com.au

Sightseeing by Ferry

Australian Travel Specialists (ATS)
Wharf 6, Circular Quay, Darling Harbour. **Map** 1 B3. **Tel** 9263 1100. 🌐 atstravel.com.au

Captain Cook Cruises
Tel 1800 804843.
🌐 captaincook.com.au

Matilda Cruises
Tel 8270 5188.
🌐 matilda.com.au

National Parks and Wildlife Service
Tel 9253 0888.
🌐 environment.nsw.gov.au/nationalparks

Water Taxis

H2O Taxis
Tel 1300 420 829.
🌐 h2owatertaxis.com.au

Water Taxis Combined
Tel 9555 8888.
🌐 watertaxis.com.au

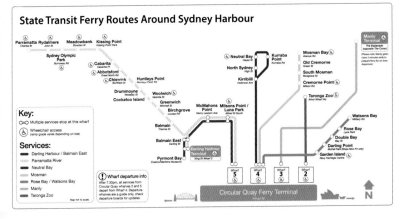

State Transit Ferry Routes Around Sydney Harbour

Parramatta (Charles St), Rydalmere (John St), Meadowbank (Bowden St), Kissing Point (Kissing Point Park)

Sydney Olympic Park (Burroway Rd)

Cabarita (Cabarita Pt), Abbotsford (Great North Rd), Chiswick (Bortfield Dr)

Huntleys Point (Huntleys Point Rd)

Drummoyne (Thompson St), Woolwich (Valentia St), Greenwich (Mitchell St)

Cockatoo Island, Birchgrove (Louisa Rd)

Neutral Bay (Hayes St), North Sydney (High St), Kirribilli (Holbrook Ave), Kurraba Point (Kurraba Rd)

Mosman Bay (Avenue Rd), Old Cremorne (Green St), South Mosman (Musgrave St), Cremorne Point (Milson Rd)

Taronga Zoo (Athol Wharf Rd)

McMahons Point (Henry Lawson Ave), Milsons Point / Luna Park (Alfred St South)

Balmain (Thames St), Balmain East (Darling St)

Pyrmont Bay (Casino/Maritime Museum), Darling Harbour Terminal (King St Wharf 3)

Watsons Bay (Military Rd), Rose Bay (Lyne Park), Double Bay (Bay St), Darling Point (Mona Park (Stops Mon–Fri only)), Garden Island (Navy Heritage Centre)

Key:
⊂⊃ Multiple services stop at this wharf
♿ Wheelchair access (ramp grade varies depending on tide)

Services:
— Darling Harbour / Balmain East
— Parramatta River
— Neutral Bay
— Mosman
— Rose Bay / Watsons Bay
— Manly
— Taronga Zoo
Map not to scale.

ⓘ **Wharf departure info**
After 7.30pm, all services from Circular Quay wharves 2 and 5 depart from Wharf 4. Departure wharves are a guide only; check departure boards for updates.

Wharf 5 | Wharf 4 | Wharf 3 | Wharf 2

Circular Quay Ferry Terminal (Wharf 6)

Manly Terminal (The Esplanade, opposite The Corso) (Please note: Manly gates close 2 minutes early to prepare ferry for on-time departure)

N

Travelling by Bus

Sydney Buses provides a punctual service that links up conveniently with the city's rail and ferry systems. As well as covering city and suburban areas, there are regular routes that serve the airport *(see p228)* and privately owned hop-on hop-off sightseeing buses. The Transport Infoline *(see p231)* can advise you on routes, fares and journey times for all Sydney buses. Armed with the pull-out map from the inside back cover of this book and a MyMulti ticket, you can avoid the difficulties and expense of city parking.

Automatic stamping machine for validating bus tickets

Using Sydney Buses

The public transport system, including **Sydney Buses**, has been overhauled, and the fleet upgraded. Buses are blue and white, and environmentally friendly "bendy" buses operate on several lines. The route name and number are shown on the front and side of the bus, and the number is also displayed on the rear. An "X" in front of the number means that it is an express bus.

About 25 routes are "prepay" only, so you must buy a ticket before boarding. All Central Business District (CBD) bus stops are also prepay only from 7am–7pm on weekdays to ease congestion. During weekends and outside these hours, you can pay with cash – try to have the right change for the fare.

Among the permanent prepay routes is the popular 333 bus to Bondi Beach and on to Watsons Bay. When using a prepay MyBus or MyMulti ticket, insert it in the automatic stamping machine as you board. Ensure the arrow is facing you and pointing downwards. Free 555 CBD Shuttle buses travel in a loop around the CBD from Circular Quay to Central Station along Elizabeth and George streets every 10 minutes.

Front seats on buses must be given up to elderly or disabled people. Eating, drinking, smoking or playing music is prohibited on buses. To signal that you wish to alight, press one of the stop buttons, which are mounted on the vertical handrails, well before the bus reaches your stop.

Bus Stops

Bus stops are indicated by yellow and black signs displaying a profile of a bus and a boarding passenger. Sometimes the numbers of the buses travelling along the route are listed below this symbol.

Timetables are usually found on the bus stop sign or are displayed in the nearby shelter. The Sunday timetable also applies to public holidays. While efforts are made to keep bus stop timetables as up-to-date as possible, it is always best to carry a current bus timetable with you. They can be collected from some tourist information facilities and are also available at Sydney Buses Transit Shop kiosks found at Circular Quay, Wynward, the Queen Victoria Building and Railways Square in the city, as well as at Bondi Junction and the Manly ferry wharf. Maps and timetables can also be downloaded from the Sydney Buses website.

Sightseeing by Bus

The brightly coloured Sydney Explorer *(see pp230–31)* buses operate a daily hop-on hop-off service that visits 24 Sydney sights in a loop from Circular Quay. The whole journey takes 90 minutes if you don't get off. Stops include Kings Cross, the Botanic Garden, the Australian Museum and Darling Harbour.

The same company runs the Bays & Bondi Explorer that departs from Central Station and calls at 10 stops including Bondi Beach, Double Bay, Rose Bay and Paddington.

The first buses leave at 8:30am and the last finish at 7:30pm, with buses departing every 20 minutes. A combined ticket for both the city and Bondi tours is A$40 for 24 hours, or A$60 for 48 hours.

The great advantage of these services is that you can explore at will, getting on and off the buses as often as you wish. The best way to make the most of your journey is to choose the sights you most want to see and plan a basic itinerary.

Tickets can be bought on the buses at any stop, or from Sydney Visitor Centres *(see p221)*, hotels, travel agencies and ATS at Circular Quay *(see p235)*. They can also be bought online in advance.

Hop-on hop-off Sydney Explorer bus in front of the Opera House

Travelling Beyond Sydney

Sydney is close to several areas of scenic beauty and an excellent wine region. The best way to explore the nearby regions of the Blue Mountains, Hunter Valley and the Southern Highways, or national parks on the edge of Sydney is by car and train. The far north coast New South Wales beach towns and outback and regional centres of western New South Wales are between 1 and 1½ hours away by plane.

Blue Mountains National Park

Domestic Flights

Qantas and its subsidiary Qantas Link, Jetstar and Virgin Australia are the main domestic airlines. REX – Regional Express Airlines operates to regional areas in New South Wales from T2 in Sydney Airport *(see pp228–9)*.

Fares can be quite low on competitive routes, and the cheapest rates can often be found online, so shop around before booking. Domestic flights depart from Sydney Airport's terminals 2 and 3; the latter is used exclusively by Qantas.

Country and Inter-Urban Trains

The Sydney Trains network *(see p232)* includes InterCity trains that travel to the Blue Mountains, the South Coast (via five stations near the Royal National Park), the Southern Highlands and Newcastle, and the Central Coast. All these services depart from Central Station *(see p229)*.

While the network also includes the Hunter regional line, this does not service the popular wineries near the town of Pokolbin. Passengers wanting to visit the wineries should take the train to Morrisett (on the Newcastle and Central Coast line), then a Rover Coach to Pokolbin. NSW Trains *(see p229)* is a rail network that covers more than

360 destinations in New South Wales, along with Brisbane and Melbourne. On its way out west, the train travels through the Blue Mountains, and trains to Melbourne stop at some Southern Highlands towns.

Tickets can be bought at Central Railway station, suburban stations in Sydney and at many travel agents. They can also be booked over the phone or online. Trains depart from the main concourse of Central Station, which is upstairs from the suburban train platforms.

Long-Distance Bus Travel

Long-distance bus travel can be cost effective but many journeys are long: for example a coach to Coffs Harbour (considered the mid-way stop between Sydney and Brisbane) takes over 7 hours. **Greyhound Australia** covers the nation, while other operators, such as **Firefly Express** and **Murrays Coaches**, run services on certain routes.

Competition on the Sydney–Melbourne route means fares are usually quite good and can be as little as A$70 one-way, although it is a long 12- to 14-hour trip. Coaches leave from Central Railway Station. Greyhound Platinum business-class coaches have extra leg room and additional facilities.

Road Travel

Highways in Sydney and New South Wales are improving all the time. The biggest challenge is knowing which route to take out of the city, so hire a car with a GPS system. Many areas of scenic beauty are within 2 hours' drive of Sydney. Ensure that your hire car comes with road-side breakdown assistance. For more on driving, *see pp230–31*.

Car Hire

Rates offered by the major agencies *(see p231)* range from about A$75 a day for a small car to A$100 a day for a larger vehicle. These rates become cheaper over a week's rental and usually include comprehensive insurance. Be sure to read the fine print on hire agreements. **Bayswater Car Rental** has the best rates in Sydney and can be as low as A$28 a day for a week's hire, excluding "extras" like insurance.

You must be over 21 years old to hire a car from some companies and if you do not have a credit card, you will need to leave a deposit.

DIRECTORY

Using Sydney Buses

Sydney Buses
Tel 131 500.
w sydneybuses.info

Long-Distance Bus Travel

Firefly Express
Tel 1300 730 740 or
(03) 8318 0318.
w fireflyexpress.com.au

Greyhound Australia
Tel 1300 473 946.
w greyhound.com.au

Murrays Coaches
Tel 132 251.
w murrays.com.au

Sydney Coach Terminal
Eddy Avenue and Pitt Street,
Sydney. **Map** 4 E5. **Tel** 9281 9366.

Car Hire

Bayswater Car Rental
Tel 02 9360 3622.
w bayswatercarrental.com.au

SYDNEY STREET FINDER

The page grid superimposed on the *Area by Area* map below shows which parts of Sydney are covered in this *Street Finder*. Map references given for all sights, hotels, restaurants, shopping and entertainment venues described in this guide refer to the maps in this section. All the major sights are clearly marked so they are easy to locate.

A complete index of the street names and places of interest follows on pages 246–9. The key, set out below, indicates the scale of the maps and shows what other features are marked on them, including railway stations, bus terminals, ferry boarding points, emergency services, post offices and tourist information centres.

Sydney Harbour Bridge *(see pp72–3)*, viewed from North Sydney Olympic Pool

Key

- Major sight
- Place of interest
- Other building
- Sydney Trains station
- Bus terminus or coach station
- Ferry boarding point
- *i* Tourist information office
- Hospital with casualty unit
- Police station
- Church
- Synagogue
- Mosque
- Freeway
- Railway line
- Ferry route
- Pedestrianized street

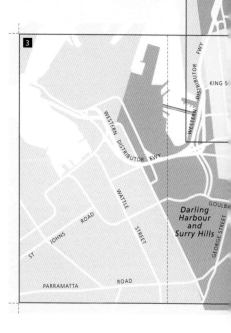

0 metres 250
0 yards 250

0 metres 500
0 yards 500

Sundial in the Royal Botanic Garden *(see pp106–7)*

Statues on the Art Deco Anzac Memorial in Hyde Park *(see p88)*

Enjoying coffee outside Bar Coluzzi in Darlinghurst *(see p192)*

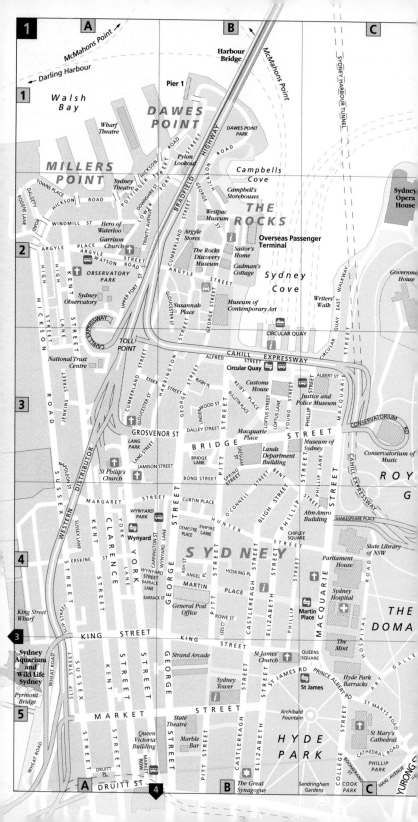

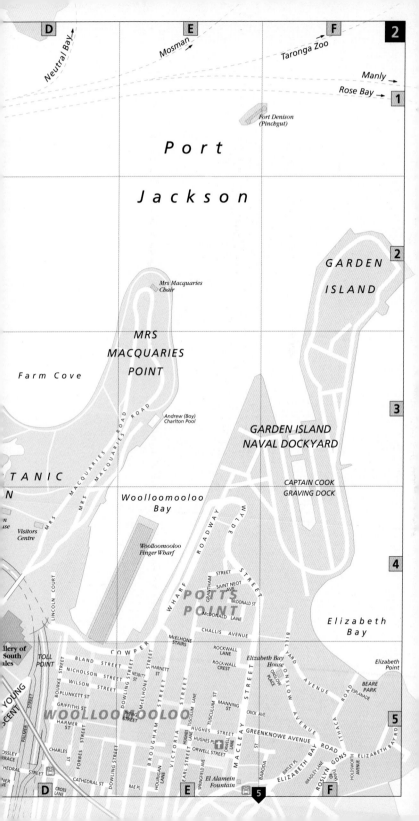

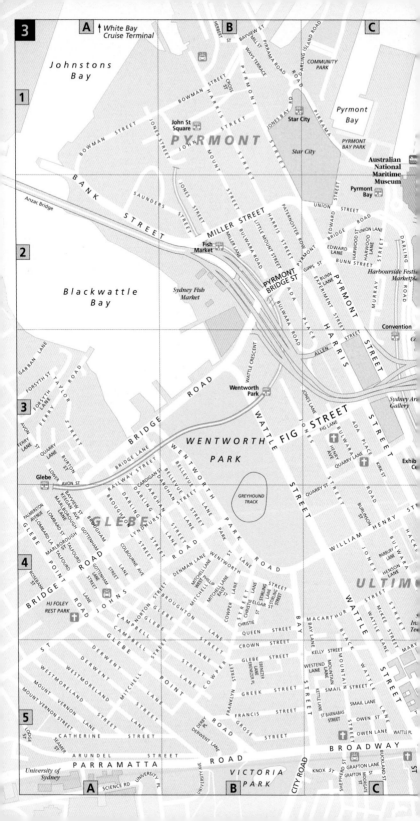

A ↑ White Bay Cruise Terminal

B

C

1

Johnstons Bay

BOWMAN STREET

HERBERT ST

BAYVIEW ST

MILL ST

PIRAMA ROAD

DARLING ISLAND ROAD

COMMUNITY PARK

WAYS TERRACE

PYRMONT STREET

CROSS STREET

HARRIS STREET

JONES STREET

BOWMAN STREET

John St Square

JOHN STREET

PYRMONT

JONES BAY RD

Star City

PIRAMA ROAD

Pyrmont Bay

Star City

PYRMONT BAY PARK

Australian National Maritime Museum

BANK STREET

SAUNDERS STREET

JONES STREET

MOUNT STREET

JONES STREET

HARRIS STREET

PATERNOSTER ROW

LITTLE MOUNT STREET

PYRMONT STREET

UNION STREET

EDWARD STREET

BRIDGE ROAD

HARWOOD STREET

UNION LANE

HARWOOD LANE

DARLING

Pyrmont Bay

2

Anzac Bridge

MILLER STREET

Fish Market

MILLER LANE

BULWARA LANE

PYRMONT BRIDGE ST

GIPPS ST

BUNN LANE

EXPERIMENT STREET

BUNN STREET

MURRAY STREET

EDWARD LANE

Harbourside Festival Marketplace

Blackwattle Bay

Sydney Fish Market

BULWARA ROAD

ADA PLACE

HARRIS STREET

ALLEN STREET

Convention

3

GARRAN LANE

FORSYTH ST

TAYLOR ROAD

FERRY ROAD

FORSYTH LANE

BRIDGE ROAD

WATTLE CRESCENT

Wentworth Park

WATTLE STREET

JONES LANE

FIG STREET

FIG LANE

HENRY AVE

BULWARA PLACE

ADA PLACE

QUARRY LANE

KIRK ST

Sydney Arts Gallery

Exhib Ce

AVON LANE

FERRY LANE

QUARRY LANE

BURTON STREET

STREET

Glebe

LOWER AVON ST

BRIDGE STREET

RAILWAY STREET

WENTWORTH PARK ROAD

WENTWORTH PARK

QUARRY STREET

STREET

GREYHOUND TRACK

QUARRY ST

BURINSON ST

WILLIAM HENRY

JONES

PARBURY LANE

HENSON LANE

4

PALMERSTON AVENUE

BAYVIEW AVE

KEEGAN AVE

MARLBOROUGH ST

LOMBARD ST

LOMBARDIA LANE

HALFORD ST

BROUGHAM STREET

CARDIGAN ST

O'CARDIGANS LANE

DARLING STREET

DARLING LANE

BELLEVUE STREET

BELLEVUE LANE

DARGHAN STREET

LYNDHURST STREET

COLBOURNE AVE

DENMAN LANE

WENTWORTH PARK ROAD

MITCHELL LANE WEST

PHILLIP ST

WENTWORTH STREET

MITCHELL ST

MITCHELL LANE EAST

CHRISTIE LANE

CHRISTIE ST

ELGAR ST

STIRLING LANE

STIRLING STREET

ULTIM

WATTLE STREET

MCKEE STREET

WATTLE LANE

MARY

GLEBE

BRIDGE ROAD

GLEBE POINT ROAD

JOHNS ROAD

GOTTENHAM ST

GOTTENHAM LANE

NORTON STREET

GLEBE STREET

BROUGHTON STREET

COWPER LANE

ST PHILLIP ST

CHRISTIE STREET

QUEEN STREET

MACARTHUR LANE

BAY LANE

BAY STREET

BLACKWATTLE LANE

HJ FOLEY REST PARK

ROSEBANK ST

BRIDGE POINT ROAD

CAMPBELL STREET

GLEBE POINT ROAD

CAMPBELL LANE

COWPER STREET

CROWN STREET

GLEBE STREET

KELLY STREET

WESTEND LANE

MOUNTAIN STREET

SMAIL STREET

KETTLE LANE

WATTLE STREET

In Te

5

MOUNT VERNON STREET

MOUNT VERNON LANE

LODGE ST

SEAMER ST

WESTMORELAND STREET

WESTMORELAND LANE

DERWENT STREET

DERWENT LANE

MITCHELL STREET

GLEBE POINT ROAD

CATHERINE STREET

COWPER STREET

DERBY PL

DERWENT LANE

GLEBE LANE

EBENEZER LANE

EBENEZER STREET

GREEK STREET

FRANCIS STREET

GROSE STREET

FRANKLYN STREET

SMAIL LANE

ST BARNABAS STREET

OWEN ST

OWEN LANE

WATTLE LN

BROADWAY

University of Sydney

ARUNDEL STREET

PARRAMATTA ROAD

SCIENCE RD

UNIVERSITY AVE

UNIVERSITY PL

VICTORIA PARK

CITY ROAD

KNOX ST

SHEPHERD ST

GRAFTON LANE

GRAFTON STREET

BUCKLAND ST

MACQUARIE ST

A

B

C

Street Finder Index

A

Abercrombie Street	3 C5
Ada Place	3 B2
Albert Square	6 D3
Albert Street	
(Edgecliff)	6 F2
Albert Street	
(Paddington)	6 D3
Albert Street	
(Sydney)	1 C3
Alberta Street	4 F4
Albion Avenue	5 A3
Albion Place	4 E3
Albion Street	4 F5
continues	5 A3
Albion Way	4 F5
Alexander Street	
(Paddington)	5 C4
Alexander Street	
(Surry Hills)	5 A4
Alexandra Lane	5 A5
Alfred Street	1 B3
Allen Street	3 C3
Alma Street	6 D2
Alton Street	6 F4
Amos Lane	5 C1
Angel Place	1 B4, 4 E1
Ann Street	4 F5
Anzac Parade	5 B4
Argyle Centre	1 B2
Argyle Place	1 A2
Argyle Street	1 A2
Arnold Place	5 A2
Art Gallery of New	
South Wales	2 D5
Art Gallery Road	1 C5
Arthur Lane	5 A4
Arthur Street	
(Edgecliff)	6 E2
Arthur Street	
(Surry Hills)	5 A4
Arundel Street	3 A5
Ash Street	1 B4, 4 E1
Ashton Lane	6 D3
Australian Broadcasting	
Corporation	4 D4
Australian Museum	4 F3
Avon Street	3 A3

B

Bank Street	3 A1
Barcom Avenue	5 B2
Barlow Street	4 E4
Barncleuth Lane	5 C1
Barncleuth	
Square	5 C1
Barnett Lane	5 A1
Baroda Street	2 F5
Barrack Lane	1 A4
continues	4 E1
Barrack Street	1 A4
continues	4 E1
Bartlett Lane	5 B3
Bates Avenue	5 C3
Bathurst Street	4 D3
Batman Lane	4 F5
Bay Lane	3 C4
Bay Street	
(Double Bay)	6 F2
Bay Street (Glebe)	3 B4
Bayswater Road	5 B1
Bayview Street	
(Glebe)	3 A4

Bayview Street	
(Pyrmont)	3 B1
Beare Park	2 F5
Beattie Lane	4 E5
Beauchamp Lane	4 F5
Begg Lane	5 C3
Bellevue Lane	
(Glebe)	3 B3
Bellevue Lane	
(Surry Hills)	4 F5
Bellevue Street	
(Glebe)	3 B3
Bellevue Street	
(Surry Hills)	4 F5
Belmore Lane	4 F5
Belmore Park	4 E4
Belmore Place	5 C3
Belmore Street	4 F5
Bennett Place	5 A4
Bennett Street	5 A4
Bennetts Grove	
Avenue	6 D3
Bent Street	
(Paddington)	6 D4
Bent Street (Sydney)	1 B3
continues	4 F1
Berwick Lane	5 A1
Bethel Lane	5 B3
Bijou Lane	4 D5
Billyard Avenue	2 F4
Birtley Place	2 F5
Blackburn Street	4 E4
Blackwattle Lane	3 C4
Bland Street	2 D5
Bligh Street	1 B4
continues	4 F1
Bond Street	1 B3
Boomerang Street	1 C5
continues	4 F2
Bossley Terrace	2 D5
Boundary Lane	5 B2, 5 C2
Boundary Street	5 B2
Bourke Street	5 A5
Bowden Street	6 F4
Bowes Avenue	6 E2
Bowman Street	3 A1
Bradfield Highway	1 B1
Bradley Lane	2 F5
Bridge Lane (Glebe)	3 A3
Bridge Lane	
(Sydney)	1 B3
Bridge Road (Glebe)	3 A4
Bridge Street	1 B3
Brisbane Street	4 F4
Britannia Lane	6 E4
Broadway	3 C5
Brodie Street	5 C3
Brooklyn Lane	6 F2
Broome Avenue	6 F5
Brougham Lane	
(Glebe)	3 A4
Brougham Lane	
(Potts Point)	5 B1
Brougham Street	2 E5
continues	5 B1
Broughton Lane	3 B4
Broughton Street	
(Glebe)	3 A4
Broughton Street	
(Paddington)	6 D3
Brown Lane	5 C2
Brown Street	5 C3
Browns Place	5 C2
Buckland Street	3 C5
Bulletin Place	1 B3

Bulwara Road	3 B2
Bunn Lane	3 C2
Bunn Street	3 C2
Burdekin Lane	5 A4
Burlinson Street	3 C4
Burnell Place	5 A1
Burrahore Lane	5 A1
Burton Street	
(Darlinghurst)	5 A2
Burton Street (Glebe)	3 A3
Busby Lane	5 A1

C

Cadman's Cottage	1 B2
Cahill Expressway	1 B3
Caldwell Street	5 B1
Caledonia Lane	6 E4
Caledonia Street	6 D4
Cambridge Lane	6 D2
Cambridge Street	6 D2
Cameron Street	6 E2
Campbell Avenue	5 B2
Campbell Lane	3 A4
Campbell Street	
(Glebe)	3 A4
Campbell Street	
(Haymarket)	4 E4
Campbell Street	
(Surry Hills)	5 A2
Campbell's	
Storehouses	1 B2
Capitol Theatre	4 E4
Cardigan Street	3 A4
Carrington Drive	6 E5
Carrington Street	1 A4
continues	4 E1
Cascade Lane	6 D2
Cascade Street	6 D3
Castlereagh Street	1 B5
continues	4 E5
Cathedral Road	1 C5
continues	4 F2
Cathedral Street	2 D5
Catherine Street	3 A5
Cecil Lane	6 E3
Cecil Street	6 E3
Centennial Lane	6 D5
Centennial Park	6 E5
Centennial Square	6 E4
Central Railway	
Station	4 E5
Central Street	4 E3
Centre for Contem-	
porary Craft	1 B2
Challis Avenue	2 E4
Chalmers Street	4 E5
Chapel Street	5 A1
Chaplin Street	5 B2
Chapman Lane	5 A4
Chapman Street	5 A4
Charles Street	
(Surry Hills)	5 A5
Charles Street	
(Woolloomooloo)	2 D5
Charlotte Lane	4 F3
Chelsea Street	5 A5
Chifley Square	1 B4
continues	4 F1
Chinatown	4 D4
Chinese Garden	4 D3
Chisholm Street	5 A3
Chiswick Lane	6 F3
Christie Lane	3 B4
Christie Street	3 B4

Church Place	6 D4
Church Street	5 A3
Circular Quay East	1 C3
City Road	3 B5
Clapton Place	5 B1
Clare Street	5 A3
Clarence Street	1 A4
continues	4 E1
Clarke Street	4 F3
Clement Street	5 C1
Cleveland Street	5 A5
Clifton Reserve	5 A3
Colbourne Avenue	3 A4
College Street	1 C5
continues	4 F3
Collins Lane	5 A4
Collins Street	5 A4
Comber Street	5 B3
Commonwealth	
Street	4 F5
Community Park	3 C1
Conservatorium of	
Music	1 C3
Conservatorium	
Road	1 C3
Convention and	
Exhibition Centre	3 C3
Cook Park	1 C5
continues	4 F2
Cook Road	6 D5
Cooper Lane	4 F5
Cooper Street	
(Double Bay)	6 F1
Cooper Street	
(Paddington)	5 C2
Cooper Street	
(Surry Hills)	4 E5
Corben Street	4 F5
Corfu Street	5 A1
Coulton Lane	5 A4
Cow Lane	5 B2
Cowper Lane	3 B4
Cowper Street	3 B5
Cowper Wharf	
Roadway	2 D5
Craigend Street	5 B1
Crane Place	1 B3
Crick Avenue	2 E5
Cross Lane	2 D5
Cross Street	
(Pyrmont)	3 B1
Cross Street	
(Double Bay)	6 F1
Crown Lane	5 A1
Crown Street	
(Glebe)	3 B5
Crown Street	
(Woolloomooloo)	2 D5
continues (Surry	
Hills)	5 A3
Cumberland Street	1 A3
Curtin Place	1 B4
continues	4 E1
Customs House	1 B3

D

Dalgety Road	1 A2
Dalley Street	1 B3
Darghan Lane	3 B3
Darghan Street	3 A3
Darley Place	5 B2
Darley Street	5 B2
Darling Drive	3 C2

Darling Harbour	
Passenger	
Terminal	1 A4
	& 4 D1
Darling Island Road	3 C1
Darling Lane	3 A4
Darling Point Road	6 E1
Darling Street	3 A4
Darlinghurst Court	
House	5 A2
Darlinghurst Road	5 A2
Davies Street	5 A4
Davoren Lane	5 A4
Dawes Point Park	1 B1
Day Street	4 D3
De Mestre Place	1 B4
continues	4 E1
Denham Street	5 A3
Denman Lane	3 B4
Derby Place	3 B5
Derwent Lane	3 A5
Derwent Street	3 A5
Devonshire Street	5 A4
Dillon Lane	5 C2
Dillon Street	5 C2
Dixon Street	4 D3
Domain, The	1 C4
Dorhauer Lane	6 E4
Douglas Lane	4 E3
Dowling Street	2 D5
continues	5 B1
Downshire Street	1 A2
Driver Avenue	5 B4
Druitt Lane	4 D3
Druitt Place	1 A5
continues	4 D2
Druitt Street	1 A5
continues	5 E2
Dudley Street	6 D3
Duxford Street	6 D3
Dwyer Lane	6 E4
Dwyer Street	4 D5

E	
Eagar Lane	4 E3
Earl Place	5 B1
Earl Street	2 E5
continues	5 B1
Eastern Distributor	5 A2
Ebenezer Lane	3 B5
Ebenezer Place	3 B5
Eddy Avenue	4 E5
Edgecliff Road	6 F2
Edgely Street	5 A5
Edward Lane	3 C2
Edward Street	3 C2
Egan Place	5 A1
El Alamein Fountain	2 E5
Elfred Street	5 C3
Elger Street	3 B4
Elizabeth Bay House	2 F5
Elizabeth Bay Road	2 F5
Elizabeth Place	6 D4
Elizabeth Street	
(Paddington)	6 D4
Elizabeth Street	
(Sydney)	1 B5
continues	4 E5
Empire Lane	1 B4
continues	4 E1
Entertainment Centre	4 D4
Erskine Street	1 A4
continues	4 D1
Esplanade	2 F5
Essex Street	1 A3
Esther Street	5 A4
Evans Road	2 F5
Experiment Street	3 C2

F	
Factory Street	4 D4
Fanny Place	5 A4
Farrell Avenue	5 B1
Faucett Lane	5 A1
Ferry Lane	3 A3
Ferry Road	3 A3
Fig Street	3 B3
Fitzroy Place	5 A3
Fitzroy Street	4 F5
continues	5 A3
Five Ways	5 C3
Flemings Lane	5 A3
Flinders Street	5 A3
Floods Lane	5 A3
Foley Street	5 A2
Forbes Street	
(Darlinghurst)	5 A2
Forbes Street	
(Paddington)	6 E3
Foreshore Road	3 B1
Forsyth Lane	3 A3
Forsyth Street	3 A3
Fort Denison	2 E1
Forth Street	6 F4
Foster Street	4 E4
Foveaux Street	4 E5
continues	5 A3
Fox Studios	6 D5
Francis Lane	5 A1
Francis Street	
(Darlinghurst)	4 F3
Francis Street	
(Glebe)	3 B5
continues	5 A1
Franklyn Street	3 B5
Fullerton Street	6 F3
Furber Lane	6 D5
Furber Road	6 D5

G	
Garran Lane	3 A3
Garrison Church	1 A2
George Lane	6 D4
George Street	
(Paddington)	6 D4
George Street	
(Sydney)	1 B5
continues	4 E4
Gipps Street	
(Paddington)	5 B3
Gipps Street	
(Pyrmont)	3 B2
Glebe Island Bridge	3 A2
Glebe Lane	3 A4
Glebe Point Road	3 A4
Glebe Street	
(Edgecliff)	6 E2
Glebe Street	
(Glebe)	3 A4
Glen Street	5 C2
Glenmore Road	5 B3
Glenview Lane	5 C2
Glenview Street	5 C2
Gloucester Street	1 B2
Goderich Lane	5 B1
Goldman Lane	6 F1
Goodchap Street	4 F4
Goold Street	4 D5
Gordon Lane	6 D4
Gordon Street	6 D4
Gosbell Lane	5 C2
Gosbell Street	5 C2
Gottenham Lane	3 A4
Gottenham Street	3 A4
Goulburn Lane	4 F4

Goulburn Street	4 D4
continues	5 A2
Government House	1 C2
Grafton Lane	3 C5
Grafton Street	3 C5
Grand Drive	6 E5
Grantham Street	2 E4
Great Synagogue	1 B5
Great Thorne Street	6 E2
Greek Street	3 B5
Green Park	5 B2
Greenknowe Avenue	2 E5
Greenoaks Avenue	6 E1
Greens Road	5 B3
Gregory Avenue	5 B5
Gresham Street	1 B3
Griffin Street	4 F5
Griffiths Street	2 D5
Grose Street	3 B5
Grosvenor Street	1 A3
Guilfoyle Avenue	6 F1
Gumtree Lane	6 F2
Gurner Lane	6 D2
Gurner Street	6 D3

H	
Hackett Street	3 C4
Haig Avenue	1 C5
continues	4 F2
Haig Lane	1 C5
Halls Lane	6 E4
Hamilton Drive	6 E5
Hampden Street	6 D2
Hands Lane	4 F4
Hannam Street	5 A3
Harbour Street	4 D3
Harbourside Festival	
Marketplace	1 C2
Hardie Street	5 B2
Hargrave Lane	
(Darlinghurst)	4 F3
Hargrave Lane	
(Paddington)	6 D3
Hargrave Street	6 D3
Harmer Street	2 D5
Harnett Street	2 E5
Harrington Street	1 B3
Harris Street	
(Paddington)	6 E3
Harris Street	
(Pyrmont)	3 B1
Harris Street Motor	
Museum	3 C3
Harwood Lane	3 C2
Harwood Street	3 C2
Hay Street	4 D4
Hayden Lane	5 B2
Hayden Place	5 B2
Heeley Lane	5 C3
Heeley Street	5 C3
Henrietta Street	6 F2
Henry Avenue	3 C3
Henson Lane	3 C4
Herbert Road	6 E2
Herbert Street	3 B1
Hercules Street	4 F5
Hero of Waterloo	1 A2
Hickson Road	1 A2
High Lane	1 A2
High Street	
(Edgecliff)	6 E2
High Street	
(Millers Point)	1 A2
Hill Street	5 A3
HJ Foley Rest Park	3 A4
Hoddle Street	6 D2
Holdsworth Avenue	2 F5

Holdsworth Street	6 E3
Holt Street	
(Double Bay)	6 F2
Holt Street	
(Surry Hills)	4 F5
Hopetoun Lane	6 D3
Hopetoun Street	6 D3
Hopewell Lane	5 B3
Hopewell Street	5 B3
Hoskin Place	1 B4
continues	4 E1
Hospital Road	1 C5
continues	4 F2
Hourigan Lane	2 E5
Hughes Lane	2 E5
Hughes Place	2 E5
Hughes Street	2 E5
Hunt Street	4 F4
Hunter Street	1 B4
continues	4 E1
Hutchinson Lane	5 A3
Hutchinson Street	5 A3
Hyde Park	4 F2
Hyde Park Barracks	1 C5

I	
Ice Street	5 B2
Iris Street	5 B4
Ithaca Road	2 F5

J	
James Lane	
(Darling Harbour)	4 D3
James Lane	
(Paddington)	6 D2
James Street	
(Darling Harbour)	4 D3
James Street	
(Woollahra)	6 E4
Jamison Street	1 A3
Jenkins Street	1 A3
Jersey Road	6 D4
Jesmond Street	5 A3
John Street	
(Pyrmont)	3 B1
John Street	
(Woollahra)	6 E4
Jones Bay Road	3 B1
Jones Lane	3 C3
Jones Street	3 A1
Josephson Street	5 B4
Judge Lane	5 B1
Judge Street	5 B1
Junction Lane	2 D5
Juniper Hall	5 C3
Justice and Police	
Museum	1 C3

K	
Keegan Avenue	3 A4
Kellett Street	5 B1
Kells Lane	5 A2
Kelly Street	3 C5
Kendall Lane	5 A4
Kendall Street	5 A4
Kennedy Street	5 A1
Kensington Street	4 D5
Kent Street	1 A2
continues	4 D1
Kettle Lane	3 C5
Kidman Lane	5 B3
Kilminster Lane	6 F4
Kimber Lane	4 D4
King Street	1 A4
continues	4 D1
Kings Cross Road	5 B1

Kings Lane	5 A2	McLachlan Avenue	5 C2
Kippax Street	4 E5	McLaughlan Place	5 C3
Kirk Street	3 C3	Macleay Street	2 E5
Kirketon Road	5 B1	Macquarie Place	1 B3
Knox Lane	6 F1	Macquarie Street	1 C4
Knox Street		*continues*	4 F1
(Chippendale)	3 C5	Maiden Lane	5 A3
Knox Street		Manning Road	6 F2
(Double Bay)	6 F1	Manning Street	2 E5
		Mansion Lane	5 C1
L		Marathon Lane	6 E1
		Marathon Road	6 E1
Lacrozia Lane	5 B2	Marble Bar	1 B5
Lands Department		Margaret Street	1 A4
Building	1 B3	*continues*	4 D1
Lang Park	1 A3	Market Row	1 A5
Lang Road	6 D5	*continues*	4 E2
Lang Street	1 A3	Market Street	1 A5
Lawson Lane	6 D2	*continues*	4 D2
Lawson Street	5 C2	Marlborough Lane	3 A4
Lee Street	4 D5	Marlborough Street	3 A4
Lees Court	1 B4	Marshall Street	5 A4
continues	4 E1	Martin Place	1 B4
Leichhardt Street	5 B2	*continues*	4 E1
Leinster Street	5 C4	Martin Street	5 C4
Lincoln Court	2 D4	Mary Ann Street	3 C5
Lincoln Place	6 F2	Mary Lane	4 F5
Lindsay Lane	5 C2	Mary Place	5 B3
Little Albion Street	4 F5	Mary Street	4 E5
Little Bloomfield		Melrose Lane	6 D4
Street	5 A2	Merchants' House	1 B2
Little Bourke Street	5 A2	Mill Street	3 B1
Little Cleveland		Miller Lane	3 B2
Street	5 A5	Miller Street	3 B2
Little Comber Street	5 B3	Mitchell Lane East	3 B4
Little Dowling Street	5 B3	Mitchell Lane West	3 B4
Little Hay Street	4 D4	Mitchell Street	
Little Mount Street	3 B2	(Centennial Park)	6 D5
Little Oxford Street	5 A2	Mitchell Street	
Little Regent Street	4 D5	(Glebe)	3 A5
Little Riley Street	4 F5	Mona Lane	6 D1
Little Stewart Street	5 C4	Mona Road	6 E1
Little Surrey Street	5 B2	Moncur Lane	6 E4
Liverpool Lane	5 A1	Moncur Street	6 E4
Liverpool Street	4 E3	Moore Park	5 A4
continues		Moore Park Road	5 B4
(Darlinghurst)	5 A1	Moorgate Street	3 C5
Liverpool Street		Morrell Street	6 E4
(Paddington)	5 C3	Mort Lane	5 A5
Loch Avenue	6 F5	Mort Street	5 A5
Lodge Street	3 A5	Morton Lane	6 F4
Loftus Lane	1 B3	Mount Street	3 B1
Loftus Road	6 E1	Mount Vernon Lane	3 A5
Loftus Street	1 B3	Mount Vernon Street	3 A5
Lombard Lane	3 A4	Mountain Lane	3 C5
Lombard Street	3 A4	Mountain Street	3 C5
Lower Avon Street	3 A3	Mrs Macquaries	
Lower Fort Street	1 A2	Chair	2 E2
Lyndhurst Street	3 A4	Mrs Macquaries	
Lyons Lane	4 F3	Road	2 D4
		Murray Street	3 C2
M		Museum of	
		Contemporary Art	1 B2
Macarthur Avenue	5 B5	Museum of Sydney	1 B3
Macarthur Street	3 C4		
Macdonald Lane		**N**	
(Paddington)	5 C2		
McDonald Lane		Napier Street	5 B3
(Potts Point)	2 E4	Napoleon Street	1 A3
Macdonald Street		National Maritime	
(Paddington)	5 B2	Museum	3 C2
McDonald Street		National Trust	
(Potts Point)	2 E4	Centre	1 A3
McElhone Place	5 A4	Neild Avenue	5 C2
McElhone Street	2 E5	Nelson Lane	6 F4
continues	5 B1	Nesbitt Street	2 E5
McGarvie Street	6 D4	New Beach Road	6 D1
McKee Street	3 C4	New McLean Street	6 E2
Mackey Street	4 F5		

New South Head		Perry Lane	5 C3
Road	6 D1	Phelps Street	5 A4
Newcombe Street	6 D4	Phillip Lane	1 C4
Nichols Street	5 A3	Phillip Park	1 C5
Nicholson Street	2 D5	*continues*	4 F2
Nickson Lane	5 A5	Phillip Street (Glebe)	3 B4
Nickson Street	5 A5	Phillip Street	
Nimrod Street	5 B1	(Sydney)	1 B4
Nithsdale Street	4 F4	*continues*	4 F1
Nobbs Lane	5 A4	Pickering Lane	6 F4
Nobbs Street	5 A4	Pier Street	4 D4
Norfolk Lane	6 D3	Pitt Street	1 B5
Norfolk Street	6 D3	*continues*	4 E4
Norman Street	4 F4	Plunkett Street	2 D5
Norton Street		Poate Lane	6 D5
(Glebe)	3 A4	Poate Road	6 D5
Norton Street		Point Piper Lane	6 E4
(Surry Hills)	4 F5	Poplar Street	4 F4
		Pottinger Street	1 A2
O		Powerhouse	
		Museum	4 D4
O'Briens Lane	5 A1	Premier Lane	5 B1
O'Connell Street	1 B4	Prince Albert Road	1 C5
continues	4 E1	*continues*	4 F2
O'Loughlin Street	4 E5	Pring Street	2 E5
O'Sheas Lane	5 A3	Prospect Street	
Oatley Road	5 C4	(Paddington)	5 B3
Observatory Park	1 A2	Prospect Street	
Ocean Avenue	6 F2	(Surry Hills)	5 A4
Ocean Street	6 E2	Pyrmont Bay Park	3 C1
Octagon Road	6 E1	Pyrmont Bridge	1 A5
Olive Street	5 C3	*continues*	4 D2
Olivia Lane	5 A4	Pyrmont Bridge	
Omnibus Lane	4 D4	Road	3 B2
Old Gaol,		Pyrmont Street	3 B1
Darlinghurst	5 A2		
Onslow Avenue	2 F5	**Q**	
Onslow Place	2 F5		
Ormond Street	5 C3	Quambi Place	6 F2
Orwell Lane	2 E5	Quarry Lane (Glebe)	3 A3
Orwell Street	2 E5	Quarry Lane	
Osborne Lane	6 F4	(Ultimo)	3 C3
Oswald Street	6 D1	Quarry Street	
Overseas Passenger		(Paddington)	6 E3
Terminal	1 B2	Quarry Street	
Owen Lane	3 C5	(Ultimo)	3 C4
Owen Street	3 C5	Quay Street	4 D4
Oxford Square	4 F4	Queen Road	6 D4
Oxford Street	4 F3	Queen Street	
continues	5 A2	(Glebe)	3 B4
		Queen Street	
P		(Woollahra)	6 E4
		Queen Victoria	
Paddington Bazaar	3 C5	Building	1 B5
Paddington Lane	6 D3	Queens Avenue	5 C1
Paddington Street	6 D3	Queens Square	1 C5
Paddington			
Town Hall	5 C3	**R**	
Paddington Village	5 C3		
Paddy's Market	4 D4	Rae Place	2 E5
Palmer Lane	5 A1	Railway Square	4 D5
Palmer Street	2 D5	Railway Street	3 A4
continues	5 A2	Rainford Street	5 A4
Palmerston Avenue	3 A4	Randle Lane	4 E5
Parbury Lane	3 C4	Randle Street	4 E5
Park Lane	3 B4	Raper Street	5 A4
Park Street	4 E2	Rawson Lane	4 E5
Parker Lane	4 E4	Rawson Place	4 E4
Parker Street	4 E4	Reddy Street	6 D1
Parkes Drive	6 E5	Regent Street	
Parkham Lane	5 A4	(Chippendale)	4 D5
Parkham Place	5 A5	Regent Street	
Parkham Street	5 A5	(Paddington)	5 C4
Parliament House	1 C4	Reiby Place	1 B3
Parramatta Road	3 A5	Renny Lane	5 C4
Paternoster Row	3 B2	Renny Street	5 C4
Peaker Lane	6 E4	Reservoir Street	4 E4
Pelican Street	4 F4	Richards Avenue	5 A4
Pennys Lane	5 B1	Richards Lane	5 A4

Ridge Lane 5 A5
Ridge Place 5 A5
Ridge Street 5 A5
Riley Street 1 C5
continues 5 A2
Rockwall Crescent 2 E5
Rockwall Lane 2 E5
Rodens Lane 1 A2
Rosebank Street 3 A4
Rosella Lane 5 A1
Rosemont Avenue 6 F3
Roslyn Gardens 2 F5
continues 5 C1
Roslyn Lane 5 C1
Roslyn Street 5 C1
Rowe Lane 5 C3
Rowe Street 1 B4
continues 4 E1
Royal Agricultural
  Society (RAS)
  Showground 5 C5
Royal Botanic
  Gardens 1 C3
Roylston Lane 6 D2
Rush Street 6 E4
Rushcutters Bay Park 6 D1
Ryder Street 5 A2

S

Sailors' Home 1 B2
St Andrew's
  Cathedral 4 E3
St Barnabas Street 3 C5
St James' Church 1 B5
St James Road 1 B5
continues 4 F2
St James Road 6 F5
St Johns Road 3 A5
St Marks Road 6 E1
St Mary's Cathedral 1 C5
St Marys Road 1 C5
continues 4 F2
St Neot Avenue 2 E4
St Peters Lane 5 A1
St Peters Street 5 A1
St Philip's Church 1 A3
Samuel Street 4 F4
Sandringham
  Gardens 1 C5, 4 F2
Sands Street 4 D3
Saunders Street 3 A2
Science Road 3 A5
Seale Street 5 A1
Seamer Street 3 A5
Sega World 4 D3
Selwyn Street 5 B3
Seymour Place 5 A3
Shadforth Street 5 C3
Shakespeare Place 1 C4
continues 4 F1
Shepherd Street 3 C5
Sherbrooke Street 5 A2
Short Street
  (Darling Point) 6 F1
Short Street
  (Paddington) 5 A3
Shorter Lane 5 A1
Sims Street 5 A3
Sir John Young
  Crescent 2 D5
Sisters Lane 6 F2
Slip Street 1 A5, 4 D2
Smail Lane 3 C5
Smail Street 3 C5
Smith Street
  (Surry Hills) 4 F5

Smith Street
  (Woollahra) 6 E4
Sophia Lane 4 F5
Sophia Street 4 E5
Soudan Lane 6 E3
South Avenue 6 F1
South Dowling Street 5 A5
South Lane 6 F1
South Street 6 D2
Spence Lane 5 A1
Spicer Street 6 E3
Spring Street
  (Double Bay) 6 F1
Spring Street
  (Paddington) 5 B3
Springfield Avenue 2 E5
Stafford Lane 5 C3
Stafford Street 5 C3
Stanley Lane 5 A1
Stanley Street
  (Darlinghurst) 5 A1
Stanley Street
  (Redfern) 5 A5
State Library of NSW 1 C4
State Theatre 1 B5
Stephen Lane 5 C2
Stephen Street 5 C2
Stewart Place 6 D4
Stewart Street 5 C4
Steyne Park 6 F1
Stirling Lane 3 B4
Stirling Street 3 B4
Strand Arcade 1 B5
Stream Street 5 A1
Sturt Street 5 A2
Suffolk Street 6 D3
Surrey Lane 5 B1
Surrey Street 5 B1
Susannah Place 1 B2
Sussex Lane 1 A4, 4 D1
Sussex Street 1 A3, 4 D1
Sutherland Avenue 6 D3
Sutherland Street 6 D3
Suttor Street 5 A1
Sydney Aquarium 1 A5, 4 D1
Sydney Art Gallery 3 C3
Sydney Cricket
  Ground 5 C5
Sydney Dance and Theatre
  Company 1 A1
Sydney Fish Market 3 B2
Sydney Football
  Stadium 5 C4
Sydney Harbour Bridge 1 B1
Sydney Harbour
  Tunnel 1 C2
Sydney Hospital 1 C4
Sydney Jewish
  Museum 5 B2
Sydney Mint Museum 1 C4
Sydney Observatory 1 A2
Sydney Opera House 1 C2
Sydney Theatre 1 A2
Sydney Tower 1 B5
Sydney Town Hall 4 E2
Systrum Street 4 D4

T

Talbot Place 5 A1
Talfourd Lane 3 A4
Talfourd Street 3 A4
Tara Street 6 F3
Taylor Square 5 A2
Taylor Street (Glebe) 3 A3
Taylor Street
  (Paddington) 6 E4

Taylor Street
  (Surry Hills) 5 A3
Terry Street 4 E5
Tewkesbury Avenue 5 B1
Thomas Lane 4 D4
Thomas Street 3 C5
Thomson Lane 5 A1
Thomson Street 5 A2
Thorne Street 6 E2
Thurlow Lane 5 A5
Tivoli Street 6 D4
Towns Place 1 A2
Trelawney Street 6 F3
Trinity Avenue 1 A2
Trumper Park 6 E2
Tumbalong Park 4 D3
Turner Lane 2 D5
Tusculum Lane 2 E5
Tusculum Street 2E5

U

Ulster Street 6 D4
Ultimo Road 4 D4
Underwood Street
  (Paddington) 5 C3
Underwood Street
  (Sydney) 1 B3
Union Lane
  (Paddington) 6 D3
Union Lane
  (Pyrmont) 3 C2
Union Street
  (Paddington) 6 D3
Union Street
  (Pyrmont) 3 B2
University Avenue 3 B5
University Place 3 A5
University of Sydney 3 A5
Upper Fig Street 3 C3
Upper Fort Street 1 A2
Uther Street 4 F5

V

Valentine Street 4 D5
Vaughan Place 5 A5
Verona Street 5 B3
Vialoux Avenue 6 D2
Vials Lane 6 D4
Victoria Avenue 6 E4
Victoria Barracks 5 B4
Victoria Park 3 B5
Victoria Place 6 D4
Victoria Street
  (Paddington) 6 D4
Victoria Street
  (Potts Point) 2 E5
continues 5 B2

W

Waimea Avenue 6 F4
Waine Street 4 F4
Walker Avenue 6 D2
Walker Lane 5 C3
Walker Street 5 C3
Wallis Street 6 E5
Walter Street 5 C4
Waratah Street 5 C1
Ward Avenue 5 C1
Waterloo Street 4 F5
Watson Road 1 A2
Watson Street 6 D4
Wattle Crescent 3 B3
Wattle Lane 3 C4
Wattle Place 3 C5
Wattle Street 3 B3
Ways Terrace 3 B1

Weedon Avenue 5 C3
Weldon Lane 6 F4
Wellington Street 6 F3
Wemyss Lane 4 F4
Wentworth Avenue 4 F4
Wentworth Park 3 B3
Wentworth Park
  Road 3 B3
Wentworth Street
  (Glebe) 3 B4
Wentworth Street
  (Paddington) 6 D4
West Avenue 5 B2
West Lane 5 B2
West Street 5 B3
Westend Lane 3 C5
Western Distributor 1 A4
continues 4 D1
Westin Hotel 1 B4
Westmoreland Lane 3 A5
Westmoreland Street 3 A5
Westpac Museum 1 B2
Wharf Theatre 1 A1
Wheat Road 1 A5
continues 4 D2
Whelan Lane 6 E4
White Lane 6 D3
Whitlam Square 4 F3
William Henry Street 3 C4
William Lane 5 A1
William Street
  (Darlinghurst) 4 F3
continues 5 A1
William Street
  (Double Bay) 6 F1
William Street
  (Paddington) 6 D3
Wilmot Street 4 E3
Wilson Street 2 D5
Windmill Street 1 A2
Windsor Lane 6 D3
Windsor Street 6 D3
Wisdom Lane 5 A1
Womerah Avenue 5 B2
Womerah Lane 5 C2
Woods Avenue 6 F4
Woods Lane 5 A1
Woolloomooloo
  Finger Wharf 2 D4
Wright Lane 4 E4
Writers' Walk 1 C2
Wylde Street 2 E4
Wynyard Lane 1 B4, 4 E1
Wynyard Park 1 A4
continues 4 E1
Wynyard Street 1 A4
continues 4 E1

Y

York Lane 1 A4
continues 4 E1
York Lane
  (Bondi Junction) 6 F5
York Place 6 F5
York Road 6 F5
York Street 1 A4
continues 4 E1
Young Street 1 B3
Young Street
  (Paddington) 5 C3
Yurong Lane 5 A1
Yurong Street 4 F3

General Index

Page numbers in **bold** refer to main entries.

A

Abbey's Bookshop 206, 207
ABC Shop 206, 207
ABN-AMRO Tower 43
Aboriginal and Pacific Art 206, 207
Aboriginal peoples
  art 113, 206, 207
  Australian Museum 90
  community 45
  culture 38–9
  history 21, 22–3
  land rights 33
  Museum of Sydney 87
  rock art 22–3, 156, 167
  segregation 28
Abseiling 55
Access Sydney 172
Accessories shops 204–5
Across the black soil plains
  (Lambert) 112
Admiralty House 134
Admission prices 219, 221
Adventure sports **55**
Air Canada 229
Air New Zealand 229
Air travel
  domestic 237
  international 228–9
Airport Connect 229
Airport Link 228, 229
Akira Isogawa 204, 205
Akuna Bay 156
Allan, Percy 100
Allianz Stadium 43
AllPhones Arena 214, 215
Ambulances 223
American Express 224
American Revivalism 42–3
Andrew (Boy) Charlton Pool 59
Andrew McDonald 205
Annandale Hotel 214, 215
ANZ Bank 224
ANZ Stadium 54, 140
Anzac Day 52, 53, 86
Anzac Memorial 13, 31, 40, 43,
  88
Anzacs 30
Apartments 172, 173, 174
Apia Sydney International 51
Arcades 198–9
Archibald Fountain 13, 80, **88**
Archibald Prize 30
Archibald, Wynne and Sulman
  Exhibitions 53

Architecture **40–43**
  Elizabeth Bay House 26–7
  Sydney Opera House 79
  Sydney's Best 40–41
area map 154–5
Argyle Cut 13, **66**
Argyle Stores 42, **70**
Argyle Terraces 29
Ariel (bookshop) 206, 207
Armani 204, 205
Armistice 30
ARQ 215
The Arrest of Bligh 25
Art Gallery of New South Wales
  11, 12, 19, 35, **110–13**
  Asian art 113
  Australian art 112
  contemporary art 113
  European art 112
  photography 112–13
  prints and drawings 113
  shop 206, 207
  Sydney's Best 37, 38
  Yiribana Gallery 38–9, **113**
ArtExpress 52
ATMs 224
Auburn Mosque 44
Audley 166
Australia Day 53
Australia Day Concert 51
Australia Ensemble 212, 213
Australia Square 43
Australian Accommodation
  Services 173
Australian Ballet 213
Australian Beach Pattern
  (Meere) 37
Australian Brandenburg
  Orchestra 212, 213
Australian Chamber Orchestra
  212, 213
Australian Customs & Border
  Protection 219, 221
Australian Geographic 206, 207
Australian Museum **90–91**
  shop 206, 207
  Sydney's Best 37, 38–9
Australian National Maritime
  Museum 12, 36, 38, 39, 40,
  43, **96–7**
Australian Regency 42
Australian rules football **54**
Australian Travel Specialists 235
Australian Women's Weekly 31
Australian Youth Choir 213
Australiana 206, 207
Autumn Racing Carnival 52
Autumn in Sydney 52

Avalon 57
Avis 231
AWA Radiolette 31

B

Baby changing facilities 219
Backpackers World Travel 173
The Balcony (2) (Whiteley) 112
Bali bombing memorial 33
Bally 204, 205
Balmain **133**
  fire station 145
  guided walk **144–5**
  market 133, **203**
  post office 145
  town hall 145
Balmain Court House 145
Balmain East Wharf 144
Balmoral 56, 57
Balmoral Sailing School 56
Bangarra Dance Theatre 213
Bank Hotel 215
Bank of New South Wales 26
Bank notes 225
Banking **224**
Banks, Sir Joseph 21, 86, 106,
  140
Barnet, James 74
  Australian Museum 90
  Lands Department Building
  86
Barney, Lieutenant Colonel
  George 129
Barrington 24
Bars see Pubs and Bars
Barton, Edmond 30
The Basement 214, 215
Bashir, Dame Marie 33
Basic hotels 176
The Basin 57
Basketball **54–5**
Bass, George 25, 86
Bathurst 1000 50
Bayswater Car Rental 237
Beaches 35, **56–7**
  Beaches and Browsing **11**
  map 57
  Sydney's Top 30 Beaches 57
HMS Beagle 27
Beare Park **122**, 123
Beckmann, Max, Old Woman in
  Ermine 112
Bed and Breakfast NSW 173
Bed and breakfasts 172, 173,
  175
Beer 185
Belinda 204, 205

Bell Shakespeare Company 210, 211
Belvoir Street Theatre 210, 211
Bennelong 24
Berkelouw Books 206, 207
Berrima 164
Berry 165
Between the Flags 204, 205
Beyond Sydney 153–67
  Hawkesbury **158–9**
  hotels 178, 179
  Hunter Valley **160–61**
  Pittwater and Ku-ring-gai Chase **156–7**
  restaurants 197
  Royal National Park **166–7**
  Southern Highlands Tour **164–5**
  travel information 237
Bicentenary 32
Bicentennial Park 46, 49
Bicycle New South Wales 231
Bicycles 55, 231
Biennale of Sydney 53
Big Top 134
Bilgola 57, 157
Bilgola Beach 57, 157
Bill Hicks Jewellery 206, 207
Birchgrove 145
Birchgrove Park 145
Birdland 207
Blacket, Edmund 89
  Garrison Church 71
  Justice and Police Museum 74
  St Philip's Church 75
  University of Sydney 132
Blackheath, restaurants 197
Blanchard, Jacques, *Mars and the Vestal Virgin* 110
Blaxland, Gregory 86, 162
Bligh, Governor William 24, 25
Bligh House 42
Blue Mountains 13, **162–3**
  history 22
  sports 55
Blue Mountains National Park **162–3**
  camping 173
  map 162–3
Blue Parrot Backpackers 172, 173
Blues 214, 215
Boats
  Australian National Maritime Museum 95
  HMS *Beagle* 27
  The Borrowdale 24

Boats (cont.)
  Dunbar 28, 138, 150
  HMS *Endeavour* 36
  Endeavour (replica) 97
  ferries 234–5
  ferry sightseeing cruises 235
  harbour and river cruises 235
  Lady Juliana 24
  Matilda Cruises 235
  National Maritime Museum 96–7
  HMAS *Onslow* 97
  Orcades 96
  Pittwater and Ku-ring-gai Chase 156–7
  Royal National Park 166–7
  sailing 56, 58
  HMS *Sirius* 74, 96
  HMAS *Vampire* 95, 97
  water taxis 235
  The Waverly 29
Boer War 28
Bondi Baths 146
Bondi Beach 11, 13, 97, **139**
  Aboriginal art 23
  beaches 56, 57
  Bondi Beach to Clovelly Walk **146–7**
  market **203**
  Sculpture by the Sea 50
  Surf School 56
Bondi North 146
Bondi Pavilion 146, 211, 213
Bondi Surf Bathers' Life Saving Club **139**, 146
Bondi Surf Co 56, 204, 205
Bonza Bike Tours 231
The Bookshop Darlinghurst 206, 207
Bookshops 206, 207
Boomalli Aboriginal Artists' Cooperative 206, 207
Boomerangs 23
Botanic Garden and The Domain **104–17**
  area map 105
  hotels 177
  restaurants 191–2
  Royal Botanic Garden **106–7**
Botany Bay 21, 24, 75, 140
Boutique hotels 176–7
Bowral 164
Boy in Township (Nolan) 112
Boyd, Arthur 112
Bradfield, Dr John 73, 100
Bradleys Head 47, 48
Bradman, Donald 31
Breakbeats 214, 215

Brett Whiteley Studio 38, **132**
The Bridge Hotel 214, 215
BridgeClimb 55, 73
Brighton-Le-Sands 56
British Airways 229
Broken Bay 156
Brokenwood 160
Bronte
  beaches 56, 57
  Bondi Beach to Clovelly Walk 146–7
Bronte Gully 147
Bronte House 147
Bronte Park 147
Brown Hayes, Sir Henry 138
Bubonic plague 61
Budget (car hire) 231
Budget accommodation 172, 173
The Bulletin 29
Bundanoon 164
Bundeena 167
Bungalow 8 (club) 214, 215
Bungaree 27
Bunny, Rupert
  A Summer Morning 112
  Summer Time 112
Bureaux de change 224
Burke (Nolan) 112
Busby, John 89
Busby's Bore Fountain **89**
Buses 236
  long distance 237
  safety 222
  sightseeing by 236
  tickets 230
  to/from airport 228
Bushfires 33
Bushwalking 55

C

Cabbage Tree Bay 147
Cabramatta 22, 44
Cadi Jam Ora 107
Cadigal people 69
Cadman, Elizabeth 67, 70
Cadman, John 67, 70
Cadman's Cottage 10, 25, 42, 67, **70**
  Sydney's Best 39, 40
Café of the Gate of Salvation 213
Cafés 180, 181
Cambodian community 44
Camilla 204, 205
Camp Cove 56, 57, 150, 151
Campbell, Robert 68, 141
Campbell Parade 146

Campbell's Storehouses 10, **68**
Camping 173
Cancer Council 223
Candy's Apartment 214, 215
Canyoning 55
Capital L 204, 205
Capitol Theatre **101**, 210, 211
Captain Cook Cruises 235
Captain Cook's Landing Place **140**
Car hire 231, 237
Carey, Peter 74
Cargo Bar 214, 215
Carols in the Domain 51
Cars
  car hire 230, 231, 237
  driving regulations 231
  driving in Sydney 230–31
  driving to Sydney 229
  parking 231
Cascade Street 127
Cassowary, southern 99
Castlereagh Street 201
Cat and Fiddle Hotel 214, 215
Cathedral of Ferns (Blue Mountains) 162
Cenotaph 83, **86**
Censorship, films 210
Centennial Park 19, **129**
  cycling 55
  Sydney's Best 47
Centennial Park Cycles 55
Central Railway Station 31, 221, 229, 233
Chain hotels 177
Challis Avenue 121
Chamber music **212**, 213
Chanel 204, 205
Charlton, Andrew "Boy" 31, 59
Chaucer at the Court of Edward III (Madox Brown) 112
Chauvel Cinema 210, 211
Chifley Plaza 199
Children
  clothes shops 204–5
  Family Fun **11**
  in hotels 172–3
  Kidspace (Australian Museum) 91
  theatre 210, 211
  travelling with 220
Chilli Coral 205
Chinatown 13, 35, **101**
  markets 200
Chinese community 45
Chinese Garden of Friendship 13, 94, **100–101**
Chinese Laundry (club) 214, 215
Chinese New Year 51

Chisholm, Caroline 27, 29
Choral music **213**
Churches
  Ebenezer Uniting Church 158
  Garrison Church 10, 66, **70–71**
  St Andrew's Cathedral **89**
  St Andrew's Church 145
  St James Church 10, 27, 40, 42, **117**
  St Mary's Cathedral 29, 42, **88**
  St Nicholas Church 45
  St Philip's Church **75**
Cinema Paris 210, 211
Circular Quay
  Ferry Terminal 234
  Overseas Passenger Terminal 67, 229
  see also The Rocks and Circular Quay
City Centre **80–91**
  apartments 174
  area map 81
  hotels 176–9
  restaurants 187–9
  shops and markets 201
  street-by-street map 82–3
City Circle Railway **89**
City Mutual Life Assurance Building 43
City Recital Hall 212, 213
City to Surf Race 53
Clifton Gardens 48, 57
Climate **50–53**, 218
Clontarf 144
Clothes shops **204–5**
Clovelly
  beaches 57, 147
  Bondi Beach to Clovelly Walk **146–7**
Coach services 229
Coal and Candle Creek 156
Cockatoo Island **108**
Cockle Bay 93
  street-by-street map **94–5**
Cockle Bay Wharf 95
Coffee 185
Coins 225
Collaroy beach 56
Collins Beach 48, 149
Colo River Drive 158
Colombian 215
Colonial architecture 42
Colonial history 39
Comedy Store 211
Comedy venues 211
Commonwealth Savings Bank 31, 43
Communications **226–7**
Concerts, free **212**

Conder, Charles, *Departure of the Orient – Circular Quay* 112
Conrad, Joseph 74
Conservatorium of Music 13, **108**
Consulates *see* Embassies and consulates
Contemporary architecture 43
Conversion table 221
Convict labour 24, 25
  abolition of transportation 27
Coo-ee Aboriginal Art Gallery 206, 207
Coogee 23
  beaches 56, 57
Coogee Surf Carnival 51
Cook, Captain James 21, 140
Cook and Phillip Park Centre 81
Cook's Obelisk 140
Cooper, Robert 128
The Corso (Manly) 135, 148
Cosmopolitan Shoes 204, 205
Cossington-Smith, Grace *The Curve of the Bridge* 112
Country Road 204, 205
Cowell, Brendan 210
Cox, Philip 43, 96
Credit cards 224
  in restaurants 181
Cricket **54**
  Donald Bradman 31
  test matches 51, 54
Crime 222
Cronulla 167
Crumpler 205
Cultures
  Aboriginal Peoples 22–3
  Sydney's Many Cultures 44–5
Culwalla Chambers 30
Curl Curl 57
Curracurrang 167
Currency **225**
The Currency Lass (Geoghegan) 27
The Curve of the Bridge (Cossington-Smith) 112
Customs House 64, **74**
Customs information 218
Cycling **55**, 231
  in Sydney 230, **231**

D

Dance **213**
Darling, Ralph 138
Darling Harbour and Surry Hills 35, **92–103**
  apartments 174
  area map 93
  B&Bs 175

Darling Harbour and Surry Hills (cont.)
   Darling Harbour street-by-street 94–5
   hotels 176, 177, 179
   restaurants 189–91
   shops and markets 200, 201
   visitors centre 221
Darling Street 144–5
Darlinghurst Court House 41, 42, **123**
Darwin, Charles 27, 74
David Jones 27, 198, 199, 204, 205
David Jones Spring Flower Show 50
Dawn (Louisa Lawson) 29
Dawson, Alexander 74
Dayes, Edward *A View of Sydney Cove* 24–5
de Groot, Francis 72
Debit cards 224
Dee Why 57
Deer Pool (Royal National Park) 167
Del Rio 121
Delfin House 43
Dellit, Bruce 40, 43
Dendy (cinemas) 210, 211
Dental Hospital 223
Dentists 223
Department of Immigration & Citizenship 218, 221
Departure of the Orient - Circular Quay (Conder) 112
Departure tax 218
Desmond, a New South Wales Chief (Earle) 20
DFO 199
Dialling codes 227
Dinosaur Designs 205, 206, 207
Diprotodon 22
Disabled travellers 220
   entertainment 209
   in hotels 171, 173
Discount agencies 171, 173, 209
Dive Centre Manly 56
Dixon Street 101
Dobell, William 112, 123
Dobell Memorial Sculpture (Flugelman) 86
Dodd, Henry Edward 141
The Domain 11, 12, 47, **109**, 212
   area map 105
   Symphony in The Domain 51
   see also Botanic Garden and The Domain

Doyles On the Beach (restaurant) 138, 150
Dragon Boat Races Festival 52
Dragstar 204, 205
Dr Chau Chak Wing Building 132
Drinking fountains 219
Driving regulations 230–31
Drysdale, Russell 112
   Sofala 110
Dugong Hunt (Wurrabadalumba) 38
Dunbar 28, 138, 150
Durack, Fanny 147
Duxford Street 126
Dwyer, Michael 147
Dymocks 206, 207

E
Earle, Augustus
   Desmond, a New South Wales Chief 20
   View from the Summit 26
Early Colony 24–5
EarthCheck 221
East Balmain 144
East Sail 56
Eastside Arts 212, 213
Ebenezer Uniting Church 158
Edge of the Trees (Laurence and Foley) 87
Edward, Prince of Wales 30
El Alamein Fountain **122**
Electricity 221
Elizabeth Bay 19, 121
Elizabeth Bay House 26–7, 42, **122**
   street-by-street map 121
   Sydney's Best 37, 39, 41
Elizabeth Farm 25, 39, **140–41**
Elizabeth II, Queen 32, 78
Embassies and consulates 221
Emden gun **89**
Emergency services 223
Emirates 229
HMS *Endeavour* 36, 97, 140
Enmore Theatre 214, 215
Ensemble Theatre 210, 211
Entertainment **208–15**
   buying tickets 208
   children's theatre 210
   comedy 211
   disabled visitors 209
   discount tickets 209
   free 209, 212
   gay and lesbian pubs and clubs 215
   information 208
   music venues and nightclubs 214–15

Entertainment (cont.)
   opera, orchestras and dance 212–13
   theatre and film 210–11
Entertainment Quarter **128**
Entertainment Quarter Village Markets **203**
Environmental hazards 223
Eora people 22–3, 87, 96
Eternity, Mr (Arthur Stace) 33
Etiquette 219
Evans, Len 160
Eveleigh Market **203**
Event Cinemas 210, 211
Ewenton 144
Experiment Farm Cottage 25, 39, **141**

F
Fairfax and Roberts 206, 207
Fairy Bower 57, 148
Family Jewels 205
Farage Women 204, 205
Farm Cove 59
Farmers' Markets 221
Fashion 204, 205
Federation 30
Federation architecture 30, **43**
   Sydney's Best 42
Female Factory 27
Ferries **234–5**
   Bundeena 167
   Circular Quay Ferry Terminal 234
   harbour 35
   Hawkesbury River 155
   Manly Fast Ferry 234
   Portland 159
   RiverCat 234
   Sackville 158
   sightseeing by ferry 235
   Sydney Ferries Information 234, 235
   tickets 234
   Webbs Creek 159
   Wisemans 159
Ferrython 51
Festival of Sydney 51
Festival of the Winds 50
Festivals and events **50–53**
Fiesta (festival) 50
Film **210**, 211
   festivals 51, 53, 211
Firefly Express 237
First Fleet 24, 75, 141, 159
First Fleet Ship (Holman) 24
Fish Fine Music 206, 207
Fishermans Beach 57
Fitzroy Falls 164
Fitzroy Hotel 214, 215

Five Ways 126, **128**
Flame Opals 206, 207
Flats 172, 173
Flickerfest 51, 211
Flinders, Matthew 25, 26, 27, 86
  statue 114
Flugelman, Bert, Dobell
  Memorial Sculpture 86
Flying Fruit Fly Circus 210, 211
Foley, Fiona, *Edge of the Trees* 87
Folk music 214, 215
Food and drink
  festivals 53
  Flavours of Sydney **182–3**
  licensing laws 181
  what to drink **184–5**
  see also Restaurants
Footbridge Theatre 210, 211
Foreign currency exchange
  224
Forest Path (Royal National
  Park) 166
Fort Denison **109**
The Founding of Australia
  (Talmage) 75
Fourplay 212, 213
Fowkes, Francis, *Sketch and
  Description of the Settlement
  of Sydney Cove* 21
Fox Studios 128, 203
Franklin, Miles 74
  My Brilliant Career 30
Freshwater 57
Funfairs, Luna Park 31, 130, **134**
Funnel-web spider 48, 91
Further Afield **130–41**
  apartments 174
  B&Bs 175
  hotels 176–9
  restaurants 195–7
  shopping 199

G

Gaelic Club 214, 215
The Galeries 198, 199
Gallipoli 30
The Gap 138, 139, 150, 151
Garden Island 58
Garden Palace 28–9, 102
Garie Beach 155, 166
Garigal National Park 46, 48
Garrison Church 10, 66, **70–71**
Gay and Lesbian Tourism
  Australia 172, 173
Gay and Lesbian Travellers
  220–21
Gay and lesbians
  accommodation 172, 173
  pubs and clubs 215
G'day Backpackers 172, 173

General Pants 204, 205
General Post Office (GPO) 42,
  86, 227
The Gentle Dentist 223
Geoghegan, Edward, *The
  Currency Lass* 27
George Street **68**
Georgian Era 26–7
Gibbs, May 39, 134
  Snugglepot and Cuddlepie 134
Gillard, Julia 33
Ginn, Henry 71
Giorgio Armani 204, 205
Girls With Gems 204, 205
Giulian's 206, 207
Glasser, Neil 84
Glebe **133**
  market 133, **203**
Gleebooks 206, 207
Glenbrook Crossing 22
Global Gossip 226
Glover, John, *Natives on the
  Ouse River, Van Diemen's Land*
  111, 112
Gold rush 28
  "Welcome Stranger" gold
  nugget cast **91**
*The Golden Fleece (Shearing at
  Newstead)* (Roberts) 111, 112
Golden Oldies **213**
Golf **54**
The Good Old Days 213
Goossens, Sir Eugene 78
Gordons Bay 56, 57
Government House 13, 60, **108**
Governor Phillip Tower 40, 43, 87
Govett's Leap (Blue Mountains)
  162
Govinda's cinema and
  restaurant 211
Great Depression 30
Great Synagogue 42, **88**
Greek community 45
Green, Alexander "The
  Strangler" 123
Green bans 33, 122
Green travel 230, 231
Greenway, Francis **116**
  Conservatorium of Music 108
  Hyde Park Barracks 116
  Macquarie Lighthouse 26, 139
  Macquarie Place obelisk 74
  St James' Church 40, 117
Greer, Germaine 74
Greycliffe House 138
Greyhound *see* McCafferty's
  Greyhound
Greyhound Australia 237
Griffin Theatre 210, 211
Grose River/Valley 162, 163

Grotto Point 47
GST 198
Guided tours and excursions
  230, 231
  ferry sightseeing cruises
  235
  harbour and river cruises
  235
Gumbooya Reserve 23
Gurindji people 33

H

Hacking River 166
Halls of residence 172, 173
Hambledon Cottage 39, **141**
Hampton Villa 144
Harbour cruises 60, 235
Harbourside Complex 94
Harbourside Shopping Centre
  199
Hardy Brothers 206, 207
Hargrave, Lawrence 147
Harris, John 141
Harry's Café de Wheels 59
Hawkesbury River 156, **158–9**
  ferry 155
Haymarket 101
Health **222–3**
Helen Kaminski 205, 2045
Helplines 223
Herb Garden (Royal Botanic
  Garden) 106
Hero of Waterloo 66, **71**
Hertz 231
Hip hop 214, 215
Historic hotels 178
History 20–33
  Early Colony 24–5
  Georgian Era 26–7
  Postwar Sydney 32–3
  Sydney Between the Wars
  30–31
  Sydney's Original Inhabitants
  22–3
  timeline 22–33
  Victorian Sydney 28–9
Hodgkinson, Frank 123
Holey dollar 26
Holman, Francis, *First Fleet Ship* 24
Homestay 172, 173
Homestay Network 172, 173
Hope Estate 154, 161
Hordern Pavilion 214, 215
Hornby Lighthouse 151
Horse riding **55**
Hospitals **222–3**
Hostels 172, 173, 178
Hotel Bondi 146
Hotels **170–79**
  aparthotels 172

Hotels (cont.)
basic 176
boutique 176–7
chain 177
children 171–2
disabled travellers 171
discount rates 171
hidden extras 171
historic 178
how to book 170
luxury 179
special offers 171
where to look 170
The Hour Glass 206, 207
House music 214, 215
Hovell, William 26, 86
Hoyts (cinemas) 210, 211
Hume, Hamilton 26, 86
Humphries, Barry 74
Hunter Valley **160–61**
Hutchence, Michael 33
Hyde Park 13, 46, **88–9**
Hyde Park Barracks 27, 42
Hyde Park Barracks Museum
10, 12, **116–17**
Sydney's Best 37, 39, 41
Hype DC 204, 205

I
Ideas Incorporated 173, 209
IMAX Darling Harbour 94, **100**,
210
Immigration 218
Imperial Hotel 215
Implement blue (Preston) 112
Inline skating **55**
Insurance
car hire 237
travel and medical 223
International College of
Tourism and Hotel
Management 149
International Student Identity
Card 220
International Travel
Vaccinations Centre 223
Internet access 226
Interwar architecture 43
Irish community 45
Islamic community 44
Islay, statue of 84
Italian community 45
Itineraries **10–13**
2 Days in Sydney **12**
3 Days in Sydney **12**
5 Days in Sydney **13**
Around the Harbour **10**
Art and Opera **10–11**
Beaches and Browsing **11**
Family Fun **11**

J
Jack London 204, 205
Jacob's Ladder 150, 151
James, Clive 74
Jan Logan 205, 206, 207
Japan Airlines 229
Jazz 214, 215
Jenolan Caravan Park 173
Jenolan Caves **162**
Jetstar 228, 229
Jewellery 206, 207
Jewish community 45
Great Synagogue 88
Sydney Jewish Museum 39,
123
Jibbon Head 167
Johnson, Richard 133
Juniper Hall **128**
Just Jeans 204, 205
Justice and Police Museum 39,
74

K
Kaliver 204, 205
Kamay Botany Bay National
Park 140
Kame Kngwarreye, Emily 113
Kangaroo Valley 164
Kangaroos 25
Kate Owen Gallery & Studio
206, 207
Katoomba 162
hotels 178, 179
restaurants 197
Keba 145
Kelman Vineyard 161
Ken Done Gallery 206, 207
Kiama 154, 165
King Street Wharf **100**
Kings Cross and Darlinghurst
118–23
apartments 174
area map 119
B&Bs 175
hostels 178
hotels 176, 177
Potts Point street-by-street
120–21
shops and markets 205
King's Cross Travellers' Clinic
223
Kingsford Smith, Charles 31
Kirchner, Ernst, *Three Bathers* 112
Kirribilli House 134
Kirribilli Point **134**
Koalas 99, 137
KST Sydney Airporter 228, 229
Ku-ring-gai Chase National
Park **156–7**
Aboriginal carvings 23

Ku-ring-gai Chase National
Park (cont.)
camping 173
Kurnell Point 56

L
Lady Bay Beach 150, 151
Lady Carrington Drive (Royal
National Park) 166
Lady Juliana 24
Lake, Max 160
Lake Mungo 22
Lakemba 44
Lake's Folly 161
Lambert, George *Across the
black soil plains* 112
Land Titles Office 117
Lands Department Building 42,
86
Lane Cove National Park 46, 48–9
Laurence, Janet, *Edge of the
Trees* 87
Lawson, Henry 28, 88, 147
Lawson, Louisa, *Dawn* 29
Lawson, William 86, 162
Lebanese community 44
Legs on the Wall 213
Leichhardt, Ludwig 86
Lesley Mackay's bookshop 207
Let's Go Surfing 56
Leura 162
Leura Garden Festival 50
Lewin, John, *Waratah* 25
Lewis, Mortimer 90, 123
Life savers 56, **139**
Lindemans 160
Lindsay, Norman 163
Lingiari, Vincent 33
Little Manly Cove 149
Little Marley 167
Locomotive No. 1 103
London Hotel 145
London Tavern 126
Long Reef 56, 57
Long-distance bus services 237
The Looking Glass 206, 207
Lord Nelson Brewery Hotel 18
Lost property 222, 223, 229
Louis Vuitton 204, 205
Love and Hatred 206, 207
Lower Fort Street 42
Lucas, Penelope 141
Luna Park 31, 130, **134**
Luxury hotels 179
Lyrebirds 27

M
Macarthur, John and Elizabeth
140
McCubbin, Frederick 112

McElhone Stairs 120
Mackellar, Dorothea 147
MacKennal, Bertram 86, 88
Mackenzies Point 146, 147
Macleay, Alexander 26, 37, 121, 122
Macquarie, Elizabeth 26, 108
Macquarie, Governor Lachlan 26, 27, 74, 108
Macquarie Place **74**
Macquarie Street 10, **114–17**
Macquarie Chair, 26
Macquarie Lighthouse 26, 27, **139**, 150
McRae, George 43, 84
Madox Brown, Ford, *Chaucer at the Court of Edward III* 112
Magazines 227
Magistic Cruises 219
Maitland House 144
Malls 198–9
Manly 10, 12, **135**
  food and wine festival 53
  guided walk **148–9**
  viewing platforms 148
Manly Beach 56, 57, 148
Manly Bike Tours 231
Manly Fast Ferry 234
Manly International Jazz Festival 50
Manly Sea Life Sanctuary 12, **135**
Manly Surf School 56
Manly Wharf 148
Maojo Record Bar 206, 207
Map World 230
Maps
  18th-century Sydney 21
  Australia 14–15
  beaches 57
  Blue Mountains 162–3
  Bondi Beach to Clovelly walk 146–7
  Botanic Garden and The Domain 105
  Central Sydney 18–19
  Central Sydney and suburbs 16–17
  City Centre area map 81
  City Centre street-by-street 82–3
  Darling Harbour street-by-street 94–5
  Darling Harbour and Surry Hills 93
  Early Colony 24
  Exploring Beyond Sydney 154–5
  ferry routes 235
  Further Afield 131

Maps (cont.)
  Georgian Era 26
  Greater Sydney and Environs 15
  guided walks 143
  Hawkesbury River Tour 158–9
  Hunter Valley 160–61
  Kings Cross and Darlinghurst 119
  Paddington area map 125
  Paddington street-by-street 126–7
  Pittwater and Ku-ring-gai Chase 156–7
  Postwar Sydney 32
  Potts Point street-by-street 120–21
  The Rocks and Circular Quay 65
  The Rocks street-by-street 66–7
  Royal Botanic Garden 106–7
  Royal National Park 166–7
  Southeast Asia and Pacific Rim 14
  Southern Highlands Tour 164–5
  Street Finder 238–49
  Sydney Between the Wars 30
  Sydney Harbour 58–61
  Sydney Trains route map 232
  Sydney's Original Inhabitants 22–3
  Taronga Zoo 136–7
  Victorian Sydney 28
  Walk Around Balmain 144–5
  Walk Around Manly 148–9
  Walk in Watsons Bay and Vaucluse 150–51
Marble Bar 82, **84**
Mardi Gras Festival 32–3, 51
Mardi Gras Film Festival 211
Marian Street Theatre for Young People 210, 211
Market City 199
Markets **203**
  Balmain 133, 145, **203**
  Bondi Beach **203**
  Entertainment Quarter 128, **203**
  Eveleigh Market **203**
  Glebe 133, **203**
  Paddington Markets 11, **128**, 201, **203**
  Paddy's Markets **101**, **203**
  The Rocks Market 67, 201, **203**
  Sydney Fish Market **133**, 200, **202**, 203

Markets (cont.)
  The Sydney Morning Herald Growers' Market **203**
  Sydney's Best **200–201**
Maroubra 23, 56, 57
The Marquee 214, 215
Mars and the Vestal Virgin (Blanchard) 110
Marsden, Samuel 117, 141
Martin Place 29, 83, **86**
Matilda Cruises 235
Media **227**
Medical treatment **222–3**
Medina 173
Medlow Bath, hotels 178
Meere, Charles, *Australian Beach Pattern* 37
Melbourne Cup Day 50
Merlin Entertainment Group 219, 221
The Merton 214, 215
Metro Theatre 214, 215
Middle Harbour 48
Middle Head and Obelisk Bay 47
Midnight Shift 214, 215
The Mint 10, 12, 27, 39, **116**
Mitchell, Dr James 71
Mitchell, Sir Thomas 26, 86
Mitchell Library 114
MLC Centre 43, 199
Mobile phones 226
Modern architecture 43
Molvig, Jan 123
Money **224–5**
Monorail 232
Moonlight, Captain 29
Moore, Henry *Reclining Figure: Angles* 10, 112
Moore Park 47, 54
Moreton Bay fig (Ficus macrophylla) **49**
Mort Bay Reserve 144
Moshtix 214, 215
Mount Tomah Botanic Gardens 163
Mount Wilson 163
mountain biking 55
Mrs Macquaries Chair 11, 28, 58, **108**
Mundey, Jack 69
Murrays Coaches 237
Museums and galleries (general)
  admission prices 219, 221
  Sydney's Best **36–9**
Museums and galleries (individual)
  Art Gallery of New South Wales 11, 12, 37, 38, **110–13**

Museums and galleries (cont.)
  Australian Museum 37, 38–9, **90–91**
  Australian National Maritime Museum 12, 36, 38, 39, 40, 95, **96–7**
  Brett Whiteley Studio 38, **132**
  Cadman's Cottage 25, 39, **70**
  Elizabeth Bay House 26–7, 37, 39, 121, **122**
  Elizabeth Farm 25, 39, **140–41**
  Experiment Farm Cottage 25, 39, **141**
  Hambledon Cottage 39, **141**
  Hyde Park Barracks Museum 37, 39, **116–17**
  Justice and Police Museum 39, **74**
  Macleay Museum (University of Sydney) 132
  Museum of Contemporary Art 12, 13, 36, 38, 66, **75**
  Museum of Sydney 36, 39, **87**
  Nicholson Museum (University of Sydney) 132
  Norman Lindsay Gallery & Museum (Blue Mountains) 163
  Nutcote 39, **134–5**
  Old Government House 27, 39, **141**
  Powerhouse Museum 29, 31, 36, 38, 39, **102–3**
  Pylon Lookout 12, **70**
  The Rocks Discovery Museum 12, 67, **68–9**
  Sailors' Home 39, **69**
  S.H. Ervin Gallery 39, 75
  Sherman Gallery 127
  Susannah Place Museum 29, 39, **69**
  Sydney Jewish Museum 37, 39, **123**
  Vaucluse House 39, **138**
  Victoria Barracks **129**
  War Memorial Art Gallery (University of Sydney) 132
Music 212–15
  chamber 212
  choral 213
  festivals and events 50–53
  free concerts 212
  house, breakbeats & techno 214, 215
  jazz, folk and blues 214, 215
  live music venues 214, 215
  opera, orchestras and dance 212–13

Music (cont.)
  rock, pop and hip hop 214, 215
  shops 206, 207
Musica Viva 212, 213
My Brilliant Career (Franklin) 30
Myall Creek massacre 27
Myer 198, 199, 204, 205

N

NAIDROC (National Aboriginal and Torres Strait Islander) Week 53
Napoleon Perdis Cosmetics 206, 207
Narrabeen 56, 57
National Herbarium of New South Wales 106, 107
National Mutual Building 42
National parks
  Blue Mountains National Park **162–3**
  camping 173
  Garigal National Park 46, 48
  Kamay Botany Bay National Park 140
  Ku-ring-gai Chase National Park 23, 48, 55, **156–7**, 173
  Lane Cove National Park 46, 48–9
  Royal National Park 11, 12, 23, 48, **166–7**, 173
  Sydney Harbour National Park 135, 138, 149, 150
National Parks and Wildlife Service 235
National Trust Centre **75**
National Trust Heritage Festival 52
Natives on the Ouse River, Van Diemen's Land (Glover) 111, 112
Naval Memorial Chapel 150
Ned Kelly (Nolan) 33
Nepean River 22
New Brighton Hotel 148
New South Wales Corps (Rum Corps) 24, 25
New Year's Eve 51, 85
Newport Beach 57
Newspapers 227
Nielsen, Juanita 122
Nielsen Park 47, **138**
Nightclubs 214, 215
No. 10 Darling Street 144
Nolan, Sydney
  Boy in Township 112
  Burke 112
  Ned Kelly 33
Noonuccal, Oodgeroo 74

Norman Lindsay Gallery & Museum (Blue Mountains) 163
North Arm Walk 46, 49
North Bondi Classic Ocean Swim 51
North Head 12, 47, 48, **135**, 150
North Head Reserve 149
Nowra, Louis 210
NSW TrainLink 171, 173
NSW Trains 222, 223, 229
Nude in a Rocking Chair (Picasso) 112
Nutcote 39, **134–5**

O

Obelisk **89**
Obelisk Bay 57
O'Keefe, Johnny 32
Old Gaol, Darlinghurst **123**
Old General Cemetery 159
Old Government House (Parramatta) 27, 39, **141**
Old Great North Road 159
Old Manly Boatshed 211
Old Woman in Ermine (Beckmann) 112
Olsen, John, *Salute to Five Bells* 78
Olympic Games 33, 140
Onkaparinga 144
HMAS *Onslow* 97
Opal cards 230
Opal Fields 206, 207
Opals 206, 207
Opening hours
  banks 224
  restaurants 180
  shops 198
Opera **212**, 213
Opera Australia 212, 213
Opera in the Domain 51
Optus 226
Orcades 96
Orchestral music **212**, 213
Orson & Blake 206, 207
Oswald, Debra 210
Out Travel 221
Overseas Passenger Terminal 67, 229
Oxford Hotel 215
Oxford Street 35, 119, 125, 129
Oz Bed & Breakfast 173
Oz magazine 33

P

Pacific International Hotels 173
Paddington 13, 35, 41, **124–9**
  area map 125
  B&Bs 175

Paddington (cont.)
  hotels 176, 178
  restaurants 194–5
  shops and markets 201
  street-by-street map 126–7
Paddington Markets 11, **128**, 201, **203**
Paddington Street **128**, 42, 127
Paddington Town Hall **129**
Paddington Village **129**
Paddy's Markets **101**, **203**
Padmapani 111
Palace Cinemas 210, 211
Palm Beach 56, 57, 157
Palm Beach Wharf 157
Palm Grove (Royal Botanic Garden) 106
Parade Theatre 210, 211
Park, Ruth
  The Harp in the South 132
  Poor Man's Orange 132
Parkes, Henry 28
Parkhill Sandstone Arch 149
Parking 231
Parks and reserves (general) **48–9**
  city parks 49
  coastal hinterland 48
  open eucalypt forest 48–9
  rainforest and moist forest 48
  wetlands 49
Parks and reserves (individual)
  Beare Park **122**
  Bicentennial Park 46, 49
  Birchgrove Park 145
  Blue Mountains National Park 55, **162–3**, 173
  Bradleys Head 47, 48
  Bronte Park 147
  Captain Cook's Landing Place **140**
  Centennial Park 47, 49, 55, **129**
  Chinese Garden of Friendship 13, 94, **100–101**
  Clifton Gardens 48, 57
  The Domain 47, 49, **109**
  Fitzroy Falls 164
  Garigal National Park 46, 48
  Grotto Point 47
  Gumbooya Reserve 23
  Hyde Park 13, 46, 49, **88–9**
  Kamay Botany Bay National Park 140
  Ku-ring-gai Chase National Park 23, 48, 55, **156–7**, 173
  Lane Cove National Park 46, 48–9
  Macquarie Place **74**
  Middle Harbour 48

Parks and reserves (cont.)
  Middle Head 47
  Moore Park 47, 54
  Mort Bay Reserve 144
  Mount Tomah Botanic Gardens 163
  Nielsen Park 47, **138**, 151
  North Arm 46, 49
  North Head 47, 48, **135**, 149, 150
  Obelisk Bay 47, 57
  Royal Botanic Garden 35, 48, 49, 59, **106–7**
  Royal National Park 11, 12, 23, 48, **166–7**, 173
  Seven Mile Beach 165
  South Head 47, 48, 150–51
  Sydney Harbour National Park 135, 138, 149, 150
  Sydney's Best **46–7**
  Taronga Zoo **136–7**
  Yurulbin Point Reserve 145
Parliament House 10, 27, **114–15**
Parramatta 22, 27, 39, **140–41**
Parsley Bay 57, 151
Paspaley Pearls 206, 207
Passports 218, 221
Pemulwy 25
Pepper's Convent 161
Percy Marks 206, 207
Performance Space 213
Personal security **222–3**
Pharmacies 222–3
Phillip, Captain Arthur 21, 66, 75, 133
Phonecards 226
Picasso, Pablo, *Nude in a Rocking Chair* 112
Pilot boats 151
Pinchgut (Fort Denison) 109
Pink House 172, 173
Pitt Street Mall 13, 204, 205
Pittwater 157
Pittwater and Ku-ring-gai Chase **156–7**
  Aboriginal rock art 156
  camping 173
  history 23
  horse riding 55
Platypuses 98
Police 222, 223
Pollution, beaches 56
Pop music 214, 215
Il Porcellino (Sydney Hospital) 115
Port Jackson 58
Portland Reach 158
The Possum Dreaming (Tjakamarra) 76

Postal services 226–7
Poste restante 227
Poster for the Vienna Secession (Schiele) 113
Postwar Sydney 32–3
Potts Point, street-by-street map 120–21
Power, John 75
Powerhouse Museum 29, 31, **102–3**
  Sydney's Best 36, 38, 39
Poynter, Edward, *The Visit of the Queen of Sheba to King Solomon* 112
Prada 204, 205
Premier Cabs 237
Preston, Margaret
  Implement blue 112
  Western Australian Gum Blossom 112
Pride Centre 221
Primavera 50
Prince Alfred Hospital 28
Private homes, accommodation in 172, 173
Pro Dive Coogee 56
Public holidays 53
Public telephones 226
Pubs and bars
  blues 214, 215
  cabaret venues 215
  gay and lesbian venues 215
  jazz 214
  rock music 214, 215
Pukumani Grave Posts Melville Island 111, 113
Pylon Lookout 12, **70**
Pyrmont Bridge 12, 95, **100**

Q

Q Bar 214, 215
Qantas Airways 32, 228, 229
Quarantine regulations 218
Quarantine Station 135
Queen Victoria Building (QVB) 12, 18, 29, 42, **84**
  arcades and malls 198, 199
  street-by-street map 82
  Sydney's Best 40, 200
Queen Victoria Statue 82, 83
Queen's Birthday Weekend 53
Quintus Servinton 26

R

Radio 227
Rail travel
  arriving by train 229
  country and inter-urban 237
  Powerhouse Museum 103
  safety 222

Rail travel (cont.)
 Sydney Trains and Light Rail
  232–3
 tickets 230
 to/from airport 228
 Zig Zag Railway 162
Rainfall 52
Reclining Figure: Angles (Moore)
 10, 112
Record shops 206, 207
The Record Store 206, 207
Red Eye Records 206, 207
Responsible tourism 221
Restaurants **180–97**
 Beyond Sydney 197
 Botanic Garden and The
  Domain 191–2
 City Centre 187–9
 credit cards 181
 Darling Harbour and Surry
  Hills 189–91
 dress codes 181
 eating with children 181
 Flavours of Sydney **182–3**
 Further Afield 195–7
 how much to pay 180
 Kings Cross and Darlinghurst
  192–4
 licensing laws 181
 opening times 180
 Paddington 194–5
 reservations 180
 smoking in 181
 tax and tipping 181
 The Rocks and Circular Quay
  186–7
 what to drink in Sydney
  184–5
 where to eat 180
The Revenge 24
REX – Regional Express Airlines
 228, 229
Riley, Edward and Mary 69
Rip Curl 204, 205
RiverCat ferry 234
R M Williams 206, 207
Road travel
 arriving in Sydney by car 229
 beyond Sydney 237
 car hire 231, 237
 driving in Sydney 230–31
Robby Ingham Stores 204, 205
Roberts, Tom 29
 The Golden Fleece (*Shearing at
  Newstead*) 111, 112
Rock climbing 55
Rock music 214, 215
The Rocks and Circular Quay
 35, 61, **64–79**
 apartments 174

The Rocks and Circular Quay
 (cont.)
 area map 65
 B&Bs 175
 history 25
 hostels 178
 hotels 176–9
 market **203**
 restaurants 186–7
 The Rocks Aroma Festival 53
 The Rocks street-by-street
  map 66–7
 shops and markets 201
 tourist information 221
The Rocks Discovery Museum
 12, 67, **68–9**
Rockwall 121
Rollerblading **55**
Rowe, Thomas 88
Roxbury Hotel 211
Royal Botanic Garden 11, 12,
 35, 48, 49, 59, **106–7**
Royal Clock 84
Royal Hotel 128
Royal National Park 11, 12, 48,
 155, **166–7**
 Aboriginal carving 23
 camping 173
Rugby league **54**
 grand final 50
Rugby union **54**
 grand final 50
Rum Corps (New South Wales
 Corps) 24, 25
Rum Hospital 115
Rum Rebellion 25
Ruse, James 141

S

Safety **222–3**
 beaches 56
Sailing **56**, 58
Sailors' Home 39, **69**
St Andrew's Cathedral **89**
St Andrew's Church 145
St James' Church 10, 27, 42,
 117
 concerts 212–13
 Sydney's Best 40
St John's Cemetery **141**
St Mary's Cathedral 29, 42, **88**
St Nicholas Church 45
St Patrick's Day Parade 52
St Patrick's Seminary 42, 148
St Philip's Church **75**
St Vincent's Hospital 223
Salute to Five Bells (Olsen) 78
Sandringham Garden **88**
Sani, Tomaso 86
Sass & Bide 204, 205

Scanlan & Theodore 204, 205
Schiele, Egon, *Poster for the
 Vienna Secession* 113
Scrimshaw 24
Scuba diving **56**
Sculpture, Art Gallery of New
 South Wales 112
Sculpture By The Sea 50
Sea Life Sydney Aquarium 12,
 95, **98**
Sea travel 229
Seidler, Harry 43
Self-catering accommodation
 172, 173
Self-catering agencies 173
Seniors Week 52
Settlers Arms Inn (St Albans)
 159
Seven Mile Beach 165
Seven Shillings Beach 57
Sewell, Stephen 210
Seymour Theatre Centre 210,
 211, 214, 215
S H Ervin Gallery 38, 75
Shakespeare Australia 210,
 211
Shark Bay 151
 beaches 56, 57
 Watsons Bay and Vaucluse
  Walk 151
Sharp, Martin 134
Sharp, Ronald 78
Sharp, William 122
Shelly Beach 56, 57, 148
Sherman Gallery 127
Ships *see* Boats
Shop & Save Tours 199
Shops and markets **198–207**
 arcades and malls 198–9
 Beaches and Browsing **11**
 clothes and accessories
  204–5
 department stores 199
 further afield 199
 how to pay 198
 markets **202–3**
 sales 198
 shopping hours 198
 specialist shops and
  souvenirs 206–7
 Sydney's Best: Shopping
  Streets and Markets 200–201
 tax-free sales 198
Sicard, François 88
Sightseeing
 by bus 235
 by ferry 235
Signal Station 150
Singapore Airlines 229
HMS *Sirius* 74, 96

Sketch and Description of the Settlement of Sydney Cove (Fowkes) 21
Skin protection 223
Slide 214, 215
Smith, Henry Gilbert 148
Smith, Richard 29
Smoking 219
  in restaurants 181
Snails Bay 145
Snowy Mountains 26
Snugglepot and Cuddlepie (Gibbs) 134
Sodersten, Emil 43
Sofala (Drysdale) 110
Solander, Daniel 140
South Head 47, 48, 150–51
Southern Highlands **164–5**
Souvenir shops 206, 207
Specialist shops 206, 207
Spectrum 214, 215
Spencer, John 86
Spinal Cord Injuries Australia 171, 173
Spirit of Australia 38
Splendour in the Grass 53
Sporting Sydney **54–7**
Sportsgirl 204, 205
Spring Racing Carnival 50
Spring in Sydney 50
STA Travel 220, 221
Stace, Arthur **33**
The Star 210, 211
State Library of NSW 10, 12, 31, **114**
  Bookshop 206, 207
State Theatre 13, **84**, 210, 211, 214, 215
  street-by-street map 82
Statues
  Matthew Flinders 114
  Prince Albert 117
  Queen Victoria Statue 82, 84
  Thomas Mort 74
Stephenson, Robert 103
Stonewall 215
Strand Arcade 13, 42, **86**
  arcades and malls 198, 199
  street-by-street map 83
The "Strasburg" Clock 29
Streeton, Arthur 29, 112
Student Travel Association *see* STA Travel
Suez Canal (The Rocks) 66
A Summer Morning (Bunny) 112
Summer in Sydney 51
Summer Time (Bunny) 112
Sun protection 223
Sunshine 51
Surf Dive 'n' Ski 204, 205

Surf Life Saving NSW 56
Surfection 204, 205
Surfing **56**
  history 30
  surf shops 204, 205
Surry Hills **101**
  see also Darling Harbour and Surry Hills
Susannah Place Museum 39, 42, **69**
Suzie Q Coffee + Records 206, 207
Swimming **56**
  safety 223
Swimming pools 57
  Bondi Baths 146
Sydney airport 228
  airport information 229
Sydney Between the Wars 30–31
Sydney and Bondi Explorer 230, 231
Sydney Buses 23, 222, 223, **236**
Sydney City Council One-Stop-Shop 220, 221
Sydney Coach Terminal 229, 237
Sydney Comedy Festival 211
Sydney Cove 60
Sydney Cricket Ground 54
Sydney Dance Company 213
Sydney Electric Bikes 230, 231
Sydney Fernery 106
Sydney Ferries 222, 223, **234**
Sydney Ferries Infoline 234, 235
Sydney Ferries Information Office 234, 235
Sydney Festival 209, 210
Sydney Film Festival 53, 211
Sydney Fish Market **133**, **202**, 203
  Sydney's Best 200
Sydney Gazette 25
Sydney Half Marathon 52
Sydney Harbour
  Around the Harbour **10**
  cruises 60, 235
  Garden Island to Farm Cove 58–9
  Sydney Cove to Walsh Bay 60–61
Sydney Harbour Bridge 10, 12, 34, **72–3**
  BridgeClimb 55, 73
  City shoreline 60
  history 30–31
Sydney Harbour National Park 135, 138, 149, 150
Sydney Harbour Tunnel 33
Sydney Hospital 115, 223

Sydney International Boat Show 53
Sydney Jewish Museum 37, 39, **123**
Sydney Light Rail 232–3
Sydney Living Museums Pass 219, 221
Sydney Mint *see* The Mint
The Sydney Morning Herald Growers' Market **203**
Sydney Observatory 66, **71**
Sydney Olympic Park **140**, 214, 215
Sydney Opera House 2–3, 11, 12, 35, **76–9**
  architecture 43
  City shoreline 60
  Concert Hall 77, **78**, 212
  Dame Joan Sutherland Theatre 76, **78**
  design **79**
  disabled visitors 209
  Drama Theatre 78, 210
  history 32
  information and booking 209
  Northern Foyers 76
  opera, orchestras and dance 212, 213
  The Playhouse 76, **78**
  restaurant 77
  roofs 77
  Sydney's Best Architecture 41
Sydney Philharmonia Choirs 213
Sydney Regatta 52
Sydney Royal Easter Show 52
Sydney Swans 54
Sydney Symphony Orchestra 209, 212, 213
Sydney Theatre 210, 211
Sydney Theatre Company 71, 210, 211
Sydney to the Gong Bicycle Ride 50
Sydney to Hobart Yacht Race 32, 51
Sydney Tower 11, 35, **85**
  street-by-street map 83
Sydney Town Hall 29, 42, **89**
  concerts 212, 213
  Sydney's Best Architecture 40
Sydney Trains 222, 232–3
Sydney Trains Information 233
Sydney University **132**, 172, 173
Sydney Visitor Centre 173, 208, 209, 218, 220, 221
Sydney Writers' Festival 52
Sydney Youth Orchestra 212, 213

Sydney's Top Ten Attractions 35
Symphony in The Domain 51
Synergy 212, 213

T

Talmage, Algernon, *The Founding of Australia* 75
Tamarama
  beach 57
  Bondi Beach to Clovelly Walk 147
Tank Stream 61
Taronga Zoo 11, 13, 35, **136–7**
Tasman, Abel, map 114
Taxes 219
Taxis 231
  safety 222
  to/from airport 228
  water taxis 235
Tebbutts Observatory 158
Techno 214, 215
Telephones 226–7
Telestial 226
Television 227
Telstra 226
Temperature 53
Tennis **54**
Thai Airways 229
Thai community 44
Theatre Royal 210, 211
Theatres 210, 211
Theft 222
Three Bathers (Kirchner) 112
Three Mimis Dancing (Wagbara) 113
Three Sisters (Blue Mountains) 13, 154, **162**
Thrifty 231
Thunderbolt, Captain 108
Ticket-of-leave 25
Ticketek 54, 55, 209
Ticketmaster 209
Tickets
  entertainment 208, 209
  ferry 234
  public transport 230
  train 233
Tidal Cascades Fountain 94
Time Flys Travel 171, 173
Time zones 220
Tipping 219
  hotels 171
  restaurants 181
Tivoli Theatre 29
Tizzana Winery 158
Tjakamarra, Michael Nelson, *The Possum Dreaming* 76
Tjapaltjarri, Clifford Possum, *Warlugulong* 113

Tjapaltjarri, Tim Leura, *Warlugulong* 113
Toilets 219
Tourism Australia 218
Tourism NSW 208, 209
Tourist information 218–19, 221
Tours
  Hawkesbury Tour 158–9
  Southern Highlands Tour 164–5
Traffic signs 231
Trains *see* Rail travel
Trams 232–3
Transport Infoline 220, 231, 233
Transport Management Centre 231
Travel Concierge 219, 221
Travel information 228–37
  air 228, 229, 237
  beyond Sydney 237
  bicycle 230
  car 229, 237
  coach 229
  customs 218
  cycling 231
  departure tax 218
  disabled travellers 220, 221
  driving in Sydney 230–31
  ferry 234–5
  getting around Sydney 230–31
  guided tours and excursions 230
  monorail 232–3
  public transport 230–37
  rail 229, 232–3, 237
  sea 229
  student travel 220, 221
  taxis 231
  tickets and travel passes 230
  Transport Infoline 231, 233
  water taxis 235
Travelex 224
Traveller's cheques 224
Travellers Information Service 171, 173
Tropfest 51, 211
True Local 208, 209
Tulip Time Bowral 50
Turkish community 44
Tusculum Villa 42, 120
Twain, Mark 74
Tyrrell, Murray 160

U

Ulm, Charles 31
United Airlines 229
University of Sydney **132**, 172, 173

Utopia Records 206, 207
Utzon, Jørn 41, 43, 78, 79
  tapestry 77

V

HMAS *Vampire* 95, 97
The Vanguard 214, 215
Vaucluse, Watsons Bay and Vaucluse walk **150–51**
Vaucluse House 39, **138**
  history 27
  Watsons Bay and Vaucluse Walk 151
Vegemite 182
Verge, John 41, 117, 122
Vernon, WL 110
Victoria Barracks 27, 41, 42, **129**
Victoria, Queen 27, 29
  statue 82, 83
Victoria Street 120, **122**
Victorian architecture 42
Victorian Sydney 28–9
Victorian terrace houses 29
  Paddington Street 126–7, 128
  Potts Point 120
  Sydney's Best Architecture 41
Vidette 145
Vietnam War 32
Vietnamese community 44
View from the Summit (Earle) 26
A View of Sydney Cove (Dayes) 24–5
Viewing platforms (Manly) 148
Virgin 226, 227
Virgin Australia 228, 229
Visas 218, 221
The Visit of the Queen of Sheba to King Solomon (Poynter) 112
Vivid Festival 52
Vodafone 226

W

Wagbara, Samuel, *Three Mimis Dancing* 113
Walking
  Balmain Walk **144–5**
  Bondi Beach to Clovelly Walk **146–7**
  Four Guided Walks **143–51**
  Manly Walk **148–9**
  in Sydney 230
  Watsons Bay and Vaucluse Walk **150–51**
Wallabies 99
Walsh Bay 60
Waratah (Lewin) 25
Wardell, William 88
Warlugulong (Tjapaltjarri) 113
Warwick 127

Watch House 145
Water sports **56**
Water taxis 235
Waterman's Cottage 144
HMAS *Watson* Military Reserve 150
Watson, Robert 151
Watsons Bay **138**
  beaches 57
  guided walk **150–51**
  pilot boats 151
Wattamolla Lagoon (Royal National Park) 167
Waverley Cemetery 147
The Waverly 29
Waves, types of **57**
Weather **50–53**, 218
Wentworth, D'Arcy 141
Wentworth, WC 86, 138, 162
Wentworth Falls 163
Werrington 120
Western Australian Gum Blossom (Preston) 112
Western Union 224
Westfield Bondi Junction 199
Westfield Sydney 83, 198, 199
Whale Beach 57, 157
The Wharf 210, 211
Wharf Beach (Watsons Bay) 151
Wharf Theatre 61, **71**
Wheels and Dolly Baby 206, 207
White, Patrick 32

White Bay Cruise Terminal 229
Whiteley, Brett 32
  The Balcony (2) 112
  Studio **132**
Whitlam, Gough 33
Wildlife
  Australian Museum 91
  Manly Sea Life Sanctuary 12, **135**
  parks and reserves 48–9
  Sea Life Sydney Aquarium 12, 95, **98**
  Taronga Zoo 11, 13, 35, **136–7**
  Wild Life Sydney 12, **99**
Williams, Fred 112
Williamson, David 210
Williamson, JC 122
Windsor 158
Windsor Street (Paddington) 127
Windsurfing **56**
Wine
  Hunter Valley 160–61
  Manly Food and Wine Festival 53
  Tizzana Winery 158
  what to drink **184–5**
Winter Magic Festival 53
Winter in Sydney 53
Wiring Money 224
Wiseman, Solomon 159
Wisemans Ferry 159
Witchery 204, 205

Wolgan Valley, hotels 179
Wombats 136
Woodward, Robert 94
Woollahra, shopping 201
Woolloomooloo Finger Wharf 58, **109**
World Bar 214, 215
World Square 199
World War I 30
World War II 31
  El Alamein Fountain 122
Wright, Judith 74
Writers' Walk **74**
Wurrabadalumba, Jabarrgwa, *Dugong Hunt* 38

Y

YHA Australia 172, 173
Yiribana Gallery (Art Gallery of NSW) 38–9, **113**
Youth hostels 172, 173
Yulefest 53
Yurulbin Point 145

Z

Zambesi 204, 205
Zig Zag Railway 162
Zimmermann 204, 205
Zoo Emporium 204, 205
Zoos, Taronga Zoo 11, 13, 35, **136–7**

Acknowledgments

Dorling Kindersley would like to thank the following people whose help and assistance contributed to the preparation of this book.

Main Contributors
Ken Brass grew up on Sydney's Bondi Beach. He began his career in journalism with the *Sydney Morning Herald* and later worked as a London correspondent before becoming a staff writer on national daily newspapers in the United Kingdom. Returning home, he worked on the *Australian Women's Weekly*, *Weekend Australian* newspaper and *Australian Geographic* magazine. His photographs appear regularly in Australian magazines.

Kirsty McKenzie grew up on a sheep station in outback Queensland. She entered journalism after completing an arts degree. After making Sydney her home in 1980, she worked on a number of lifestyle and travel publications. Since becoming a freelance writer in 1987, she has regularly contributed to food, interior design and travel magazines.

Additional Text and Research
Angus Cameron, Leith Hillard, Kim Kitson, Siobhán O'Connor, Rupert Dean.

Additional Photography
Claire Edwards, Leanne Hogbin, Esther Labi, Siobhán O'Connor, Ian O'Leary, Carol Wiley.

Additional Illustrations
Leslye Cole, Stephen Conlin, Jon Gittoes, Steve Graham, Ray Grinaway, Helen Halliday, David Kirshner, Alex Lavroff, Iain McKellar, Chris Orr, Oliver Rennert.

Additional Cartography
Land Information Centre, Sydney.
Dorling Kindersley Cartography, Sydway.

Editorial and Design
Deputy Editorial Director Douglas Amrine
Deputy Art Directors Gillian Allan, Gaye Allen
Map Co-ordinators Michael Ellis, David Pugh
Production David Proffit
Picture Research Wendy Canning,
DTP Designer Leanne Hogbin
Maps Gary Bowes, Fiona Casey, Casper Morris, Anna Nilsson, Christine Purcell, Richard Toomey (Era-Maptec Ltd)
Editorial and Design Assistance: Emma Anacootee, Charis Atlas, Vandana Bhagra, Jenny Cattell, Louise Cleghorn, Sherry Collins, Stephanie Driver, Mariana Evmolpidou, Joy Fitzsimmons, Clare Forte, Anna Freiberger, Caroline Gladstone, Emily Green, Vinod Harish, Julia Harris-Voss, Gail Jones, Lisa Kosky, Esther Labi, Phoebe Lowndes, Jim Marks, Sam Merrell, Rebecca Milner, Sonal Modha, Kylie Mulquin, Rachel Neustein, Scarlett O'Hara, Louise Parsons, Helen Partington, Alok Pathak, Susie Peachey, Marianne Petrou, Clare Pierotti, Pure Content, Marisa Renzullo, Ellen Root, Sands Publishing Solutions, Azeem Siddiqui, Susana Smith, Deborah Soden, Rachel Symons, Tracey Timpson, Richa Verma, Ros Walford, Dora Whitaker, Carol Wiley, Sophie Wright.
Index Jenny Cattell.

Special Assistance
Art Gallery of New South Wales, in particular Sherrie Joseph; Australian Museum, in particular Liz Wilson; Ann-Marie Bulat; the staff of Elizabeth Bay House; Historic Houses Trust; Lara Hookham; Info Direct, in particular Frank Tortora; Professor Max Kelly; Lou MacDonald; Adam Moore; Museum of Sydney, in particular Michelle Andringa; National Maritime Museum, in particular Jeffrey Mellefont and Bill Richards; National Trust of Australia (NSW), in particular Stewart Watters; Bridget O'Regan; Royal Botanic Gardens, in particular Anna Hallett and Ed Wilson; State Transit Authority; Sydney Opera House, in particular David Brown and Valerie Tring; Diane Wallis.

Photography Permissions
Dorling Kindersley would like to thank all those who gave permission to photograph at various cathedrals, churches, museums, restaurants, hotels, shops, galleries and other sights too numerous to thank individually.

Picture Credits
a-above; b-below/bottom; c-centre; f-far; l-left; r-right; t-top.

Works of art have been reproduced with the permission of the following copyright holders:
© **Museum of Sydney** 1996: *Edge of the Trees* Janet Laurence and Fiona Foley, on the site of **First Government House**: 36tr, 87b.

The publisher would like to thank the following individuals, companies and picture libraries for their kind permission to reproduce their photographs:

ACP: 31cb, 32bc; **Adge Boutique Apartment Hotel**: 175tr; **Admiral Collingwood Lodge**: David Young 170c, 177br; **Alamy Images**: John Buxton 222br; Maurice Crooks 235bc; CulturalEyes-AusGS 232cla; Chad Ehlers 34; frank'n'focus 228cra; Daniel Hewlett 222cr; *Aboriginal art painted on urban brick wall* by Danny and Jamie Eastwood Suzanne Long 8-9; Network Photographers 182cl; Debbie and Nigel Picknell 13clb; Alan Smithers 219cla; Diane Stoney 197br; Travel-shots 183tl; Mike V 216-7; David Wall 183c; Rob Walls 124; Wildlight Photo Agency/Rob Cleary 219tr; Worldwide Picture Library 10br; **Andrew (Boy) Charlton Poolside Cafe**: 59tl, 193br; **Art Gallery of New South Wales**: *Portrait of Arthur Streeton* (date unknown) Grace Joel oil on canvas on hardboard, 55.6 x 40.7 cm, gift of Miss Joel 1925: 29cb; © Bundanon Trust 1996 *The Expulsion* 1947–48 Arthur Boyd (1920–99), oil on hardboard 99.5 x 119.6 cm: 35c; © Ms Stephenson-Meere 1996 *Australian Beach Pattern* 1940 Charles Meere (1890–1961) oil on canvas 91.5 x 122 cm: 37tl; © estate of the artist, courtesy Anindilkawa Land Council *Dugong Hunt* (1948) Jabarrgwa (Kneepad) Wurrabadalumba natural pigments on bark 46 x 95cm, gift of the Commonwealth Government 1956: 38b; *Bridge Pattern* Harold Cazneaux (1878–1953), gelatin silver photograph 29.6 x 21.4 cm, gift of the Cazneaux family 1975: 60bc(d); © AGNSW 1996 *Sofala* 1947 Russell Drysdale (1912–81), oil on canvas on hardboard 71.7 x 93.1 cm 110bl; *Mars and the Vestal Virgin* 1638 Jacques Blanchard 110cl; © Tiwi Design Executive 1996 *Pukumani Grave Posts, Melville Island* 1958 various artists, natural pigments on wood 165.1 x 29.2 cm, gift of Dr Stuart Scougall 1959: 111tc; *The Golden Fleece* (1894) Tom Roberts (1856–1931), oil on canvas, 104 x 158.7 cm: 111br; *Natives on the Ouse River, Van Diemen's Land* 1838 John Glover, 111crb; © Wendy Whiteley 1996 *The Balcony 2* 1975 Brett Whiteley (1939–92), oil on canvas 203.5 x 364.5 cm: 112bl; *Three Bathers* 1913 Ernst Ludwig Kirchner 112tr; *The Curve of the Bridge* 1928-9 Grace Cossington Smith 112cla, © reproduced by courtesy of Aboriginal Artists Agency *Warlugulong* 1976 Clifford Possum Tjapaltjarri (1932–2002) and Tim Leura Tjapaltjarri (1939–84), synthetic polymer

paint on canvas 168.5 x 170.5 cm: 113tr; *Poster for the Vienna Secession 49th Exhibition* (1918) Egon Schiele (1890–1918), colour lithograph, 67.8 x 53.7 cm: 113bl; **Arts Hotel Sydney:** 176tr; **Australian Information Service:** 33tl(d); **Australian Museum:** C. Bento 22tl, 22clb, 22cb, 23tl, 23c, 23crb; 37bl, 90cr, 90crb, 91cra, 91crb; **Australian Picture Library:** John Carnemolla 32clb; **AWL Images:** Walter Bibikow 119; Andrew Watson 62–3, 104.
Greg Barrett: 209bc; **Bartel Photo Library:** 162bc; **Beppi's Restaurant:** 195tr; **Bet's B&B:** Peter Koudounas 172tl; **Big Hostel:** 179tr; **Mervyn G Bishop:** 24crb; Courtesy of **Bluetongue Brewery:** 185cl; **Bonza Bike Tours:** 230cla; **Botanic Gardens Trust, Sydney:** 106bc, Jaime Plaza 50bl; **Bruce Coleman:** John Cancalosi 47br; Francisco Futil 46tr; **Bridgeclimb Sydney:** 70br, 73tl; **Bula'bula Arts:** Tony Dhanyula *Nyoka* (Mud Crabs), circa 1984, ochres and synthetic polymer on bark, J.W. Power Bequest, purchased 1984 by the Museum of Contemporary Art, Sydney 36cb; **Bridgeman Art Library:** private collection *Ned Kelly, Outlaw* (1946), oil on panel, Sir Sidney Nolan (1917–92) 33ca; **Botanical Gardens Trust, Sydney:** 106cla, 106bc.
Café Nice: 186bc; **Captain Cook Cruises:** 234cla; **Centrepoint Management:** 85br; courtesy **City sightseeing:** 236br; **Corbis:** Richard Cummins 88tl; E. O. Hoppé 67cra; Reuters/ Mick Tsikas 231tl; **Anthony Crickmay:** 78cla; David Jones (Australia) P/l: 27crb(d).
Rupert Dean: 184cl, 184crb; **Dixson Galleries, State Library of New South Wales:** 22tr, 24blb(d), 28cla, 72tr, 140br; **Destination NSW-Tourism:** Hamilton Lund 221tl, 237cla; Phase IX 154tr; **Dreamstime.com:** Andrew Chambers 12br; Pierre Jean Durieu 92; Sadequl Hussain 12tc; Jackmalipan 13tr; Kjuuurs 64; Lev Kropotov 95tc; Chee-onn Leong 152–3; Pominoz 233tl, Mark Ward 2–3; David May 130; Gordon Tipene 80; **Max Dupain:** 79br.
Fairfax Photo Library: 30bl; 54cra; 73br; 116cl(d); 79tc; ASCUI 53br; Dallen 33cra; Gerrit Fokkema 32br; Ken James 209tr; McNeil 122bl; White 45clb; **Fire and Rescue NSW (FRNSW):** 222crb; **The Four in Hand Dining Room:** 180bl; **Four Seasons Hotel Sydney:** Elbow Room Productions 170br. **Getty images:** AFP PHOTO/Greg Wood 226cl; Paco Alcantara 154tr; Oliver Strewe 142; **Global Gossip Group:** 226br; **Government Printing Office Collection, State of New South Wales:** 28clb, 30clb, 78bl; **Guillaume Brahimi/ The Cru - Media + Communications:** 194bc.
Happy Medium Photos: 45tr; **C Moore Hardy:** 208br; **Hood Collection, State Library of New South Wales:** 73bl, 139br (d); **Hotel London, Paddington, Australia:** 126bc. **Lake's Folly Vineyards:** 161cr; **The Langham, Sydney:** 171tr; **Leura Gardens Festival Inc:** 50cr; **Liberty Wines:** 160cla; **Lonley Planet Images:** Juliet Coombe 11tr; **The Lord Nelson Brewery Hotel:** 172br, 187tr; **Lucio's Italian Restaurant:** 181bl; Courtesy **Luna Park Trust:** 134cl, 134tc. **Madame Nhu:** 188tr; **Maya Restaurant:** 181tr, 196br; **Mazz Images:** 32–3; **The Mercantile Hotel:** Martin Brady 173tc; **Meriton Serviced Apartments:** 174bc; **Mitchell Library, State Library of New South Wales:** 23br, 23bcb, 24br(d), 24–5, 25tl, 25ca(d), 25cb, 26clb(d), 26cb(d), 26bl, 27tl, 27ca(d),

27bl(d), 28cr, 28bc, 28br, 29tl, 29br, 31ca(d), 31blb, 33cb, 73cr 114tl; **David Moore:** 32cla; **Mount Franklin:** 185br; **MoVid Sydney:** 191tr; **Multiplex Property Services:** 100c; **Museum of Contemporary Art, Sydney:** 36cl, 66bl; Alex Davies 75tl **National Library of Australia, Canberra:** 26cla, 27brb(d), 29bc; **National Maritime Museum:** 24cl, 97cra; **Nature Focus:** Kevin Diletti 49br(d); John Fields 46bl; Pavel Germar 49tr; **Norman Lindsay Gallery:** Photo courtesy National Trust of Australia 163cr; **NSW Police Force:** 222cla.
Otto Ristorante/BLACK Communications: 192tr.
Pablo and Rusty's: 189br; **Parliament House:** The Hon Ma Willis, RFD, ED, LLB, MLC, President, Legislative Council, Parliament of New South Wales. The Hon J Murray, MP, Speaker, Legislative Assembly, Parliament of New South Wales. Artist's original sketch of the historical painting in oil by Algernon Talmage, RA, *The Founding of Australia*. Kindly loaned to the Parliament of New South Wales by Mr Arthur Chard of Adelaide: 75bl; **Parramatta City Council:** S. Thoma 44tr; **Pier One Sydney Harbour:** 178bc; **Photolibrary.com:** David Messent 11bl, 229tl; images reproduced courtesy of **Powerhouse Museum:** 25br, 26bcb, 30cla, 30cb, 30bc, 31crb, 31bc, 36br; 102–3 all, John-Francois Lanzarone 102c Tyrrell Collection 108tc.
Radisson Blu Plaza Hotel: Gerry O'Leary 171bl; Reproduce with permission from Railcop NSW Australia: 233br; Phil Carrick 233cra, 233cr; **The Rocks Discovery Museum:** 67tl **Sepia Restaurant:** 190bc; **Simon Johnson Purveyor of Quality Foods:** 221bl; **Southcorp Wines Europe:** 185tr; **State Library of Tasmania:** 24clb; **Stopmotion:** 162tr; **Suzi Thomas Publishing:** Thomas O'Flynn 76bc, © DACS, London 2011, 78clb; **Superstock:** Digital Vision 10cl; **Sydney Attractions Group:** 98br; **Sydney Film Festival:** 53cb, **Sydney Freelance:** J Boland 51cl; **Sydney Harbour Foreshore Authority:** 218br; **Sydney Jewish Museum:** 37br; **Sydney Opera House Trust:** 76tr, 76cla, 77tc, 77br, 77bl, 78br, 79cla, 79ca, 79cra, 79c; Willi Ulmer Collection 79bc; **Sydney Restaurant Group:** 196tr; **Sydney Theatre:** 208cl; **Sydney Wilderness Tours:** 154tr.
Taronga Zoo: 136tr, 137cra; **Tebutt's VII Restaurant and Function Centre:** 158clb.
University of Technology, Sydney/uts.edu.au: Coptercam 132br.
Vintage Estates: 161ca.
Westfield Sydney: 83crb; **Wild Life Sydney:** courtesy of Merlin Entertainments Group 99 all.
Yalumba Wines: 184cra.

Front Endpaper: **Alamy Images:** Rob Walls Rcr; **AWL Images:** Walter Bibikow Rcra; Andrew Watson Rtc; **Dreamstime.com:** Pierre Jean Durieu Lbc; Kjuuurs Lcl; Gordon Tipene Lclb;
Map cover: **Getty Images:** Scott E Barbour.
Jacket – Front and spine top: **Getty Images:** Scott E Barbour.

All other images © Dorling Kindersley.
For further information see: www.dkimages.com

Special Editions of DK Travel Guides

DK Travel Guides can be purchased in bulk quantities at discounted prices for use in promotions or as premiums. We are also able to offer special editions and personalized jackets, corporate imprints, and excerpts from all of our books, tailored specifically to meet your own needs.

To find out more, please contact:
in the United States **SpecialSales@dk.com**
in the UK **travelspecialsales@uk.dk.com**
in Canada DK Special Sales at **general@ tourmaline.ca**
in Australia **PCorporatesalespenguin randomhouse.com.au**

Sydney Transport Map

Balmain West,
Parramatta

McMahons
Point

Milsons
Point

Goat
Island

Walsh
Bay

Sy
Ha
Br

KEY

Major sight
Sydney Trains station
Sydney Light Rail station
Ferry boarding point
Ferry route
— Sydney Explorer
— Bondi & Bays Explorer
— Bus route

Terminal 1 Circular Quay

309, 310 Port Botany
373, 374 Coogee
380 Watson's Bay (Via Bondi)
389 Bondi
392 Little Bay
394, L94 La Perouse
396, 397 Maroubra
422 Kogarah (Via Newtown &
Tempe)
423 Kingsgrove (Via Newtown)
426 Dulwich Hill (Via Newtown)
428 Canterbury (Via Newtown)
520 Parramatta

**Terminal 2 Gresham/Pitt/
Spring St**

311 Railway Square (Via Elizabeth
Bay)
391 La Perouse & Port Botany

**Terminal 3 Millers Point
(Argyle St)/ Walsh Bay**

339 Clovelly
431 Glebe
433 Balmain (Via Glebe)

**Terminal 4 Wynyard
(Carrington St)**

247 Taronga Zoo

**Terminal 5 Queen Victoria
Building (York Street)**

442 Balmain East (Darling St Wharf)
311 Gresham/Pitt/Spring St
(Via Elizabeth Bay)
372 Coogee
378 Bronte
393 La Perouse
395 Maroubra Beach
L88 Avalon
L90 Palm Beach

Terminal 6 Railway Square

311 Gresham/Pitt/Spring St
(Via Elizabeth Bay)
372 Coogee
378 Bronte
393 La Perouse
395 Maroubra Beach
L88 Avalon
L90 Palm Beach

Terminal 7 King Street Wharf

412 Campsie (Via Dulwich Hill)

Terminal 8 Woolloomooloo

441 Birchgrove

0 kilometres   500

0 miles   500

Balmain
East

442

BALMAIN

Darling
Harbour

COMMUNITY
PARK

John St
Square

Star City

PYRMONT

Pyrmont Bay

Fish Market

Australian
National Maritime
Museum

Cockle
Bay

Convention

Wentworth
Park

WENTWORTH
PARK

Powerhouse
Museum

Paddy's
Markets

WATTLE STREET

HARRIS STREET

Exhibition
Centre

DARLING
HARBOUR

VICTORIA
PARK

431-433

412

431-433

422-423-
426-428

BROADWAY

412-422-423-426-428-431-433

ABERCROMBIE ST

CLEVELAND STREET

LEE STREET

PRINCE
ALFRED
PARK

309-310-372-393-395

CLEVELAN

372-393-3

Redfern

GIBBONS ST

309-310

OBSERVATORY
PARK

Circu
Qua

339-431-433

433

339-431-433

3

241-L88-L90

Pyrmont
Bay

Darling
Harbour

Wynyard

4

7

YORK ST

CLARENCE ST

GEORGE ST

412

247

412

441-
442

441

441-442-520

5

Town
Hall

L88-L90

GEORGE ST

412-426-428-431-433

PITT ST

339

Capitol
Square

BELMORE
PARK

Central

HAYMARKET

6

309-310-
311-372-378-
393-395-422-
423-426-428

412-
422-
423-
426-428

422-
423-
426-428

309-310-339-
422-423-426-428

ELIZABETH ST

CASTLEREAGH ST

422-423-426-428

M

SUR
HI

309-310
311-339
372-374
378-391
393-395

309-
310-339-
422-423-
426-428

412

CI
CEN

2

311-
BRIDG

BRIDGE

309-310

422-423-
426-428

520

339-
520

309-310-339-
422-423-
426-428

M

441-
442-520